Chicago's
New Negroes

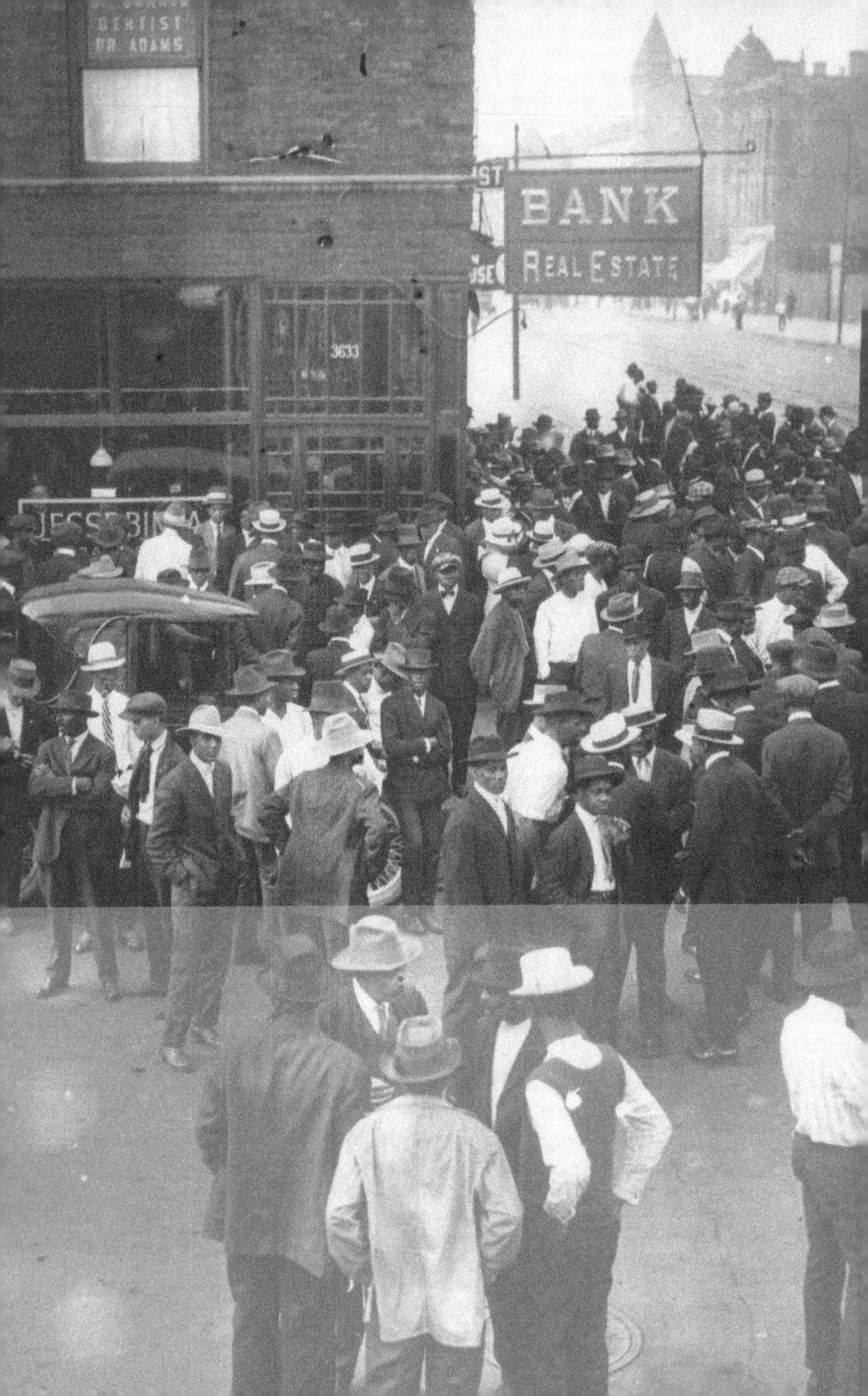
DENTIST
DR. ADAMS
BANK
REAL ESTATE
3633

Chicago's *New* Negroes

Modernity, the Great Migration, & Black Urban Life

DAVARIAN L. BALDWIN

The University of
North Carolina Press
Chapel Hill

Designed by Jacquline Johnson
Set in MT Walbaum
by Keystone Typesetting, Inc.

Frontispiece: Courtesy of the
Chicago Historical Society.

This book was published with the assistance
of the Z. Smith Reynolds Fund of the
University of North Carolina Press.

The paper in this book meets the guidelines
for permanence and durability of the Committee on
Production Guidelines for Book Longevity of
the Council on Library Resources.

Library of Congress Cataloging-in-Publication Data
Baldwin, Davarian L.
Chicago's new Negroes : modernity, the great migration,
and Black urban life / Davarian L. Baldwin.
p. cm.
Includes bibliographical references and index.
ISBN-13: 978-0-8078-3099-4 (cloth: alk. paper)
ISBN-13: 978-0-8078-5799-1 (pbk.: alk. paper)
1. African Americans—Illinois—Chicago—History—20th
century. 2. African Americans—Illinois—Chicago—Social
conditions—20th century. 3. African Americans—
Migrations—History—20th century. 4. Migration,
Internal—United States—History—20th century.
5. Chicago (Ill.)—History—1875- . 6. Chicago (Ill.)—
Social conditions—20th century. 7. Chicago (Ill.)—
Population—History—20th century. 8. Chicago (Ill.)—
Race relations—History—20th century. I. Title.
F548.9.N4B35   2007
305.896'07307731090452—dc22   2006027378

cloth   11 10 09 08 07   5 4 3 2 1
paper   11 10 09 08 07   5 4 3 2 1

To the New Negroes
in my life

Muldrow and Mora
Olivia and Ford
Mary Jo and Robert

Contents

Illustrations

Acknowledgments

This was truly a collective undertaking that would not have been possible without the improvisational forms of support, encouragement, and critique that forced me to at least try to do justice to this powerful story. The process of working on this project has reaffirmed my confidence in the human spirit. I want to thank the institutions that offered financial support: Boston College's Research Incentive Grant from the College of Arts and Sciences, the Carter G. Woodson Institute for African and African American Studies Postdoctoral Fellowship at the University of Virginia, the W. E. B. Du Bois Institute for American and African American Research at Harvard University, the American Studies Program at New York University, the Erskine Peters Dissertation Fellowship and the Program of African-American Studies at the University of Notre Dame, and the Minority Faculty Fellowship and the Lily Library's Everett Helm Visiting Fellowship at Indiana University. I am especially grateful for the dollars and credit cards of family members who funded my first trip "back" to Chicago.

This project was first brought to life by the fabulous archivists and the institutions they represent who translated my random queries and bursts of excitement into legible possibilities. Archie Motley at the Chicago Historical Society was simply an unending wealth of local Chicago resources and references: may he rest in peace. Wilma Gibbs at the Indiana Historical Society was instrumental in helping me navigate the Madam C. J. Walker archives. Timothy Wiles at the National Baseball Hall of Fame Research Library expertly tailored his breadth of knowledge to help me in my earliest forays into sports studies. Finally, Michael Flugg at the Carter G. Woodson Branch of the Chicago Public Library and his staff are a Chicago institution. They knew my project better than I did and many times took me to archival corners and cultural figures in Chicago's black metropolis that I would have never known without their knowledge and true care for the people I attempt to represent.

I must also sing the praises of the independent scholars who write and teach as a labor of love and were so generous to me with their masterworks. Both Pearl Bowser and A'Lelia Bundles offered me powerful insights and training that far exceeded the bounds of the classroom and even shared their now-landmark texts on Oscar Micheaux and Madam C. J. Walker respectively before they had been published.

While my project is about Chicago, the conceptual and spiritual vision that framed it couldn't have happened, at the time, anywhere else but New York City and particularly through the force of the collective minds assembled around New York University. My intellectual vision was literally assembled by the dissertation dream team of Robin D. G. Kelley, Andrew Ross, and Nikhil Pal Singh. Robin has remained a model mentor, leading by example in a range of areas from his understanding of graduate student labor, to his insistence on the centrality of social relevance to academic work, to his bibliographic knowledge about *everything*. I could not have had a better advisor. He is the man through whom I measure both intellect and social responsibility. Despite all of his administrative duties and ridiculous research and writing profile, Andrew kept me on task with an intimate knowledge of my vision that came from memorable moments, including line editing my proposal at a coffee shop to next-day express shipments of my chapters when he could sense my anxiety. He was more than a director; he was a friend to all of the dispossessed graduate students who refused to be "disciplined." Nikhil was truly a fellow traveler in the quest to expand what it means to "do" intellectual history. I hope I live up to our shared desires for the academy and the world. I also can't forget Lisa Duggan, who was simply fantastic, not only because of the power of her work but also because of her ability to train graduate students through teaching and offering realistic maps for navigating life both inside and outside academia.

The sixth floor at 269 Mercer will one day stand as a historical marker because of all that it has provided for so many people. Both Africana and Asian/Pacific/American studies sponsored a wealth of programs, parties, and individual projects that kept countless students sane. I must specifically recognize intellectual activist John Kwo Wei Tchen and especially Manthia Diawara, mentor, gentleman scholar, and host of the "living room," who created a life force for NYU graduate students that became a home away from home. It is amazing to see the cadre of fellow travelers who have emerged from these spaces that helped create circles of affiliation and affection that I continue to treasure. Donnette Francis, Jerry Philogene, Mabel Wilson, Michele Brown, Rosamond King, and Jafari Allen know there aren't enough words.

With this project there was always an extended family of committee members, readers, and comrades stretching across a stream of experiences and encounters from New York, to Indiana and Chicago, down to Virginia, and back to Boston. In particular, I want to thank Alyssa Hephburn, Philip Brian Harper, George Yudice, Wahneema Lubiano, Kobena Mercer, Cathy Cohen, Tara Scott, John Richey, Danielle McGuire, Darlene Clark Hine, Alberto Torchinsky, John Bodnar, John McCluskey, Claude Clegg, Quinton Dixie, Phyllis Klotman, Wallace Best, Beverly Love-Holt, Hugh Page, Richard Pierce, Gail Bederman, Tiwanna Simpson, Michelle Taylor, Cymone Fourshey, Glenda Gilmore, John Jackson, Mark Anthony Neal, Roderick Ferguson, Victoria Wolcott, Reginald Butler, Corey Walker, Marlon Ross, Tyrone Simpson, Candace Lowe, Ethan Blue, and Tracy Sharpley-Whiting for their varying degrees of support and counsel. Indiana also introduced me to my brother from another mother, Thabiti Lewis, who has become a reader, sounding board, and real friend. Colleagues at Boston College have been particularly great in helping me make the transition to the professoriat, especially David Quigley, Lynn Johnson, Lynn Lyerly, Deborah Levenson, and Crystal Feimster, while my students at NYU, Monroe College, Indiana University, and Boston College and especially my research assistants Peter Markovics, Katherine Lummis, and Leah Tseronis importantly remind me what this academia thing should be about: service.

Portions of the book have been presented at various conferences and invited lectures. In different form, parts of the introduction and chapter 1 appeared in the journal *American Studies*, and parts of chapters 3 and 4 appeared in an essay in the CD-ROM collection *African Americans in Cinema: The First Half Century*, edited by Phyllis Klotman (Urbana: University of Illinois Press, 2003).

My editor at North Carolina, Sian Hunter, has been absolutely stunning throughout this process, bearing with all of my intensity, insecurities, and idiosyncrasies. She has been a true shepherd, immediately understanding the story I wanted this project to tell and, most important, how I wanted to tell it. Encouragement, support, critical awareness, and basic kindness were unending. I want to also thank Julie Bush for her prodigious labors in what was surely a challenging task of editing.

In the end, if it weren't for early high school and college mentors like Raymond Schoenfield, Danny Goldberg, Myra George, and M. Shawn Copeland, I wouldn't have even made it to graduate school. Last words are saved for the inner circle of family. Charles and Robert, you know the time, Six Feet Deep forever! High school conversations with Joseph Hill and Christopher

Parham in "the bucket" began this all. Both Brenda Atlas and Pastor Anne Barton have shined the light for my journey. I also have the best family network, from Beloit to Racine, Wisconsin, from Clovis, New Mexico, to where it all began, Houston, Mississippi. To my mother, Mary Jo Baldwin, you have always been my role model. I could never work to be the master storyteller that you are without effort. When I first thought to examine how "everyday people" theorize themselves, it was your life that inspired such a vision. Your resilience, brilliance, beauty, and stubbornness are all the things I continue to work so hard to honor in my life and work. Finally, to Bridgette, words can't describe what we have been through together, and I know that you were the only one I would have ever wanted to ride with on this crazy journey. You have been my lover, comrade, best critic, partner in parenting, and friend. This book is such a limited representation for all that we have been through, but in the lives I describe I hope to honor the life that we are trying to build. From research trips on credit cards to necessary vacations from the world in your arms and in your eyes, you keep me both grounded and flying. I'm sorry for all mistakes made in the past, and I can't wait to see what life has in store for us. Our creation of Nylan Xavier and Noah Elias keeps us laughing, tired, inspired, and confused. But when I see you study, parent, teach, build, and love, I am both humbled and constantly reminded what this is all about. I am so proud of who you are and who you inspire me to be. Finally, to Nylan and Noah, you may never read this book, but know that your life worlds are between these pages, and even when I didn't know it, your scrutiny, joy, suspicion, inquisitiveness, and majesty are what boomerangs us all forward.

Chicago's
New Negroes

"Chicago Has No Intelligentsia"?

CONSUMER CULTURE AND INTELLECTUAL
LIFE RECONSIDERED

Those who would restrict intellectual history to the educated,
the intelligentsia, the elite, would do well to look carefully at
the richness of expression, the sharpness of perception, the
uninhibited imagination, the complex imagery that
form . . . the mind of the black folk.
—Lawrence Levine,
Black Culture and Black Consciousness, 1977

Jack Johnson foreshadowed, and in some ways
helped to create, the "New Negro."
—Jeffrey Sammons, *Beyond the Ring*, 1990

By 6 P.M. on the Fourth of July 1910, black communities all over the country had exploded into an unexpected and seemingly synchronized outburst of race pride and national patriotism. In Philadelphia, "Lombard Street, the principal street in the negro section, went wild." *New York Age* columnist Lester Walton observed, "I have never seen so many colored people reading newspapers." The *Boston Globe* reported, "Youngsters scarcely more than pickanninies, young girls, women and old men, walked up and down the streets with heads erect and chests protruding," and in Hutchinson, Kansas, "prayers broke loose into street singing and dancing." Along this line of an almost religious jubilee, Ruby Berkley remembered that "Negroes were jubilant. . . . The older people laughed and cried, and the children danced around and knocked each other about in good fun." Her entire DuQuoin, Illinois, family sang, "Hallelujah, hallelujah, the storm is passing over, Hallelujah." Essayist George Schuyler recalled that he was "bursting with pride and enthusiasm."[1]

Chicago was particularly on fire as the *Chicago Daily Inter Ocean* proclaimed it "the wildest night in the Black Belt." This paper continued, "The negroes drunk with happiness . . . [tossed] their hats, canes and other independence day finery into the air" until State Street became "a river of black people, surging up and down aimlessly." Supposedly the "uproar started in a hundred places at once," according to the Indianapolis *Freeman*, until State Street revelers reached 35th, where an "impromptu parade" started and the entire "Stroll," especially Robert Motts's Pekin Theatre, was "transformed." Black people filed out of "coliseums, bars and gambling dens onto the street with large firecrackers and other noisemakers" until police officers were sent in to "warn them not to go too far." Yet one police officer conceded, "It's their night. . . . Let them have their fun." Observers concluded that on this night, "the negroes were given a free reign to enjoy themselves."[2]

But this was Jim Crow America, where the slightest infraction of the codes of black public humility and deference could result in jail time or death. How had *any* moment—but especially the Fourth of July—become "their night" with "a free reign"? It was because Chicago resident and boxing great Jack Johnson, touted as the "Negro's Deliverer," had just defeated the "Great White Hope" Jim Jeffries to retain the heavyweight boxing championship title. Two years earlier, Johnson had chased then-champion Tommy Burns "around the world" to become the first internationally recognized black heavyweight champion of the world. His title roused an immediate call for legendary retired champion Jeffries to come back and, as he said, prove "that a white man is better than a negro." It has been well documented that this "Fight of the Century" was overtly shaped as a battle over racial supremacy. While Johnson's unquestionable dominance over Jeffries was exhibited in the ring, it still did not seem to "make sense" in the white world where "in one swift blow" white victory was denied, money was lost, scientific theories were challenged, and "far more interest was taken in the aftermath of the fight at Reno than in the observance of the national holiday."[3]

Black "exuberance" in the streets that followed Johnson's victory exacerbated white feelings of racial impotency, which were expressed in arguably the first ever nationwide race riots in U.S. history, extending from the "Deep South" through even northern "liberal" states including Illinois, Ohio, Pennsylvania, and New York. On the ground, white anxiety and violence in the deepest South were a response to both the "disorderly celebration of Johnson's victory" and a very real economic loss as black betters collectively "filled their purses" with an estimated $150,000 to $500,000. Black people seized the opportunity to not just celebrate but also physically retaliate against long-standing racial restrictions on public space and behavior. Black male and female revelers all over the country "shouted" at whites in their cars, jostled them on sidewalks, made "threats," and blocked traffic. Collective and even armed black resistance challenged white attempts to enter communities to arrest "over-zealous" celebrants, while, periodically, black residents and white soldiers on leave waged gun battles in the streets.[4]

To add insult to injury, then and over the following years, Johnson openly flaunted his desire for white women and celebrated their desire for him, one of a number of his racial transgressions both in and out of the ring. While many within the black masses immortalized such defiance through Johnson folk tales and fight film screenings, the black "better class" would continue to warn him to live in a "modest manner." Then, in 1912 Johnson was charged with violating the Mann Act—described as the trafficking of white women across state lines for immoral purposes. No laws were violated, but the *Chicago Tribune* was filled with letters and statements from southerners inquiring about a "Johnson persecution fund," a pastor announcing that lynching Johnson "would be light punishment for his sins," and former Texas state treasurer Sam Sparks calling for a delegation of one hundred hand-picked Texans to head to Chicago to "chastise" or "attend Jack Johnson." In defiant response, the *Chicago Broad Ax* warned Sparks to "not invade the black belt of the Windy City" with any select group of Texans. Even the Tuskegee-owned *New York Age* added, "The Negro bruisers of the Northern and West-

Jack Johnson sitting in the driver's seat of an automobile, Chicago, 1910.
(Courtesy of the Chicago Historical Society)

ern cities will fight" if any white invasion occurred. If only for a moment, the many masks and strategies of deference and accommodation were collectively discarded as a new aggressive race consciousness emerged through the events surrounding a black boxer.[5]

With notable exceptions, discussions about Johnson's controversies and their violent aftermath focus primarily on what his ascendancy meant for white anxieties about race, manhood, and civilization in the "Progressive Era." Yet it is also telling that according to mainstream newspapers, the white "mob spirit seemed to rise wherever a negro cheered for Johnson . . . or permitted his exultation over the victory to grow to an extent that made it offensive." We rarely invert the lens to investigate how Johnson exceeded his stature as a boxer to become a "Magnificent Vicarious Experience" for black communities. Placing the Johnson story within its black context crystallizes how he did more than challenge Social Darwinism but, in the words of historian Jeffrey Sammons, "foreshadowed, and in some ways helped to create, the New Negro." Reverend Reverdy Ransom, founder of Chicago's Institutional Church and Social Settlement, articulated that precise point when he predicted in a famous 1909 sermon, "What Jack Johnson seeks to do to Jeffries in the roped area will be more the ambition of Negroes in every domain of human endeavor." He prophetically asserted that alongside Johnson, the Negro singer, poet, sculptor, and scholar would "keep the white race busy for the next few hundred years . . . defending the interests of white supremacy."[6]

Taking the lead from Johnson, this book examines the mass consumer marketplace as a crucial site of intellectual life. Despite a growing body of scholarship that powerfully proves otherwise, popular memory resiliently associates the term "New Negro" with the literary and visual artists and intellectuals of the Harlem Renaissance.[7] Therefore, to place a Chicago migrant and mass cultural icon like Johnson at the center of the "New Negro" movement forces a serious rethinking of the relationship between consumer culture and intellectual life in the early twentieth century. This approach recognizes that the "Renaissance" actually provided only one small piece of a much larger New Negro sociocultural transformation marked by the race, class, and cultural contestations between white observers, black cultural producers, critics, activists, reformers, and—centrally—black migrant consumer patrons. By looking at the consumer marketplace, this book gives life to "the folk" as more than just the objects of black modernist art and writings waiting for aesthetic construction but as subjects creating and crafting their own ideas that would forever alter the course and shape of the modern world.[8]

These migrants powerfully show that to develop any comprehensive framework for examining the production of knowledge, one must consider all of the realms and forms in which ideas are created, have force, and engage with other ideas. My notion of a marketplace intellectual life recovers the actual existing interface between urban migrant cultural practices and the mass consumer marketplace as a problematic but fertile field for New Negro critique and action. Here the "richness of expression" and the "sharpness of perception," found on Chicago's city streets and in its cinemas, beauty salons, Sanctified churches, and sports stadiums, arguably loom larger than the traditional mediums of pen, paint, and paper. This was so particularly for those who did not have access to or simply did not desire entrée into the traditional channels of intellectual life.[9]

A full understanding of the New Negro experience requires an examination of how black consumer practices in cities like Chicago converted acts of desire into a political and intellectual life of distinction and defiance against traditional ways of life. In order to achieve this understanding, the marketplace intellectual life highlights how a variety of cultural formations—often understood within the division of labor between "high" and "low" culture—actually overlap and intersect. The "life of the mind" is therefore situated within the political economy of all knowledge-producing institutions and spaces; the diverse and changing rules of aesthetic taste, form, and behavior managed by critics and reformers; and the unevenly expressed needs, interests, and actions of philanthropic, social movement, and consumer patrons, even when manifested in the words and deeds of an individual thinker.[10] As an example, the *cerebral physicality* Johnson exhibited in the ring through his boxing genius and self-conscious crafting of black bodily display was given further meaning by the two-year-long "Johnson Affair." Through Johnson, the country was swept up in ideological debates about appropriate expressions of masculinity, racial assertiveness, and mass cultural pleasure.

Outside the ring, various postfight celebrations and castigations enacted a call and response between black feelings of restlessness and resistance against Jim Crow America and the spectacle of Johnson as a mass cultural object of both erotic desire and detestation that extended far beyond his sport. The marketplace intellectual life that surrounded Johnson foretold, in an extreme form, the larger wave of black migrants soon to come. Male and female migrants continued using consumer culture to challenge both white and black conceptions of "northern freedom," a freedom that was put to the ultimate test in a series of race riots just nine years after Johnson's defeat of Jeffries.[11]

As much as the explosive "Johnson Affair" marked a coming-out party for twentieth-century New Negroes, it merely served as prophetic prologue to the grand narrative-altering forces that shaped the historical crucible of 1919. The popular arts and ideas that emerged from Chicago's marketplace intellectual life in the interwar period were directly embedded within the social "chaos" of the Great Migration, World War I, a series of race riots, and the combined economic and cultural race consciousness emerging all over the country and throughout the African Diaspora in the early twentieth century. Chicago is an especially appropriate site for reexamining New Negro intellectual life because this black "City of the Big Shoulders" has been so soundly and almost singularly associated with an industrial lifestyle and entrepreneurial spirit. In the "shadows of the stockyards," even University of Chicago–trained black sociologists E. Franklin Frazier and Charles Johnson jointly lamented, "Chicago has no intelligentsia."[12] Yet it was precisely under these shadows, within the very circuits of Chicago's industrial capitalism, where black working-class migrants attempted to use the mass consumer marketplace to challenge the dehumanizing effects of capitalism and etch out a world of leisure that could cater to their labor demands. This dangerous locus of consumer capitalism became the unintended conduit for the creation of a black intellectual life and for the seeds of political dissent situated directly within the daily industrial realities of the New Negro era.[13]

The marketplace became a significant space where New Negroes sought race-based cooperative and capitalist strategies as possible solutions toward autonomy and self-control. Five years before Alain Locke's famed proclamation of the Harlem Renaissance and in direct response to the race riots of 1919, word began to spread in Chicago about the rise of a New Negro. America's "race" paper, the *Chicago Defender*, immediately dismissed the adjective "new" as a misnomer but recognized that "the same old tainted individual was roused into self-consciousness" and "awakened . . . with new desires, new hopes for the future." The more politically leftist *Chicago Whip* added, "New Negroes are those who have conceived of a new line of thought . . . that the intrinsic standard of beauty does not rest in the white race." They went on to highlight that white dollars had compromised or heavily informed black cultural and intellectual visions. The *Whip* argued that black control over both mental and manual labor could be achieved only through a "general pooling together of race finance." Chicago historian Frederic H. H. Robb summed up the quest for cultural and economic autonomy best: "The New Negro . . . does not seek philanthropy but an opportunity."[14]

The overt desire for autonomous black cultural production through economic control, and specifically through consumer strategies, was arguably the most salient aspect of Chicago's New Negro consciousness. Chicago writer Howard Phelps foresaw that "the stability of the Negro rests upon his financial independence. Independence means the employment of race men and women by race business men and women." Sharing a national quest to break from the chains of white economic dependence (an approach made popular by black nationalist Marcus Garvey), Chicago's black entrepreneurs, war veterans, laborers, artists, entertainers, politicians, and intellectuals attempted to build a separate economic and institutional world—and worldview— known in their time as simply "the metropolis." The metropolis model was to be driven by a symbiotic relationship between black producers and consumers to secure community control over intellectual and industrial labor. In retrospect, Chicago-trained social scientists St. Clair Drake and Horace R.

Cayton pointed out that while diverse in opinion, there was a general interest in Chicago about the possibilities of a "Black Metropolis." For some it was a fatalistic attempt to deal with the limitations created by American racism; to others it was a tactical position from which to galvanize strength toward eventual integration. Still for others, like gospel singer Mahalia Jackson, it was a collection of moments when one "could lay down his burdens of being a colored person in the white man's world and lead his own life." Most agreed, however, that the metropolis was more than a simple description of space and place; it was an ideology, instrumental in galvanizing Chicago's Black Belt into what Frazier termed a "race conscious community." That residents turned to the metropolis as a solution to white economic control over black manual and mental labor forces us to rethink where and how knowledge is produced.[15]

BLACK MODERNITY: NEW NEGROES MAKING A NEW WORLD

The national rise of the culture industries played a significant role in the emergence of a marketplace intellectual life by creating entire professions and classes driven by "mental" labor. Outside of the labor produced by and for corporate and academic research laboratories, the culture industries primarily took the form of leisure and entertainment. Such industries drew from the new technologies of moving pictures, recorded sound, broadcasting, and mass spectator sports. The ideas and commodities from these media spheres were further advertised and exchanged through the accelerated commercial networks of trains, ships, newspapers, and airwaves. By the late nineteenth century, the more stabilized distinctions between "high" and "low" culture were already collapsing under the weight of the industrialized production of cultural entertainments and artifacts. But it was the modern revolution in commercialized sight and sound after World War I that increasingly made cultural production, exchange, and interpretation relatively inexpensive and hence more accessible to a wider variety of people and perspectives. This shift also posed a direct challenge to the Victorian era authority of the written text, the museum, the formal theater, and their designated critics.[16]

As all Americans turned to the mass consumer marketplace, it became an especially hopeful and harrowing site for a diversity of New Negroes. The new technologies of sound, celluloid, and print could more efficiently disseminate now mass-produced racist ideas across the globe. At the same time, however, these mediums could be used to free up black cultural production from the literally patronizing confines of white patriarchy, patronage, and/or philanthropy through a consumer-based control over black labor and leisure. The important shift from white philanthropy to the black metropolis, and its dependence on a diversity of black consumer patrons, also transformed the marketplace into a public sphere of dialogue and debate over competing visions of the New Negro world. Importantly, the very notion of a race discourse was largely circulated and contested within the marketplace. The worlds of race papers, race records, race films, and race entrepreneurship were essential spheres where cultural producers, critics, and patrons engaged the arena of commercial exchange to rethink the established parameters of community, progress, and freedom.[17]

At the center of debate were competing ideas about the appropriate displays of black migrant bodies and behaviors in especially public commercial arenas, where the possible implications for "the race" were magnified. Simply put, Chicago's New Negroes shared hope in the potential viability of the mass consumer marketplace, but struggles emerged over varying interpretations of what the *Chicago Defender* and *Chicago Whip* called the "bad deportment" of "newcomers" within that space. The marketplace dictates of an "old settler" sensibility marked public images of labor efficiency—temperance, bodily restraint, and functional modesty in dress—as indicators of respectability. A range of moral leaders and recent migrants hoped such images could combat restrictions on black mobility, challenge industrial stereotypes of dysfunction, and craft images of a "better class." At the same time, those residents who adopted a "new settler" outlook felt as oppressed by the limited guarantees of an old settler puritan work ethic as they did by domestic surveillance and industrial dehumanization. Many people turned to leisure spaces within the mass marketplace seeking public displays of pleasure, bodily release, and decorative self-mastery, which created different visions of community and alternative labor sources and hence their own New Negro visions of respectability. The dialectic of disgrace and desire, over the transforming mass consumer tastes, styles, and habits of urban migrants, became the driving force behind Chicago's "New Negro" intellectual life. Yet the story of Chicago's New Negroes did not stand alone but was part of an epic tale of the "Darker Races" and their quest to forge a black modernity.[18]

More than a literary metaphor, the New Negro was a product and producer of the global transformations that generated "Modern Times."[19] At the turn of the twentieth century, New Negroes represented people within intellectual circles who generally debated various strategies toward racial integration—a debate that took place during the earliest black elite migration of "the talented tenth" north.[20] Yet, the New Negro became a more progressive "movement" in both senses of the word between the Great Migration of over 1 million African Americans north and west beginning in 1910 and the convergence of proletarian and black radical internationalisms in the mid-1930s. Domestic migration followed the exodus of immigrants from the colonial poles of southern/eastern Europe, Asia, and the Caribbean to U.S. industrial cities. These immigrations and migrations were symbolic of larger processes, including the growth and expansion of industrial capitalism searching for new labor and markets and the long march of black resistance against subservience, offering new definitions of freedom and enlightenment.[21]

The two inextricably tied forces of capitalism and black resistance struggles came to an apocalyptic head during World War I in ways that transformed the political and cultural concerns associated with the New Negro. Cultural critics, activists, and general observers saw in the war a violent struggle between European industrial nations over colonial markets. For example, both Hubert Harrison's essay "Our International Consciousness" and W. E. B. Du Bois's 1915 *Atlantic Monthly* piece "The African Roots of War" highlighted that one of the unintended consequences of global capitalism was that white-on-white violence on the world stage exposed the dark underside of patriarchy and progress while undermining a blind faith in the racial supremacy of rational-industrial nations.[22] Wartime black internationalisms brought a particular urgency to the 1919 Pan-African conference alongside a number of organizations, including the Negro Equal Rights League, the Hamitic League, and the short-lived International League of Darker Peoples, all trying to place black grievances on the platform of the Versailles peace treaty meetings. This black internationalist moment signaled a shift in New Negro consciousness toward a varied denouncement of the interconnections between Euro-American enlightenment, colonialism, global capitalism, racial science, and racist social formations in transnational metropolises.[23]

On one side, wartime suspicions of "the West" strengthened visions of resistance that pulled from images of the Great Migration, the Mexican Revolution, anti-colonial rebellions in Ireland, China, and Trinidad, and even the imperial advance of Japan against European expansion. Furthermore, radicals in the United States and abroad interpreted the Bolshevik Revolution of 1917 as a "slave movement," while V. I. Lenin himself saw direct parallels between the conditions of Russian peasants and black sharecroppers' endurance of Jim Crow terrorism. On the other side, *The Rising Tide of Color* in many white minds seemed to wash over every corner of the planet. This moment of almost fatalistic uncertainty spawned T. S. Eliot's aptly titled poem "The Waste Land," which served as the lingua franca of white expatriates who fled to Europe, flew up to their cities on hills, or stormed the capital agitating for anti-immigration and anti-miscegenation laws. Despite alarmist tales about red scares, yellow perils, brown hordes, and black problems, the literal complexion of the globe was changing.[24]

The demographic and conceptual shifts in this era spilled the private lives of a "dark" proletariat out onto the public streets of global cities. The post-migration centrality of specifically black people and their culture haunted the American consciousness and its cityscapes while intersecting with a general moral ambivalence about the future of Western civilization. Many notable future black scholars and activists were student agitators as part of the New Negro's collegiate arm of rebellion against white control over black colleges. Importantly, black soldiers also returned home from World War I with an internationalist sense of New Negro militancy. Du Bois pointed out in his 1919 packed-to-capacity speech at Chicago's Wendell Phillips High School that returning black soldiers "will never be the same again. You need not ask them to go back to what they were before. They cannot, because they are not the same men anymore." Upon return, one soldier boldly confirmed, "We were the first American regiment on the Rhine. . . . We fought for democracy, and we're going to keep on fighting for democracy 'til we get our rights here at home. The black worm has turned."[25]

Though President Woodrow Wilson could not imagine reasons for a domestic brand of race militancy, it is telling that he worried that returning black soldiers would be "our greatest medium in conveying bolshevism to America." While most were not "Bolshevik," many soldiers quickly "return[ed] fighting" alongside newly arriving migrants and established residents in the struggle against long-standing white restrictions on black labor, leisure, and living. White angst and annoyance with a growing black presence quickly erupted into what writer James Weldon Johnson termed the "Red Summer" of 1919 with over forty race rioting "hot spots" as far away as Liverpool, England. However, as white mobs attacked, black people fought back, adding resonance to Claude McKay's timely poem "If We Must Die."[26]

This international and riot-induced New Negro spirit found institutional form within old and newer nationalist/leftist/liberal organizations, including the National Association for the Advancement of Colored People (NAACP), the Universal Negro Improvement Association (providing the first reported use of the term "Negro Renaissance"), the National Association of Colored

Women, the African Blood Brotherhood, the Brotherhood of Sleeping Car Porters and Maids, the Moorish Science Temple, the Negro Sanhedrin Movement, the Ligue de Défense de la Race Nègre, the Sociedad de Folklore Cubano, and the renamed African National Congress, and through general expressions of entitlement in factories and nightclubs and on streetcars. Periodicals as diverse as *Negro World* and the *Messenger* in New York, Chicago's *Defender* and *Whip*, and the *California Eagle* and *Kansas City Call* confirmed this changing tide. Their diasporic counterparts included *Les Continents* and *La Voix des Nègres* in Paris, *Workers Herald* and *African World* in Cape Town, *African Times and Orient Review* in London, and *Diario de la Marina* in Havana. By 1920, the *Messenger, Negro World, Whip,* and *Defender* were collectively and explicitly articulate about defining the "New Negro" vision as one addressing the issues of race and class by resisting the white philanthropic control of black labor and culture.[27]

White leftist papers, including the *Call* and the *Freeman*, also announced, "The New Negro is here" and praised black radical periodicals like the *Messenger* for their analysis of the relationship between race and class toward an interracial proletarian movement. Concurrently, white artists, intellectuals, and consumers turned to, in their minds, the premodern vitality, spirit, rhythm, and communalism of Africa and its now urban descendants, helping to inaugurate the primitivism movement in art and culture. The living artifacts of a non-Western "Africa" in America were excavated and exoticized as a "folk" alternative to and critique of the overindustrialized and atomized modernity of the Western, postwar world. Even when the call was for antiracism, everyone from visual artist Pablo Picasso, classical composer Antonín Dvořák, gangster Al Capone, cultural broker Carl Van Vechten, and folklorist John Lomax to social scientists Franz Boaz and Robert Park were all in a sense white "slummers" seeking rejuvenation from "The Souls of Black Folk." Plantation cafés (or cotton clubs), bricolage art pieces, and theories of cultural relativism all derived a direct sense of inspiration and profit as early "samplers" of what many perceived as the unique primitivisms and "esprit" of African and southern folk cultures that could soothe the Western soul. This mix of interracial solidarity and primitivist fascination created the space for various intellectual and cultural ideas, including the Harlem Renaissance, cubism, New Africanism, "Chicago School" sociology, Afrocubanismo, surrealism, and the "metropolis" model.[28]

On the other side of the veil, the spotlight from white attention intersected with the postmigration rise in black militancy to create art and ideas containing both primitive stereotypes and modern innovations. Race films, race records, race newspapers, Negro baseball leagues, Negro art, Negro history, and race relation studies throughout the African Diaspora became ironic positions of strength in the creation of a New Negro consciousness. Within these marketplace spaces, competing black and white interests converged to struggle over a multiracial, if inequitable, modern identity. From such larger contexts and New Negro ways of "being" in the world, residents of Chicago's black metropolis began to contest the conventional theories of race, class, and national belonging.

CHICAGO AND THE NEW NEGRO

Chicago's central location in the production and distribution of industrial commerce and mass culture helped set the stage for the New Negro's marketplace intellectual life. The national reach of the Illinois Central Railroad and the locally made Pullman cars shuttled industrial and human capital out from the ominous "shadows of the stockyards," meatpacking plants like Armour and Swift, U.S. Steel mills, and the Sears and Roebuck mail-order house. These industries simultaneously received orders back from local sites of consumption along with the harvested raw materials in faraway outposts with an unparalleled efficiency and speed. However, while industrialization and mechanization became symbols of infinite progress, abundance, and interconnectedness, these developments also brought disastrous effects to social groups caught in the gears of the new urban machinery.[29] Industrialization and subsequent immigrant flows made visible the intimate and sharpening contrast between urban prosperity and poverty directly along racial lines. Neoclassical preserves like the Opera House, the Art Institute of Chicago, and Lincoln Park sat in sharp contrast to the growing "towns" and "belts" of cramped and unsanitary shanties, shacks, and slums constructed to pen in the rising tide of European, Asian, and black races. Such conditions created a provocative laboratory of inquiry for muckraking journalists, crusading reformers, and disinterested social scientists alike.[30]

Alongside its manufacturing empires and before the consolidation of local social sciences, Chicago's internationalizing culture industries blurred lines between entertainment, instruction, and enterprise in the creation of an emerging sacred/secular moral order literally built on black bodies and souls. Religious leader Dwight L. Moody brought together ties to businessmen including Marshall Field, his leadership over the local Young Men's Christian Association (YMCA), and stewardship over his Chicago Bible Institute and large revival camp meetings into a powerful Christian economy.

These exploits inspired a mass appeal revivalism that influenced athlete-turned-evangelist Billy Sunday, who later informed the music ministry of the gospel sound. Wrapped in both a language of science and the conventions of the carnival, the World's Columbian Exposition used visual mediums of exhibition and film to instruct visitors on the Social Darwinist hierarchy of races. As the first physical educator in the country to hold an academic position, Amos Alonzo Stagg preached the gospel of "Muscular Christianity" at the University of Chicago while excluding many black athletes from his divine providence. Finally, the already successful Chicago-based J. E. McBrady and Company expanded its appeals to female beautification with a halfhearted attempt to capitalize on the race market with their line for "Brown Skin People." The relegation of new migrants to shanty-style living and scab-status labor and the academic and popular cultural attempts to justify such life "choices" foretold the racial logic that would be used as local black population growth weighed heavier on Chicago's big shoulders.

Between 1910 and 1935, within what was called the Black Belt, at least 250,000 new migrants forced Chicago's older residents to engage intimately the rapid transformation of the black community in the city. While Harlem has been heralded as the center of early-twentieth-century black culture, when most migrants connected freedom with the urban North, "the mecca was Chicago." Shortly after Jack Johnson's defeat of Jim Jeffries in 1910 and the resulting riots, black moviegoers in the "better class" won a landmark antidiscrimination suit against a prominent downtown theater, and Wendell Phillips High School hired its first black teachers. These events helped provide an infrastructure of black possibility in Chicago for the migrants to come; yet it was during the 1919 moment that a black modernity more fully materialized. This alternate modern landscape was made real through, for example, the barnstorming Chicago American Giants baseball team on luxurious private Pullman cars, the international transportation of "race" images and ideals through locally produced records and films, and of course the circulation of the *Chicago Defender* via black Pullman porters to future migrants in southern cities and countrysides. Chicago eventually became such a powerful symbol of prosperity and freedom that blues singer Robert Johnson literally relocated the city within the much older American mythos of the Western frontier, singing, "Ooh, baby don't you want to go? / Back to the land of California, to my sweet home Chicago." Positions of north and south, east and west, rural and urban, were transformed into provisional expressions of a national "race" consciousness and imagined community. In fact, the term "race" was popularized (similar to "black" over fifty years later) by *Defender* editor Robert Abbott as a galvanizing and modern alternative to what he saw as derogatory outdated labels.[31]

The effects of cultural mediums such as the *Chicago Defender* were both material and far-reaching, but nothing seemed to cohere a national and local New Negro outlook as much as the Red Summer of 1919. Chicago's black workers were at once fighting against racist labor unions and joining the interracial meatpackers union in unprecedented numbers (6,000 out of the possible 18,000 black workers). At the same time, the social "problems" of racial incorporation and national belonging were especially acute at the sensitive lines of demarcation between black migrants and their white ethnic immigrant counterparts in South Side living and leisure spaces. The black working class took the full brunt of the double meaning of the word "red" that summer in the bloody suppression of black mobility and leftist political organizing. With earlier upheavals in Springfield and East St. Louis, Illinois, and "red scares" in the city, there were prophetic warnings that Chicago was about to explode. Gun battles erupted in Chicago's streets during the summer of 1919 where white violent aggression ensued, and black people took up arms to defend their lives and communities.[32]

In the September 1919 *Crisis*, Du Bois announced that the strategy of "Passive Resistance" had to be laid down in favor of the "terrible weapon of Self-Defense" in the struggle for "Freedom or Death." While men, women, and children had joined this struggle, he went on to bestow "endless and undying Honor, to every man, black or white, who in Houston, East St. Louis, Washington and Chicago gave his life for Civilization and Order." The *Messenger* devoted almost its entire September 1919 issue to discussing events in Chicago. The black radical *Crusader* journal also made direct links between Chicago and revolts in the rest of the "darker" world, declaring, "Whether the caucasian reads the news dispatches from Egypt or from West Africa, from the Capital of the United States or from the West Indies, from *Chicago* or from Panama, it must be dawning upon his junker mind that his self-constituted lordship of the world is at an end" (emphasis added). Initial sparks for the fiery uprisings were found in interracial contests over crowded housing, limited labor, and/or racist recreation spaces. Notably, the violence began that summer in Chicago when black teenager Eugene Williams accidentally floated "across the imaginary" racial line and into "white water" at the 29th Street Beach. He was subsequently stoned to death for "trespassing," and violent battles erupted to maintain white order. The global importance of local events in 1919 Chicago made it clear that whatever the sparks, struggles over both labor and leisure were central.[33]

Crowds in the street in front of Jesse Binga's bank during the 1919 race riots.
(Courtesy of the Chicago Historical Society)

In fact, during Chicago's race riots, the *Messenger* found Chicago's cabarets along the black leisure/business district the "Stroll" to be a "dynamic agent of social equality" that offered promising contact within the working class across the color line without the intrusions of the wealthy who encouraged antagonisms. Their understandings about the cabaret were a bit utopian, ignoring the very real divisions between black workers and black and white patrons at cabarets. But the *Messenger*'s observations about the political potential within Chicago's mass culture were telling and wouldn't be the last. The Stroll, while not solely a place of leftist politics, became an important site where many working-class migrants acquired alternative sources of labor and created new kinds of leisure and hence their own routes and rites of respectability. In the world of mass culture, Chicago became, among other things, "the home of black recording companies in the 1920s." By the 1930s, many cultural workers who were once deemed community pariahs had now ascended to respectability—unfortunately with their own exclusionary rules, regulations, and codes of conduct.[34]

These competing visions of labor, leisure, and racial respectability were put on explicit display in the appropriately titled pamphlet *Chicago and the New Negro*. In 1927, Carroll Binder, staff writer for the mainstream newspaper the *Chicago Daily News*, consolidated a series of news articles into this ten-cent pamphlet. Binder's primary goal in this project was to assuage local white fears about the threat of another race riot in the city. From the start, the pamphlet dismissed the well-known violent interracial struggles over neighborhood boundaries as a thing of the past and replaced them with images of black home ownership, entrepreneurship, satisfactory labor performance, and supervised leisure. What was once a "Negro invasion of white territories" was now described as a peaceful New Negro residential evolution through social, economic, and political "stability." In retelling the story of the New Negro, Binder in fact appropriated the term "New Negro" as a reformist top-down signifier of community self-discipline and as a metaphor of interracial cooperation between the better-situated of each race.[35]

However, this linguistic takeover was so self-conscious that Binder's heavy-handed condemnations of questionable entrepreneurial and leisure activities actually highlighted the significance of their threat to the reformist social order he seemed to desire. For example, Binder celebrates the increase in the interracial work of "reform and cultural movements," but this is discussed in the face of the admittedly more popular "interracial intercourse" in cabarets and gambling houses. Alongside his showcasing of the respectable race entrepreneurs Anthony Overton and Jesse Binga, Binder was forced to acknowledge the power of decentralized and lower-"grade" black amusements, dance halls, and Prohibition-era policy gambling and bootlegging as equally "impressive . . . industries of the race." In the end, working-class migrant leisure practices remained "unbound" from Binder's attempt at reform and criticism. He could at best demonize or retell but never fully suppress the power of the "less fortunately situated" of the race and their centrality to Chicago's New Negro ascendancy.[36]

To better situate the "less fortunately situated," this book is an intellectual history in which ideas are embodied and explained through a collection of scholars, critics, urban spaces, cultural producers, and the consumer patrons who supported their work. This marketplace intellectual life is refracted through the lenses of beauty culturist Madam C. J. Walker, filmmaker Oscar Micheaux and the actual exhibition spaces of black film culture, musician/composer Thomas Dorsey, and athletes Jack Johnson and Andre "Rube" Foster, who were all "thrown up" from the Stroll as simply framed articulations of the incomplete yet collective visions of their mass consumer patrons.

Their articles, compositions, and textbooks, their educational, media, and community institutions, and their varied support of political causes and social movements helped facilitate a makeover of the black metropolis.[37]

Importantly, Chicago's New Negro intellectual life demonstrates how marketplace and consumer support were used not just to push cheaper products on black publics. Individual figures invested their commercial successes in group institutions and individual interests to widen the scope of black political and intellectual possibilities. The visions and desires of sharecroppers, entertainers, and factory, domestic, clerical, and sex workers were put in conversation with traditional intellectuals and leaders, including Du Bois, Ida B. Wells, Woodrow Wilson, Fannie Barrier Williams, Booker T. Washington, D. W. Griffith, Marcus Garvey, and Richard Wright, among others. The form, style, and sites of these conversations challenge traditional representations of intellectual life and force us to reexamine the larger New Negro world where knowledge was produced in ways that suggest lessons for our future.

This book comprises six chapters. "Mapping the Black Metropolis" surveys the literal construction of Chicago's marketplace intellectual life by examining debates over the behaviors, styles, and spaces of leisure and enterprise. The remaining chapters explore distinct cultural formations as part of an intersecting matrix of popular art and imagination. These chapters do not follow a linear progression of time but contain overlapping chronologies. Each chapter serves as a snapshot within the larger collage of a shared New Negro moment in time. "Making Do" traces the rise of a distinctly black beauty culture and its role in fashioning a modern womanhood at the intersection of "old settler" resistance, migrant adornment practices and innovations, and new urban technologies. "Theaters of War" collectively engages those who crafted, recycled, and displayed themselves and their ideas within local film exhibition spaces, hence serving as the real actors within Chicago's pioneering black film culture. "The Birth of Two Nations" shifts from the exhibition space to chronicle the "Golden Age" of race film production within its central Chicago context. Through the emergence and circulation of gospel music, "Sacred Tastes" explores the aesthetic, institutional, and commercial agendas that gained voice through early-twentieth-century black sacred music. "The Sporting Life" focuses on the promises and pitfalls of athletics, or commercialized physical culture, and the sporting production of new public displays of black masculinity. The epilogue, "The Crisis of the Black Bourgeoisie, Or, What If Harold Cruse Had Lived in Chicago?" demonstrates, through a conversation between the ideas of E. Franklin Frazier and Harold

Cruse, the consistent links that traditional black intellectuals have made between race consciousness, agency, and consumerism in devising projects of political and social possibility.

The consumer marketplace and intellectual life did not stand at odds within the black metropolis. The discourse and debate over hairstyles, musical rhythms, cinematic images, and "sporting" recreations are what gave life to the black metropolis as a physical space and as an intellectual vision. It is precisely in these consumer-based amusements, alongside the traditional intellectual spheres of church and academe, where class struggles were waged, theoretical insights were produced historically, and many of the thoughts of the "people" are now revealed to the historian. The pairing together of "autonomous" thought and "mindless" consumption within a reconstructed notion of New Negro and Renaissance suggests new directions for the study of ideas within American life. Within this mass consumer space, Chicago's "New Negroes" self-consciously negotiated, struggled over, and upheld the categories of race, class, gender, nation, and intellect literally, as academics like to say, "on the ground" in ways that offer lessons for the present. Even though these marketplace intellectuals and their consumer patrons would not use this language, they understood such identities as socially (even commercially) constructed while both spatially and historically specific.

In the end, this book resists the impulsive search for narratives of linear progress, consolidation, and unification. For both migrants and established residents, the interwar period was a moment of community building, class formation, and cultural conflict over a variety of desires for a different future. Placing the lives and thoughts of black migrants at the center of analysis maps out the socioeconomic transformation of the urban and national terrain between the two world wars. New Negro sensibilities illustrate a much larger set of social and cultural processes that Harlem Renaissance aesthete Locke himself admits were part of "a racial awakening on a national and perhaps even world scale," where "the professional man, himself [is] migrating to recapture his constituency."[38]

Chapter One

Mapping the Black Metropolis

A CULTURAL GEOGRAPHY OF THE STROLL

We can end this review of the institutions, businesses and life
of the Negro in Chicago with much self-contentment, if the
review of this big city has unsealed the eyes of many,
regardless of where they live, who contend that the race
has no field for its capital.
—Howard A. Phelps, "Negro Life in Chicago,"
Half-Century Magazine, May 1919

The Map of Colored Chicago: Showing the Streets, Street
Car Lines, and especially featuring the Colored section,
giving the location of all the principal Colored Churches,
Colored Hospitals, Lodges, Colored Clubs, Colored Y.M.C.A.,
Colored Y.W.C.A., and other public places of amusement,
recreation and interest.
—Progressive Book Company advertisement,
Half-Century Magazine, April 1922

Chicago . . . was a real us-for-we, we-for-us community. It was
a community of men and women who were respected, people
of great dignity—doctors, lawyers, policy operators, bootblacks,
barbers, beauticians, saloonkeepers, night clerks, cab owners
and cab drivers, stockyard workers, owners of after-hours
joints, bootleggers—everything and everybody.
—Edward Kennedy "Duke" Ellington,
Music Is My Mistress, 1931

Six years before cultural critic Alain Locke made an almost identical (and more famous) claim about the Harlem Renaissance, the impact of the Great Migration encouraged writer Howard Phelps to remark, "Professional men are leaving the South on the trail of their clients and patients who have settled in Chicago." In the same 1919 essay, Phelps offered an extensive documentation of prominent black church and amusement landmarks complemented by the individual accomplishments of black entrepreneurs and leaders as indications of racial respectability in the city. His *Half-Century Magazine* essay, "Negro Life in Chicago," was followed by the Progressive Book Company's 1922 advertisement for a map of the same community. Finally, when musician/composer Duke Ellington visited in 1931, he was equally impressed by Chicago's black institutions and its "community of men and women who were *respected*" (emphasis added). These various cultural mappings highlight the consistent symbolic importance of black "enterprise" in constructing notions of race pride and in securing the desire for a many times elusive respectability. And yet on first sight, Ellington's inclusion of policy (illegal lottery) operators, saloon keepers, and bootleggers as enterprising might seem out of place and glaringly incommensurate with both Phelps's and the Progressive Book Company's vision of racial respectability.[1]

Such divergent mappings of the same place and the inclusion of different figures and institutions under the same banner of respect and dignity are significant. They reveal the larger spatial transformations, class conflicts, and ideological struggles that took place in both the physical and conceptual space of the emerging black metropolis. The contested highlights and oversights in the various geographical representations of the metropolis by white observers and black old and new settlers reveal contested interpretations of what a black modernity could mean. These embattled mappings became the terrain upon which Chicago's New Negro life was built.

At the center of the emerging "metropolis" vision stood Chicago's black commercial amusement and business district, the "Stroll." This chapter examines the same space and time of the Stroll from three different conceptual vantage points, three simultaneously generated and overlapping planes of existence, each competing for community (re)cognition. The space and meaning of the Stroll was pushed and pulled as a battleground over the three basic images of black primitivism, racial respectability, and leisure-based labor. Amid this representational struggle, the Stroll became the spatial articulation of different New Negro intellectual positions on the meaning and use of the black metropolis as both a built environment and an ideal. Yet, the Stroll was not an island unto itself but must be understood as a spectacular manifestation of the international transformations affecting both the community and the city at large.[2]

FROM BLACK BELT TO BLACK METROPOLIS:
SLUMMERS, SOCIAL SCIENTISTS, UPLIFTERS, AND ENTERPRISERS

By 1910 and especially after 1915, the ranks of Chicago's black citizenry were rapidly swelling within the cramped spaces of what was called the Black Belt, a narrow strip of land on the south side of the city from 18th Street to 39th Street and bounded by State Street on the east and the Rock Island Railroad tracks and LaSalle Street on the west. As the population exploded from 44,130 in 1910 to 233,903 by 1930, a trend of spatial consolidation restricted the Black Belt's expansion primarily to the south, west to Wentworth, and a few streets east with some black residents as far east as Cottage Grove. Black residents were faced with the "dynamic of choice and constraint" and therefore, unlike other immigrants, were more restricted to residential space along the lines of ethnicity instead of class.[3]

The force of racist restrictive covenants and racial violence helped materialize the notion of racial restraint quite clearly. Restrictive covenants became legally binding agreements, usually between white real estate agents and owners, to prevent the renting or sale of housing to nonwhites, with threat of civil action. The neighboring Hyde Park, Kenwood, and Woodlawn areas to the south had more available and less expensive housing, but organizations like the notorious Hyde Park and Kenwood Property Owners' Association went as far as to call on employers to deny jobs to black residents who would dare "invade" white areas. Their general rationale was the protection of property values, but with the financial help of the neighboring University of Chicago, this meant keeping Hyde Park all white. The housing stock left to black residents was in some of the city's most dilapidated neighborhoods. With the rule of restrictive covenants, landlords could extract the highest rents for the worst housing from the most economically disenfranchised population. This reality gave rise to overcrowded housing in the black community and to kitchenettes, where apartments were cut up into single rooms, rented without a lease or, ironically, a kitchen, sometimes including a hot plate for cooking. By 1919, the Black Belt suffered a housing shortage while there was abundant surplus in other parts of the city. Such urban boundaries for housing and leisure mobility were at the same time shaped by racial

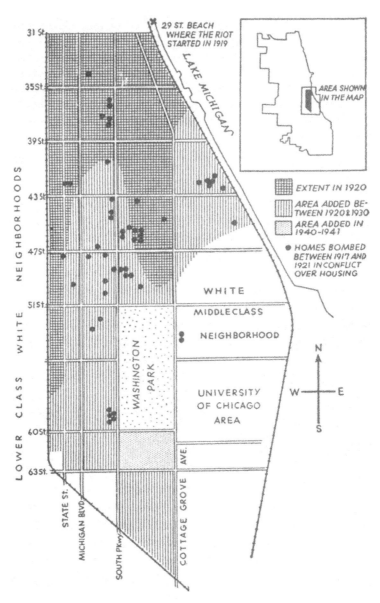

31 St.

29 ST. BEACH
WHERE THE RIOT
STARTED IN 1919

35 St.

LAKE MICHIGAN

39 St.

AREA SHOWN
IN THE MAP

N
E
I
G
H
B
O
R
H
O
O
D
S

43 St.

▦ EXTENT IN 1920

▦ AREA ADDED BE-
TWEEN 1920&1930

▦ AREA ADDED IN
1940-1941

47 St.

● HOMES BOMBED
BETWEEN 1917 AND
1921 IN CONFLICT
OVER HOUSING

W
H
I
T
E

51 St.

WHITE

MIDDLECLASS

NEIGHBORHOOD

N

WASHINGTON PARK

UNIVERSITY
OF CHICAGO
AREA

W—E

S

C
L
A
S
S

60 St.

L
O
W
E
R

63 St.

AVE.

STATE ST.

MICHIGAN BLVD.

SOUTH PKWY.

COTTAGE GROVE

Map of the Black Belt. From St. Clair Drake and Horace R. Cayton,
Black Metropolis: A Study of Negro Life in a Northern City
(New York: Harcourt, Brace, 1945).

24 / MAPPING THE BLACK METROPOLIS

violence in the form of young white "athletic clubs" patrolling neighborhood lines and the anonymous firebombing of black homes. Between July 1917 and March 1921, fifty-eight homes in Chicago were bombed, with the predominant victims being South Side black people who had moved into white areas and the black and white agents who had sold to them. This use of restrictive covenants and racial violence racially structured labor, leisure, and living spaces while providing the backdrop for the city's explosive Red Summer of 1919.[4]

In the midst of the rapid growth and spatial consolidation of the black community, white reformers, reporters, and thrill seekers were not just repelled from (and repelled by) its quarters. They also turned a new eye to what they called the Black Belt and particularly its leisure district, the Stroll, as a site of urban primitivism and pleasure. In response, black leaders hoped to showcase the more respectable "race" enterprises in what they called the metropolis. But all had to concede that the music clubs, movie theaters, beauty parlors, and "sporting dens" on the Stroll were some of the most popular and profitable institutions in the community and so ultimately became the structural foundation for Chicago's New Negro intellectual life.

Located along State Street from 26th to 39th Street, the Stroll was the spatial articulation of New Negro intellectual life within the black metropolis vision. Its major intersection of theaters, restaurants, dance halls, and businesses centered around 35th and State until the late 1920s, when it moved farther south to 47th. This area was variably lauded as "the Bohemia of Colored Folk," "the black man's Broadway and Wall Street," and "just like Times Square." However, these celebratory proclamations were not without context. The *Chicago Defender* announced that the Stroll was "not so bad as painted—reputable business men and women make up this wonderful thoroughfare." The paper's sarcastic retort "a careful investigation—or, I might say, visit . . . will show less that tend to be bad" was a direct response to "the white plague" of slummers and pleasure seekers who, according to the *Chicago Whip*, entered the Stroll "first to scoff and then remain to play" under the guise of uplift, journalism, and/or sociology.[5]

In newspapers, legislative investigations, and academic studies, black Chicago, among other ethnic enclaves, was represented as the antithesis of Progressive Era industriousness and productivity. At the beginning of the Great Migration, white newspapers screamed "HALF A MILLION DARKIES" bring "PERIL TO HEALTH." Migrants were demonized as helpless peasant refugees ignorant of urban life with a culture that needed adjustment, containment, and discipline.[6] Yet there was still a mix of fascination and fear of the "foreign" culture these migrants carried with them from the South that was simply reinforced by the physical concentration of more black bodies in a confined space. Articles focused on the primitive release and premodern pleasure white tourists thought they found in the race-mixing sites of black-and-tan clubs, buffet flats, and brothels along or near the Stroll. One sensational story described a night at the famous black-owned Pekin Theatre as a miscegenated cauldron of "lawless liquor, sensuous shimmy, solicitous sirens, wrangling waiters, all tints of the racial rainbow. . . . A brown girl sang. . . . Black men with white girls, white men with yellow girls, old, young, all filled with the abandon brought about by illicit whisky and liquor music." Reporting on a show of famed jazz musician Joe "King" Oliver, *Variety* described his set as "loud, wailing, and pulsating," a jazz with "no conscience." Even those like white jazz musician Eddie Condon, who truly celebrated the Stroll, described this space of black nightlife as having a primitive flair of inherent musicality, as if the "midnight air on State Street was so full of music that if you held up an instrument the breeze would play it." Black urban space was further depicted as a foreign reserve when the *Chicago Tribune* described a nearby streetcar line as "African Central."[7]

Ironically, as early as 1911, the Vice Commission of Chicago made clear that the link between black life and vice was not a racial inheritance but an intentional project of municipal rezoning that put Chicago's red light district in the black community. Just as in other cities, the rapid growth of Chicago's black population, combined with residential and employment segregation, racist zoning practices, and white violence, confined all black classes, leisure, vice, religion, and so on to the same racially confined space, making the Stroll a perceived model for urban dysfunction and disorganization. The white ownership, operation, patronage, and protection of vice in the Black Belt challenges charges that vice was a "Negro Problem." However, the spatial fixity of the majority of Chicago's vice and amusement to the geographical location of the Stroll physically marked and conceptually mapped deviance as a "Negro" trait. White tourists could enter, partake of, and enjoy the "vitality" and "spirit" of the African safari in the city, as both a threat and balm that existed outside of and away from their own overindustrialized "white" civilization.[8]

This nightlife picture of black primitivism was reinforced as "scientific" through the findings of the University of Chicago's "Chicago School" of sociology and its eventual chair and former Urban League president, Robert Park, in particular. The University of Chicago developed a social scientific analysis of urbanization, positing a process of eventual cultural assimilation among different races, to counter the prevalent Social Darwinist theories of inherent biological racial difference and conflict. The integrated emergence of manufacturing industries, urban expansion, ethnic/racial immigration and migration, and conflict made Chicago the perfect "laboratory" for race relations scholarship and reform. Through his human ecology theories, Park argued that social relationships naturally progressed from simple to complex, agrarian to industrial, and primitive rural to civilized urban. The city was seen as a liberating force of natural growth from the confines of the past, and those who did not evolve were unfortunately the dysfunctional causalities of progress.[9]

At the time, most social scientists used the term "race" where we would now use "ethnicity." In Park's work, he designated, for example, Jews, Poles, Irish, and Negroes as distinct races with their own "temperaments" that determined the state and speed at which each group would assimilate into the "American" social order. Park built on the popular assumptions of employers to rationalize that all "foreign" racial groupings had deviant temperaments. But in the context of Chicago's entrenched racial violence, it also became clear that the "racial uniform" of "nonwhite" social groups prevented a natural incorporation into the national whole simply through acculturation. However, instead of focusing on the very real systemic and personal resistance on the part of both white citizens and European ethnic immigrants toward black migrant incorporation, Park turned to the Negro's temperament as a rationale. He wrote that black people manifested "an interest and attachment to external, physical things rather than to subjective states and objects of introspection, in a disposition for expression rather than enterprise and action. . . . He is, so to speak, the lady among races." So if the industrial symbols of "enterprise and action" designated a culture of "civilization," the Negroes' specific "disposition for expression" was the natural explanation for their slow advance and their spatial location in urban vice districts. Park later suggested that perhaps the only route to Negro assimilation was through biological miscegenation. He argued that the mixture of white blood and culture was what, for example, made mulattoes like Frederick Douglass and W. E. B. Du Bois less docile and more "aggressive and ambitious." Negroes could be assimilated, but unlike Poles, Jews, or the Irish, the Negroes' racial temperament—more so than racism—fixed them as the negation of civilization from the start.[10]

In *The City*, the most important co-edited work of urban sociology, Ernest Burgess took Park's theories about "racial temperaments" and literally mapped them out on urban space. The Black Belt and its leisure district, the

Stroll (never named), were represented as an unassimilable mass of "free and disorderly life," different and distinct from the "immigrant colonies—The Ghetto, Little Sicily, Greektown, Chinatown—fascinatingly combining old world heritages and American adaptations." While he witnessed the possibility of European immigrant "adaptations," Burgess marked the "excessive increase . . . of southern Negroes into northern cities since the war" as the standard by which to measure disturbance in the natural "metabolism" of urban order.[11]

The Black Belt appeared to constitute a structurally homogeneous and socially deviant community primarily because of both the legal and informal modes of racial restrictions on mobility. But within the black community, preexisting and newly developing cultural codes profoundly shaped structural realities. Underneath racist visions of the Black Belt as an undifferentiated racial mass existed varied responses to economic, residential, and ideological discrimination attempting to directly refute Park's theory that the Negro had no disposition for "enterprise and action." Alongside journalistic and sociological observations, black institutions, social mores, and cultural codes continued to develop in black neighborhoods. These enclaves became attractive to those who either chose or were forced into relative exclusion from the white properties of social and physical mobility, especially during the Great Migration.

Across the nation, the years of the Great Migration signaled a moment of "ideological, political and cultural contestation between an emergent black bourgeoisie and an emerging working class." In Chicago, the same period, roughly between 1910 and 1935, highlighted a point of structural/cultural contact and transformation between the self-described "better class" and the masses, giving life to competing "old" and "new" settler ideologies. The "old" and "new" markers of distinction within the black metropolis first referred to a turn-of-the-twentieth-century rift between an emerging middle class and an older elite. The middle class attempted to capitalize on the growing concentration of black residents in the physical ghetto, whereas the older elite feared this turn inward could justify segregation, impede their business relationships of service to the white elite, and force them to associate with black people who did not possess their refinement. However, after 1915, these two groups merged in response to the much larger Great Migration from the "Deep South." Within the postwar New Negro culture, the terms "old" and "new" became much less about when one arrived in Chicago and began to signify one's relationship to ideas about industrialized labor and leisure as expressions of respectability.[12]

All black people shared relative positions of marginality within Chicago's socioeconomic structure, but community members drew lines of distinction around the markers of refinement and, most important, respectability. Here, class and particularly the distinction of an old settler respectability was established through representational markers of "bourgeois status." In the broadest sense, old settler notions of respectability located the industrial standards of labor function and efficiency within the outward appearance and behavior of economic thrift, bodily restraint, and functional modesty in personal and community presentation. However, these distinctions were not as rigid as they may appear. For example, notable mass cultural entrepreneurs like newspaperman Robert Abbott and beauty culture mogul Anthony Overton were migrants but also highly critical of many rural and urban "folk" traditions that were thought to inspire conspicuous consumption and excessive displays of public behavior. Whether migrant or long-term resident, those who adopted an old settler respectability wanted to present a unified and positive public image of the race to counteract the cultural assumptions of white supremacy. At the same time, they believed that a leadership class could help better the conditions of working-class migrants.[13]

Many of those very migrants, however, had just come from lives where they were already defined strictly by their function within a labor system and, along with older residents, found a resiliently racist division of labor in northern industrial life. A "new settler" ideology emerged that equally worked within the black metropolis model but turned primarily to the Stroll's commercialized leisure world to create alternative kinds of labor, routes to upward mobility, and visions of the racial community. Women were especially excluded from industrial and white-collar jobs, making their work in the leisure industries an important option outside the largely domestic labor made available. In this context, general desires for self-worth, family survival, and race pride were, in the extreme, expressed through brash public displays of nonfunctional fashions, up-tempo rhythms, theatrical personalities, and muscular confrontations. Such displays also served as moments of possible dissent against white supremacy, black reform, and a labor identity of subservience.

But again, the term "new settler" was an ideological vision that did not simply mean new migrant. In fact, an old settler like Ida B. Wells supported beauty culturist Madam C. J. Walker, the policy-backed Pekin Inn, and Oscar Micheaux's controversial films on the grounds of race pride, while working-class migrants in the demonstrative Sanctified churches were harshly critical of worldly amusements on the grounds of religious virtue. But even if all did not agree, leisure industries helped construct a new settler respectability through clean work, economic alternatives, the possibility of geographical mobility, and a liberating identity outside the dehumanizing conditions of factories and relatively free of the intimate sexual harassment found working in white homes. The mass consumer marketplace of moving pictures, radio and records, advertising, and athletics helped instigate a struggle over the broad terms of respectability as a world of bodily restraint versus bodily release.[14]

As one version of Chicago's New Negro culture, those who identified with the old settler ideology attempted to capitalize on their forced proximity to migrant voters and consumer patrons to focus on a respectable and hence daytime image of the Stroll in creating the black metropolis. At the same time, the physical structure of the black community forced them "to live with those of their color who [were] shiftless, dissolute and immoral" and to witness "the brazen display of vice of all kinds." Old settlers then both depended on and distinguished themselves from the black migrants they felt reinforced white visions of black deviance, most clearly embodied in Stroll nightlife. Moreover, when those of the self-described "better class" wanted to engage in recreation, they resented the limited option of being "mixed with the undesirable or remain[ing] at home in seclusion." Many understood the "racial amusement problem" to be one of "boisterousness and defiance of public sentiment." In fact, after the race riots of 1919, some old settlers argued that it was the vulgar behaviors and southern ways migrants brought with them "like a disease" that brought on racial tensions and violence.[15]

Park's "lady among races" phrase begins to help clarify how the politics of respectability was centrally played out within the mass consumer marketplace and took on overtly gendered meanings. Within the public theater of the city, Chicago's vice was centrally located in the Black Belt, while black men and women were predominantly relegated to the industrial roles of unskilled factory and service work and domestic labor. These urban social realities collapsed any widespread possibilities for the black acquisition of the desirable Victorian divisions between public/private, male/female, and producer/consumer. Such conditions reinforced the idea that black males were seemingly not manly economic producers and consequently could not keep "their" women in the home or prevent race, sex, and class mixing in their communities. In this context, the black community appeared fully penetrated, compromised, and miscegenated and hence was spatially gendered as a "lady." Moreover, women became the most public and targeted displays of racial respectability as the designated cultural caretakers of black metropolis homes, streets, and local institutions where bodily restraint and traditional gender/class/sex roles were learned.[16]

Appropriate womanhood and domesticity became such powerful symbols for the success or failure of old settler respectability that the decades prior to the Great Migration were known as the "woman's era" of reform politics. A heightened focus on culture, as opposed to biology, meant that group status was not fixed but open to evolutionary change, or literally cultivation. In response to persistent biological stereotypes of black female promiscuity and general immorality, leaders attempted to craft a new positive cultural image of black womanhood within the bounds of Victorian femininity. Reformers pushed for images of female virtue and sanctity in the domestic sphere as a positive reflection on the public "virility" of the race. But like its white counterpart, the club- and churchwoman arm of black leadership also turned its restrictive and private role of provider and nurturer into a public calling for racial uplift and moral betterment through reform and temperance movements. If women were valuable for the nurturing homes and moral culture they provided for the present-day and future (male) citizens of the race, then they must be at the center of any public or private discourse about the race. African American female reformers extended this general logic to include the particular goal of racial empowerment, which included women's struggles for wage work, a belief in black female morality, and women's protection from racial and sexual harassment and violence.[17]

However, as black working-class female migrants turned north with "southern ways," the more general "politics of respectability" took on a class-specific approach to racial uplift. The reform of particularly migrant women's "dress, demeanor, and deportment" became a reflection of the race's sexual purity, social orderliness, and industrial efficiency. Again, with many women as urban leisure and service workers, migrant behaviors, styles, and attitudes were obstacles to the cause of racial uplift and required temperance and reform by an "appropriate" race leadership. For example, Chicagoan Fannie Barrier Williams, a founding member and leader of the National Association of Colored Women, utilized a "politics of respectability" to instill an old settler regimen of social purity in black women to discourage connections between immorality and race womanhood. Instead of advocating for change in labor relations, many reformers focused on professionalizing domestic work and black women workers to some "acceptable" level of utility and efficiency. Toward this end, Nannie H. Burroughs's National Training School for Girls associated discipline in public laboring behavior with private virtue to dispel myths about black working-class female laziness, unreliability, and incompetence. In Chicago, among other settlement houses and training schools, the Phillis Wheatley Home (3526 Rhodes Ave.) had provided living accommodations and classes in the domestic arts since 1886. This approach helped define a distinct New Negro leadership class set against the masses in need of reform. Old settlers highlighted a daytime image of the Stroll built on the institutional foundation provided by clubs, churches, social programs, and businesses that materially aided migrants and institutionally structured the larger community.[18]

Black clubwomen's organizations compensated for the (in most cases) outright exclusion of newcomers by Chicago's mainstream lodging homes and social agencies. The network of women's clubs became so strong that they were able to consolidate their many activities into the influential Women's Conference of Chicago. Black women organized settlement programs with childcare, educational, and domestic arts facilities in institutions like the Frederick Douglass Center and the Wendell Phillips Settlement. However, at the height of the Great Migration, the Wheatley Home primarily attended to the needs of the "already" respectable women migrants who, they observed, had been improperly led to "disreputable homes, entertainment and employment," primarily in nearby brothels. And while Ida B. Wells's Negro Fellowship League (2830 S. State) was one of the few organizations that catered to all migrants regardless of their leisure habits, she still warned that the Stroll contained "not a single uplifting influence." The leisure solution for many settlement homes and clubwomen was to hold card parties, musicales, luncheons, and charity balls for themselves while hosting youth clubs, dances, picnics, and other recreations to both raise funds for their important charity work and to lure young women away from Stroll enticements.[19]

In Chicago's dynamic and diverse black sacred sphere, churches ranging from Presbyterian to Pentecostal embodied a wide spectrum of social positions based on the parish's specific form of worship and relationship to the community. Some 5,000-person "Old Line" African Methodist Episcopal (AME) and Baptist churches, but also small storefront churches, offered spiritual counsel along with decorous service- and industry-sponsored programs of social adjustment to attract migrants looking for assistance and those desiring social positions of service and mobility. Examples of this combined civic uplift and spiritual reform included Bethel AME pastor Reverend Reverdy Ransom's Institutional Church and Social Settlement (3825 S. Dearborn) and Olivet Baptist's (3101 S. Parkway Ave.) extensive array of programs that served as alternatives to the nearby Stroll. Yet, many churches offered

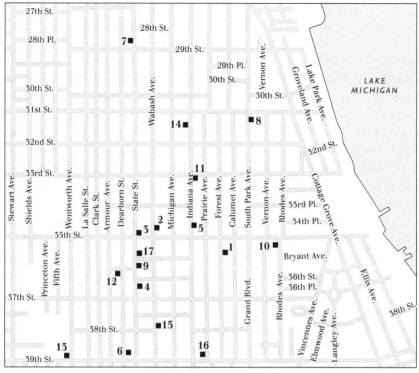

1 8th Regiment Armory, 3533 S. Giles Ave.
2 Appomattox Club, 3632 Grand Blvd. (now MLK Jr. Dr.)
3 Binga Bank, 3452 S. State St. (originally located at 3633 S. State St.)
4 Chicago Bee Building, 3647-55 S. State St.
5 Chicago Defender Building, 3435 S. Indiana Ave. (originally located at 3159 S. State St.)
6 Institutional Church and Social Settlement, 3825 S. Dearborn St.
7 Negro Fellowship League, 2830 S. State St.
8 Olivet Baptist Church, 3101 S. Park Ave. (now MLK Jr. Dr.)
9 Overton Hygienic Building, 3619-27 S. State St. (also housed Douglass National Bank,
    the first African American bank granted a national charter; the Victory Life Insurance
    Company; *Half-Century Magazine*; and the *Chicago Bee* until 1931; tenants also
    included the Theater Owners Booking Association and the Chicago Music Company,
    a music publishing firm owned by J. Mayo Williams)
10 Phillis Wheatley Home, 3526 Rhodes Ave.
11 Pilgrim Baptist Church, 3301 S. Indiana Ave.
12 Provident Hospital, 16 W. 36th St./36th St. and Dearborn St.
13 Schorling Park, 39th St. and Wentworth Ave.
14 Unity Hall, 3140 S. Indiana Ave.
15 Wabash Avenue YMCA, 3763 S. Wabash Ave.
16 Wendell Phillips High School, 244 E. Pershing Rd./39th St. and Prairie Ave.
17 Your Cab Company, 3535 S. State St.

Daytime Stroll

youth clubs, athletic leagues, and literary societies to provide fun recreations while also reforming migrant behaviors. In many ways, some churches also presented programs structured by heightened orderliness and bodily restraint to discipline souls and combat the perceived migrant worship practices linked to the southern slave past. Intellectual sermons and reverent, classically composed Negro spirituals reinforced the view of Walters AME Zion pastor W. A. Blackwell that "singing, shouting and talking" are "the most useless ways of proving Christianity" because they reinforced an image of primitive spiritualism.[20]

As the Great Migration increased, white philanthropic or factory-sponsored institutions, like the YMCA, NAACP, and Urban League, also sought to reform leisure spaces and behaviors to fight any cultural "disorganization" that could compromise an efficient black labor corps. The *Chicago Defender* celebrated the opening of the all-black Wabash Avenue YMCA (3763 S. Wabash) as equal to the Emancipation Proclamation. However, years later, the radical *Chicago Whip* and Wells reflected that it simply catered to the "better styled cod fish aristocracy of the race," never reaching those "farthest down and out." The YMCA never did reach a wide audience, but it devised a series of leisure activities including glee clubs, baseball leagues, and efficiency clubs that tied recreation to labor. Even the stridently integrationist and elitist NAACP got into the act with a three-page flyer pairing "refined and gentle manners" with voting and citizenship rights.[21]

The Chicago Urban League was the most comprehensive, far-reaching, and well-funded old settler organization, seeking employment for both black working and professional classes as laborers and researchers in the city. The heavy-handed industrial influence of the Urban League was exemplified in the words of black sociologist and Urban League researcher Charles S. Johnson. He urged northern employers to focus more on a black desire for employment instead of on the oppressive southern racial climate when considering reasons for the migration. For Johnson, such an approach distinguished "wholesome and substantial life purpose" from the "symptom of a fugitive incourageous opportunism." The local Urban League maintained a strong job referral system, pro-union stance, and race-first advocacy. Equally important, however, were the cultural values it emphasized, reflected by instructional cards and "dos and don'ts" lists published in the *Chicago Defender* warning migrants, for example, to "not carry on loud conversations in street cars and public places."[22]

Old settler expressions of a New Negro race consciousness are further revealed in the link made between industry, the social sciences, and race enterprise. University of Chicago–trained black sociologists Johnson and E. Franklin Frazier worked with Park at the university and at the Urban League. In their important New Negro studies *The Negro in Chicago* and *The Negro Family in Chicago*, neither Johnson nor Frazier agreed with Park that the race was averse to "enterprise" or "action." Johnson did not posit a "racial temperament," yet he did remain optimistic that black migrants could excise their rural traits of "disorganization." In *The Negro in Chicago*, Johnson gave historical context to the 1919 riot that, combined with a wealth of information on the living conditions of black people, challenged misconceptions, misinformation, and prejudices that for Johnson produced many of the "race problems" in the city. However, his detailed and innovative analysis of newspaper articles and public opinion about race suggested, like Park, that better understanding and more accurate reporting were solutions equal to adequate housing, employment, and policing.[23]

Frazier was more directly critical of Park's inability to recognize the broader socioeconomic forces that prevented black assimilation. Unlike Park, Frazier argued that the Negro's "social disorganization" was not the result of racial temperament but extended from slavery and a continued racial discrimination. In *The Negro Family in Chicago*, Frazier challenged the image of the Black Belt as a homogenous mass by examining its socioeconomic diversity despite structural constraints. However, both Johnson's and Frazier's notions of assimilation were still based on the norms of white cultural standards of industriousness and efficiency within a capitalist social order. This reinforced the idea that black folk culture was something that ultimately had to be reformed, disciplined, and normalized.[24]

At the same time, black historian Carter G. Woodson ironically used the space of the industry-sponsored Wabash YMCA offices to found the Association for the Study of Negro Life and History (ASNLH) in 1915. Through this organization, Woodson moved from a racial uplift to black radical analysis to conclude that black workers and entrepreneurs were making progress in the city because of their ancestral legacy from African and southern cultures, and any regression was the responsibility of the U.S. nation-state. In "Fifty Years of Negro Citizenship as Qualified by the United States Supreme Court," *The Negro in Our History, The Negro as Businessman, The Negro Wage Earner*, and *The Negro Professional Man and the Community*, Woodson detailed the strides and setbacks of all black workers within a serflike economic system. From the YMCA basement and later in Washington, D.C., Woodson and the ASNLH pioneered annual Negro History Week celebrations, published the *Journal of Negro History*, served as a clearinghouse of information for scholars and the general public, and continued to provide a forum for research presentation and publication.

During this time, local historian Frederic H. H. Robb published the landmark *Intercollegian Wonder Book*, also known as *The Negro in Chicago: 1779 to 1927*. The Washington Intercollegiate Club of Chicago was a young professional alternative to the NAACP that produced 1927 and 1929 editions of the *Wonder Book* to survey selective educational, athletic, entrepreneurial, and labor interests within the community.[25] This old settler expression of race pride, through a focus on enterprise and action, reflected a larger ideological shift directly tied to the black metropolis model.

The prominent connection between enterprise and race pride is best examined through the public sphere of Chicago's black newspapers and periodicals. Even before they left the South, migrants knew about the wonders of the black metropolis and were incorporated into a transregional racial community by consuming the stories and images in black newspapers. As soon as they arrived, the same newspapers were key instruments of urban enticement and instruction in navigating the leisure and labor opportunities in the city. With basic reportage, editorials, and sections on entertainment, employment, society, and politics, newspapers were the most overt and far-reaching black public sphere of discourse and debate in the making of "the race."[26]

Until the turn of the century, black leaders maintained Chicago's abolitionist tradition of radical integration best exemplified in the pages of Ferdinand Barnett and Ida B. Wells-Barnett's *Chicago Conservator* alongside the politically Democratic *Chicago Broad Ax*.[27] However, around 1900 and particularly after the bloody summer of 1919, leaders reinterpreted Booker T. Washington's "economic self-help" philosophy into an aggressive response to segregation and disenfranchisement.[28] Newsletters and brochures for Oscar Brown's Black Chamber of Commerce and its "Sustain Black Business" campaign used the story of black trader Jean Baptiste Point DuSable, Chicago's first non-Indian settler, to proclaim black citizens' inherent right to enterprise.[29] Institutional landmarks, including Provident Hospital (16 W. 36th / 36th and Dearborn), the Eighth Regiment Armory (3533 S. Giles), and the Appomattox Club (3632 Grand Blvd.), became physical symbols of interracial cooperation and military and civic race manhood in the black metropolis. Furthermore, journalists celebrated and exaggerated the productive successes of the daytime Stroll activities of Jesse Binga's banking and real estate empire (3452 and 3458 S. State), Anthony Overton's Overton Hygienic/ Douglass National Bank Building (3619–27 S. State), the Your Cab Company (3535 S. State), Abbott's *Chicago Defender* (3435 S. Indiana Dr.), and Claude

Barnett's Associated Negro Press. These institutions and the boom in black-owned insurance companies symbolized race pride and served as instructional guides for migrants to emulate.[30]

From the middle-class conservatism of the Overton-sponsored *Half-Century Magazine* (later the weekly *Chicago Bee*) to the economic radicalism of the *Chicago Whip*, an ethic of race pride and economic nationalism was articulated in a diversity of journalistic formats. While *Half-Century* and the *Bee* fought to secure a more conservative readership by instructing migrants on respectable consumption habits, the *Whip* supported the organization of consumers into the "Don't Spend Your Money Where You Can't Work" boycott campaign in 1929, which became a national movement. *Half-Century* offered a more conservative argument that migrant behavior might be the "cause of race prejudice," while the *Whip* hoped to redirect the energy migrants placed on street activities, like parades and strolling, toward "labor organizations and behind Negro business."[31] These two intellectual factions differed in platform, but they converged in the class-based concern that working-class migrants needed to be instructed and uplifted toward varying notions of racial consciousness.

The uplift approach in the widely popular *Chicago Defender* was not much different from any other paper. Founded in 1905 at his landlady's kitchen table, migrant Abbott's *Defender* newspaper was eventually a primary advocate of black migration north and at the same time imposed "middle class deportment among the migrants" in public dress and behavior. However, its identity as a "mass appeal" race paper required as broad a reach in content as it hoped for in circulation. This approach also brought with it another set of restrictions. For example, *Half-Century Magazine* readers were appalled by the *Defender*'s "over the top" sensationalist race paper approach. At the same time, the *Defender*'s reliance on white advertisers restrained its support of race conscious projects like the *Whip*'s "Don't Spend" campaign.[32] On many issues, the *Defender* held an ideological middle ground by combining a pride in separate institutions with an analysis of politics through the lens of race.

Ironically, the connections made between racial self-sufficiency and a racial market denied leaders the ability to fully impose their habits, desires, and ideologies on the race. Despite Abbott's criticisms of migrant behaviors, embodied in the reprint of Urban League "dos and don'ts" lists, his sensationalist and militant coverage of local and national politics was literally on the same page as ads for love potions, dream books, race records, and beauty systems. This combination brought him a larger consumer base while offending both middle-class conservatives and economic radicals. The paper took on a "mass appeal" format by serving as community watchdog and cultural tastemaker in its coverage and commentary on everything from southern lynching and race riots to love scandal stories and Stroll nightlife.[33]

Billed as "The World's Greatest Weekly," the *Chicago Defender* was "fearless, sensationalist, and militant" and arguably without peer as the most instrumental medium for consolidating an "official" race outlook in the nation by both aggressively shedding light on injustice and showcasing a broader spectrum of black urban experiences in its pages. Moreover, the display of such a diversity of consumer tastes in black metropolis race papers is where one gets a strong sense of the lifestyles of working-class migrant men and women. Under the shroud of old settler institutional expressions of enterprise and productive action, the realm of consumer culture became a key site where new settler ideology emerged. Migrant consumer practices within marketplace spaces helped re-map the Stroll and hence the New Negro with alternate interpretations of enterprise, race pride, and respectability.[34]

"THE NEGRO PEASANT TURNS CITYWARD"?:
THE MIGRANT IMAGE OUTSIDE THE NORTHERN MIND

Centrally, black migrants were a group of individuals with a diversity of reasons for leaving the South, informing the various lifestyles and urban experiences that emerged in Chicago. It has been well established that the decision to will oneself out of the southern reign of terror took great courage and financial sacrifice and came with varying levels of ambivalence. All along the path to Chicago, migrants were required to negotiate transforming modes of social interaction and personal development. The sometimes liberating, sometimes unsettling experience created a space in between an always changing "ancestral" past and a racially restrictive northern industrial present. The new settler framework became the repository for dynamic ideas about migrant mobility and community stability that altered what local expressions of the New Negro meant. In the process, both migrants and many older residents developed consumer-based styles and institutions on the Stroll, transforming the shape and substance of the black metropolis.[35]

Most important, images of a naive mass of rural peasants turning cityward were far from the actual migrant experience. The Chicago Commission on Race Relations (CCRR) found that only 25 percent of Chicago's migrants had been agricultural laborers. A significant number in the remaining 75 percent had between five and ten years of experience in a combination of lumbering,

railroading, iron, and steel industries and a significant rate of literacy. Therefore, most migrants had lived in southern cities and towns and hence were
familiar with urban conditions before they arrived at Chicago.[36] Life chances
might not have compared with the scale of possibility in a place like Chicago,
but part of migrants' early engagement with the urban South and their
motivation to move forward included participation in commercialized leisure. While sociologists, labor recruiters, and newspapers like the *Chicago
Defender* painted a picture of sharp contrast between the modern glitz and
glamour of Chicago and the bleak, primitive life available in the South, such
depictions hardly reflected existing conditions. In fact, by World War I, two-
thirds of those who read about the Stroll in the *Defender* lived outside
Chicago.[37]

Moreover, Chicago's Stroll was not a unique phenomenon but part of a
larger circuit of city strips, strolls, and jukes that included Storyville in New
Orleans, Decatur Street in Atlanta, and Beale Street in Memphis. Gertrude
"Ma" Rainey and W. C. Handy reported travels on southern vaudeville tours
as early as 1902. These tours were later formalized through grueling and
oppressive performance circuits like the Theater Owners' Booking Association (also known as Tough On Black Acts or even Black Asses) that were
transformed into assets for the later successes of northern race film and race
records industries. The *Chicago Defender* also kept readers up on the progress of Chicago's own black baseball team, the American Giants. However,
southern readers were already quite aware of the Giants because National
Negro League (NNL) teams went on frequent barnstorming trips to take
advantage of the warmer climate and larger black consumer base provided in
southern states. The North may have offered images of cultural freedom, but
it was southern dollars and desires that made Chicago's black consumer
culture so viable.[38]

Many migrants already found consumer culture to be an important place
where they could express individual desires and even collective forms of
dissent against the dreams deferred in urban industrial life. Such a funda-
mental disconnect existed between the ideals of the American work ethic and
the very real inequities African Americans faced in factories, unions, and
schools in northern and southern cities. With few exceptions, Chicago's
powerful trade unions consistently excluded black workingmen who had
acquired skilled trades in southern cities, except in foundries where the work
was heavy, hot, and dangerous. Black men made significant wartime ad-
vances in the steel industry but in most trades were at best considered a last
option and until 1916 usually only hired as strikebreakers, furthering tensions

with labor unions. Those who found work started primarily as short-term employees on the bloody, slippery killing room floors of stockyards and meatpacking plants like Armour and Swift. A large segment of black male workers were still restricted to unskilled nonindustrial labor and service positions as porters, waiters, janitors, general laborers, and the like.[39]

Conditions for black women, on the bottom rung of the employment ladder, were even less promising. While Chicago was one of the few wartime cities where black women could struggle to leave domestic labor, they primarily moved to dangerous low-paying, unskilled industrial positions in mechanical laundries and stockyards. Yet even by 1920, at least 64 percent of documented black women workers in Chicago were still restricted to domestic labor. Some black male and even fewer black female workers found solace in the Chicago Federation of Labor's Local 651 and 231 respectively, but because these locals were reserved primarily for the Black Belt (and not by trade), they became another form of industrial marginalization. Migrants were sold a tale of freedom, but their Chicago experience was continually influenced by the inability to move freely. From the workplace to union affiliation, migrants were heavily restricted by domestic surveillance, the suspicions of white unions, hourly and piece productivity rates, and standardized and subdivided tasks. Even the leisure time provided by the workplace, like company picnics and industrial baseball leagues, were racially segregated and designed to instill the labor-centered values of sobriety and efficiency.[40]

The stage was set for a new settler outlook, at least partially due to the insecurity of consistent labor and the broken promises of thriftiness, worker brotherhood, and education. Such conditions reconfirmed interests in public spheres of personal and communal expression outside industrial and domestic workplaces. For example, many reformers and social scientists saw the buffet flats and brothels near the Stroll as a social threat, but they were also understood as an opportunity for women to leave "the low-wage, low-status domestic labor that left them vulnerable to sexual harassment." Even the 1913 vice commission reasoned, "Is it any wonder that a tempted girl who receives only six dollars per week working with her hands sells her body for $25 per week?" One Chicago buffet flat prostitute confirmed, "When I see the word *maid*—why, girl, let me tell you, it just runs through me! I think I'd sooner starve." Beyond wages, the status of maid was collectively resisted because, as one woman stated, there was no "place to entertain your friends but the kitchen, and going in and out of the back doors. I hated all that. . . . They almost make you a slave." The subservient memory of "slavery" or slavelike labor was still fresh in migrants' heads, and many women in particular developed various strategies, from sex work to beauty culture, to "never work in nobody's kitchen but my own anymore."[41]

New settler ideology advocated hard work and encouraged social mobility through industrial labor but was also open to what scholar C. L. R. James later termed the "popular arts" in ways that complicated old settler prescriptions about appropriate labor and leisure. James prophetically saw in the popular arts—films, comic strips, soap operas, detective novels, jazz and blues music—complex levels of creativity that reflected the masses' desire for the same kind of autonomy and free association they wanted in the labor process.[42] While both old and new settlers believed in black cultural and economic autonomy as part of their New Negro philosophies, there were various disagreements about where labor and leisure could take place and how one's physical "standing" altered definitions of respectability.

First, various mass-appeal political, media, religious, and educational organizations took shape or reorganized themselves in response to postmigration realities. These intermediary institutions demonstrate the intricate and intimate relationship between a solidly industrial logic and seemingly deviant consumer culture in the creation of both Stroll pleasures and social movement politics within Chicago's New Negro intellectual life. For example, even before black southerners came to Chicago, they heard about (and sent their children to) Wendell Phillips High School (244 E. Pershing Rd./39th and Prairie), with its modern facilities, integrated classes, and night school programs that included early courses in Negro history and literature by 1920. Later, Phillips's music programs offered training for future Stroll musicians, and its basketball team served as a pipeline to Xavier University's championship five and both the Savoy Big Five and Harlem Globetrotters.[43]

At the same time, an altered New Negro consciousness emerged through the reading groups, public protests, and street corner and Washington Park debates within the wide spectrum of nationalist and leftist organizations in the city. In the face of strong opposition from the *Chicago Defender*, Marcus Garvey's Universal Negro Improvement Association (UNIA) gained a strong foothold in the black metropolis. With some financial backing from beauty culturist Madam C. J. Walker, Garvey's *Negro World* newspaper reached as far away as Australia and local jazz musicians Roy Palmer and James "Steady Roll" Johnson played in the Chicago branch UNIA band and organized Saturday night musical events. Later, Timothy "Noble" Drew Ali's Moorish Science Temple offered a mystical "eastern," even "Orientalist" black identity through the lure of exotic fezzes, gowns, and public healings that played on the recognizable signs of the medicine show, fraternal order, and policy gambling dream book. Moorish Science gained enough status that Abbott, alderman Louis Anderson, and policy-backed politicians Oscar De Priest and Dan Jackson attended the 1928 Moorish Conclave in Chicago.[44]

Of the black migrants who turned to the political left, Harry Haywood and Lovett Fort-Whiteman went as far as to study in the Soviet Union. Upon return, Fort-Whiteman was known to stroll through the black metropolis in a flamboyant Russian *rubaschka* (blouse), displaying a leftist New Negro alternative that by 1931 had a communitywide impact when the Communist Party fought in defense of the Scottsboro Boys. At the same time, many created their own path that focused equally on race and class. Musicians contested the color line of their parent federation to create the "Musicians' Protective Union, Local 208, AFM" as early as 1902. Like most turn-of-the-century guilds, 208 focused on perhaps more old settler concerns with craft and skill but also fought for equitable job opportunities in Stroll ballrooms, nightclubs, and theaters, while Stroll regular Milton Webster was a key local figure in the national Brotherhood of Sleeping Car Porters and Maids, one of the most powerfully independent unions in black labor history. Finally, the *Chicago Whip*, with its Marxist Free Thought Society, is most known for a pro-economic radical and race-first stance and support for the local African Blood Brotherhood, but it was initially described as "an information sheet for the cabarets" as much as it was a radical paper. This mass cultural convergence between race and class consciousness came together most expertly in the 1929–30 "Don't Spend Your Money Where You Can't Work" campaign. The "Don't Spend" movement was an important mass protest and boycott strategy to secure jobs for black workers that started on Chicago's Stroll and expanded to cities across the country.[45]

By the late 1920s and early 1930s, the struggles between "old" and "new" settler solutions to the shared "Negro problem" were also waged through the equally crucial mediums of visual and literary art and radio, which continued to find both aesthetic inspiration and institutional support from the Stroll consumer marketplace. As an example, Archibald Motley used the formalist training he acquired from the Art Institute of Chicago to shift from the dominant respectable images of southern folk landscapes (consider the important work of Henry O. Tanner) toward the urban streetscapes of a new settler life. He powerfully depicted Stroll nightlife in his paintings *Black Belt* and *Barbecue* (both in 1934); nightclub and vaudeville scenes in *Blues* (1929), *Saturday Night* (1935), and *Between Acts* (1935); and Sanctified church life in *Tongues (Holy Rollers)* (1929). In the literary realm, Richard Wright's day-in-the-life novel set on Chicago's South Side, *Lawd Today!* (1935), leveled a trenchant critique of the American Dream, while Marita Bonner's three-part story, "A Possible Triad on Black Notes" (1933), was a complex narration of race, ethnicity, and color hierarchy on fictional Frye Street and part of her never-completed book, aptly titled *Black Map*. Clearly, more traditional arts and letters were not removed from or residing above the messiness of the consumer marketplace but were aesthetically inspired and institutionally funded by the Stroll's commercial world. These "high art" visual and literary products testify to the impact of urban migrant and mass consumer culture on the overlapping frequencies of black life in the city.[46]

Finally, struggles over race pride and racist representations took on new meaning in the overwhelmingly mass-mediated realm of radio because of the popular and broad reach of the airwaves both within and beyond the black metropolis. The remote jazz and blues broadcasts of Earl "Fatha" Hines from the Grand Terrace and the music of Dave Peyton and Albertine Pickens on WGN in the 1920s encouraged some white listeners to move beyond an aural voyeurism and "physically traverse the remapped metropolitan landscape" to actually venture onto the Stroll. But alongside the Chicago-based and very popular (for black and white listeners) *Amos 'n' Andy* show also stood powerful innovations in Chicago's New Negro forms of "race radio." Described as the "undisputed patriarch of black radio in the United States," migrant Jack Cooper debuted his *All Negro Hour* in 1929 as the first black-produced radio program in the country. Cooper consistently expressed an old settler respectability with calls for black commercial ownership and a "standard" professional broadcast style with no dialect. In fact, the *All Negro Hour* had its own parody of southern black migrants in Chicago, *Luke and Timber*, but also embraced the new settler "gospel sound" challenging the traditional sacred tastes of appropriate music and behavior.[47]

These social movements and cultural formations powerfully link the various mappings of the black metropolis. They are haunted by white fascinations with black primitivism while reinforcing older notions of labor discipline and reform alongside offering leisure-based forms of labor and activism. The New Negro worlds of "old" and "new" settlers were intimately connected through the black public sphere of the mass consumer marketplace, as it profoundly shaped the direction of a black intellectual life. No matter how formalist in aesthetic choices or critical of mass consumerism and working-class tastes, not one of these arenas could claim any pure distinction from the Stroll or the New Negro intellectual life that emerged from these commercial spaces.

Under the labels of "reserve labor" by industry, "nigger scabs" by unions, the "Negro Problem" by sociologists, and "undesirables" by old settlers, those who adopted a new settler philosophy were finding in mass-produced consumer culture a third plane of existence with a possibility to create truly representative work and identities. Comments by a Chicago essayist echoed Locke's observations that the New Negro resisted being a "social problem." But for this essayist, it was on the Stroll that for a minute or so one forgets the " 'Problem.' It has no place here. It is crowded aside by good cheer." While not rigid, old and new settler struggles about respectable spaces as sites of labor or leisure, of function or fashion, of the puritanical or profane, reflected a contest for the direction of the race. Moreover, the diversity and volume of old settler recreational projects signaled the failure of reformers and their attempts to cultivate black migrants strictly in accordance with industrial labor dictates. When one migrant was asked if he had gone to work every day, he replied, "Goodness no. . . . I had to have some days of the week off for pleasure."[48] In the face of white images of urban primitivism, old settlers upheld the "manly" daytime Stroll activities of banking and insurance as authentically representative of racial respectability. But actually it was the new settler nighttime Stroll of an interconnected leisure world of "sporting" and entertainment that provided the socioeconomic and conceptual base for the black metropolis.

FROM DAY TO NIGHT: RETHINKING
RESPECTABILITY ON THE STROLL

When migrants like pianist Lil' Hardin (who would later become the wife of Louis Armstrong) and writer Langston Hughes took the time to document their impressions of Chicago, they were immediately arrested by the convergence of seemingly contradictory impulses that met on its Stroll. Hardin made it her "business to go out for a daily stroll and look this 'heaven' over. Chicago meant just that to me—its beautiful brick and stone buildings, excitement, people moving swiftly, and things happening." Hughes remarked that South State Street was crowded with "theaters, restaurants and cabarets. And excitement from noon to noon. Midnight was like day. The street was full of workers and gamblers, prostitutes and pimps, church folks and sinners." Even before Duke Ellington came to the city, he heard "very romantic tales about the nightlife on the South Side . . . and the apparently broken-down neighborhoods where there were more good times than any place in the city." William Everett Samuels, leader of the Musicians' Protective Union, Local 208, added, "You could stand at 35th Street and see people from any place you wanted to see because they came here to go." While these various reflections exhibit a collective sense of race pride, they also begin to reveal how the new consumption habits, traditions, and desires of migrants combined with changing social realities to transform the city and give added form to the New Negro experience.[49]

Like the larger black metropolis, its central artery the Stroll was more than simply a stretch of buildings, amusements, sidewalks, and signposts but the public showcase for black "expressive behavior." To stroll on the Stroll meant to take part in a moving theater where freedom often meant the mobility of men with women as objects of acquisition, among a wide array of other commodities, and where black people were staging new visions of blackness in the particular ways they looked and were looked at within a structured space of local exhibition. Here, race, class, gender, and sexuality (among countless identities) were unequally expressed and enforced through public displays of dress, language, affiliation, and behavior. The nighttime Stroll physically consolidated the promises and pitfalls of brothels and battle royals, ballrooms and buffet flats, storefronts and policy stations, kitchens and kitchenettes, the saunter and the shake, as a collectively combustible archive for the new settler refashioning of respectability.[50]

The fact that leisure activities became the cultural and economic foundation of the black metropolis serves as a commentary on the power of black consumer culture and the profound exclusion of black professionals from the mainstream world of labor, leisure, and political influence. Despite reform leaders' frustrations, the so-called underworld of vice and leisure made old settler institutions of respectability possible. Studies of Chicago's black policy gambling make clear that "the creative excitement of black entertainment, the emergence of black gambling syndicates and the rise of black politics— were closely interrelated and had a broad impact." Better-paying industrial jobs surely provided the disposable income for leisure activities, but it was the nickels and dimes used to buy drinks in local dance halls and put on lucky numbers at policy wheels that recirculated within the community to support the black metropolis. The way policy gambling continued older southern and diasporic traditions of black gaming made it both a cultural and economic institution in the North by serving as another popular art form in the city. Amid low status employment in the formal economy, the predominantly white ownership of Stroll businesses, and the inspiration of social movements, the world of illegal policy gambling (now legalized as state lottery), leisure, and recreation served as the centerpiece of the black metropolis.[51]

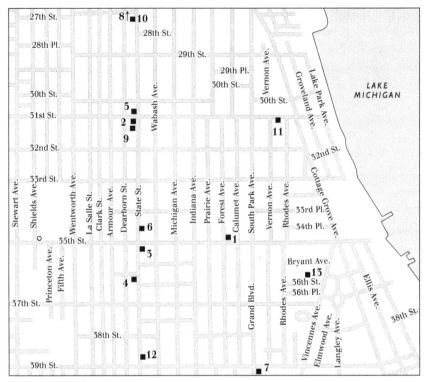

1 Apex Club, 35th St. between Prairie Ave. and Calumet Ave.
2 Café de Champion, 41 W. 31st St.
3 De Luxe Café, 3503 S. State St.
4 Dreamland Ballroom/Café, 3618 S. State St.
5 Elite No. 1, 3030 S. State St.
6 Elite No. 2, 3445 S. State St.
7 Grand Terrace Café, 3955 S. Parkway (now MLK Jr. Dr.)
8 Emporium Saloon, 464 S. State St.
9 Grand Theater, 3110 S. State St.
10 Motts' Pekin Theatre, 2700 S. State St.
11 Royal Gardens Café, 459 E. 31st St. (after 1921 known as Lincoln Gardens)
12 Star Theater, 3835-37 S. State St.
13 Vincennes Hotel and Platinum Lounge, 601 E. 36th St.

Nighttime Stroll

In the last decade of the nineteenth century, John "Mushmouth" Johnson (so-nicknamed due to his use of profanity) took his earnings from work as a porter in a white gaming establishment and opened his own saloon and gambling house, the Emporium Saloon at 464 South State Street. Johnson's gambling house foreshadowed a popular arts sensibility by creating games for patrons with both "deep" and "shallow" pockets and featured the game of policy brought to the country by Spanish-speaking "black" immigrants and to the city reportedly by Alabama migrant "Policy Sam" Young. Johnson's appeal to diverse gambling tastes attracted many poor black migrants. When historian and businessman Dempsey Travis's father, Louis Travis, looked back on Johnson's establishment, he remembered: "Where else could a country boy go just ten days out of Georgia and feel like a big time gambler for only a nickel?" The opportunity to feel "big time" in the world of leisure is an overlooked moment of social respectability that had as deep an impact as the Urban League or Olivet Baptist Church did. Moreover, Johnson was able to amass enough wealth to make his enterprise one of the largest gambling syndicates in the city and himself one of the largest real estate moguls on the South Side. The attention Johnson gave small-time gamblers benefited him while also serving the cause of black-owned banking, real estate, and entertainment growing on the Stroll.[52]

One such "gambler," Robert T. Motts, opened the Pekin in the heart of the Stroll at 2700 South State. This cultural institution, which Dempsey Travis called "the formal cradle of Negro drama in the United States," was also considered one of the first northern venues to feature jazz musical performance. Built in 1892, the Pekin started out as a beer garden, then became a gambling hall and a nightclub, and in 1906 was converted into a theater, which also served as a key place for social gathering and political organizing. The Pekin sponsored a controversial benefit for Ida B. Wells's Negro Fellowship League, endorsed sporting entrepreneur Beauregard Moseley for Cook County commissioner, and hosted the 1912 founding of the Colored Press Association. Such activities were made possible because of Motts's background in gambling, having worked under "Mushmouth" Johnson. Johnson's influence continued to expand even after his death, when his sister Eudora inherited 60 percent of his wealth. She married Jesse Binga in 1912 and, with her brother's policy money, provided significant economic support for Binga's bank and his larger real estate empire.[53]

Across the street, Johnson's brother Elijah leased property at 3618 South State, where he built the Dreamland Ballroom, later converted into the famous Dreamland Café. When Motts died in 1911, Dan "The Embalmer" Jackson married Motts's sister Lucy Lindsey, who used her brother's gambling inheritance to reclaim the Pekin for reasons of race pride, profit, and preservation until the space was taken over by white owners, marking a rapid decline in its significance. Jackson's undertaking business next door to the Pekin was also funded by his own gambling activities and in 1925 became the prominent Metropolitan Funeral Systems Association. As a Second Ward politician, Jackson protected both his illegal and legal business interests. Later, Jackson's disciple Robert Cole took over Metropolitan and diversified its holdings by funding the early black magazine the *Bronzeman* and building a recording studio for Jack Cooper's *All Negro Hour* and his other radio programming. At the same time, the Kelley brothers (Walter, Ross, and Ily) ran the Tijuana Policy Wheel and Walter was a stockholder in the Binga Bank, again proving that the line between old and new settler respectability was fluid at best.[54]

In this interwar period, Chicago also became the "melting pot for jazz and blues" as much because of the convergence of musical styles from different parts of the south as for the employment possibilities musicians could take advantage of in Chicago's black-owned and policy-supported cabarets, dance halls, vaudevilles, and theaters. When "good time" mayor William "Big Bill" Thompson took office in 1915, the Stroll became the logical next site for the aesthetic and institutional development of black music, especially when jazz musicians were driven from New Orleans with the closing down of Storyville in November 1917. Chicago's black gamblers and entrepreneurs took advantage of the consolidation of the city's vice on the South Side to make the Stroll a mecca for cultural innovation. Once dubbed the "South Side's Sweetheart," blues great Alberta Hunter recalled that "if you had worked in Chicago and had been recognized there, you were somebody, baby. New York didn't count then." By 1917, the Dreamland Café was under the ownership of William Bottoms, former saloon keeper at boxer Jack Johnson's "sporting set" black-and-tan cabaret, the Café de Champion (41 W. 31st St.). Under the direction of Bottoms, the Dreamland arguably became the center of black musical development, featuring under one roof Hunter, Joe "King" Oliver, and the young Louis Armstrong in Lil' Hardin–Louis Armstrong's Dreamland Syncopators.[55]

During this time, policy gambling baron Henry "Teenan" Jones, who occasionally wrote a column for the *Chicago Defender*, took control of the Stroll's entertainment world. Teenan helped sporting entrepreneur Frank Leland fund his first baseball team. With his brother Charlie "Giveadam" Jones, Henry opened up the Elite No. 1 (3030 S. State), where pianist Earl "Fatha" Hines was featured, and later the Elite No. 2 (3445 S. State). The Elite No. 2, also called Teenan Jones' Place, became a popular after-hours spot for musicians who played feature shows at venues like the Dreamland. Politically, Jones served as an organizer in the Republican Party and as president of the Colored Men's Retail Liquor Dealers' Protective Association. When Jones took ownership of the Star Theater (3835–37 S. State) in 1916, it was lauded as "the only house in Chicago owned and operated entirely by members of the Race," and in 1917 he hired pioneering Chicago filmmaker and writer William Foster as its manager.[56]

Entrepreneur Bottoms, who was also a small-time policy operator, was now quickly becoming a major force on the Stroll beyond the Dreamland. Along with Frank Preer, husband of actress Evelyn Preer (principle actress in numerous Oscar Micheaux films), Bottoms offered financial assistance to Liberty Life Insurance director and policy wheel owner Virgil Williams to open the De Luxe Café (3503 S. State). These three also helped fund the black radical newspaper the *Chicago Whip*, with lawyer Joseph Bibb as one of its editors (his sister Eloise Bibb Thompson was the Chicago representative for the black-owned Black Swan recording company). Then Bottoms and Williams joined forces with then Second Ward alderman Louis Anderson to buy the Royal Gardens Café (459 E. 31st). From here, Williams also founded and directed the Royal Gardens Moving Picture Company. These institutional foundations helped make Chicago "home of black recording companies in the 1920s."[57] The central role of policy gambling in the development of black music pales only by the obvious permeability between formal and informal economies in the creation of a wide spectrum of community institutions.

Policy and gambling, as part of the larger culture of the "sporting set," also played a direct role in the emergence of black commercialized athletics. In 1910, Motts and "Teenan" Jones headed the reception committee in Chicago after Jack Johnson defeated Jim Jeffries. Bottoms, with the help of Abbott, sponsored a celebrated 1922 football game where an all-black team was victorious over their all-white opponents; policy baron Julian Black managed the boxing career of Joe Louis; and Bottoms served as Louis's dietitian. Many policy barons also used their support of black baseball teams to "launder" respectability (and their money) while providing economic stability to capital-intensive sporting industries that black entrepreneurs were excluded from because of limited finances. "Teenan" Jones and Bottoms supported early NNL ventures, and gambler Robert Jackson served as the treasurer of the famed Chicago American Giants (Schorling Park at 39th and Wentworth), while policy banker Ily Kelley was a stockholder.[58] In 1932, when Giants manager Andrew "Rube" Foster had a nervous breakdown, the president of the Metropolitan Funeral Systems Association, Robert Cole (partner with gambler Dan Jackson), took his gambling earnings and bought the team specifically to keep this community institution in black hands.[59]

At the same time, political leaders, put in place with migrant votes, protected illegal and legal activities while business dollars bought political favors in the age of Mayor "Bill." As much as white politicians, the political careers of black figures like Oscar De Priest, the first black member of the city council, and Second Ward boss Dan Jackson were supported by the new settler world of policy. Jackson used politics to protect his legal and illegal race enterprises. While from his Unity Hall post (3140 S. Indiana), De Priest used policy dollars in the form of campaign contributions to galvanize his People's Movement Club and become the first black congressman from the North. Even the work of noted Harlem Renaissance poet Fenton Johnson was underwritten, from beyond the grave, by his uncle "Mushmouth" Johnson. Many residents agreed that if anyone, policy bankers were most accurately living out the black metropolis vision.[60]

On a smaller scale, struggling black businesses like beauty salons, barbershops, and lunch counters served as legal "fronts" and benefited from increased customer circulation while employees made extra money serving as "numbers runners." Even leaders in the religious world of Spiritualist and Pentecostal churches understood the logic of policy for their predominantly new settler parishes. From Elder Lucy Smith's small concession to not "hold it against the people if they play policy numbers" because "conditions here are not good," to Reverend Clarence Cobbs's open relationship with "policy kings," the structural power of policy offered new visions of respectability. Moreover, women created indirect economies benefiting from policy, by giving consultations and selling dream books and other lucky products as spiritualist mediums.[61] The high point of the symbiosis between the informal economy and race respectability took place when policy barons the Jones brothers (Edward, George, and McKissack) created their economic dynasty, including various charities, the Chicago Crusaders professional basketball team, the National Brotherhood of Policy Kings in 1933, and the 1937 opening of the South Side's first Ben Franklin store at 436 E. 47th Street.[62]

The "official" history of Chicago's black business world credits "old settler" Jesse Binga's business acumen for the creation of the Black Belt's "Broadway and Wall Street" where, in fact, it was the underworld of policy gambling that stabilized the city's black economy and social world, especially during the Depression. From policy baron Julian Black's Apex Club (35th between Prairie and Calumet) to Elizabeth and "Pops" Lewis's Vincennes Hotel and Platinum Lounge (601 E. 36th), policy bankers underwrote a vibrant urban culture of theaters, dance halls, and athletic and traditional business enterprises. Many reformers argued that gambling deluded working people into wasting their money on a long-shot dream, and city officials made attempts to thwart its corrupting affects. For sure, policy was a blend of exploitation and enterprise, both capitalizing on the dire economic conditions of black residents and circulating money back into the black community. However, many migrants also saw direct parallels between their bets and the investments whites placed in the stock market, except that policy didn't discriminate. Moreover, policy provided a relatively higher rate of return while becoming another avenue toward race advancement, especially in the discriminatory job market of the 1930s.[63]

Scholars of the black metropolis St. Clair Drake and Horace R. Cayton were forced to concede, even in light of legitimate criticisms, that policy bankers in Chicago were the ones who had "given some reality to the hope of erecting an independent economy within black Metropolis." In fact, policy barons gained the status of respectable "race leaders" during the Depression because they offered employment and supported "legitimate" establishments and charitable activities. The moral ambivalence and yet socioeconomic centrality of policy for the metropolis foreshadows the eventual co-optation and legalization of the game by many states in the United States.[64] Even indirectly, policy provided both the physical and conceptual space where Chicago's New Negroes would work out many of the cultural styles, forms, and institutions that were initially critiqued and are now celebrated within black communities.

A constant surveillance of community institutions through old settler ideologies of behavioral reform and bodily restraint encouraged many migrants and some residents to readily embrace this diverse world of brash exhibition, leisure-based labor, and emotional and "rational" release in the mass marketplace. The new settler possibilities offered by the blurring lines between labor and leisure served as the catalyst for a different set of New Negro "popular arts" and institutions that both paralleled and even funded cultural production within the famed Harlem Renaissance. Alongside Chicago's more noted New Negro popular arts of jazz and blues, the Stroll set the stage for the rise of gospel music on "race records," "race films," a black beauty industry, and professional athletics as sites of leisure, labor, and knowledge production.

The continual reconstruction of the black metropolis as both a built environment and as an ideal helps us to get at a more comprehensive New Negro movement and at the diversity of ideas produced within that world. The transition from pen, paper, and paint in ivory towers to record, radio, and celluloid on city streets did not signal the demise of creative agency. This modern canvas for the creation of ideas was situated directly within and not in evasion of twentieth-century socioeconomic realities. The following chapters survey the struggles over "different" visions of a black modernity within the mass consumer cultures of beauty, film, gospel music, and athletics. They reveal that in many cases, the consumer marketplace of the Stroll was one of the only sites where New Negroes could buy and sell culture, dreams, and products of self-transformation and create both personal and communal desires for a different black metropolis and a different world.

Chapter Two

Making Do

BEAUTY, ENTERPRISE, AND THE "MAKEOVER" OF RACE WOMANHOOD

Surely you are not going to shut the door in my face. I feel
that I am in a business that is a credit to the womanhood of our
race. I went into a business that is despised, that is criticized and
talked about by everybody—the business of growing hair. . . . I am
a woman who came from the cotton fields of the South. I was promoted there to the washtub. Then I was promoted to the cook
kitchen, and from there I *promoted myself* into the business of
manufacturing hair goods and preparations.
—Madam C. J. Walker before the Annual Convention of the
National Negro Business League, 1912 (emphasis in original),
Madam C. J. Walker Collection,
Indiana Historical Society, Indianapolis

We, the representatives of the National Convention of
the Mme. C. J. Walker Agents, in convention assembled, and in
a larger sense representing twelve million Negroes, have keenly felt
the injustice done our race and country through the recent lynching
at Memphis, Tennessee, and the horrible race riot of East St. Louis.
Knowing that no people in all the world are more loyal and patriotic
than the Colored people of America, we respectfully submit to you this
our protest against the continuation of such wrongs and injustices in
this "land of the free, and home of the brave" and we further respectfully urge that you as President of these United States use your great
influence that congress enact the necessary laws to prevent a
recurrence of such disgraceful affairs.
—Telegram from Madam C. J. Walker Hair Culturists Union of
America to Woodrow Wilson, 1917, Madam C. J. Walker Collection,
Indiana Historical Society, Indianapolis

In 1912, Booker T. Washington presided over the three-day annual convention of his National Negro Business League (NNBL) held that year at the Institutional Church and Social Settlement, founded on Chicago's South Side just twelve years earlier by black socialist reformer Reverend Reveredy Ransom. The young upstart "beauty culturist" Madam C. J. Walker also came to Chicago, arriving in a chauffeur-driven Model T convertible touring car, with hopes of addressing this distinguished group of race entrepreneurs about her business accomplishments. However, throughout the conference, Washington pointedly denied her any opportunity to speak from the floor and refused to acknowledge those who attempted to speak on her behalf. After multiple efforts to gain Washington's attention, Walker on the final morning defiantly seized the floor. She proclaimed her right to be there and be heard based on the traditionally masculine narrative of the rise from poverty to wealth. In bold fashion, Walker announced she was promoted by others "from the cotton fields of the South" to "the washtub" and finally acquired self-promotion in "the business of manufacturing hair goods and preparations." Within the year, Walker successfully fought to become a part of this world of race entrepreneurs and to attain the social status that came with such affiliation. Yet, Washington's initial avoidance of this particular beauty culturist was not surprising. He had long been known to lump together spiritualists, palm readers, and beauty culturists as peddlers of "meaningless stuff." Moreover, his dismissal was part of a growing concern with the black consumption of beauty products—presumably to straighten the hair and lighten the skin—as destructive acts of excessive adornment and white emulation.[1]

The racist ideologies of Social Darwinism were quite effectively disseminated to wider, non-elite popular spheres through white beauty/cosmetics advertisements, packaging, and procedures. Images of women with straight(ened) hair and white(ned) skin were prized as aesthetically and morally superior to women with "darker" features. For a black woman like Walker to defiantly promote herself in the male-dominated public sphere of race enterprise—as, first and foremost, a beauty culturist and as a conscious "race woman"—was surely disruptive and considered by some treasonous. At the same time, historical hindsight reveals that both black female beauty culturists who worked for white women and black male beauty entrepreneurs had spoken at NNBL meetings. Yet there were not many race women like Walker, who had come from the "cotton fields" and the "washtub," defying male authority all along the way, to build a race industry driven by the cultural tastes and social practices of working-class black women. There-fore, in the case of Walker, Washington's reticence toward this beauty cultur-ist was perhaps less about peddling products of white emulation and more about his reservations with her particular brand of modern race womanhood. Under the veil of race pride and authenticity, struggles over questions of class, gender, and clientele point to a much more complicated set of mean-ings and history surrounding beauty culture within black communities.[2]

The mere existence of a figure like Walker reveals that beauty culture did not mean the same thing to everyone who engaged in cosmetic or adornment practices. One could interpret black women as victims or complicit dupes in a desire for white femininity in a bottle. However, black urban migrants seized the mass consumer marketplace to alter the implied intentions of white firms and the uses of their beauty products. Old settler prescriptions of bodily restraint and modesty in dress and behavior were powerfully challenged by the elaborate hairstyles many in the working class created as a physical and ideological response to a work-based image of servitude. Moreover, positions as beauty culturists and agents served as lucrative employment alternatives to domestic labor where black women were overwhelmingly relegated. Based on the migrant-oriented manipulations of identity, technology, and labor through Chicago's beauty culture, this chapter examines how black women "made do."[3] The way they implanted an alternative set of values and visions of the world within their adornment practices is what made a Madam Walker possible. The ideological exchange expressed in the circulation of beauty-related products, advertisements, and social possibilities helped solid-ify this cultural formation as a key space within the marketplace intellectual life. Here, the specific consumption habits, tastes, and desires for beautifica-tion among black women in cities like Chicago instigated the "makeover" of a twentieth-century beauty culture that was supposedly not "made" for them into a medium of personal and collective transformation.

During the Great Migration, Chicago witnessed a moment of contact and contestation between old and new settler sensibilities that were powerfully worked out in struggles over the appropriate practice and consumption of hairstyles and bodily adornment. In the process, beauty culture became an important locus for the development of a contested New Negro womanhood. The relationship between old settler resistance, new settler consumption practices and urban innovations, and the engagement with new modern technologies served as the foundation for a distinctly black beauty culture in Chicago. Migrants such as Walker, Anthony Overton, Annie Turnbo Malone, and Marjorie Stewart Joyner along with their agents, critics, and consumer patrons manipulated beauty culture for a variety of reasons. A survey of the production and consumption of Overton Hygienic, Poro Industry, and Walker System cosmetics highlights the emergence of black beauty not just as an enterprise but also as a vibrant intellectual discourse about alternative expressions of New Negro womanhood. Only six years after Walker took the floor from Washington at the NNBL meeting, an estimated 20,000 agents in the United States and abroad were in her employ and organized into the Madam C. J. Walker Hair Culturists Union of America that would specifically "protest against" the East St. Louis race riots of 1917 and later even against the capitalist business practices of Walker herself.[4] Black working-class migrant women transformed an industry of white emulation into a powerful black public sphere of leisure, labor, and politics.

NATURAL VERSUS ARTIFICIAL BEAUTY:
NEGOTIATING GENDER AND CLASS THROUGH ADORNMENT

Turn-of-the-century white beauty/cosmetic company ads in black newspapers for products including "Black-No-More" and "Kink-No-More" suggested that what was popularly understood to be black genetic inferiority could be remedied by changing black people's physical features. While these marketing campaigns were aimed at the entire race, they targeted women in particular as the symbolic reflection and literal face of races and nations. Victorian notions of feminine chastity, moral restraint, and purity underscored the racial hierarchy of Social Darwinism. Black women's dark skin and "kinky" hair, in contrast to that of their white Victorian counterparts, were seen as physical manifestations of an excessive and morally questionable racial character. The "scientific" connection made between color and character seemed to visually rationalize the scientific fact of black women's sexual impurity and "biological" immorality. Typically, black women were bombarded with "before and after" advertisements that featured a "dark-skinned, woolly-haired" primitive juxtaposed with a more refined "high-class lady" who had undergone the scientific treatment of a skin whitener or hair straightener.[5]

In direct response, many black leaders and reformers directly attacked beauty products as a non-productive obsession with artificial self-indulgence that presumed an inherent link between white physical features and feminine virtue. In a series of essays started in 1904 for the elite journal *Voice of the Negro*, Fannie Barrier Williams and Nannie Helen Burroughs argued that "the colored girl" must focus not on "color but character." They attacked men who chose mates based on skin tone and also women who were lured by the marketplace artifice of hair straighteners and skin whiteners. By combining race pride with a Victorian focus on inner beauty, Burroughs specifically argued that black women should be proud of their natural selves and should labor at being pure of heart instead of focusing on external features.[6]

To dispel Darwinist myths of black female impurity and minstrel stereotypes of laziness, the reform-oriented or old settler image of the "New Negro woman" linked the values of hard work, temperance, and moral virtue to a prescription of physical "naturalness." This reform vision was on full display in John Adams's *Voice of the Negro* essay, "Rough Sketches: A Study of the Features of the New Negro Woman." Black women had been conceptually and physically excluded from civilization and represented as the negation of "the moral stamina, the purity of heart, the loftiness of purpose and the sober consciousness of true womanhood." But here Adams, painter and professor of art at Morris Brown College, directly inserted black women into the Victorian image of womanhood that had been the preserve of white women without question simply by nature of their skin. While Adams puts a black face on feminine purity and virtue, his accompanying sketches of this New Negro womanhood tell an equally important story.[7]

Adams rejected an association of womanhood with whiteness but could not excise the general "pose, expression and features" of womanhood that were still governed by the white Victorian imagination. In a sense, putting black women within the space of civilized or refined womanhood did not challenge the Euro-American aesthetic standards of beauty and behavior that defined that identity. So for example, New Negro women were literally sketched in Adams's essay with a posture of feminine deference, not looking directly into the frame but up and away, clothing covering the entire body (with one exception), no makeup, and hair in an un-straightened, simply adorned bun style or pulled back off the face. Moreover, Adams reclaimed an analytical style of "reading" the sketches that was typical of the era: a kind of aesthetic Darwinism where the physical depiction of the subjects in the sketches served as indicators of their mental ability and moral worth. A sketch of "Lena" tied her seemingly kind and affectionate face with "an 'industrious turn of mind.' " A college president's daughter, "Lorainetta," was a product of "careful home training and steady schooling," as indicated by her "beautiful" eyes. Women like "Gussie" both admired art and kept a good home and, if appreciated by the properly deserving man, would serve as a "death-knell to the dude and the well dressed run-around."[8] This last comment is significant because it reveals that reformers were threatened by the

This beautiful eyed girl is the result of careful home training and steady schooling. There is an unusual promise of intelligence and character rising out of her strong individuality. A model girl, a college president's daughter, is Lorainetta.

You cannot avoid the motion of this dignified countenance. College training makes her look so.

John H. Adams, "Rough Sketches: A Study of the Features of the New Negro Woman," *Voice of the Negro* 8 (August 1904).

kinds of images associated with the modern male dandy or black flapper. In reality, the old settler attention to self-presentation was not so different from the dandy or flapper but simply existed along a spectrum of adornment with excessive displays of artifice at the other end.

Moreover, the announcement of the "death-knell" was more a hope than a guarantee because a black flapper could easily argue that she shared in the quest for personal grooming and hygiene. However, those who held reform visions of New Negro womanhood would retort that grooming was meant to subdue, not highlight, physical features (neat, natural, and modestly adorned). Reformers rejected the idea that the race was inherently devoid of virtue but also worried that perhaps some behaviors ascribed to the entire race did actually exist within the "lower" classes. Again, Victorian prescriptions about behavior, even if determined by white aesthetic standards, were not necessarily called into question. Reformers simply protested the inherent exclusion of black women on the basis of skin color who at the same time met those Victorian behavioral standards. Despite present-day assumptions that authentic or "natural" blackness is rooted in visions of the "folk" or the "people," we see that the notion of "natural" black beauty was directly tied to emerging leadership struggles over Victorian versus modern definitions and images of black female respectability.

The surveillance of migrant black bodies and behaviors was in many ways an attempt by the "better class" to establish a hierarchy of distinction that provided distance from but also dominion over the newly arriving migrant masses. Furthermore, the identification and description of "unnatural" behaviors as non-elite or mass-produced placed black reformers in relative proximity to their white middle-class peers. The bottom line is that connections between a particular physical stature and social status were not inherent, especially in a community whose very marginalization was (and is) heavily informed by visual representation.

As a case in point, the "better class" was not the only social group that held disdain for "artificial beauty." A relationship between bodily temperance and moral virtue also existed in the "otherworldly" ideology of many black working-class religious practitioners as well. Emerging urban Sanctified churches encouraged emotional and physical forms of worship (rhythmic music, speaking in tongues, spirit possession) that ran counter to reformist views of order and restraint. However, these new denominations also argued that the body should be freed from restraint only in labor for the Lord, not for personal pleasure. The perspective of devout working-class women reveals the development of a competing definition of respectability, where for example they found card playing or the wearing of jewelry among middle-class reformers appalling. Many of these churches vehemently censured any overt focus on the personal satisfaction of the flesh, like the use of cosmetics ("the devil's paint"), but did so for reasons of religious sanctification and not necessarily for racial uplift in the secular world.[9]

The common thread running through elite reform and working-class religious critiques of beauty culture was a response to the presumption that black people did not have an inherent ability to be moral and good. All parties resisted the connection that mainstream beauty made between chemical or genetic enhancement and black women's virtue.[10] Race leaders specifically fought for the world to see that black women were "naturally" virtuous and moral, regardless of their proximity to white physical features. However, within the race, what I call the *cult of the natural* also signified boundaries and restrictions and reinforced static notions of gender and class difference. The physical restriction of women to a "natural" state of beauty, in the face of modern desires for dress and artifice, made beauty culture an important "style war" over distinctions of gender and class.

Fashion and style became physical markers that helped justify a gendered division of labor as natural. Women were unrealistically considered more natural than men as "products and prisoners" of their physical functions and reproductive capacities and, hence, biologically restricted to the domestic realm, whereas men seemed to have an innate ability to master nature, providing them with the power to control and manipulate themselves and their physical surroundings (including women). Not coincidentally, many of the findings about these gendered divisions of labor were derived from experiments conducted within the physical education arm of the "sporting life."[11] Therefore, most attempts by a woman to move from the sacred hearth of home and domesticity, whether through labor or artifice, were interpreted as going against her "nature." According to various sacred and secular standards, beauty products took women out of their "natural" state, representing an adulteration of female sanctity and purity.

The behavioral and cosmetic indicators of female respectability naturalized distinctions between men and women, sinners and saints, while also crystallizing previously mentioned struggles between the "better class" of women and their working-class counterparts. While male and female leaders rallied against white emulation and artificial beauty for the less enlightened, their personal stance on general adornment seemed less clear. Louis George, a freelance writer and sometime Walker employee, argued directly that the relegation of black women to a state of "remaining" natural was hypocritical, especially coming from the "better class." In an article for the *Messenger*, George charged that while reformers may not use beauty products, "these extreme race loyalists artfully avoid the unkempt, unimproved hair and the poorly 'attended-to skin.'"[12] George went on to challenge leaders and reformers to forgo the excessively artificial cultivation of homes, clothing, food, and, most important, personal hygiene to which they had grown so accustomed. By pointing out race leaders' and reformers' reliance on "unnatural" goods while they condemned the masses for making their own consumption choices, George exposed underlying class assumptions about what appeared to be general definitions of style and artifice within the race.

In many ways, all black people were paying more attention to hygiene and self-presentation. But debates over what kind of adornment—excessive modesty or artifice—determined the beauty standards of the race are what helped mark competing fashion practices as emerging class struggles. George suggested that leaders were less concerned about the racial treason of adornment than with the belief that only those of a certain class or cultivation had the right to determine such luxury. The number of fashion pages and/or beauty columns in elite, genteel black magazines since the 1890s reveals an extremely self-conscious leadership class always aware of how they looked to their white peers in ways that also helped maintain distinctions between themselves and working-class migrants. Moreover, the fact that race reformers continually had to campaign for a degree of decorum in migrant styles and dress exposed "modesty" as an equally unnatural process that required hard work and its own form of self-indulgence.[13] In this context, when working-class migrant women dressed "up," they helped contest any static image of the migrant masses as a group of primitive or rural folk while challenging the very idea that the behavioral or beauty prescriptions of old settlers defined the New Negro.

A narrative of women's "natural" position proved extremely difficult to hold on to, as working-class migrants gained a growing access to instruments of technological innovation during World War I. Despite race leaders' goals, many migrant women traveled from southern town to city and finally left the South altogether with the deferred hopes of breaking the constraints associated with domestic subservience, bodily temperance, and parental control. Mainstream beauty culture reinforced a white standard of aesthetic norms, but black women's culturally specific engagement with adornment technologies also helped fashion alternate expressions of a modern gender and race consciousness through physical manipulation.

The process of adornment was part of a long struggle for various forms and spaces of personal agency that took on new political meanings during slavery and can be traced back to techniques of physical manipulation and enhancement partially derived from an African past. This legacy continued and became one of the opportunities to create a sense of individuality and self-presentation for slave men and women. Women used whatever was on the plantation, but especially cotton, to "roll" or "wropt" their hair for easier styling while also using animal shears for cutting and shaping. Madam Walker provided an interesting account of this old relationship between plantation labor and slave leisure in her manual for beauty culture students. She argued that the process of straightening the hair was generally termed "pressing" because of its similarity to labor performed by many black women: the pressing and ironing of clothes.[14]

In slave societies, the poor condition of one's hair became a material marker of one's status. On a very practical level, the health and diet of those in or escaping bondage did not allow hair growth for desired styles. The earliest forms of hair relaxing were, in many ways, attempts to stretch the hair out long enough to put it in elaborate styles that were a hybrid of African cultural forms and the emulation, or even parody, of white adornment.[15] Black beauty culture was part of the legacy to reclaim personhood from servitude, a status that had historically derived, in part, from body cultivation. Therefore, during the Great Migration, cities like Chicago became a battleground between old and new settler sensibilities over divergent meanings and practices of beauty culture. What emerged was an alternative conception of New Negro womanhood and respectability that included, for many, the use of "artificial" adornment materials.

The beauty salons, kitchens, and porches of Chicago's black metropolis were important venues where women finalized the process of reconstructing themselves as sophisticated and modern when they were so obviously excluded from mobility within modern labor. Black women had made clear strides in their migration to Chicago, but they were still constricted in occupation and pay. In the 1920s, black women could earn between twelve and eighteen dollars a week in Chicago factories, compared to between two and four dollars in southern states. Some black women were even hired as temporary wartime help by Sears and Roebuck and Montgomery Ward. However, the increase in wages did not account for the cost of living increase in the city or for the fact that women were restricted to unskilled labor positions in the factory. The reality was that while factory jobs had opened up between 1910 and 1920, black women worked in the worst conditions, and at least 64 percent of documented black women workers were still restricted to domestic service.[16]

In this context, working-class black women's engagement with the artifice and recreational leisure of beauty culture signaled both aesthetic and actual breaks from their traditional status as simply and completely mothers, wives, and domestics. Beauty culture's artificiality and the collective acts of self-conscious fashioning (waved and dyed hair) signified, for many, women's growing possibilities for personal liberation from tradition and toward modernity in bodily display, profession, and politics. Even in the South, when beauty agent Mamie Garvin Fields saw powerful women like Walker and educator Mary Church Terrell speak, her evaluation of their modernity included both ability and appearance. Walker's elegant dress represented "a go-ahead, up-to-date black woman," and Terrell's "beautifully done hair" signified "she *was* that Modern Woman." Interviews from Paul Edwards's rare 1932 black consumer study tellingly concluded that it was precisely "products of the Madam Walker Company" that "pictured the Negro as he [*sic*] really is, not caricatured, degraded, or made fun of; that here the Negro was dignified and made to look as he is striving to look, and not as he looked in ante-bellum days; that here was the *new Negro*" (emphasis added).[17]

Letters to the Walker company reveal that, beyond extravagant spectacles of glamour, a beauty culture modernity was most acutely expressed in demands for a complete beauty system that could remedy practical or serious problems, including scalp disease, skin blemishes, and limited hair growth. At the same time, black *and* white newcomers to the urban North used black beauty products to conform their skin tone, hair texture, and grooming habits to unwritten requirements established by northern industrial and professional businesses. For the majority who remained in domestic jobs, they reinscribed beauty culture with a meaning of resistance to servitude, as a symbol of race pride, and as a form of labor-based leisure. Edwards's study also confirmed that many black women specifically used beauty culture to separate themselves from identification with labor efficiency and the servitude that aprons and head rags signified. This vision was reinforced by what black women in Washington, D.C., aptly called "freedom bags," in which they carried work clothes so they would not have to wear them on the street.[18]

In the hands of migrant women, who usually served someone else, the time and space offered through beauty culture was also much less about pure hedonism and more an issue of personal attention and affirmation within a black world of leisure outside of labor dictates. At the same time, the demand for this alternative space of leisure helped turn the practice of beauty culture into a viable source of labor as culturists. One of Walker's agents, Maggie Wilson, argued that beauty culture "made it possible for thousands of women to give up the washtub, the cook kitchen, the scrub work and that drudgery that was the only way for them to make a living." These working women's concerns with healthy scalps, exciting "non-functional" styles, and an economic "way out" overshadowed anxieties over white emulation. More than simply a politics of "Straight vs. Natural" hair, beauty exposed class conflicts over working migrant women's bodies. These complex and fractured struggles over appropriate aesthetic and economic choices gave meaning to the beauty culture and industry that emerged within Chicago's black metropolis.[19]

SELLING BLACKNESS: BEAUTY ENTERPRISE IN
THE MIDWESTERN BLACK METROPOLIS

Even before the Great Migration, black women in Chicago continued the southern practice of dressing white women's hair as an alternative labor source. Jary Gray opened the first hair salon downtown in 1856, and a Mrs. Joe Stanley had five people in her employ at a Chicago hairdressing shop during the Civil War. The best-documented black beauty establishment in Chicago of the pre-migration era was the shop run by Grace Garnett-Abney. In 1896, she opened a parlor at 2808 South State Street that was one of the first to have a clientele of both elite white and black women who desired wigs and/or suffered from the threat of hair loss.[20] However, it was the intersection between old settler reformers, new migrant sensibilities, and larger processes of urbanization that provided the Chicago area with the fertile ground for a thriving culture of black beauty industries, agents, advertisements, and consumers.

Black migrants like Overton, Malone, Walker, and Joyner continued and improved on the work of Garnett-Abney and helped to give form to beauty culture's role in shaping Chicago's marketplace intellectual life. Despite their ability to capitalize on new settler adornment desires, this new generation of beauty culturists had to contend with old settler anxieties over migrant women's growing interest in forms of artificial beauty and self-indulgence. As a response, beauty magnets and the enterprises they inspired attempted to nullify the controversies surrounding "artificial" beauty as white emulation, emphasizing in different ways how their businesses were an expression of race pride and respectability. Beauty culturists and their consumers variably focused on the value of men in cultural and financial control of race issues, the service and supporting role that female beauty agents provided for uplifting the race, and the control that working women could have over their civic, economic, and aesthetic choices.

The way that black beauty entrepreneurs, critics, and consumer patrons shaped the meaning of various mass consumer beauty companies and their products resulted in divergent expressions of a New Negro consciousness. After migrating to Chicago in 1911, Overton set up his Overton Hygienic Company when he realized that his "High Brown" face powder was more lucrative than his baking powder. His business, which focused on outer beauty, was in conflict with many race leaders' version of "uplift." However, Overton found common ground through his conservative ethic of race conscious economic nationalism that rested on black men's right to enterprise. Overton presented his business as a symbol of race pride, protecting black womanhood from white companies not concerned with refining and uplifting the public image of the race, as evidenced by the dangerous and cheap products they pushed on the community.[21]

Overton never owned or published the journal *Half-Century Magazine* officially, but the sheer strength of his advertising dollars guided the conservative business and beauty focus of its articles and columns. It is in between the pages of this magazine that we find the ideological position of Overton and his particular appeal to critics and consumer patrons. *Half-Century*'s old settler support of a strict gendered division of labor was evidenced in its early subtitle, "Colored Monthly for the Business Man and the Home Maker." Articles aimed at men focused on race enterprise, whereas specific columns like "Beauty Hints," "Domestic Science," "Fashions," and "Etiquette" addressed women in the home. The journal also shared concerns about the detrimental impact that migrant culture had on racial uplift while also recognizing the consumer dollars that migrants brought to urban centers. Toward this end, Overton products and *Half-Century* columns served as another kind of reform to discipline female migrants in their "adjustment" to the North according to old settler visions of respectability.[22]

The erection of the Overton Hygienic/Douglass National Bank Building on 36th and State in 1923 became a material symbol of race man progress by housing Overton's many business interests and offering rental space for other black professionals. As part of the nouveaux riches of his era, such activities helped secure Overton's place in the circles of respectability among race leaders who were skeptical about his chosen profession. Beauty industrialists who marketed to black consumers were initially denied membership into

Booker T. Washington's NNBL. Washington's biographer, Louis Harlan, argues that Washington felt beauty products fostered the imitation of white beauty standards. However, an alliance was made between Overton and Washington's NNBL because of the shared desire for black male enterprise to fashion black female conduct and beauty.[23]

For black businesswomen like Walker and Malone, who both battled overzealous men in their personal and professional lives, working within the identity of "race manhood" proved difficult. They were initially on the margins of the black metropolis (both physically and conceptually) and had to develop alternative strategies toward legitimacy through their controversial business interests. With Walker in Indianapolis and Malone not arriving from St. Louis until 1929, it could be argued that they were not central figures in the development of Chicago's New Negro culture. However, their proximity and property holdings in Chicago, their association with Chicago's Claude Barnett and his Associated Negro Press (ANP) and also the *Chicago Defender*, and the eventual number of Walker and Poro (Malone's company) agents, clubs, and patrons in the black metropolis solidified their impact on the community. Moreover, Walker's future national supervisor, Marjorie Stewart Joyner, strengthened the network of contacts with black colleges, Walker agents, and national media from her Chicago headquarters. As part of Chicago's New Negro intellectual life, both Malone and Walker found ways to work within and challenge the Victorian belief that a black beauty industry equaled white emulation or at best was the sole preserve of race men entrepreneurs. They sought and redefined racial respectability by variably placing attention on the hygienic nature of their beauty systems, the employment opportunities for women agents, and the philanthropic involvement of their companies in black communities.

Like many clubwomen, Malone worked within the "woman's sphere" of Victorian domesticity by combining Christian values and maternal domesticity with a race pride advocacy for African adornment practices. While women like Burroughs attacked beauty products and encouraged pride in "natural" features, Malone argued that it was African women who originated beauty culture. She maintained that her company's name, Poro, derived from a West African society committed to, in her own words, "disciplining the body." Malone charged that beauty culture, like the larger black community, needed to be equally uplifted and scientifically improved so that it would get the respect it deserved. For Malone, her "Wonderful Hair Grower" and other products were not in conflict with but in service to the cultivation of black women's character. Her strategy of a matronly public persona and equation of beauty entrepreneurship with nurturing support to the race were best revealed behind the doors of her million-dollar factory and educational complex in St. Louis and later on her "Poro block" on Chicago's famed South Parkway Boulevard.[24]

Like the Overton building, Malone's factory and "Poro block" were self-conscious symbols of race advancement. She provided dining and lodging for black celebrities and offered space for presentations during the 1933 World's Fair in Chicago. Most notably, it was in a Poro music room that Thomas Dorsey and Theodore Frye penned the famous gospel song "Precious Lord." Malone also offered many women the opportunity to pursue high school and college educations while offering them lodging and jobs through Poro. However, as in settlement houses across the country, once on Poro's campus, women could not escape Malone's maternal surveillance. Under the guise of motherly care, Malone required "the highest efficiency" in work and thrift, godliness in activity, and regimented obedience without dissent. Employees wore crisp blouses and black skirts, while many were further refined and cultured through their participation in the Poro Girls Orchestra, which specialized in church music and uplifting Negro spirituals.[25]

Malone also carried the role of "race mother" (nurturer and servant) into the public arena when her second husband unjustifiably attempted to take her business away in an ugly divorce battle. With the journalistic aid of ANP founder Barnett, she supported the magazine *The Light and Heebie Jeebies* to gain public sympathy in the kind of debate that would normally see race men filing behind the man of the business. She successfully presented herself as a poor, matronly woman of her race who had supported an ambitious and womanizing husband who was attempting to undermine a great race enterprise.[26] By crafting the image of a victimized race mother, she sidestepped the predictable charge that it was her success that was emasculating and would have driven any man into another's arms.

Finally, Malone was also heavily involved in civic charities and community events, funding two students at every land grant black college and aiding Max Yergan's YMCA interests in South Africa. Her biggest passions, the Women's Christian Temperance Union and a St. Louis orphan's home, solidified her place in the women's sphere of reform and respectability.[27] Through a mixture of benevolent service and autocratic control, Malone turned the image of a nurturing, supporting, private woman into a public role of prestige and power. However, Walker, Malone's one-time employee, would revolutionize the impact of a black beauty culture, turning many traditional images of black female domesticity inside out.

Walker worked within the same constrictions of a separate female sphere of service. However, Walker capitalized on the already expressed desires of her female mass consumer patrons to shift beauty culture's ideological focus from the powerful sphere of domesticity into the forthrightly public spaces of race enterprise and even race politics. From the start, Walker juxtaposed her washerwoman origins with her enormous wealth in an effort to place herself within the male-dominated public world of business by appealing to a wide and varied consumer base and by organizing a massive network of sales agents and institutions. The growing agency of the Walker System's female employees and consumer patrons was central to her success, even though they challenged her own authority, and in the process the black beauty marketplace broadened the concerns generally associated with "New Negroes."

Walker's marketing techniques, advertisements, and social organizations reveal strategies not only for increased profit margins. She invested the space around her products with messages and images of personal adornment, spiritual/scientific empowerment, health and well being, economic self-sufficiency, and a woman's-centered race politics that captured the already existing ideological desires of her consumer patrons' vision of a black modernity. Walker used different aspects of her story as personal advertisements and collective organizing strategies that appealed to working-class and even professional black women. Where Malone's utilization of African heritage and stories of a preslave civilization appealed to Victorian notions of discipline and order, Walker's "creation story" combined formal notions of race pride with a more "Pentecostal" style of divine dream revelation.

Walker claimed the answer to her personal woes as a domestic came in the form of a dream where "a big black man appeared to me and told me what to mix for my hair. Some of the remedy was from Africa, but I sent for it, mixed it, put it in my scalp and in a few weeks my hair was coming in faster than it had ever fallen out. I tried it on my friends; it helped them. I made up my mind I would begin to sell it." The belief in the power of religious signs and symbols spoke directly to many migrant women in a recognizable cultural context. This story pushed to the background Walker's engagement with chemistry (a field presumably alien to migrant women) and skirted rumors that she stole the formula from Malone. At the same time, the combination of spirituality and science also offered an alternative narrative of modernity that evoked the more scientific notion of a beauty system without rejecting the older rituals of mystical healing. Her reference to the supernatural world as the source of her remedy also indirectly provided her a higher power of authority over "man's" indictment of a woman leaving the home to peddle "unnatural" beauty products.[28]

Walker's resistance to preexisting gender relations was not merely rhetorical. Unlike Overton, Malone and Walker could not gain commercial space for their products in the white male–dominated preserve of the retail store, which forced them to develop alternative strategies of distribution and communication. These women created their own commercial market through advertisements in black papers and via church and club networks within the black community. Moreover, they provided "live" models for the aesthetic and economic desires of women through their company agents. In early advertisements that were heavily distributed in papers like the *Chicago Defender* and in speeches at sacred and secular women's meetings, Walker continued to reconstruct her own story and image in a number of ways to directly address consumer desires.

From the outset, she was very conscious of many women's reservations to patronize her system because of the "hair straightening" stigma. Walker's early ad campaign argued that her product "Makes Short Hair Long and Cures Dandruff." Contrary to popular belief, Walker never advocated hair straightening and in one interview made great efforts to "correct the erroneous impression held by some that I claim to straighten hair. I want the great masses of my people to take a greater pride in their personal appearance and to give their hair proper attention." Unlike ads for Overton Hygienic, she did not place glamorous light-skinned women with straight hair on her ads as objects of male desire. Walker offered her own dark-skinned image, the growth and health of her own hair, and the success of her enterprises as the object of black *female* desire.[29]

Bald patches and scalp diseases functioned as the scarlet letter of poverty for many women in this era, and Walker recognized that "good" hair was about long and healthy locks as much as it was about straight and stringy texture. Walker's ads and interviews reveal that her appeal was driven both by profit and politics but also suggest that she ultimately did not believe the goal of her system was turning black people white. At a time when poor and working-class black women were restricted to servicing others, this kind of advocacy for personal attention, leisure time, and later economic autonomy is important to note. Walker's vision of beauty included a holistic method of physical cleanliness, rest, a soothing and relaxing setting for customers at parlors, and a proper diet as prerequisites "if the patron is to get the most beneficial results." Furthermore, she did not sell skin-lighteners and argued that straight hairstyles were only one of many options after employing her more complete ritual of grooming and treatment. An advertisement began to circulate around 1914 that stated her system does "not handle false hair nor straightening tongs. No curling irons; an entirely new method used. No burning or singeing, but a beautiful head of hair in *natural* condition" (emphasis added).[30]

Walker masterfully continued to use the marketplace to craft alternative images of a New Negro womanhood through the direct address of community lectures that showcased her wealth and the creation of a corps of Walker agents. The connection Walker made between personal female prosperity and beauty products became material when women were able to see and touch the success of which the ads spoke. Walker was very conscious of the personal form of address that she needed for each forum. She employed Alice Kelley to tutor her in Greek, Latin, speech, grammar, and etiquette for some venues and employed agrarian metaphors for others: "Do you realize that it is necessary to cultivate the scalp to grow hair as it is to cultivate the soil to grow a garden?"[31] Walker also required a well-thought-out and relevant approach from her workers. She instructed agents to "acquaint yourself with the history and life of Madam C. J. Walker, get on the tip of your tongue the strong points that you will find in the story of her personal experience, tell your prospective customer about her, do so in an intelligent and emphatic way, watch his or her face, note what statement or statements impress most. . . . Imagine yourself a *missionary* and *convert him*" (emphasis added). In private, Walker dictated this letter to someone with better verse, but in public she embodied success, control, and—for the masses—a material form of salvation. Walker commanded respect when her chauffeur-driven, 40-horsepower, 6-cylinder Cole automobile arrived at both high and low civic and religious settings. She entered meetings draped in fine clothing, including a full-length mink coat, with well-crafted speeches spreading the "gospel of beauty." All of the elements of her carefully constructed presentations served as encouragement to the women in the audience, though for the men, as a warning of things to come.[32]

Walker's use of a relatively new technology—colored glass slides in a Stereopticon projector—further enhanced her sermonic approach and dynamic appeal. She fully realized the power of the images and remarked, "The pictures are the most important thing for it is that that arouses such keen interest." Walker awed crowds with a pictorial collage of her humble sharecropper shack origins in Louisiana complete with solo shots of washtubs and irons contrasted with images of her property, cars, and salons. In mostly religious settings, this sharp juxtaposition provided evidence of the riches that could be had in "this world" versus waiting for salvation in the hereafter. Walker used her origins as a laundress to create a level of semblance between herself and the many women in the audience who held the same service positions.[33]

The form and content of Walker's presentation and slides helped make her beauty industry more acceptable and appealing to women of all walks. For example, despite Booker T. Washington's dislike for beauty culture, Walker's illustrated lectures placed images of herself and her financial holdings alongside images of Washington and other race men to create a narrative of beauty culture respectability. Moreover, the simple fact that Walker owned and operated a slide projector noted success and urbanity, as movies were still a novelty in many areas.[34]

Walker offered financial advice and encouraged consumers to support particular black entrepreneurs who she felt were doing a good job, such as Chicago's Royal Life Insurance. When Walker visited the company in 1916, she was impressed that the president had come from a modest background like herself and that through his firm, "a Negro could buy as many shares as the white man." She immediately asked for slides of the company and included Royal Life in her talks.[35]

Walker marketed beauty culture as a way out of servitude for black women and created a sphere of public discourse where the same women could exchange information that met their particular needs. For women who lived in areas that didn't have a train depot, Walker threw out promotional booklets from the window of her luxurious passenger train car along with the mail pouches. These packages contained a listing of her real estate holdings and the still-famous early picture of Walker behind the wheel of a Ford Model T. This image of her in a car staring almost defiantly into the camera became a new and powerful symbol of the modern and upwardly "mobile" black woman in control of her destiny and image.[36]

Walker's beauty industry helped materialize a new identity for working-class women, but she also understood that a relationship with elite organizations provided another market for promoting her products and ideals. However, Walker also knew that her peasant origins, choice of profession, and defiant self-assertion into the world of race (read male) enterprise went against many of the uplift ideals of the "better class." In the face of resistance, she used her sheer wealth and celebrity status as a means through which to boost product visibility and win the seal of respectability from influential

Madam C. J. Walker at the wheel of her Model T in front of her Indianapolis home in 1912. (Courtesy of the A'Lelia Bundles/Walker Family Collection [www.madamcjwalker.com])

race organizations. After fighting her way into the entrepreneurial circles of the NNBL in 1912, Walker canvassed the Baptist, AME, AME Zion, Knights of Pythia, Court of Calanthe, and National Association of Colored Women's (NACW) annual conventions. She made donations to legal defense campaigns, scholarships, and organizational support and was noted as the "first colored woman in the United States to give $1,000 to a colored YMCA building." Leaders began to realize her philanthropic power, and Walker used these donations to secure endorsements, which distinguished her from other beauty figures, including her mentor, Malone.[37] In 1913, three respectable organizations endorsed Walker's products as "the best on the market." In 1914, Walker finally received approval from Washington as "the foremost businesswoman of the race." That same year, she even made the bold reminder to the NNBL convention that, "if the truth were known, there are many women who are responsible for the success of you men." The power of Walker's wealth and celebrity status helped her not only gain approval from but also challenge the gender and class ideals of organizations that, for various reasons, had previously been staunchly opposed to beauty culture.[38]

The strategies of personal address and philanthropy in black institutions helped Walker strengthen her market in Chicago's black metropolis. Walker spoke at Olivet Baptist Church in 1918, one of the many traditional Chicago churches that were going through social and cultural transformations due to an influx of migrants from the South. The fact that this parish invited her showcased a changing tide in the rules of respectability. As in similar settings, Walker secured entry into the church by coming under the auspices of the pastor's aid society, revealing the hopes of the church leadership that she would possibly make a donation to the church. *Chicago Defender* city editor Cary Lewis reported that Walker included her Stereopticon slide presentation but localized the reach of her success by displaying a slide of her "very valuable piece of property . . . located at 3316 Calumet Avenue." The article made special note that it was "one of the finest decorated homes in Chicago." Walker followed this by talking about how the wealth she acquired through beauty culture allowed her to buy property where people of her race could "take advantage of steam heat and electric lights and modern bathrooms."[39] The speech at Olivet is a perfect example of how Walker promoted beauty culture by focusing on the prospects of prosperity, race pride, and modernity while hardly mentioning female appearance.

With this trip, Walker consolidated her substantial presence in Chicago. In a letter to an agent, Walker's lawyer noted the growth of the black community and, after pointing out a few prominent churches, told the agent, "You could do a big business over there." One of the most important elements of these lectures for black women, and the reason for big business, was not just the display of the individual success of Walker but also the encouragement for them to "Learn to Grow Hair and Make Money."[40] Even if women could not be agents themselves, their use of the system and patronage of the local agent made them part of a personal and collective transformation of New Negro womanhood.

Walker's beauty network was so viable because it was "employing hundreds of Negro girls and women all over this country as agents, clerks and otherwise." She convincingly argued that the Walker System was making it possible for "many colored women to abandon the washtub for a more pleasant and profitable occupation." Walker was chosen as one of the featured speakers for the NNBL's 1914 annual convention, a bastion of race manhood, where she delivered the pointed remarks: "I am not merely satisfied in making money for myself, for I am endeavoring to provide employment for hundreds of the women of my race. I had little or no opportunity when I started out in life, having been left an orphan. . . . I had to make my own

Learn To Grow Hair and Make Money

MADAM C. J. WALKER
President of the Madam C. J. Walker Manufacturing Company and the Leila College, 640 N. West Street, Indianapolis, Ind.

Complete Course by mail or by personal instructions. A diploma from Leila College of Hair Culture is a passport to prosperity. Is your hair short, breaking off, thin or falling out? Have you tetter, eczema? Does your scalp itch? Have you more than a normal amount of dandruff?

MME. C. J. WALKER'S

Wonderful Hair Grower

Write for booklet which tells of the positive cures of all scalp diseases, stops the hair from falling out and starts it at once to growing.

Beware of imitations—all of the Mme. C. J. Walker Preparations are put up in yellow tin boxes.

A six weeks' trial treatment sent to any address by mail for $1.50. Make all money orders payable to Mme. C. J. Walker. Send stamps for reply. Agents Wanted. Write for terms.

See your nearest Walker Agent or Write

THE MADAM C. J. WALKER MFG. CO.

640 North West Street,　　　　　　　　　　　Indianapolis, Ind.

Madam C. J. Walker Mfg. Co., "Learn to Grow Hair and Make Money," *Chicago Defender*, October 21, 1916.

living and my opportunity! But I made it! That is what I want to say to every Negro woman present, don't sit down and wait for the opportunities to come. . . . Get up and make them!" These comments echoed what she had said two years earlier: "I am not ashamed of my past; I am not ashamed of my humble beginning. Don't think because you have to go down in the wash-tub that you are any less a lady!"[41] Her wealth and patronage allowed her to encourage working women while staring resistant race leaders in the face with a black female vision outside the normative ideology captured in an adage like "Behind every great man is a great woman." Walker chose not to stand behind but shoulder to shoulder with (some would say in front of) her male peers.

Walker defiantly marketed the idea that becoming an agent or opening up a shop would "secure prosperity and freedom" for black women. She spoke to black women where they existed in the social hierarchy by explicitly encouraging them to "rise above the laundry and kitchen . . . and to aspire to a place of commerce and trade." Walker boasted in ads that her system was "a real opportunity for women who wished to become independent."[42] This proclamation may have been exaggerated for marketing appeal, but no one could deny that beauty culture employed women in a field where they were making a living serving themselves, other black women, and the larger community within the constraints of consumer capitalism. Beauty culture offered a limited opportunity for many of these women who had come north with professional skills but in Chicago were either relegated to low-wage labor or tired of working in someone else's kitchen and "going in and out of back doors." The life and labor made possible through a profitable beauty industry provided important degrees of relative autonomy.

By 1916, Walker employed a reported 20,000 agents in the United States and abroad. In 1918, top sales agents and distributors earned around $100 a month, not including their 50 percent commission. But, even on a smaller scale, the average agent, like Mrs. Williams of Columbus, Ohio, made "$23 a week." Women could realistically make more money as an agent and were therefore also freed from the horrible conditions of factories, the surveillance of a house mistress, and the general stigma of servitude. Walker agent Lizzie Bryant wrote, "I have all I can do at home and don't have to go out and work for white people in kitchens and factories." For women in a severely restrictive labor economy, Walker's claim that working as an agent or beautician could be their "passport to prosperity" was more fact than sales hype.[43]

Walker also achieved respectability from major organizations, revealing both her entrepreneurial and personal desires to be within the elite "inner circle" of the race. At the same time, her modest origins and the logic of the marketplace intellectual life, where she had to address the specific desires and tastes of her consumer patrons, left Walker ambivalent about old settler respectability. In a letter to her lawyer, F. B. Ransom, during a tour, Walker scoffed, "You should have seen the dictey who did not notice the washerwoman falling on their faces to see her, and everyone wanted to entertain me, but I didn't accept one social call." Walker's reliance on a narrative of common origins with her consumer patrons and agents and the unconventional stances she took on gender norms and hierarchies encouraged her to redefine respectability. Walker continued to actively take part in organizations like the NACW. Yet at the same time, she encouraged clubwomen "to get closer in touch with our women in the factory."[44]

Instead of fully buying into the cultural codes of old settler respectability, Walker used her wealth to create a space where she and other women could exist outside of prevalent gender and class restrictions. An examination of Walker's agents union, her support for *Woman's Voice* magazine, and her political and civic affiliations reveal a simultaneous desire for and ambivalence about the terms on which social mobility could be gained. Walker dignified herself through the field of beauty culture, and now her goal was to establish the same civic responsibility and public recognition for her agents. Through the coordination of her lawyer, her tutor Alice Kelley, and others, Walker established a powerful network of national directors, spokespersons, supply stations, and agents. In 1916, she decided to formalize her extensive network of agents into the Madam C. J. Walker Hair Culturists Union of America. While one of the biggest goals of the organization was to protect Walker and her agents from being undersold, the union also encouraged political and civic service on the part of its members.[45]

The structural logic of Walker's first beauty culturists' convention in 1917 resonated with the interests and setbacks of Walker's own attempts to inspire a New Negro womanhood. Here was an organization of black women (not of the NACW elite) who were business-minded (but not as apolitical as the NNBL), putting their economic might to service for the race. This convention was most concerned with organizing agents into a political bloc with their national statement protesting the injustice of the East St. Louis Riots of 1917, while her 1918 convention in Chicago proved that Walker had roused a political consciousness in agents that could not be fully controlled, even by Walker herself.

Walker's decision to place her products in retail stores, in response to dwindling wartime profits, caused a huge stir within the agents union. Even before the Chicago convention, a group of local agents argued, "We . . . do not have the proper protection from you by placing your goods in the drugstore. In this way our sale of goods has been greatly cut down." In response to this tension, Walker attempted to calm the agents with a hollow missive that suggested that "plans are now under way to enable the agents to share in the profits of the business, as I am exceedingly anxious to put my business on a cooperative basis." This policy was never instituted, and even if it had been, some agents had long grown skeptical about what they saw as a growing focus on increased profits over the integrity of the company's philanthropic foundations. This debate came to a head at the 1918 Chicago convention with a protest from the floor questioning Walker's loyalty to her agents. Walker eventually won the debate, but the creation of a retail mediator undermined the kind of power that the direct sales method provided for working-class black women, and agents continued to complain about the new policy. Ironically, Walker's organization of working-class and migrant women into a political/civic bloc set the stage for the Chicago agents and their dissent from her business decisions.[46] Once this conflict was momentarily resolved, the convention focused on Walker agents becoming a refuge for the female migrant in Chicago's black community. The Chicago convention gave direction to the many individual efforts that were going on in the city on behalf of the company.

Alongside the Phillis Wheatley Home and the Urban League, Walker wanted her recently opened shops on 4656 South State Street and 3115 South Prairie to play a significant role in public advocacy for female migrants, since many of the agents were recent arrivals themselves. The convention also heard speeches from *Chicago Defender* founder Robert Abbott and alderman Oscar De Priest. Agents were encouraged to get out into the streets and back alleys to help migrants from the South. This collection of speeches was reminiscent of older forms of racial uplift and rhetoric about the Herculean will of black enterprise.[47] However, through words and deeds, Walker and her agents continued to encourage a level of political engagement in the city that exceeded the goals of social work and moral betterment programs.

Walker, like Thomas Dorsey and Oscar Micheaux, was explicitly interested in the relationship between identity, enterprise, and mass media technologies, from slide presentations to film technologies. Walker contemplated purchasing a magazine to promote her company and race ideals and the opinions and concerns of her agents. She felt that her wealth could keep a magazine solvent while the press that printed it served the company by cutting down on advertising costs. These motivations led her to purchase *Woman's Voice* magazine. As magazines became one of the key mediums within an evolving black public sphere, Walker's wealth subsidized an important voice. Unlike Overton's *Half-Century Magazine*, which contained the traditional and segregated "woman's page," *Woman's Voice* was a woman-edited, fully integrated magazine that contained profiles of black women, a section on the African diaspora, and a current news section that addressed women within a larger spectrum of not only the home but also business and politics. Front covers with provocative figures including blueswoman Bessie Smith and entrepreneur Maggie Lena Walker amplified the importance of this forum "For Women, By Women, Of Women" that was possible solely because of wealth created by Walker's consumer patron base.[48] This magazine was just one of many of what might be considered unfathomable accomplishments that emerged from Walker's wealth.

In the arena of "formal" politics, Walker's affluence allowed her to entertain political visions that might be seen as divergent but for her were different means to a general goal of advancing the race. Walker and her agents supported people all along the political spectrum, from Washington's Tuskegee Institute to W. E. B. Du Bois's NAACP. When she, along with others, grew weary of the NAACP's white leadership, Walker joined William Monroe Trotter's National Equal Rights League (NERL). Her advertising dollars also helped support such newspapers as the radical *Chicago Whip* and *Messenger*, which had divergent editorial aims from the more centrist-agitator organs such as the *Chicago Defender* and the *Crisis*. Famously, former Walker student Lucille Green Randolph's beauty earnings underwrote the radical *Messenger* magazine published by her husband, A. Philip Randolph; he admitted, "Without her money . . . we couldn't have started *The Messenger*." The economic and cultural capital provided by beauty culture allowed both Walker agents and Walker herself "the independence [needed] to choose causes and issues rather than sides and personalities" on a local, national, and international scale.[49]

As Walker's company expanded globally, she used these very same capitalist networks to develop a black internationalist politics. As early as 1913, she had canvassed the United States and the Caribbean selling her products, promoting her training agents, and eventually setting up a foreign sales bureau that conducted business in French, Spanish, and Portuguese. When it came to her products, by 1919 Walker ads boasted "A Million Eyes Turned Upon it Daily" because "WE BELT THE GLOBE." At the same time, World War I brought different elements of the black world together in unthinkable ways, and Walker's beauty industry gave her political prominence in advocacy for the globally oppressed. Most recognize Du Bois's efforts to attend the Paris Peace Conference on behalf of the millions unrepresented in the African Diaspora, yet few know that Walker and Ida B. Wells, after staunch male opposition, were chosen as "auxiliary" delegates to travel to the Paris conference on behalf of the NERL's National Race Conference for World Democracy.[50]

Walker's New York State mansion was also the birthplace of the short-lived International League of Darker Peoples (ILDP) that included Marcus

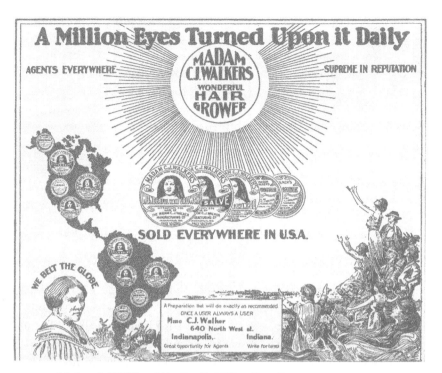

Madam C. J. Walker Mfg. Co., "A Million Eyes Turned upon It Daily,"
The Crisis (March 1919).

Garvey, Adam Clayton Powell Sr., and A. Philip Randolph. She explicitly stated that the ILDP was organized to "engage world opinion" far beyond the aims of the Paris conference. While ill-fated, Walker met with a Japanese delegation in Harlem in the "spirit of race internationalism" with hopes they would place the "race issue" on the Paris platform. Her more conservative lawyer, F. B. Ransom, shunned her alliance with "highly questionable characters," particularly "the Trotter bunch," and warned that "anything that borders on Bolshevikism is to be avoided." Sure enough, Walker caught the attention of the War Department's Military Intelligence Division and was added to their wartime list of "Negro Subversives." The State Department denied Walker's request for a passport to France, yet she still put her support behind Du Bois's delegation and, most important, remained open to a variety of political options for her black working-class women's constituency when their options had been so few.[51] These formal political activities reinforced the more general role of beauty institutions and ideas within an emergent new settler modernity.

After the war, beauty culture had solidified its influence in Chicago's changing black metropolis. Black women as agents and patrons entered into a New Negro discourse about the role of consumer culture in creating personal space and time away from work and home. Walker resolved the issue of retail sales by setting up supply stations in a number of cities, including Chicago. While the convention sparked the debate over profits, her presence also strengthened the Chicago market. In a letter to Walker, Ransom remarked, "You will be surprised at the number of Parlors that have been opened up since the Convention. . . . Chicago now reminds me of New York, a Walker Parlor on every corner."[52]

Chicago's beauty culture had grown larger than the individual exploits of Overton, Malone, or Walker. Within a rapidly industrializing America, the mass production, circulation, and consumption strategies of black beauty industries served as a way of reclaiming interpersonal networks among black women that were continually being stripped away by the inhumanity of accelerated industrial labor relations. Beauty colleges, shops, and house visits became sites where black women took back their bodies and reorganized their lives through the time-consuming rituals of "doing hair."[53] Furthermore, beauty culture offered flexible hours and part-time employment and allowed women to mix labor and leisure time by performing their tasks at home while socializing with clients and friends.

While concerns about the stability of beauty culture arose when Walker died in 1919, its hold on urban Black Belts across the country only strengthened in the next decade. The informal nature of beauty culture resists the collection of even near-exact numbers, but the U.S. Census Bureau reported that between 1910 and 1920, the number of black female hairdressers rose from 3,093 to 12,666. In 1920, Ford Black's annual *Blue Book* of Chicago's race enterprises found at least 108 documented hairdressing shops in the city alone, reflecting a diverse array of active beauty companies, schools, shops, personalities, and ideas in Chicago's black metropolis.[54]

POSSIBILITIES AND LIMITATIONS: THE
PROFESSIONALIZATION OF BLACK BEAUTY CULTURE

The groundwork set by Overton, Malone, and Walker inspired other figures to toss their hat into the ring of a growing and prosperous Chicago beauty culture. By this time, glamorous ads and more strict policies of professionalism had signaled a shift within the changing meaning of beauty culture. Would it continue to serve as a means to the larger end of female autonomy, or become an end in itself driven by male desires? Heightened professionalism brought on more prominent representations of black African race pride and diasporic solidarity along with the declining significance of woman-centered entrepreneurial images. Yet, an unbending insistence remained that beauty culture maintain a viable space for some level of female agency. A group of local prominent businessmen shifted some of their capital away from other interests and into financing the cosmetics firm Kashmir Chemical Company (312 S. Clark St.) and eventually hired Claude Barnett because of his advertising and promotional skills. The Tuskegee graduate proved an ideal choice, having once worked for Richard Sears of Sears and Roebuck and as a Chicago postal clerk, which gave him familiarity with the processes of mass circulation and promotion.[55]

Barnett helped revolutionize beauty advertising and so shifted the focus of the industry's mission. Through Kashmir, Barnett developed an urbane yet cosmopolitan set of ad campaigns for its Nile Queen line that were the envy of the rest of the industry. Gone were the pictures of beauty culturists, like Malone and Walker, and in came professional layouts of models in exotic settings extolling the joys of luxury and urbanity. Men in uniforms or tuxedos admired the finely dressed "Nile Queens" in scenes with either ballroom or Egyptian and Middle Eastern motifs. On face value, these advertisements served as another early form of race pride. Barnett's Nile Valley settings were a direct reference to Cleopatra, depicted as a black woman, whose "beauty was unsurpassed." This aesthetic reclamation of diasporic pride through references to a black Nile Valley was quite prevalent at the time. Even boxer Jack Johnson had a wall-size picture of a black Cleopatra at his Chicago black-and-tan club, the Café de Champion. The representation of Cleopatra, through Nile Valley product ads, specifically relocated black women within an African legacy of beauty culture's reported origins. Furthermore, the ads gave the Nile Queen Preparations direct authority by arguing that the goods came from old Egyptian formulas, which had produced the most beautiful woman in history. This visual construction was important at a time when black scholars were arguing for the African Nile Valley as the birth of civilization.[56]

However, this new aesthetic approach within the industry positioned beauty culture as no longer a means toward other goals but as an end in itself. Women had advanced outside the home through beauty, but Kashmir's ad presentations of women in staid and languid poses of glamour shifted race pride back to a focus on male desire. In a press packet, Kashmir argued that the reason women want beauty is "to look well in the eyes of the world in

Kashmir, "Nile Queen," *The Crisis* (December 1919).

general and of some one man in particular." Beauty had fallen back into the service of looking good for a "husband or sweetheart," because if a woman did not, "he soon loses interest in her, and her very presence then will often displease him." Barnett worked closely with both the Poro and Walker industries, but his shift in focus was in sharp contrast to their appeal for women's health and employment.[57]

One ad campaign attempted to capitalize on the *Chicago Defender*'s celebration of Chicago's famous all-black "Fighting Eighth Regiment" returning from World War I and exemplifies the Kashmir approach. In these ads, the soldiers return home, having seen European women, and now only the beauty of a Kashmir girl could catch and satisfy the eyes of such a soldier's newfound "worldly" outlook. This display of postwar female elegance and male desire was matched by an alarmist ad that warned, "THE TIME IS AT HAND! You are just as much a soldier as the husband, brother, son or any that have gone to fight in this great conflict. IT DEPENDS UPON YOU whether he will come back to find you and yours healthy, happy and *pretty* or—sad, discouraged and *homely*" (emphasis added).[58] For Kashmir, this new approach of displaying beautiful, well-groomed brown (not black) women as the objects of race pride was a necessary shift that gave beauty a more modern and professional image. However, in an attempt to professionalize the industry, black women had been returned to a restrictive mantel where an industry standard of physical beauty qualified one's "race womanhood."

As another example of restricted race pride, in 1936 Malone encouraged the women graduating from Poro College to also celebrate their African heritage by wearing a cape fashioned after one worn by Ethiopian emperor Haile Selassie. This advocacy for African pride in fashion took place only a year after Italy's invasion of Ethiopia. That Malone even suggested her graduates wear an Ethiopian-inspired cape highlights an important moment in black international solidarity. But with the decline of the "Women's Era" of the early twentieth century, the Selassie cape was also meant to assuage any concerns that black men might have of Malone challenging their authority in the world of business. For example, Malone explicitly discouraged her students from wearing a cap and gown for graduations, believing that her "contribution to culture and higher learning did not warrant the same symbol as that adopted by great universities."[59] Beauty culture struggled and succeeded in redefining the kind of respectability that shaped race pride, but Kashmir and Malone foreshadowed the kind of costs that came with professional legitimacy.

What was once a fledgling enterprise on migrant women's porches and in

KASHMIR
PREPARATIONS
FOR HAIR AND SKIN
" They Can't be Beat "

Our new colored officers are as gallant and dashing and game a set as ever wore a puttee. They've a keen eye for beauty, too. Of course KASHMIR GIRLS are the ones who attract them.

There is something pleasing about the woman who has clear, smooth skin and soft, pretty hair which wins everybody's instant admiration. Learn the "KASHMIR WAY" to beautiful hair and skin. No matter what you have used before, you'll find KASHMIR better.

You can always tell a KASHMIR GIRL

Learn how to be beautiful. Send for new edition de-luxe beauty book—richly illustrated—tells all about the KASHMIR WAY. Write today for free copy. Agents Wanted.

KASHMIR COMPANY, Dept. K, 312 S. Clark St., Chicago, Ill.

Barnett Advertising Service.

Kashmir, "They Can't Be Beat," *The Crisis* (September 1918).

Poro College graduating class wearing Haile Selassie capes.
(Courtesy of the Chicago Historical Society)

their kitchens was now a community institution prominently featured all over the Stroll. Chicago was home to a number of beauty colleges and industries, including the Unique Beauty School, C. Taylor's Beauty Cosmetics (5009 S. Parkway), Scott's Beauty Culture Residence and Home Study Course (432 Oakwood Ave.) and Arroway (3423 Indiana Ave.). While in many circles beauty culture was still questionable, the Chicago Negro Chamber of Commerce highlighted Apex News and Hair Co. (412 E. 47th), Lydia's School of Beauty Culture (4655 S. Michigan), Marguerita Ward's Cosmetics (444 E. 47th), and the continued efforts of the Overton (3651 S. State St.), Poro (4414 S. Parkway), and Walker (4703 S. Parkway) industries and colleges as models of race enterprise. Even local white interests like McBrady's attempted to masquerade as race businesses. McBrady developed a special line for "Brown Skin People" to capitalize on a growing race consciousness in the city's beauty culture.[60]

The different schools and firms represented a diverse set of positions regarding black beauty culture. The older ideas of health, female autonomy, and civic responsibility persisted in companies like Sara Washington's Apex

News and Hair Co., whereas a company like Arroway, subtitled "The Aristo-crat of Toilet Preparations," embodied the newer ethic of race professional-ism with sophisticated ads that equated beauty culture with a world of male fantasy.[61] While a female space of leisure was a goal of Walker's and Ma-lone's, race companies' turn to skin bleachers and the growing focus on beauty as a female means to romance and marital bliss marked a new era. The efforts of Joyner, the eventual national supervisor of Walker Beauty Colleges, served as a bridge between the two extreme positions. She con-tinued using beauty culture as a place to "give girls a chance" in a changing world, especially during the Depression era when black women were further shut out of employment opportunities. At the same time, she disciplined young women according to the dictates of emerging professional standards.[62]

Joyner was a chief organizer in Walker's Chicago market and became a key figure in changing the terms of respectability in ways to benefit beauty as a black woman's industry. In the role of Walker beautician and eventual vice president of Walker's company, she helped cultivate relationships with black colleges and assisted in the writing of an Illinois state law governing beauty culture. Joyner became a model figure through whom the profession was catapulted from just "doing hair" to the ascendancy of women into public positions through beauty culture. Joyner became not just a beautician but an inventor and public advocate for the black metropolis and beyond.

Joyner deployed various strategies to move beauty culture from a health remedy and cure into a profession. Like most of Chicago's major New Negro figures, Joyner had migrated to Chicago. Coming from Virginia via Dayton, Ohio, in 1912, she became a student at the all-white A. B. Molar Beauty School, where she confronted the prevailing attitudes toward black people within beauty culture: "They said if you were Black you couldn't be an American. They said that right out in class one day." However, Joyner was resilient and became Molar's first black graduate in 1916. From there she opened her first shop at 5448 South State Street. She initially had an all-white clientele, but the growing desire for black women to develop a black beauty culture locally affected her in a very personal way. Joyner recalls that she attempted to "do" her mother-in-law's hair with little success. Her mother-in-law told her that Madam Walker was coming to town and gave Joyner money to take her class because Walker "is teaching how to do *black* hair" (emphasis added). This failed attempt to do black hair sparked a relationship between Joyner and the Walker company that lasted until her death.[63]

After Joyner became a Walker agent, she worked closely with Walker, becoming her chief organizer in Chicago and developing relationships with black colleges throughout the country. In contrast to Malone, Joyner helped Walker professionalize the industry by advocating the instruction of beauty culture as a central part of educational curriculums at black colleges, including Wiley University (Texas), Roger Williams (Rhode Island), and Arkansas Baptist College. At the colleges, Walker donated a beauty culture "laboratory" in exchange for employing Walker agents as faculty and certifying the Walker System at that particular college. Students worked on local women's heads at a reduced rate, and the college program became another way for Walker to cultivate new markets. Equally important, women who perhaps would not have acquired a postsecondary education now had access to this world.[64]

While Washington's Tuskegee Institute was one of the last to consent to beauty culture on campus, Mary McLeod Bethune's Bethune-Cookman College in Florida supported the Walker System from the beginning. Bethune and Walker were both relatively prominent black women with modest origins, and through the years they had witnessed each other's successes and failures in trying to gain acceptance from the black "better class." Joyner became the intermediary between Walker's desires to train black women for enterprise and Bethune's preparation of many of the same women for education. By the time of Walker's death in 1919, the company through Joyner had become a leading fund-raiser for Bethune-Cookman College. Walker company donations and Joyner's personal fund-raising efforts at Bethune-Cookman helped establish a certified curriculum of beauty culture, which went a long way toward legitimizing the industry.[65]

In Chicago, South Parkway's Walker College and Joyner's personal shop on State Street became sites where women were also disciplined into professional agents and beauticians. Beauty culture in general moved from narratives of divine revelation to the more scientific metaphors of systems, methods, and trained expertise. The demand for scientific rigor and professionalism also became a way to reinsert older Victorian ideas of female bodily temperance and public decorum. Joyner argued, "Good mannerisms accent good looks. Not one of my beauticians would dare walk down the street with a cigarette in his or her mouth. I'd snatch it out." The growing connection between professionalism and an almost medical/military form of discipline is revealed in pictures of students in white (nurselike) training uniforms, the almost clinical "practical work rooms," and graduates adorned in traditional caps and gowns. Yet, the beauty school remained a place for Joyner and other women to cultivate skills in marketing, sales, and even engineering.[66]

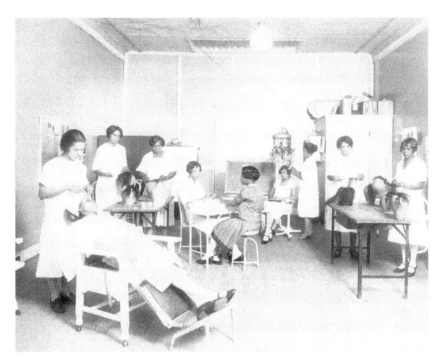

Marjorie Stewart Joyner's first salon/workroom; the permanent wave machine is in the background. (Courtesy of the Vivian G. Harsh Research Collection of Afro-American History and Literature, Carter G. Woodson Regional Library, Chicago Public Library)

When Joyner became frustrated with the time it took to set a permanent wave hairstyle, she invented a machine that allowed her to "wrap the hair in six or eight sections and apply heat at one time." She could never raise the capital to market her invention but did receive a patent and continued to use the "permanent wave machine" at the school. Joyner went on to formalize the early efforts of Walker to stop the adulteration of products and/or modification of their uses at cheaper rates. The culturists union was the first attempt to control and regulate the industry by identifying certified agents. In 1924, Joyner helped to write the first law in Illinois that regulated beauty culture and its schools and salons.[67]

The creation of standards and a uniform set of regulations protected black beauty interests from being undersold by fraudulent white companies and provided cultural authority. However, the professionalization of beauty culture also undermined some of the informality and autonomy of the field by placing the power of certification and licensing in centralized decision-making bodies. First, the professional focus on training and expertise over-shadowed the equally important skills of personality and charisma that made a black beauty industry possible. Second, by certifying the information gained through beauty culture, what was once a communal exchange of ideas was even more formally converted into a form of property.[68] The creation of unions, guilds, and experts became a form of protection, authority, and, for many black women, re-exclusion from the world of enterprise. Finally, the way Walker entered the business, by modifying a competitor's product (Malone's), proved more difficult for later women because of Joyner's advocacy for licensing and regulation. But importantly, Joyner's professional-ization of beauty culture also became a key avenue toward getting involved in mainstream civic-reform activities and Democratic Party politics.

Early in her beauty career, Joyner cultivated the eventually strong rela-tionship between the Walker company and Abbott's *Chicago Defender*. Joy-ner and Bethune escorted Abbott's nephew and successor, John Sengstacke, from Savannah, Georgia, to Chicago and lectured him about education and politics on the train ride north. Since its inception in 1929, the famous *Defender*-sponsored Bud Billiken Parade was directed by Joyner for more than fifty years, turning it into a massive community event. With the power of the Walker company behind her, Joyner then began to assert as well as strengthen her business status by helping found Bethune's Council of Negro Women in 1935 and working with First Lady Eleanor Roosevelt during the Depression.[69]

In the end, Joyner's career is symbolic of the transformed meanings of beauty culture in the mid-1930s. Despite the push toward professionalism, beauty culture remained a viable source of agency, employment, and civic responsibility for black women. Joyner boasted that at the height of the Depression, her school attendance averaged over 200 students.[70] At the same time, the new professional culture of certification and expertise, instigated by her mentor, Walker, undermined community networks that were at the foundation of the industry. Ironically, the transitional period of the mid-1930s marked a time when beauty culture would be at its most powerful, but at the same time its vision was forever changed.

Despite limitations, black working-class women's beauty culture in the early twentieth century emerged as an important and dynamic public sphere of race consciousness. Such seemingly simple acts of "making do" broadened the concerns generally associated with New Negroes by transforming accept-able representations of race, class, and gender. As much as beauty culture was caught in the racist web of white supremacy, black style and adornment practices focused on economic self-sufficiency, divine inspiration, and "race conscious" definitions of beauty and health care. The agents and patrons of beauty products desired middle-class respectability, but by bringing women outside the home, they gained it, for better and for worse, by redefining the terms. Women beauty culturists, once seen as peddlers of white emulation, used black adornment practices to "make over" the black metropolis as agents, entrepreneurs, educators, inventors, models, and political activists. As working-class black women took their bodies into their own hands to fashion arresting displays of modern womanhood, such larger-than-life performances of a New Negro consciousness were further projected and protested in the scopic realm of theater spaces and on movie screens as part of Chicago's vibrant black film culture.

Chapter Three

Theaters of War

SPECTACLES, AMUSEMENTS, AND THE
EMERGENCE OF URBAN FILM CULTURE

Long sermons against the movies, admonitions to
stay away from them, seem to result in empty pews in the
church and an augmented attendance at the picture show
around the corner. . . . Would it not be better then, to encourage
more of our people to produce pictures—films that will uplift; urge
them to build first class moving picture theaters, rather than
discourage them from attending picture shows?
—Jean Voltaire Smith, "Our Need for More Films,"
Half-Century Magazine, April 1922

Some of our citizens who claim to be so refined and up-to-date
certainly showed how they were raised. . . . While the great Albini
was trying to explain his work there was so much loud talking that
he was forced to ask them to quit. . . . We rather think it is our
newcomers to the city who think they are at a camp meeting.
—"Loud Talking at the Pekin,"
Chicago Defender, April 23, 1910

In 1915, writer Juli Jones, the pen name for Chicago's race film pioneer William Foster, made the bold proclamation, "Moving pictures offer the greatest opportunity to the American Negro in history of race from every point of view." This statement was such a declarative pronouncement that a connection between the film enterprise and race pride seemed a foregone conclusion. But Foster was not simply attracting consumer patrons to his version of an accepted black cultural institution; he was also trying to convince the race that the "moving picture business . . . is the Negro business man's only international chance to make money and put his race right with the world." Many race leaders, as discussed earlier, did not see music clubs, policy stations, beauty salons, and now theater spaces as ideal venues for the articulation of the metropolis model of race pride. However, these "nighttime" spaces on the Stroll were precisely some of the most popular and profitable enterprises in the black metropolis.[1]

For example, on any given Friday night, migrants with hard-earned leisure time jumped off the elevated train at 35th and State and landed in the middle of the blazing neon glory of the Stroll. The street was packed with black revelers (and more than a few white "participant observers"); the air was filled with music and laughter. To be sure, the streets and theaters were often dingy and many times dangerous. Sometimes illicit wares were too alluring, hawkers too aggressive, pickpockets too quick, madams too mothering, and shows too bawdy. A week's wages could be lost in a weekend. Still a veneer of freedom permeated the soul as the shroud of subservience was lifted to reveal extravagant displays of fast talk, fine clothes, and feeling good. Some ducked into the Monogram or New Grand Theater to catch a jazz set, with a few moving pictures mixed in, and if lucky avoided the threats of ushers to steal a few kisses with their sweethearts while hiding in the shadows of the rising and falling luminescence of the screen. Others headed north, dropping into the Elite Club for a cocktail and maybe some craps before jumping over to the famed Pekin Theatre, only to be accosted by some garish oglers begging them to slow down so they could get a better look, or by anti-vice uplifters telling them to speed up to save their souls or the image of the race. Little did revelers know that their saunter down the Stroll and adventures into various theatrical venues evoked such a wide spectrum of meanings, ranging from modern blackness, to "maybe baby," to bad breeding and even immorality, and yet many couldn't wait to enter this moving theater all over again. The crossroads of nighttime activities on the Stroll, as well as the varied responses to them, created the conditions that inspired filmmaker Foster's excitement and the race consciousness that propelled Chicago's burgeoning black film culture.

In this context, Foster's pronouncement about the power of black film culture can be seen as both a proclamation and a plea, as there were divergent and contested opinions about any connection between race pride and the leisure enterprise of moving pictures. Despite the economic potential in the dynamic untapped market that Foster referenced, there was a strong resistance against handing over the race's entrepreneurial future and public image to the leisure world of moving pictures. Many were leery of this new technology's ability to more powerfully tell the same old stories of black deviance and pathology with now mass-produced minstrel and lynch films, while some theater professionals worried that an increase in moving pictures might undermine the most recent viability of black stage productions. Black moral leaders, along with the 1911 Vice Commission of Chicago, were also critical of "the wicked moving picture theaters." Movie theater spaces, with their ties to the underworld and other vice activities, seemingly encouraged a wasteful use of time in a leisurely world of illusions and immorality with amusements that particularly highlighted black women's sexuality. Even the Chateau de la Plaisance, an amusement facility that featured moving pictures, presented itself as a healthy, high-class, and tasteful alternative to the popular nickelodeons on the Stroll.

Half-Century Magazine writer Jean Voltaire Smith outlined these reservations, but in an interesting twist, the primary goal of Smith's article was actually to warn *against* a strict condemnation of moving pictures. According to Smith, any flat-out dismissal of movie theaters resulted in "empty pews in the church and an augmented attendance at the picture show around the corner." With all of Chicago's black residents racially restricted to leisure on the Stroll, leaders and reformers simply could not compete with the attractions offered within theater spaces. Smith's solution, which became the general approach within old settler respectable circles, was to produce uplifting race pictures and "build first class moving picture theaters" to direct "a portion of the millions of dollars spent each year by Colored movie fans" back within the race.[2]

However, any economic success for "race" films and the possible creation of a viable race market depended on a mass audience. Therefore, the diversified leisure tastes or divergent expectations that black consumers brought to the theater tempered and even contested old settler prescriptions about what behaviors and viewing expectations were deemed appropriate and racially respectable. The dominance of the silent film genre in this era made the variety format in exhibition spaces, with its live amusement contexts, the site for a new settler approach to black film culture. Live accompaniments, sing-alongs, and other potentially participatory acts allowed audiences to shape entertainment experiences and even the narratives of the most uplift-minded "race" productions and events. Within the logic of old settler respectability, the "Loud Talking . . . newcomers" with their collective acts of "excessive boisterousness" and uncivilized manners were a real threat, because this kind of theater enjoyment potentially took place in mixed-race crowds and exceeded the official performance on the movie screen. However, the acts of "talking back," "acting up," and "showing out" in Chicago theaters signaled more than moments of unruly behavior.[3]

Desires for "films that will uplift," as opposed to a "camp meeting" atmosphere, and the range of expectations in between, marked the theater as a "theater of war," a commercialized arena of struggle over contested ideas about race, class, uplift, ownership, freedom, and representation. Conscious debates over exhibition behaviors and film texts exemplify the role of Stroll theater spaces within the larger marketplace intellectual life. A war was taking place across class lines, between old and new settlers waging campaigns for citizenship, among consumers and reformers over the racial market, and between black and white leaders over power. The desires, anxieties, and discourses that converged on black public exhibitions, spectacles, and amusements reveal an urban film culture that struggled over what can be considered the *means of projection*. The theater became a black public sphere for debates about how the race should be visually projected, as in beauty culture, but arguably in a more collectively public sense, linking grand theatrical displays to definitions of race itself. The dynamic intersection between various forms and spaces of mass spectacle within an emerging black film culture also set the stage for both the initial phase and the "golden age" of race film production.[4]

Cinema studies have historically focused on the film text as an autonomous entity, but a range of newer scholarship forces us to recognize cinema as a "social phenomenon," where the film experience acquires meaning through the specific amusement contexts where the celluloid texts are located. Therefore, this chapter offers "a critical methodology that allows us to look at [the] specificity" of black film *culture* rather than just at racial difference in films. Black film culture represents another public space, alongside the sports stadium, the beauty salon, and the tent revival, that provided alternatives to racially exclusive cinematic and social institutions and even to many of the expectations and pressures created within the race. As audience members, performers, managers, critics, and filmmakers, black Chicagoans exhibited strategies and desires for equitable participation in American life and projected both personally and collectively crafted new images of the race within their own theater spaces. Here black audiences could laugh at, desire, or ridicule screen characters even in the most mainstream white film. If too boring or offensive, individuals could turn from the screen and interact with the live entertainments, musical accompaniments, or fellow audience members in the theater. Finally, frustrations or fascinations with theatrical events were written about in the entertainment section of various local media, debated in beauty salons and on street corners, or even contested in landmark court cases. The power of black urban film culture is derived from these contextual dimensions as much as from the film texts themselves because they all collectively generated the contested meanings of the theater experience as varying expressions of race pride, release, and respectability.[5]

NIGGER HEAVENS IN THE PROMISED LAND: THE RACIAL AND SPATIAL CONSTRUCTIONS OF URBAN FILM CULTURE

Midnight Ramble, the pathbreaking documentary on early black cinema, argues, "It was in Chicago that race movies got their start," but until recently we have known very little about the black film culture that gave them meaning. Therefore, in order to understand race films more generally, we must examine the particular racial politics of theater spaces, both on and off the Stroll, that preceded and paralleled the arrival of race films.

The social-structural makeup of leisure spaces, in terms of location and patronage, had a profound impact on the formation of race and class identities. Although anyone legally had the right to sit anywhere in any of Chicago's theaters since 1885, de facto forms of segregation persisted throughout the city and particularly in the mainstream white leisure district, the Loop. However, black residents did not accept this policy as a given, and it is precisely because of their multiple forms of agitation, including protests, critical essays, and legal action, that we are able to gain a sense of the profound ways in which leisure habits and spaces shaped ideas about race.

In 1910, the *Chicago Defender* celebrated the landmark case in which Frank D. Donaldson, described as "one of our most enterprising young men," was denied entrance into the Colonial Theater after he had purchased his tickets. Donaldson actually won his case against the Colonial, which marked the first time that sanctions against racial discrimination in a theater were legally enforced in the city with penalty of a fine. The *Defender* encouraged black residents to take advantage of this legal precedent and "sue every time they are refused in theaters."[6]

Unfortunately, this case did not eliminate discriminatory practices, and a standard set of policies was implemented to discourage black patrons from coming to Loop theaters. Tactics included placing black patrons in a Jim Crow section and usually in the balcony, a practice made famous by the Carl Van Vechten novel *Nigger Heaven*, or in other less conspicuous areas, for example, in aisle seats near the wall. Mrs. T. P. Morgan and friends went to the white-owned Globe (Wabash and Pekin Court) and were ushered to seats that they did not purchase; they then realized they had been "seated in the Jim Crow section" of the theater. Only after vehement protest were these ladies given better seats. Such policies, however, were not exclusive to the Loop. Even white managers attempted to implement what Chicago historian and businessman Dempsey Travis called "super Jim Crow" in theaters on the Stroll.[7]

In the heart of the Black Belt, the Avenue Theater (31st and Indiana) preserved the main floor for white customers while restricting even "our most representative" blacks to the balcony. In this setting, where black citizens were the primary consumers, leaders were able to exert full indignation. In the context of World War I and growing sentiments of American patriotism, the *Chicago Defender* took an overtly nativist stance, contrasting the historic role of black soldiers in the U.S. military with the "foreign" ethnic identity of the theater owner: "The management should be deported to his home country—the American citizens of color who fought in all America's wars will not stand the insult."[8] Yet, most profound about theater racism was the way in which white justifications were shaped by what amounted to, at best, a series of racial mythologies.

After the bloody race riots of 1919, the Chicago Commission on Race Relations (CCRR) completed a landmark study to examine the reasons for racial antagonism in the city. Within this project, they also devoted some time to theaters where black investigators went to white theaters as customers and even attempted follow-up interviews with white managers to assess the rationale behind discriminatory practices. According to managers, the most common complaint by white patrons was that the mere "attendance of Negroes in any high-class theater was not desirable . . . especially in the presence of a lady." When pressed, managers asserted that blacks had an "odor" that could not be tolerated for "an hour or hour and a half"—long performance. Accordingly, these were the reasons blacks were "ushered" to the least conspicuous area and, if possible, never on the main floor.[9] Unfortunately, we will never know how many black residents were subject to the multiple forms of illegal discrimination that ranged from neglect to acts of violence. Yet our limited present-day knowledge of these events is shaped as much by a class politics that limited the scope of agitation as by a simple access to historical documentation.

Race leaders couched their theater protests within class assumptions that structured and limited the scope of their agitation. For example, the most consistent themes in the CCRR report were the descriptions of victims' behavior, status, or prestige. Phrases like "well-mannered, well-dressed," "a well-known prominent Negro employed by City Hall," "one of our enterprising young men," or "two of our most representative people" reveal that primarily those of the "better class" were considered the ones worthy of support and documentation. Thus, black consumers could not just be patrons; they had to be perfectly well mannered and behaved—a requirement not necessarily imposed on white moviegoers—to even register as valid complainants.

For those in the "better class," the dominant response to the racist zoning practices that confined them to live in the city's vice district and to patronize the same leisure venues as the masses was to disassociate themselves from the wide net cast over the entire community by linking specific leisure behaviors with class. As the hopeful arbiters of behavior, the "better class" attempted to reform the leisure habits of black migrants and particularly women. This approach also helped create a position of distinction on the Stroll, where the status of reformer helped identify the most "representative" of the race as possible patrons at Loop theaters. Instead of challenging the white standards of black behavior, the "better class" organized their politics around racist assumptions to prove to their white peers that not all blacks were alike. These politics of the most representative, best articulated as racial uplift ideology pervaded black notions of value, class, and community protest in leisure spaces. In addition, many new migrants had the double burden of fighting racial stereotypes while at the same time contesting the social stereotypes of the respectable class. The irony the commission report revealed is that the actions or status of black patrons never mattered to whites; the mere presence of black consumers was what was most generally objectionable.[10]

Even when those of the "better class" were allowed to sit with their white peers, many felt thrown back into the general void of blackness by the representations of the race on the screen. Early cinematic depictions of black people emerged from the cultural tropes of white supremacy, best exemplified in the popular pastime of whites in blackface minstrel entertainment.

The minstrel themes of chicken-stealing, watermelon-eating black laziness and incompetence were depicted in such films as *A Hard Wash* (1896), *Dancing Darky Boy* (1897), *The Watermelon Contest* (1900), *Wooing and Wedding of a Coon* (1907), *Uncle Tom Wins* (1909), and *Rastus in Zululand* (1910), with many marketed as authentic depictions of black people as opposed to theatrical blackface.[11]

However, Chicago's race leaders thought they gained a new weapon against these stereotypes when film exhibition came under the partial control of city censor boards as early as 1909. Chicago was one of the first cities to enact an ordinance requiring a police permit for every film shown. This law prohibited "the display of 'immoral or obscene movies.'" Films that were screened in other cities without problem had a difficult time winning approval in Chicago. Unfortunately, black reformers could find no solace in the early formation of Chicago censor boards because the interpretation of "immoral and obscene" did not include negative stereotypes of the race until 1914.[12] In this early period of film history, one could conclude that because black or sympathetic filmmakers did not own the means of cultural production or have access to distribution networks, they were exclusively at the whim of racist white filmmakers and exhibitors. Yet, parallel to the rise of mainstream film production emerged the consolidation of black leisure habits and practices that cohered around the dynamic realm of consumption, specifically through divergent styles of exhibition, or the means of projection, in segregated amusement spaces.

VAUDEVILLE REFORMERS, VARIETY FORMATS, AND THE POLITICS OF RACE-SPECIFIC EXHIBITION

Within the context of all-black theaters, vaudevilles, and movie houses in the silent movie age, even the most mainstream silent film text was appropriated, transformed, and given new meaning in the local context of Stroll theaters. The racial specificity of exhibition habits on the Stroll reveals a dynamic "appropriation of commercial entertainment" by black consumers that far exceeded the implied meanings of the films themselves.[13] There were three key factors that helped create an urban film culture on the Stroll and established the central role of the theater as a viable black public sphere within Chicago's New Negro intellectual life.

First, a number of venues were constructed on the South Side that exhibited race pride to consumers by marketing the variety format of vaudeville, music, and moving pictures. At least twelve theaters on the Stroll exhibited filmed entertainment between 1905 and 1913. This number increased to sixteen in the next decade and ballooned to more than twenty in the 1920s. At the same time, the Stroll intersection of 35th and State housed a significant cluster of smaller nickelodeons catering to both black and white audiences. Theaters were consciously recognized as a mixture of black entertainment, exploitation, and employment. Most of these theaters were part of the notorious Theater Owners' Booking Association. This grueling "chitlin circuit" of vaudevilles, primarily in the South, became the primary network through which later race films were distributed and exhibited.[14]

Second, the activities in these theaters were reported, debated, and advertised in the many newspapers and periodicals in the black metropolis. The *Chicago Defender* was the first race paper to have a freestanding entertainment section ("Musical and Dramatic"). More important, the *Defender* was a national paper, so the images reported on in this section were instrumental in motivating southerners to come north and even in inspiring readers who remained south to envision a different world. But the more regional, local, and special interest papers would not be outdone. The *Chicago Whip, Half-Century Magazine*, and even the Indianapolis *Freeman* covered activities on the Stroll in relative accordance with the political and class-based interests of their specific readerships.

Finally, as black leaders and those of the "better class" were rejected from the leisure and amusement venues of white peers, they attempted to direct the vision of performance and exhibition on the Stroll. Black reformers and leaders saw films, the emerging profession of film criticism in black periodicals, and an eventual presence on Chicago's censor boards as mediums of race pride, community formation, and moral instruction. These race leaders ran up against those developing a new settler vision of race pride that had little to do with the standards of culture exhibited on the white Loop. Many Stroll leisure houses had their own rules and styles of performance and exhibition informed by preexisting activities brought from the South, different ideologies of race pride, interaction with European immigrant forms of amusement, and consumers' engagement with the urban industrial conditions of the North. The configurations of these divergent and sometimes complementary forces are what shaped the beginnings of Chicago's black film culture.

Despite recent revisions, the period after 1905 is traditionally marked as the vaudeville era of theater in competition with the nickelodeons of working-class ethnic immigrants until the completion of the "classical system" of feature films around 1917. The most important point about this genealogy is the identification of nickelodeons as being more class-, ethnic-, and community-specific because of their low cost, location, and variety format.[15] However, racial restrictions made the supposed nickelodeon/vaudeville distinction a near impossibility within black film culture. Economic inequalities, cultural distinctions, and the exclusion of black patrons from white ethnic nickelodeons made Stroll vaudevilles, among other venues, the primary site to collectively represent "the race" and its internal differences well into the 1920s.

Robert Motts's famed Pekin Theatre proudly represented itself as "Home of the Colored Race." This race-specific form of advertising continued with the Grand ("Built for Colored People"), New Grand ("Home Theater of the South Side"), Lux ("Finest Theater in America Built for Colored People"), States ("Most Popular Vaudeville and Photo Play House on the Stroll"), and Monogram ("The Only Colored Vaudeville House on State Street") theaters. These theaters recognized that black consumers were not welcome at venues on the Loop, which encouraged them to invert racism and market "race" as a symbol of comfort and pride. The legacy of the Pekin, as the race's first modern theater, was so expansive that venues all over the country caught the "Pekin fever" by taking on the name of Chicago's famous house.

Until Ida B. Wells came to Motts's defense, many race leaders were hesitant to bestow racial respectability on the Pekin because of its ties to policy gambling. But because it was such a successful race enterprise, the *Chicago Defender* quickly deemed Motts the "Greatest Napoleon of Theatricals," and the Pekin became a symbol of race pride and solidarity by marking an important shift in black theater venues away from the honky tonk and brothel. The New Grand followed the race consciousness of the Pekin by announcing its opening in 1911 as "the finest theater in the United States . . . devoted to the Colored people." This vaudeville and moving picture house was described as an architectural work of art with a seating capacity of 800. The owners hoped that the city's black population would give their attention to a house that "has given for their exclusive use and enjoyment this new temple of amusement."[16] The advertising, marketing, and existence of these black spaces for enjoyment were instrumental in the leisure time of migrants and in the construction of black urban identities.

Ironically, most Stroll theaters, including the New Grand, were white-owned. Yet as the theaters' ads and articles show, they had to make specific appeals to their primary market by tapping into a growing political and cultural race consciousness. This did not necessarily mean just putting a black face on a white business. Stroll theaters actually had to acknowledge

View of the Pekin Café from across the street.
(Courtesy of Chicago Historical Society)

black consumer leisure habits and desires as well as employ black staff and performers who catered to the needs and interests of black consumer patrons. But the use of a race discourse by white-owned theaters was not a policy that all local black leaders found acceptable. In her early 1912 article "In Union Is Strength," Minnie Adams called on black patrons to support black-owned houses, and specifically the Pekin, over white-owned theaters on the Stroll. In the end, Adams did not disparage other venues but argued that black patrons should "hang our heads in shame" regarding the sparse attendance at the Pekin, especially in light of the collective discrimination black people faced at white-owned theaters.[17] Yet, underneath these general appeals to race pride existed a more complicated and competing set of visions. Within the racial community there was a continual push and pull between envisioning black leisure as a theater of pleasurable enjoyment or as a medium of racial uplift and moral reform.

Conceptually, many of the ideas about reform and pleasure were embedded in the aesthetic and physical structure of films and their exhibition. Some of the first known race films were non-acted documentaries and "scenics" of prominent buildings, landscapes, and exhibitions that served as an integral element within the popular genre of reform narratives. In cinema's early history, film was much more of a presentational than representational medium. Terms like "moving picture" and "photoplay" help express how audiences learned to view this new technology within the context and conventions of preexisting theatrical entertainments. As much as these early entertainments and their presentational style were ripe for more carnivalesque pleasures, they were also deployed to instruct. Within the context of old settler ideology, moving images of "race" figures, landscapes, or communities served as responses to the "authentic" minstrel presentations of black characters in mainstream comedic genres. These mass visual representations of respectability also served as primers or lessons on "acceptable" urban behavior. For example, as early as 1899, the Chicago-based, black-owned Royston Moving Picture Show toured the South screening Lubin Cineographs of black troops in the Spanish-American War as displays of appropriate manhood, patriotism, and race pride.[18]

In the same era, the *Chicago Defender* announced the Boston screening of panoramic shots of Booker T. Washington's Tuskegee Institute. Presenters attempted to "uplift" these documents from the leisure to the instructional format, but this particular film was still shot in a variety style that depicted the events as thrilling entertainment. This moving picture included a series of shots of military-style drilling and students in workshops, but the highlight was the college's marching band. The Tuskegee moving picture is an early example of how the variety format of "thrills" and "sights" was also used for uplift strategies. The *Chicago Defender* reporter made a point to note his desire to bring the film to Chicago as an instructional tool so that local "would-be leaders can see what makes Booker T. so great."[19] The documentary and panoramic genres became a perfect tool for an old settler version of New Negro dissent against the comedic depiction of black people in moving pictures. However, the popularity of thrilling attractions and comedies in Stroll theaters reveals that a strict production of serious and uplifting black images would not satisfy all black audiences. While leaders hoped to shape the presentation and interpretation of these films, they were primarily exhibited in variety contexts where a unitary "race" consciousness could not be fully imposed.

Early black film culture relied on a number of different conventions for its subject matter and styles of presentation, including street fairs, parades, carnivals, Juneteenth celebrations, vaudevilles, burlesque, air(plane) shows, boxing and wrestling matches, and minstrel, variety, and tent shows. Advertisements reveal that Stroll theaters, such as the Pekin, Grand, New Grand, States, Monogram, and Lincoln, focused primarily on vaudeville and musical comedy and slowly incorporated the unproven commodity of moving picture amusement within the guaranteed success of live entertainments. Moving pictures had grown from a technological fascination at Chicago's Columbian Exposition of 1893 to the 1910 observation by *Chicago Defender* columnist Sylvester Russell that Negroes were stampeding into the "moving picture theater craze." The Grand introduced a new policy where "a great feature picture will accompany each stage show," and the Phoenix owner commented that "people seem to like . . . the moving picture . . . and this house is doing good business."[20] Consumer patrons forced theater owners to realize that the moving picture could attract audiences and complement live acts, so they increasingly began to include films within mixed bill programs.

Within the variety format, cinematic exhibitions served to complement live events, including race lectures, orchestras, and illustrated songs. The Phoenix advertised a mixed bill of an orchestra, a featured tenor singing illustrated songs, and "sensational and highly colored pictures with incidental music." Another mode of presentation consisted of alternating activities in the exhibition venue, including vaudeville skits, amateur shows, novelty acts, and sporting events. The Grand offered a collage of amusements that included a six-reel feature film; the famous stage act of Butter Beans and Susie; comedian Boots Hope, the King of Liars; dramatic song artists; the soubrette Lizzie Wallace; and a "song and dance mélange."

The best black variety format was found at the Stroll's own Pekin Theatre. In one week, the Pekin bill announced the hypnotist Svingali, the mind reader Madam Helene, a white ventriloquist, singers, musical acts, blackface comedians, and moving pictures that changed daily. On March 18, 1911, the Pekin announced that it would shorten Jessie Ships's famous comedic play *The Test* to "give time for moving pictures and wrestling matches." This format spoke to a more engaged consumer patron whose active participation, direct response, and local desires gave class-specific meaning to the theater spectacle, reinforcing the power of this space as a dynamic sphere of race discourse and debate.[21]

ABSORPTION/DISTRACTION: EXHIBITING CLASS CONSCIOUSNESS THROUGH RECEPTION PRACTICES

Old and new settler struggles over appropriate exhibition styles resonate with what film scholars have discussed as the distinction between absorption and distraction. The activities within black vaudevilles, among other venues, resisted the emerging "high art" desires for a distant, passive, private, individualized spectator who was *absorbed* into a closed, predefined, self-explanatory feature film text with self-contained narratives. Like white ethnic nickelodeons, the black vaudeville's relatively easy access, low-cost variety format and nonfilmic events "fostered a casual, sociable if not boisterous, atmosphere. The multiple *distractions*, on and off the screen, made movie going an interactive rather than merely passive experience" (emphasis added). In the variety context, the mode of exhibition, the diversity of displays, and the conditions of reception powerfully shaped the theater experience and its meaning as much as the narrative intentions of the film did. The exhibition site and the amusements also created an important stolen moment, particularly for working-class migrants, away from the world as it was, toward an imagined place of what social relations in Chicago could be.[22]

The mixture of live and recorded visual amusements made exhibition sites a place of refuge from crowded kitchenettes, white women's kitchens, sweatshop conditions, and the generally disciplined dictates of urban industrial life. The theater became a place of fantasy and adventure as well as a social space for group interaction, negotiation of the urban experience, and, under dim lights, sexual exploration. Urban amusements held a specific use-value for urban migrants where class, regional, and generational differences within the race could be understood, expressed, and contested. Many young migrants were caught between the standards of traditional community clubs, societies, guilds, and religious affiliations and the inhumane work conditions and race hierarchies imposed upon them through modern industrial capitalism. Vaudevilles and movie houses, alongside the beauty shop and the storefront church, provided a third space of modernity through which the urban terrain could be reconceived.

The logic of thrills, pleasures, distractions, and moving pictures offered in leisure houses paralleled even the earliest migrants' own engagement with the pace and scale of northern urban technology, time, and social identity. These leisure spaces were real places within local communities, but at the same time they "opened up into a fantastic space." The variety format with its juxtaposition and jumble of the foreign and familiar paralleled the migrant experience. Some version of the migrant's continual confrontation with the shock, disorientation, and violence of urban life, starting in southern towns, could be contested, manipulated, and even inverted in the less dangerous and more playful world of black leisure. For example, the Chateau de la Plaisance (5324–26 S. State) and the Dunn and Hight "chop suey" restaurant (5050 S. State), with food brought in from nearby Chinatown, were race attractions with foreign names that offered dancing, movies, orchestra music, and seemingly exotic cuisines in local surroundings. Moreover, the Chateau de la Plaisance skating rink and a nearby combination merry-go-round/skating rink provided relatively safe ways for consumers to engage industrial technologies as mechanical thrill rides.[23]

While the daily labor of mostly male migrants consisted of their subordination to the dangerous assembly line and stockyard machines, at amusements they could enjoy being mastered by fantastic onstage storylines or even by machines with less threat of injury. Other places of refuge—the museum, library, or club meeting—focused on the stability of time, order, and control, but the world of amusements put a premium on the festive nature of excessive, inconsistent breaks from "real" time.[24] Unlike the white ethnic nickelodeon, however, black amusements did not necessarily offer reprieve from the strict scrutiny of race reformers and their behavioral codes of respectability, because there were not many class-specific black vaudeville spaces. Therefore, the very same level of active and local participation that was possible and desirable for some in black amusements were, for other patrons at the same events, threatening to old settler visions of racial uplift and moral order.

The application of old settler respectability in cinema narrative and exhibition was an attempt to reform migrant behaviors while also exhibiting the race consciousness of the "better class" rejected by their white peers. As early as 1912, the aforementioned article "In Union Is Strength" brought specific attention to this dynamic. In what was otherwise a call to racial solidarity in support of the black-owned Pekin was a specific appeal to the "better class." Here Adams conceded that black venues might not have the same "quality entertainment" as other houses but called on patrons to "give the theater your support and watch its policies improve." She argued that the "credibility" and "quality" of Pekin shows and policies would be improved if respectable citizens began to take interest in and direct the vision of the theater.[25] Like Adams, Stroll theater owners and managers were quite aware of class-based anxieties and distinctions and attempted to cater to various audiences in their mixed programs.

Theaters offered code phrases in their advertisements, like "high-class" and "safe for women and children," to gain a respectable clientele, which also helped make their amusements respectable. For example, the Phoenix Theater advertised that it catered to ladies and children while showing "selected high class motion pictures, high class vocal and instrumental music, [and a] first class colored orchestra." When Motts opened the Pekin Theatre, it was originally a place of gambling and drinking until Motts found opposition from clergy. At this time, the *Chicago Defender* noted that the Pekin renamed itself a "Temple of Music" and hoped the name would stick as a mark of "high-class endeavor," which depended on the kind of presentations offered at the theater. But attempts to assuage the "better class" while maintaining a mass consumer base proved difficult. The *Defender* reported that a "riot" almost broke out at a Pekin-hosted wrestling match "when M. Monhamer, the stalwart Turk, failed to floor Ilea Vincent, the Cuban-born German Negro in thirty minutes." After an exciting reportage of these attractions that appealed to a mass audience, the writer quickly tried to clean up the image of the event. He argued that "the entertainment is perfectly moral and conducted in a *respectable* manner, and has therefore been a grand treat to *ladies* as well as young men" (emphasis added).[26] The frequent disparity between respectable old settler aspirations and the actual behaviors in exhibition venues, however, made theaters a target of class-based criticism and reform.

Racial solidarity was promoted as a universal call for the control of leisure spaces on the Stroll, but the strategy of political and economic autonomy through a united racial front continually ran up against competing visions of theater respectability. On the Stroll, those of the "better class" were disappointed that they were "compelled to be mixed with the undesirable or remain at home in seclusion." Many identified the "racial amusement problem" as one "of boisterousness and defiance of public sentiment." The initial marginalization of the black elite and reformers from censor boards and Loop theaters helped focus complaints toward the behaviors in the exhibition space and, initially, not toward the activities on the stage and screen. An article in the *Chicago Defender* entitled "Loud Talking in the Pekin" complained about the inability of the performer to explain his work. The article went on to set up white theaters as the standard for behavior by arguing, "These same people will go to the Illinois, Grand or Lyric and in order to get their mouth open, one would have to use a crow bar. . . . Why is it then in a house managed and controlled like the Pekin is, such disgraceful scenes must occur?" As a final point of distinction, the writer laid the problem at the feet of black migrants, who were described as "our newcomers to the city who think they are at a camp meeting."[27] The problem clearly rested in competing visions about what respectable notions of leisure meant for different groups within the race. Would black film culture enforce a policy of absorption that focused solely on the film text, or maintain a participatory style of distraction that provided space for multiple meanings through a diversity of pleasures?

For many, particularly displaced migrants and those among the working class, theaters were not necessarily a medium of moral instruction but a combination amusement venue, social center, and place for sexual encounters, activities that are revealed precisely in the criticisms of such behaviors by the black press. One writer complained about a "bunch of 'smart Alecks' . . . who come in and peacock up and down the aisle" at the Vendome. The description of " 'Strollers' who strut up the aisle mannequin-like" was marked specifically as an offense to "decent guests." Another major complaint was the rise of "lip slobbering in theaters." The article paid exclusive attention to the morality of women, commenting that "the 'lady' connected with a show of this sort must have some little bit of breeding." Responses to the rise in public intimacy varied from putting more light in theaters to calls for "ushers [to] be armed with ball bats with which to tap these sapheads on the conk."[28] However, for those who participated in such acts, boisterousness could have been pride, and peacocking was perhaps distinction in direct defiance of a southern past and even the northern prescriptions represented by these very editorialists. Moreover, female participation in "lip slobbering" ran parallel to the performance and participation of some women in cabarets, burlesque houses, and theaters, all revealing alternative notions of femininity that engaged questions of sexuality, gender, and social position.

The worlds of vaudeville and burlesque, with their multiple visual sensations, were complemented by the bawdy jokes of comedians and the risqué lyrics and flamboyant dress of women cabaret singers. While women like Ma Rainey and Bessie Smith are most identified with blues music, in the first decade of the twentieth century one could find them "jassing up" cabaret music and mixing tent show comedy and blackface minstrelsy in vaudevilles. Hardly an accident, variety conventions like slapstick, double entendre, and cross-dressing found their way into blues lyrics and performances and on race records. Much of the variety format was built on the objectification of women or the transgression of perceived sexual difference, but women performers were also able to manipulate their construction as sexual objects by making a space for same-sex desires, dressing up, and talking back found in vaudeville blues. In the process, the theater, like the rent party and the sports stadium, also became a showcase for the audiences as well as a place of public privacy for stolen moments.[29] Importantly, the rise of "private" activities in "public" exhibition sites, and the responses that ensued, became a major force in the increased prominence of theater and film criticism as a profession within black newspapers.

One letter to the *Chicago Defender* commented on the "deplorable state" of black theaters and moving picture concerns and suggested "a great national journal like the *Chicago Defender* would be a most effective weapon to use in cleaning up and creating new respect for and inspiration in the Negro Theater." The writer then proceeded to offer his services to "write a series of articles on and for the Negro theater for the Defender." This gentleman was not alone but just one voice in a larger call to "use remedial devices in the form of regulation without discrimination" in black leisure spaces. The seeds of film criticism were seen in the "Musical and Dramatic" column of Sylvester Russell and his successor, Minnie Adams. Yet D. Ireland Thomas's column, "Motion Picture News," signaled the formal beginnings of film criticism in the black metropolis. Through his self-proclaimed title as "Theatrical Efficiency Expert and Motion Picture Specialist," Thomas early on tried to set standards of behavior, which evolved into a thriving career as a theater and film critic. In response to a letter, Thomas again used the white theater as a standard of civility and decorum and called on theaters to throw out disorderly patrons: "Stop the Show, turn on the light and let everyone see you do it and make them stay out." In another article, Thomas chastised black patrons for "bad language" and "loud noises" in race theaters when such actions would not take place in white balconies.[30] To achieve a standard of behavior and discipline, these comments glossed over issues of racial violence, local desires for audience participation, and the class difference between patrons of Loop theaters and those of white ethnic theaters, where similar "deviant" behaviors existed.

Evolving class and generational differences in leisure signaled the growing consciousness of race leaders and their consideration of black spectacles, amusements, and films as mediums of moral instruction, migrant uplift, and status-specific notions of race pride. At the same time, while the actual voices of new settler dissenters were not recorded, the activities in amusement spaces signaled that there would be no uniform position on the meaning of race exhibitions. Two important examples help make this point clear and inform later race film conventions: the censorship and circulation of Jack Johnson fight films and the organization of the 1912 Grand August Carnival and Fair.

THE SPECTACLES OF JACK JOHNSON AND THE 1912 GRAND AUGUST CARNIVAL AND FAIR

Films and prizefighting actually have overlapping origins. Like weight lifters and other performers, including comedic actors, wrestlers and boxers were carnival sideshows as spectacles of courage and oddities of human achievement. Elements of prizefighting and moving pictures both emerged from this larger world of entertainment. In fact, theater agents managed both actors and fighters, and in urban areas, boxing and wrestling matches were housed in theaters. However, the particular spectacle that was Jack Johnson did more than just prove the relationship between boxing and film. Johnson as an American icon expressed an important set of national/racial conflicts, especially within the context of the exhibition of his fight films.

Scholars have argued, "No discussion of race and early cinema in the United States would be complete without considering the impact of Jack Johnson's cinematic image on the racial order of things." When Johnson became the world heavyweight boxing champion, he directly challenged traditional visions of white supremacy and race pride both in Chicago and around the world. As a young migrant himself, Johnson became a larger-than-life public spectacle of black male sexuality and power in testing the promises of northern freedom. Importantly, all of the anxieties, joys, and fears of his title fights—with Tommy Burns (1908), Stanley Ketchel (1909), and Jim Jeffries (1910)—were magnified by their circulation and exhibition on film.[31]

The Johnson-Burns fight took place in Sydney, Australia, but the film premiered in the United States on March 21, 1909, at the Chicago Auditorium for a two-week engagement. The major response by the *Chicago Tribune* was that the moving pictures were "tame with Colored man always the master," making them "good pictures of a poor fight." The *Tribune* article was accompanied by a cartoon depicting Johnson as an apelike Sambo character, complete with minstrel dialect. But within black communities, the fight and the circulation of the film delivered a different set of meanings. In terms of presentation, black papers stayed away from cartoon depictions of Johnson but did include a number of "actual" photographs that were posed to display his physical prowess. At the same time, race leaders attempted to uplift the fight as a formal sign of race progress. Before the pictures had even arrived, the *Chicago Defender* and the Indianapolis *Freeman* reported on the fight while anticipating the arrival of the films.[32]

There is little formal documentation of the first set of screenings of Johnson films, but local black citizens were clearly affected by what they heard and saw. Indianapolis *Freeman* writer Harry Jackson gave a detailed report of the Johnson-Burns fight after attending a screening at the Indianapolis English Opera House in April 1909. Tellingly, the article was titled "As the Fight Pictures Told the Story," revealing the unquestionable force of Johnson's victory. For many, Johnson's fight on film was an "objective, un-

biased" account of a victory for the race that could not be erased or dis-
counted. The films became a social and scientific fact in the face of other
victories that had been taken away. In Chicago, black people were so "wild
with enthusiasm" that Johnson's friends, including hometown theater celebrity Bert Williams, "were asked to subscribe to a fund that was expected to
reach the amount of $50,000" in order to place a collective bet against any
white challenger. Black residents in "Dehomey" (a synonym for black Chicago) were reportedly so excited that they were duped on the night of
Johnson's second defense against Stanley Ketchel. According to Juli Jones
(William Foster), a man came into town advertising "First Moving Pictures
of the Johnson-Ketchel Fight" on the day of the fight. However, as Jones
observed, the screening was scheduled half an hour before the actual event
was to take place. Before fans realized they had viewed old reels of the
Johnson-Burns fight, "the wise gent had loaded up."[33] While this might serve
some as a criticism of the black community, it also revealed the anticipation
and excitement generated by the film for black consumer patrons.

Black journalists were able to exact some revenge through their reports of
the actual Johnson-Ketchel fight. Indianapolis *Freeman* reporter Uncle Rad
Kees exclaimed, "Johnson shows physical prowess of the Negro. . . . In his
fight with Johnson, Stanley was merely a child to the sight of the champion."
Throughout the article, Kees made references to the scientific objectivity of
Johnson's superiority and Ketchel's "ignorance" while identifying the symbolic capital of a black heavyweight champion: "Prize fighting has always
been a conspicuous factor in the world's sensations, but never before has a
championship title been worth so much to the white man as now."

While white audiences were frustrated by these sights, black communities
incorporated the films within preexisting leisure practices to construct a
larger counterprojection of race pride. The Johnson-Ketchel films were
owned by the Motion Picture Patents Company's empire, but through
Johnson's influence they got into the hands of the fighter's friend, Robert
Motts. Through Motts's Pekin Theatre network, the films followed the
vaudeville circuit and were screened in black communities. One report
chronicles that the Johnson-Ketchel fight was screened at the Pekin between
stage acts the night before the Jeffries bout, complete with round-by-round
commentary.[34] Yet nothing could compare to the series of events that surrounded Jeffries's decision to come out of retirement and the response to his
ensuing defeat.

Even before Jeffries decided to come out of retirement, white racial anxieties were wonderfully captured in two cinematic parodies: *The Night I*

Fought Jack Johnson and *Some White Hope*. Many white pundits shaped the fight as a battle for racial superiority. In 1910, when the superior Johnson thrashed Jeffries, the *Chicago Defender* readily appropriated the prevalent logic and announced that Johnson was "the first Negro to be admitted[ly] the best man in the world."[35] Of course, this did not sit well with many whites, and the response was to reinforce the racial order through race riots and legislation. In Chicago, effigies of Johnson hung from trolleys and electric light poles, while nationally, the visual reproduction and mass exhibition of this spectacle on film was just too much for many white spectators to see.

Three weeks after the fight, local and state suppressions of the film were bolstered by the passage of a congressional bill prohibiting the interstate circulation of "boxing films." Black communities rallied to identify the timing of this bill as more than a coincidence. The *Chicago Defender* responded with a cartoon titled "The Strong Arm of the American Law." This cartoon illustrated Uncle Sam throwing a fight film promoter into the police wagon while lynchers went free. In an article "The Nigger Unmolested," reviewer Mildred Miller continued the inquiry by comparing the exhibition of the racist melodrama *The Nigger* to the banning of the Johnson-Jeffries film. The films were eventually screened across the country but reportedly not until much later in Chicago's Black Belt.[36]

Importantly, the idea of Jack Johnson as a symbol of race progress was tempered by his activities outside the ring. His controversial ownership of the black-and-tan club the Café de Champion and his overt flaunting of black sexuality through relations with white women tested the boundaries of racial solidarity. Black leaders eventually rallied behind Johnson when he was brought up on charges through the White Slave Traffic Act. Johnson remained a folk hero both for his boxing and personal choices, while one *Chicago Defender* reporter chided, "From a racial point, we in this country would be better off if Jack Johnson would quit the United States, burning the bridges as he leaves."[37] In the end, the multiple responses toward and intentions for Johnson as a visual spectacle reveal the power of representation and image as well as the lack of a unifying vision within this emerging black public sphere. Two years later, race leaders had another chance to consolidate the rules of spectacle and amusement through their design of one of the most powerful projections of race progress within the black public sphere.

Heralded as "the greatest race achievement in the history of Chicago," the 1912 Grand August Carnival and Fair (State Street Fair) consolidated various spectacles and amusements in ways that would inform later film culture. Through an amazing blend of tradition and modernity, leisure and race

"The Strong Arm of the American Law," *Chicago Defender*, July 30, 1910.

uplift, the State Street Fair signaled a conscious moment in the construction of the race's image. The "ceremonial and ritualistic uses of the street" are an important site for exploring black urban life. Moreover, the rituals, spectacles, and amusements of street carnivals contain profound insights into the emergence of black film culture as a visual medium of racial representation. Described as "two weeks of mirth and merriment," the State Street Fair was located in the heart of the Stroll, on State between 30th and 39th Streets. Prominent local businessmen including financial mogul Jesse Binga, photographer Peter Jones, and Robert Abbott sponsored the event. The fair was called "the greatest pleasure event in local history." The festivities made over the Stroll, where "every store and residence is to be decorated while strings of many colored lights will be strung from post to post and across the streets and . . . music [will be] on every corner."[38]

State Street became a dazzling collection of spectacles, including Chiquita, the smallest lady in the world; Mazzeppa, the instrument-playing wonder horse; merry-go-rounds and Ferris wheels; a Jungleland show; and Zazelli's Old Plantation with 100 boys and girls (minstrel show). Surrounding these attractions were traveling bands and a new $20,000 calliope. The entire festival began with the formal march of organizations and societies behind

Grand August Carnival of 1912 Executive Committee, *Chicago Defender*,
August 31, 1912.

the Elks' military band and was capped off by the coronation of the "Queen of the Grand August Carnival." While this kind of event was unique to Chicago, it came out of a long tradition of black interpretations of mainstream events and the distinct black festivals of the eighteenth and nineteenth centuries. This particular event has been described as a "creative amalgam of Barnum, The Chicago World's Fair, the minstrel show, the county fair and other commercialized entertainments of the nineteenth century."[39] For a number of reasons, it is important to place the carnival within its larger social and political context.

Within a world where black people have had little access to public forms of expression, parades and carnivals have held a privileged place for personal and collective control. These were spaces where black people "shared in the material attractions of the larger world" while expressing an "alternative set of cultural values." In a post–Civil War context, black peoples' larger racist and Jim Crow realities became outward manifestations of an unequal status. Through parades and carnivals, they created moments of social parity. In their resistance to the bodily discipline that had been imposed by labor and reform, parades contained excessive caricatures of mainstream fashion and ritual, improvisational music, black militia marching groups (sometimes armed), mock trials, slave auctions, and coronations. These displays of well-dressed marchers with dignified self-presentation served as moments of utopian jubilee of another world while directly addressing the injustices of the present world. As these parades grew and migrated with black people all over the country, race leaders grew weary of the unruly and exuberant displays of black assertiveness in public places. In many regards, the State Street Fair was an amalgamation of all these competing forces, expressing the purpose and limitations of black visual representations in new urban public spaces.[40]

The State Street Fair was part of a tradition of black public presentation while also in conversation with forms of racism, inequality, and indifference specific to Chicago's urban landscape. These elements had been expertly consolidated within another Chicago "celebration" not even twenty years earlier, the Columbian Exposition of 1893. Its own vision of utopian order against the chaos of the actual city rested on displays of disparity between the civilized "white" audiences and spectacles of primitive nonwhite "others" on exhibition. While "anthropological" exhibitions of Dahomey and Javanese villages were readily available for public consumption, actual Native and African Americans were not allowed any role in the exposition. As many have argued, the spatial arrangements of the fair denied black people any existence in the "civilized" modern world. Only after the protest of Ida B. Wells and Frederick Douglass and their pamphlet *The Reason Why the Colored American Is Not in the Columbian World Exposition* was Douglass able to have a part in the fair's Haiti exhibit while spearheading the subsequent Colored Day events. The racial hierarchy of booths, set up from primitive to civilized, denied racial or ethnic diversity on both ends of the spectrum and reinforced the Social Darwinist visions of the day. While the Columbian Exposition maintained static, primitive notions of black people, the State Street Fair appropriated the pre-cinematic techniques of visual expression to emphasize the urban, modern aspects of black life as symbolic of race progress.[41]

The State Street Fair was not a direct response to the Columbian Exposition, but through brash displays of black profit and pleasure, it undermined many of the myths that had been presented as scientific fact. These events subtly spoke back to the exposition and larger issues of racial inequality. Carnival organizers advertised that it would "rival one of the streets at the World's Fair." While constructed differently, the carnival was an equally fabricated environment where black people acted out spectacles of equality, royalty, beauty, and leisure. There were special trains chartered across the country where the restrictions of Jim Crow seating were turned into a time of celebration. Once people arrived, they were introduced to a fantasy world that was seemingly divorced from the everyday ravages of racial oppression. The commissioning of special Frederick Douglass pennies were commemorations of the event and played with dreams of a separate black world with its own commerce. The crowning of "the most beautiful woman of Chicago" (never mentioning race), by vote of the people, topped off this utopian celebration. The ceremonious mixture of aristocracy and democracy spoke back to black people's marginalization in the political process while reinserting the history of black royalty. Black people could at least vote for their queen. The coronation of Hattie Holiday began at Binga's bank with the Eighth Regiment marching band. The band was followed by the queen as the "first woman of the race to ride an elephant outside of Africa," according to the *Chicago Defender*. The event was an interesting statement of black pride that included African references within its ceremonies at a time when many black people were trying to disassociate themselves from Africa altogether because of negative events like the Columbian Exposition.[42]

The closing speech by W. A. Venerable located the fair within a narrative of progress, from the nearing fiftieth anniversary of emancipation from slavery to the crowning of a queen in the city, not as "the queen of Babylon, nor of Spain, not the queen of Portugal, nor of England, but one of our own . . . that challenges the admiration and respect of all 'Africa in Chicago' and all 'Chicago in Africa.' "[43] At this exhibition, the means of projection were unified by the public display of black desires not governed by the lynch party, minstrel trope, or riot mob. However, the carnival was still within the leisure space that Chicago's black residents were restricted to throughout the year. Moreover, this particular vision of black progress and civilization might not have been a utopic endeavor for all community residents.

The State Street Fair was instrumental in rewriting the narratives of racial inferiority, but its vision of black unity also glossed over elements of difference within the race. Foremost, the coronation of a queen constructed women as "beautiful" displays, another set of objects in service to a larger narrative of race pride. Moreover, the Stroll continued to be a battleground over black amusements as mediums of pleasurable entertainment or racial uplift. The built environment of the fair was a literal overlay of Stroll streets. The display of lights and color were complemented with arches and pillars as "work[s] of Art" within a neoclassical (Greek) design.[44] These markers of civilization were visual guides that exerted a particular vision of black modernity. The fair recuperated more controversial forms of amusement, like minstrelsy and carnival sideshow attractions, to create an ordered vision of race progress. Hierarchies of difference in amusement tastes and styles were couched within the confines of the carnival space, a safe contrast to the illicit pleasures and temptations usually found in the dark allies and dimly lit theaters on the Stroll. However, focus on enterprise as race pride again required mass audiences. The initial march of civic and secret societies and the final coronation of a queen had to be filled in with Ferris wheels, human oddities, and minstrel shows. While heavily controlled, with 300 uniformed and plainclothes policemen for "safety," the need for mass audiences required an inclusion of women and "less respectable" amusements within this vision of race uplift.

The examples of Jack Johnson fight films and the State Street Fair highlight moments of struggle over the race's public image by consolidating older forms of amusement and providing the cultural/technological contexts for later "race films." However, the events surrounding fight films and festivals did more than offer sites of black exhibition; they also set the stage for two Chicago pioneers in film production: William Foster and Peter P. Jones. Foster was a sports reporter, Pekin employee, and peddler of Jack Johnson buttons, while Jones was a photographer and on the board of directors of the State Street Fair. They would both use actors from the Pekin Stock Company to star in their landmark films.

CHICAGO "RACE FILM" PIONEERS:
PETER JONES AND WILLIAM FOSTER

Jones came to Chicago from Kalamazoo, Michigan, in 1908 and began his career as one of the Black Belt's most respected photographers. He quickly gained notoriety after producing portraits of prominent Chicago figures and national leaders, including W. E. B. Du Bois, Booker T. Washington, painter Henry O. Tanner, and actor Aida Overton Walker. Jones, whom the *Chicago Defender* called "our master photographer," was showcased as succeeding in completing difficult photographs where white photographers had failed. He was known for his pictures of churches and buildings designed by black architects and of local black landmarks including the Binga Bank and Provident Hospital and for panoramic shots of thoroughfares like State and 31st Street. The work of Jones was acclaimed as revolutionizing photography through the use of "electric light," which allowed him to take pictures at night, and through his retouching and finishing abilities in his studio at 3519 South State Street. Jones set up shop on the Stroll and by 1913 had established his new Climax Post Card Studio at 3420 South State Street.[45]

In 1914, his local acclaim reportedly caught the eye of South American investors. With their capital of $100,000 and interest "in showing the Progress of the Afro-American in the United States," Jones started the Peter P. Jones Photoplay Company at 3704 Prairie Avenue (later at 3849 South State Street). Informed by Jones's work with the State Street Fair, this company's first production was a film of a Chicago Shriners parade. As a prominent photographer and civic leader, Jones's cinematic vision focused on a documentary style that showcased elite organizations and events as symbols of race pride. The *Chicago Defender* noted that this would be the "beginning of a series of our marching organizations and other features of race life that will encourage and *uplift*" (emphasis added). Those pictures were reportedly slated for exhibition in Brazil, before their screening at States Theater on June 14, 1914.[46] An attempt to track the circulation of these films would no doubt mark an important moment of black internationalist exchange.

Jones later ventured into the genre of comedy with his second film, *The Troubles of Sambo and Dinah*. The intended goal for this film was not simply entertainment but perhaps the first in the emerging hybrid genre of what could be called the *uplift comedy*. This moving picture was an attempt to use comedic cinema to counter negative racial stereotypes that had been so powerful in movie houses. Like more mainstream moving pictures, including *Uncle Josh at the Picture Show*, uplift comedies provided deviant acts (drinking, laziness, and the like) as the subject of jokes. This framework allowed the audience member, who might partake in such acts on the street, a moment of disassociation. The act of laughing at "deviant behaviors" became visual lessons for migrants and aspiring professionals on what *not* to do when they came to the city. *The Troubles of Sambo and Dinah* was specifically noted for its absence of "chicken-stealing scenes or crap games" and as a film that could "awaken the consciences of men and women to do the right thing in life and . . . discourage drunkenness, dishonesty and licentiousness."[47] This is a lot to ask of a comedy short, but it was not uncommon for reformers and reviewers to try and narrate film content when they realized they could not deter film exhibitions.

The Troubles of Sambo and Dinah was quickly followed up by the documentary *For the Honor of the Eighth Illinois USA*, which was given a celebrated debut in September 1914 at the Pekin Theatre. This film showcased the all-black Eighth Illinois Regiment in their dress parade under review by the governor of Illinois; their tour of Cuba during the Spanish-American War of 1898; and their storming of San Juan Hill and the firing of canons in victory salute. The Jones documentary used the variety format to display a collage of images and attractions in telling a story of race pride through manly military bravery.[48] Jones's background in photography and formal exhibition heavily motivated his focus on documentary film as a "realistic" corrective to comedic stereotypes in minstrelsy and other comedic films.

Foster, however, emerged from the more profit-driven vaudeville industry where comedic displays and action scenes were as important as positive "race images" in meeting audience tastes. Foster began as a publicity agent for Bob Cole and Billy Johnson's *A Trip to Coontown* and Bert Williams and George Walker's *Abyssinia*. He was initially attracted to Chicago because of Motts's Pekin Theatre, where he eventually became a booking agent. Later, Foster joined Jones in the use of Pekin Stock Company members for his films. Through the William Foster Music Company (3025 S. State Street), he supplemented his income by selling Jack Johnson novelty buttons, sheet music, and theater equipment. The *Chicago Defender* became aware of "enterprising Mr. William Foster" because of the popularity of his pictorial postcards of churches and black businesses. Once the reporter hunted down the origins of the card, he found out that Foster had mass-produced pictures taken by none other than famous photographer Jones himself. Both the cards and the business that produced them became an overt symbol of race pride in the face of white companies' refusal to publish them. Foster went on record as saying, "The colored people of Chicago were as much entitled to show the world its fine buildings as any other." By 1913, Foster expanded his desire to document race progress through his Foster Photoplay Company (3312 S. Wabash Ave.).[49]

The premiere of the two-reel comedy *The Railroad Porter* (sometimes called *The Pullman Porter*) that same year made Foster reportedly the first black motion picture producer in the country. During early screenings, Foster showcased a variety of moving pictures on the same bill, including his second comedy, *The Butler*, and a newsreel of a YMCA parade. Actual viewer numbers must be considered in light of the tendency of the *Chicago Defender* to exaggerate any symbols of race progress. Nevertheless, the debut of these films at the Grand and States theaters was shown to an estimated 4,000 patrons. The first two films must have been relatively successful, because they were quickly followed by the debut of his third comedy, *The Grafter and the Girl*, at the Phoenix. These comedies have been dismissed as similar to negative depictions of blacks in white movies or, at best, reproductions of Keystone Kops slapstick movies.[50] However, if considered within the uplift comedy genre, a more complex reading emerges.

The representations of urban black middle-class characters on State Street in *The Railroad Porter* and *The Butler* serve as counters to negative stereo-types in other films. The *Chicago Defender* lauded the films as showing "the better side of the race on canvas [rather] than always seeing some Negro making an ass of himself." Specifically, these films offered reform-oriented lessons of sobriety, thrift, and honesty through comedy. *The Railroad Porter* centers on a hardworking man who comes home to find his wife with a "fashionably dressed chap" who works at the celebrated Elite Café, and their conflict results in a comedic gunfight. Within the uplift comedy genre, black butlers and porters were portrayed as the hardworking heroes, whereas grafters and men of leisure represented the dangers of urban life. As uplift comedies, these films combined sensational entertainment with moral instruction to make the behaviors of laziness, indecency, and immodesty the subject of laughter. Moreover, these themes helped reformers appropriate vaudeville antics for the purpose of making cinema a respectable enterprise and entertainment.[51]

Between 1913 and 1916, Foster produced at least eleven comedies, including *The Fall Guy*, and a number of newsreels, like the 1914 Colored Championship Baseball Game held in Chicago. Under the pen name Juli Jones, Foster also wrote articles for the *Chicago Defender*, the Indianapolis *Freeman*, and *Half-Century Magazine* to generate a demand for black film culture and amusements. Foster articulated a politics of racial solidarity but also appeared critical of the exclusivity and complacency in race theaters. In early articles, like "Negro Theaters" and "Dehomey in Peace," he opined that the reason the white-owned Grand had taken patrons from the Pekin was because it had invested in skilled black workers. Although Foster was biased toward "first-class Negro shows," he also realized that black theaters had to "suit all kinds of people and cater to everybody." After providing what was called the "vineyard of photo plays," Foster was considered the "biggest man in the business." He attempted to generate a race films market by making appeals to consumers in his later editorials as a theatrical expert and show-man promoter. Foster proclaimed that "nothing has done so much to awaken the race consciousness of the colored man in the United States as the motion picture. It has made him hungry to see himself as he has come to be."[52] Foster had his finger on the pulse of a New Negro spirit and made appeals to this ethos to sustain the fledgling market of race films.

Foster was quite successful all along Chicago's Stroll, but his inability to secure national distribution and exhibition through white agents and movie houses forced him to stop making films by 1917. He continued to write, became a circulation manager for the *Chicago Defender*, and sold sheet music and records through the William Foster Record and Roll Supply Company. While Foster no longer made films, "the father of Afro-American photoplays" maintained that "motion pictures offer the greatest opportunity to the Ameri-can Negro in history of race from every point of view."[53] While Foster's claim might have been overstated, both black and white film entrepreneurs were beginning to recognize the economic and cultural viability of moving pic-tures. However, no one anticipated the power, reach, and controversial nature of the 1915 film *Birth of a Nation* in galvanizing, but not generating, an emerging race films market and race film consciousness. It was in fact this complex and varied convergence of critics, entertainment entrepreneurs, reformers, and consumer patrons within the preexisting black film culture that fostered the marketplace intellectual life of "race films."

This chapter has engaged the realm of black film consumption and exhibi-tion where the consumer patrons' role in crafting, re-using, and displaying ex-hibition sites made them the real actors, or agents, of knowledge production. Here, individual figures like Jones and Foster are most overtly the cultural *products* of this larger public sphere. Importantly, the conflict and contestation within spaces of visual spectacle also generated the range of ideas, assump-tions, and cultural practices that helped make the emerging world of race films possible. We now turn to focus centrally on black filmmakers and their cinematic productions within the explicitly "race films" moment.

Chapter Four

The Birth of Two Nations

WHITE FEARS, BLACK JEERS, AND THE
RISE OF A "RACE FILM" CONSCIOUSNESS

"Race" movies . . . did as much to herald the advent of
the "New Negro" as the writings of James Weldon Johnson,
Claude McKay, Langston Hughes and Nella Larsen of the
Harlem Renaissance.
—Adrienne Lanier-Seward, "A Film Portrait of
Black Ritual Expression: The Blood of Jesus,"
in *Expressively Black*, edited by Geneva Gay
and Willie L. Baber, 1987

Micheaux's photo play . . . "Within Our Gates" is the
spirit of Douglass, Nat Turner, Scarborough and Du Bois,
rolled into one but telling the story of the wrongs of our people
better than Douglass did in his speeches, more dramatically
transcendent than Du Bois in his soul [*sic*] of black folks.
—Willis N. Huggins, *Chicago Defender*, January 17, 1920

The 1915 film *The Birth of a Nation* by D. W. Griffith was pathbreaking in its ability to bring together many of the devices and conventions from older visual arts and early cinema into the form of an epic, melodramatic feature film. Furthermore, this film garnered national legitimacy by press agents and philanthropists and even official endorsement by President Woodrow Wilson, who had been a professional historian before his political career. Equally important was its 1915 release date positioned at the fiftieth anniversary of the end of the Civil War, making it a powerful cinematic and popular revision of Reconstruction history.

The film retells the Civil War and especially the period of Reconstruction with a new level of aesthetic beauty, including the massive reenactment of war scenes, an exploration of human values through visual images, and a mastery of the latest film techniques in the shaping of an epic cinematic narrative. However, it can equally be argued that "if Birth of a Nation is an epic, it is an epic of White supremacy." Uncritical celebrations of the film's aesthetic quality has historically been divorced from any discussion about how those cinematic devices of beauty and technique were built on the denigration of black people through the manipulation of visual imagery as historical fact. *The Birth of a Nation* is not some objective tale of a historical period but the "retelling of Reconstruction as a Gothic horror tale haunted by black brutes." Importantly, as much as the film is a retelling of Reconstruction, it is also an apocalyptic tale of early-twentieth-century migration and urbanization during the timely rise of Chicago's New Negroes. In fact, the film's revisionist "history of the present" unintentionally galvanized a growing "race films" consciousness within black communities, already pushing to produce a cinematic representation in the feature format model equal to the complexity of black life, during the Great Migration era.[1]

The Birth of a Nation portrays southern whites as victims of northern interference and depicts opportunistic blacks as stepping out of their place. This celluloid snapshot of history paralleled the real-time deferral of promises to black migrants in northern cities and the fortification of Jim Crow accommodations and rural black poverty in the South. In many ways, the film is a romantic tale of desire for the racial order before twentieth-century migrations. However, these anxieties are explored through a cinematic revision of events following the Civil War fifty years prior.

The entire narrative centers on the evils of both sexual and social miscegenation. The first shot is of actual black people (principle black characters were whites in blackface) in chains, explicitly marked as "the first seed of disunion." Black children are depicted as content in a peacefully pastoral southern setting, violently disrupted by the invasion of northern troops during the war. The second half of the film focuses on the consequences of Reconstruction as a black reign of terror with pornographic images of black corruption, laziness, and intellectual inferiority. Yet the scene that receives the most attention is the one in which the black character Gus is so overcome with political freedom that he can no longer contain his true primal lust and becomes a predator of the white "little sister," Flora Cameron. Eventually Gus backs her onto a cliff, but rather than be defiled by a black man, Flora jumps to her death.[2]

The story then takes on rapid pace, as aggressive black lust is finally put down by the triumphant Western-like ride-in of the Ku Klux Klan. Tellingly, the final scene, which is not in most current-day cuts of the film, show blacks boarded on ships to be sent back to Africa. With this act, the threat of miscegenation is fully contained, guaranteeing a "pure" white nation. At the time of its screening, many southerners felt defeated and many northerners were now afraid, especially in the face of a seemingly more daunting New Negro. *The Birth of a Nation* was an escape in which the traditional white power structure of the South was climatically asserted and black migrants had never come north. It has been suggested that Griffith and Thomas Dixon, writer of the book *The Clansman* on which the film was based, hoped the film would serve as a tool to socialize the many European ethnic immigrants and North and South into a disciplined order of Americanness (read: white supremacy), and in fact the film was used to bolster the northern urban renaissance of the KKK in the 1920s. But of course the film had unintended consequences.[3]

In fact, this moment actually marked the birth of *two* nations. The emerging consciousness of the race films market consolidated previous legal, political, and cinematic strategies both to respond to *The Birth of a Nation* and to offer alternative stories to Griffith's America. From the outset, race films were located within a capital-intensive industry that depended on access to networks of production and distribution, alternative forms of exhibition for black patrons, and the negotiation of censor boards and community leaders, all in the face of racial discrimination. Where the previous chapter delved into the exhibition space as a site of consciousness, here we survey the various strategies and struggles over creating race films, as the classical system of the feature format became the dominant mode of cinematic production. The ascendancy of the race-based feature film, in this context, became a powerful symbol of old settler respectability with its predetermined, self-contained fictional narrative and requirement that all exhibition activities remain in service to the screen. Yet, racially uneven access to the means of projection combined with the legacies of a specific black film culture made sure that the variety/vaudeville roots of cinema persisted through sensational advertising, raucous pit orchestra accompaniment, and film content drawn from contemporary controversies.

Ideologically, the world of race films reflected the complexity of New Negro thought, lying between pure entertainment and strict racial uplift, or what I call the dialectic of sin(sation) and sentimentality. As a case in point, the struggles, success, and failures of race filmmaker Oscar Micheaux serve as a microcosm for larger developments within Chicago's race films world. Micheaux and his films were part of the larger black public sphere that debated competing ideologies about "the race." In fact, the two general impulses of serving the sentiments of race uplift and/or sensational amusement converged in Micheaux's appropriately termed cinematic style of "sensational realism." *The Homesteader* and *Within Our Gates* heralded the race films' "advent of the New Negro" era and were explicitly celebrated as the cinematic expression of "Douglass, Nat Turner, Scarborough and Du Bois, rolled into one." At the same time, their graphic engagements with racial violence and critical depictions of race leadership brought community censure. Therefore, this "other" nation constantly struggled between the symbolic power of the feature film format and the structural demands for older black amusement forms to create a dynamic race films consciousness informed more by the politics and performance conventions from the Stroll than by Hollywood.[4]

THE BIRTH OF A RACE: FILMS AS POLITICAL CRITIQUE

While *The Birth of a Nation* inspired new critical and technological responses, black residents were already familiar with the work of Dixon and had developed a politics on racist films and performances. In 1911, the *Chicago Daily Inter Ocean* reported "Negroes in War on Thomas Dixon Play." Local leaders, including Ida B. Wells-Barnett and Quinn Chapel AME minister Reverend A. J. Carey, fought to have Dixon's play "The Sins of the Father" banned from the city. Petitions were presented to Mayor Fred Busse, and a protesting mass meeting was held under the auspices of the Negro Fellowship League. The sentiment of black leaders was bitter because Dixon reportedly threatened to come to Chicago, appear personally in his play, and make nightly speeches against the Negro race. A year later, organizers protested the photoplays *The Clansman* and *The Nigger*. Ministers even preached against these films from the pulpit, but *The Nigger* crept through the city under the name *The New Governor* at the Ziegfield Theater in the Loop. These pre-1915 forms of protest were combined with local politics, censorship boards, and film production in the fight against *The Birth of a Nation*.

One year before the release of the film, Carey was placed on the Chicago censor board to screen movies for racist themes. In 1915, Carey and the NAACP played primary roles in placing the censorship of racist films on political platforms. William "Big Bill" Thompson used this early race film consciousness to help galvanize the black vote for his mayoral race. Arguably, one of the reasons he was able to get the black vote was because, with the nudge of Carey and others, Thompson moved to ban screenings of *The Birth of a Nation* in Chicago and later throughout Illinois.[5]

The *Chicago Defender* showcased articles that countered the facts exhibited in the film with powerful ethnographic observations by people "who lived during those days." Mrs. K. J. Bills asked: "Was there ever a congress composed entirely of Negroes who passed laws to govern all the whites in the South? Was there ever a time when the southern white people were at all as submissive to the blacks as this picture would have people believe? Does anyone believe that after the war the Negroes had no other ambition than to marry white women?" Bills further asserted: "No judge or censor bureau would have permitted it if it were showing any other race than the Negro." Ironically, her condemnation was possible only because the film was still screened at the local theaters despite mayoral promises and black protest. The *Defender* chided, "Mayor was handed the 'Black Belt' vote, yet he did not stop play—leaders got jobs and they sat quietly as play continued." Even with censor boards and journalistic watchdogs like the *Defender*, black agitation could not fully eliminate factors including the renaming of films, empty political promises, and personal interests of cinematic curiosity.

Despite Carey's and later Reverend Alonzo J. Bowling's position on the censor board, racist films like *Tale of the Chicken* were still screened, and eventually *The Birth of a Nation* was shown at the Illinois and Colonial theaters in the Loop. The battle over Griffith's film revealed that the political consciousness preceding the actual film was instrumental in giving meaning to race movies as a central component of the marketplace intellectual life. At the same time, the historical focus on events surrounding *The Birth of a Nation* have obscured the way in which the larger era of "race films" was not determined simply by black people's ability to offer a cinematic response to this one film.[6]

Even direct responses to *The Birth of a Nation* can be fully understood only by examining their location within the preexisting black film culture. For example, despite earlier efforts to ban screenings of the 1910 Jack Johnson boxing victory over Jim Jeffries, the film was indeed shown in a tent at 33rd and Wabash as late as 1915 to directly counter the message within *The Birth of a Nation*. One article observed, "In the former we view the camp life of trained athletes, and subsequently their wonderful skill. In the latter a terrible picture of white men raping colored girls and women and burning of colored men at the stake." In his editorial critique of the film, M. E. Edwards ignored the actual film narrative and used the written space to reinsert the history of Reconstruction and Jim Crow from a black perspective, pointing to a larger black corrective to the "revision" offered by Griffith and Dixon. While 1915 marked the fiftieth anniversary of the Civil War for many whites, for black people it marked the fiftieth year of independence from slavery. This difference in vision found its way directly into black film exhibitions.[7]

In a large ad for a 1916 Peter Jones film exhibition, the reader immediately sees "50 Years Freedom, 50 Years Freedom." As an explicit or implicit response to the era, the film was titled *Dawn of Truth*. Following a variety format, the film did not contain one unified narrative but a collection of films by Jones paired with other footage that told a larger story of race progress. The Indianapolis *Freeman* commented on the "varied program," where Jones combined scenes from his earlier films of Chicago's *Half Century Anniversary Exposition* and *Lincoln Jubilee* (Chicago, August–September 1915), including the *Gorgeous Elks' Parade* and *Historic National Baptist Convention*. This was exhibited with his pictorials *Negro Soldiers Fighting for Uncle Sam* and the larger collage *Progress of the Negro* that included *Tuskegee and Its Builder* and *Mound Bayou, Miss., A Negro City Built by a Former Slave*. All of this footage was further combined with the earlier Jones films *For the Honor of the Eighth Illinois USA* and the comedy *The Troubles of Sambo and Dinah*. This collage of images was further framed by the consistent theme of black emancipation and progress. Another newspaper ad for this project included the dates "1865–1915," commemorating the fiftieth anniversary of slavery's abolition with an image of broken chains and the subtitle "The Re-Birth of a Nation," making it perhaps the first explicit black cinematic response to Griffith or to what his film represented.[8]

The Birth of a Race, however, was the first attempt by race leaders to enter the feature film genre, matching Griffith with an epic tale of their own. The

Dawn of Truth ad, Indianapolis *Freeman*, April 1, 1915.

Birth of a Race Corporation formed in 1917 and originally intended to adapt Booker T. Washington's autobiography *Up from Slavery* into a screenplay. The initial agreement for film production was with Edwin L. Barker of the white-owned Advance Motion Picture Company of Chicago with conditions that allowed Washington's private secretary, Emmett J. Scott, to maintain some control over the project. Vibrant advertisements promised high returns for investors and an epic vision of sentimental race pride. Local investors, including Julius Rosenwald of Sears and Roebuck, Illinois governor Frank O. Lowden, and organizations such as the NNBL, endorsed the film. *The Birth of a Race* was promised to be a symbol of race cooperation that included William Selig as the Chicago producer and primary investor and famous black singer Harry Burleigh as music composer.[9]

However, Scott also gave Barker "the right to sell his interests to a third party unbound to Scott's conditions." A year of inactivity passed, investors backed out, and as the United States entered World War I, the theme of the film changed from depicting the progress and history of the race to a sweeping history of the progress of humanity and American civilization in particular. *The Birth of a Race* opened for a month's run at the Blackstone Theater in Chicago to mixed reviews. *Moving Picture World* commented on the film's aesthetic limitations, while *Variety* went to the heart of the matter: "The venture was conceived . . . by a group of promoters who were lured by the pinnacle attained by David W. Griffith. . . . This picture was started on the premise of a nationwide defense of the Negro race." This editorial noted that a Negro theme was subsequently dropped, even though the film was still sold "largely to the colored folk on South State Street." The race failure of the film demonstrated the difficulties in navigating racist investment and distribution networks, and yet it did not deter other black people from entering the film game to offer more redemptive race images and in the process create innovative strategies for success.[10]

In 1916, on the frontiers of what was already becoming the home of U.S. film production, Noble Johnson, a small-part actor for Universal Studios, and Clarence Brooks formed the Lincoln Motion Picture Company in Los Angeles. The Lincoln company took note of Scott's failure and established backing from many in the Los Angeles black professional elite, which had a profound effect on the kind of films they produced. Lincoln "chose the route of gentle persuasion in 'uplifting' films about honor and achievement, the rewards of good character, morality, and ambition, picturing strong, positive role models to strengthen race consciousness and identity" with films including *The Realization of a Negro's Ambition, The Trooper of Troop K*, and *The Law of Nature*.[11]

Chicago film critic Tony Langston was so excited by Lincoln's uplifting themes that he quickly became the company's booking agent in Chicago and developed a network of black exhibition venues east of the Mississippi. Eventually, the demand for Lincoln films grew until Lincoln employed Johnson's brother George to establish a general booking office in Chicago. George Johnson set up branches throughout the country, established contacts with black press agents, and strengthened relations with agents like Langston. Langston requested copies of Lincoln films from Johnson so that he could "contact the managers of the Owl, State, and other Chicago theaters catering to Negro trade." This network provided the structural support for race film networks within the marketplace intellectual life, built on elite black capital, working-class consumer patronage, and the black press for its stability.[12]

Local Chicago critics and exhibitors flocked to the old settler respectability projected through Lincoln films. Langston hoped to use *The Trooper of Troop K* to counter all of "the junk that had been foisted upon the race." In the *Chicago Defender*, film exhibitor Mr. Thomas commented that *The Realization of a Negro's Ambition* and *The Trooper of Troop K* "are the best Racial pictures that I have seen." Thomas seconded the comments by Langston: "I have been disgusted with most of the Race photoplays and until I booked your pictures it had been two years since I had shown one in my house." Chester Paul, manager of the Washington Theater in Chicago, agreed that the features of Lincoln "are so far superior to the other all-colored productions that there is absolutely no comparison." In fact, in one *Defender* ad, Lincoln guaranteed satisfaction for their "classy race photoplay[s]" on the basis of their "class, photography, dignity and morals," or the patron's money would be refunded. While there is little doubt that these films were aesthetically and technologically superior, it is also telling that the above comments came from film critics and particularly exhibitors who were trying to provide a certain kind of respectability, decorum, and order for their movie houses in the face of diverse leisure habits.[13]

By creating the "black, rural family film genre, Lincoln established a new type of black protagonist, a middle-class hero who believes in the puritan work ethic." Anyone who desired upward mobility or respectability, including those in the questionable vocation of filmmaking, could relate to these narratives. At the same time, these narratives evaded the contradictions of class and racial tensions taking place in urban centers where day-to-day life was interwoven with the realities of discrimination, racial violence, and moral censure. The films channeled the combined ethos of Booker T. Washington and Theodore Roosevelt to provide a romantic vision of wide-open spaces where specifically men were able to confront and endure conflict, and eventually patience and hard work paid off. This technique of instructional narratives warned viewers against the dangerous acts of laziness, promiscuity, and even passing for white, an approach that subsequently became popular within larger race film circles.[14]

One of the race film companies in Chicago that directly followed the lead of Lincoln was the Unique Film Company (3519 S. State). In press information, the Unique Film Company explicitly claimed to have organized because of the "sensation" the Lincoln Motion Picture Company had generated from the screening of its "first production in Negro Theaters in Chicago, ILL." While information on Unique's three-reel film *Shadowed by the Devil* (1916) is sketchy, written summaries center on Jack, the son of a businessman who is possessed by the devil throughout the story. Yet, there is also an important juxtaposition between a frivolous, spoiled daughter of wealthy parents and Everett, the hardworking, industrious son of poor parents.

Though the full story line is no longer accessible (the film is unavailable to view), we know that reviewers were ecstatic over the message the film exhibited. *Champion Magazine* celebrated that the film's "theme is morality." In a lengthy *Half-Century Magazine* article, Howe Alexander didn't even review the film but lauded its potential to galvanize an uplifting "race unity that will demand high class, serious motion picture drama." Alexander called for financial backing and tellingly cited other instances, including the consumer demand for black hair preparations and black baseball, where the race pooled together its resources toward a common goal. His demand for "portraying the race in its best clothes" continued the old settler respectable politics of positive imaging that downplayed the entertainment aspect of black film culture.

Columnist D. Ireland Thomas noted, "Twelve million people want to see themselves in the *proper place* on the screen" (emphasis added). All agreed with Alexander that "too much mockery, too much cheap fun, has been made of the Colored people in the movies" at the hands of whites, but it is not clear, as discussed in the previous chapter, whether these twelve million wanted to see only proper images. While reformers and critics debated these issues, local white film companies also ventured into the market with films that were both racist and part of a black vaudeville tradition.[15]

One Chicago-based white film company—named, of all things, Ebony Pictures—also saw the potential revenue that could be generated from the growing market but had to walk cautiously on the race films tightrope between sin(sational) entertainment and sentimental uplift. Ebony Pictures (608 S. Dearborn St.) shot black-cast films that were aimed at the captive black movie house network but also attempted to cross over to the white market. However, in the aftermath of local censorship struggles over *The Birth of a Nation*, many patrons in the city were much more critical of comedic depictions of black characters. Ebony Pictures, and especially its sole black officer, Luther Pollard, who was an older brother of sports star Fritz Pollard, believed the company was a friend of the race, denouncing stereotyped black dialect while opening up dialogue with black-owned race companies, including Lincoln. However, its advertisement appeals to white consumers and the films under its distribution name told a different story. In an advertisement for *Moving Picture World*, Ebony invited filmgoers to view the inherently "natural" humor of blacks because "Colored People are funny. If Colored people weren't funny there would be no plantation melodies, no banjoes, no cake walk . . . and they are funny in the studio." In the drive to invoke sentiment for serious race conscious melodrama, there was little room for any comedic depiction of blacks, but especially ones that marketed comedy as an essentially "Colored" trait.[16]

In a 1916 *Chicago Defender* letter, Mrs. J. H. specifically cited the detrimental effect Ebony comedies like *Aladdin Jones, Money Talks in Darktown*, and *Two Knights of Vaudeville* had on the community. Notably, the letter did not question the realism of the images, but as a member of the "respectable class of theater patrons," she did not want to be exposed to "the disgraceful actions of the lowest element of the race." Langston responded in the same newspaper with a similar evaluation of the films on the grounds of old settler respectability. Langston argued that it would be in poor taste to "carry 'comedy' that causes respectable ladies and gentlemen to blush with shame and humiliation." He suggested that pressure be exerted on theaters to boycott these films by publicly listing managers that dared exhibit them. After this not-so-subtle threat of censure, he concluded that theater owners would surely "co-operate with me and show their patrons that their support is appreciated."[17]

Later, Langston proudly announced in an article, and privately to George Johnson of Lincoln Motion Picture Company, the cancellation of an Ebony picture at the Phoenix. He requested readers to notify the *Chicago Defender* of any films that insulted a "self-respecting lady or gentleman" with "moral depravity, ranging from chicken stealing and crap shooting to violating the marriage obligation." The range of scenes that were considered insulting in the name of the race tells as much about the class of the protesters and the way in which particular group ideologies determined many of the appeals to unity in support of "proper" race films. The *Defender* concluded, "We want clean race pictures or none at all."[18] In this particular battle, either the images were insulting enough to unite all groups within the race, or those in the "better class" had simply convinced Ebony that the entire race shared their notion of appropriate race films, because the company soon folded in 1919.

While Langston and others wanted only "race dramas which will uplift," it is not clear whether the masses were against these comedies and the variety format they represented.[19] Strategies like listing the names of managers who should support the cause of race uplift is perhaps an example of one moment when black critics had power over community exhibitors in the name of "race pride." This does not excuse the dissemination of racist images, but the irony is that the films cited in Langston's article were produced by Chicago's Historical Feature Film Company and distributed by Ebony Pictures, whereas Ebony films like *Spying the Spy* and *The Black Sherlock Holmes* were similar to vaudeville shows seen all along the Stroll and in fact employed many expert black comedic actors for these films while including the popular stock comedic parodies of the country rube and the city dweller. Race films rolled squarely into the emerging classical system of the feature format model during the Roaring Twenties. And the cultural conventions of the variety/vaudeville tradition persisted, where offscreen spectacles from the street and stage were transferred to the screen.

THE CINEMA OF THE SPECTACLE: PRODUCTION, GENRE, AND ATTRACTION

When columnist Thomas noted, "There is money in Race pictures," people from all walks of life with different goals and strategies engaged the technology and medium of film as a viable option to express personal and group visions. In the push away from the vaudeville/burlesque roots of cinema, the feature film, with its requirements of disciplined and focused viewing, also became a symbol of old settler styled respectability. However, within a black context, cinematic respectability was still not secured by basic feature film conventions. The history of derogatory depictions of black people found predominantly within the comedic genre required that for race films to achieve the distinction of "respectability," they preferably had to be serious dramas. Despite these lofty goals, the history of race films was neither loyal to the mainstream conventions of cinema nor to one version of racial respectability. The consistent dialectic between black people's uneven relationship to capital and alternate offscreen traditions of exhibition and entertainment helped create a different vision of cinematic modernity, somewhere between the narrative-based melodrama and variety format attractions.[20]

Before aspiring race film companies could get off the ground, they first had to motivate community interest. The lure of celebrity and capital alongside the genres of the local actuality films, non-acted documentaries, and war movies gave community significance and even narrative cues to the growing feature format of the 1920s. Many race companies appealed to the possibility of celebrity and profits (through investing or salary) to generate community interest and capital in the fledging enterprise of race films production. The Gate City Feature Film Company of Kansas City advertised in the *Chicago Whip* for "Girls and Young Men," with "NO EXPERIENCE NECESSARY . . . to Get into the 'Movies.' " Underneath these proclamations, the ad offered weekly salaries of fifty to seventy-five dollars and traveling expenses. That same year, in an ad surrounded by dollar signs, Chicago's Klimax Film Company proclaimed, "More money is made in the moving picture business than any other line of business." In the face of black people's tense relationship with U.S. financial institutions, Klimax declared that "colored films" offered "larger returns on your money than the bank."

Even industrial workers came together to form organizations, like the Railroad Men's Amusement Association. As early as 1917, this association of Chicago railroad men announced their intentions to "manufacture motion pictures employing Race people exclusively as actors and actresses" at their studio in Blue Island, a suburb of Chicago. The *Chicago Defender* reported that the company was incorporated for $300,000 and that their first order of business was to offer courses on "the art of motion picture acting" at no cost. The interest in acting was reinforced by articles that celebrated the "demand for race film actors," where "natural Negro types [were] replacing 'black face' impersonators." So many small investors and would-be actors were inspired by these possibilities that Thomas had to warn his readers of potential scam artists.[21]

The "local actuality" film, with its own appeal to possible celluloid celebrity, became a cinematic genre where the potential for race interest was embedded within its aesthetic form. Local actuality films were shot in a particular city or for an event and then screened in a local theater shortly thereafter. In 1923, the Magic Motion Picture Company announced the first "Picture Making Exhibition and Grand Ball" at the Eighth Regiment Armory in Chicago. The company first drummed up attention by going out into neighborhoods with cameras and taking pictures of local residents, urging them to attend the ball as the climatic event of the film. People were encouraged to come out in their best dress because "there will be a group of cameramen present who will make 'movies' of all those present and those pictures are to be shown, according to the promoters, at some one of the local theaters." This kind of event combined the older conventions of variety exhibition with the feature film trappings of possible celebrity and, as the article offered, potential "stardom."[22]

Non-acted documentaries and scenics, older genres of film, maintained their importance as displays of race pride because for many, such films displayed black people and communities more closely to how they lived and existed in the larger world. Such representations continued to counter negative stereotypes and in the process became community events. Film brought people together in social settings, and the moving images brought the diversity of black life from all over the world to local exhibition spaces in Chicago's Stroll theaters. For example, in 1921 the States Theater announced that it would feature two "scenics" from the Chicago-based Pyramid Pictures Company: *A Day in the Magic City* and *Youth, Pride and Achievement.* These two moving pictures showed black life, progress, and development in the thriving southern cities of Birmingham and Atlanta, respectively. The films were specifically billed as an opportunity to "see for yourself things about the south not hitherto presented to the public." Documentaries were also instrumental for the mass circulation of political ideas and for technical instruction while also exhibiting race progress. The rich pageantry, business interests, and sheer mass scale of events sponsored by Marcus Garvey and his UNIA were captured on film and screened at Morning Star Baptist Church in Chicago. This film documented the UNIA's international convention and "scenes of Africa and all the world," while in 1927 beauty magnet Annie Malone prepared a five-reel moving picture of Poro College and hair care instruction to show in Chicago at the Institutional AME Church.[23]

Probably the most popular, recycled, and yet racially meaningful genre was the war documentary. These films were so important because they documented black people's central place within mainstream American history and were visual arguments for larger calls to full manhood citizenship during World War I. William Foster proposed a film of the send-off of Chicago's all-black Eighth Regiment, showcasing family members and loved ones saying good-bye. Foster added that these films would provide "comfort and cheer to our boys at the front." In a 1919 *Half-Century Magazine* article, writing as Juli Jones, he argued for the ability of such films to confirm black masculinity through visual representations of military bravery: "The screening of the Colored men in this war has made friends for them, for us. A world that bows to the bravery of men, must think of the bravery and morality of that brave man's mother; must think of the loyalty of that man's wife and sister." The war film was also able to combine the documentary element of "reality" with the entertainment aspect of action and thrill. The first Chicago screening of official government war footage at the Atlas Theater (4715 S. State) was given the feature film title *The Colored Boys Over There* and was advertised as community property: "It is your picture." The Peter Jones Company footage of the "Fighting Eighth Regiment" was so popular that at theaters like the Grand it was interspersed with fiction-based feature films.

While this variety format persisted, the 1920s were most notable for the way in which these older strategies were relocated within the dominant feature film genre. The early 1920s were not just significant because of the larger emergence of the feature film; this time was also considered "the golden years of black film production." This era witnessed an explosion of production with thirty to forty films made at its peak in 1921. Within the larger race film movement, Chicago continued to play a key role in both the production and exhibition of black-cast films.[24]

Chicago companies like the Royal Gardens Motion Picture Company (459 E. 31st) emerged in 1920 from the Royal Gardens restaurant and show club. Under the direction of former Ebony Pictures actor and local stage writer Sam T. Jacks, Royal Gardens Motion Picture Company started out like other black companies, providing training for moving picture acting. That same year it filmed the convention of the Lincoln League at South Park Church in the middle of a snow blizzard. The company was commended for its efforts to defy the elements and film dignitaries, including black alderman Oscar De Priest and Mayor Thompson. The film was praised as a spectacle of both sociology and entertainment, observing the grace of the "better type" in the face of environmental adversity. The *Chicago Defender* argued that the weather conditions "lent animation to the entire proposition, for it gives a chance to study the characteristics of the notables who stroll through the snow on the screen."

Not even seven months later, the community celebrated the Stroll screening of the Royal Gardens' seven-reel feature, *In the Depths of Our Hearts*. This film followed in the uplift tradition of Lincoln Motion Picture Company but presented a new issue: color-caste privilege. The story centers on the trials suffered by a light-complexioned brother and sister because their mother raised them to look down on those of a darker hue. The hardworking son who rebels from his mother's teaching has to enter into hand-to-hand combat in the city's underworld to protect the honor of his sister. The film powerfully locates the story of moral instruction within the entertainment of thrilling attractions.[25]

As the catalog of black-cast films continued to grow, the older entertaining focus on spectacles and "thrills" was continually integrated into the newer feature formats. A perfect example is the continued popularity of Chicago's Jack Johnson. In 1921, he starred in the race film *As the World Rolls On*. The story line followed the typical love triangle where Joe works hard and eventually his industriousness wins the heart of Molly. However, the twist is that Jack Johnson steps in to train Joe to utilize his skills as an amateur pitcher to play in a series of Kansas City Monarch games. Long before cinema verité, the baseball scenes here contain actual footage from NNL games, including that of the Chicago American Giants. Joe's success ultimately wins him notoriety with his Elks Club, and he is given $1,000 by Johnson to begin his life with Molly. Importantly, this was one of the first race films to incorporate the spectacle of celebrity and documentary footage within the actual narrative of the feature film.[26]

The symbiosis between live amusement and feature filmmaking was equally highlighted through the career of aviator Bessie Coleman. Coleman migrated to Chicago from Texas in 1915. She started out in the beauty industry as a manicurist, then went to France to become the first African American to earn an international pilot's license and the first black woman in the world to fly a plane. Billed as "The Race's Only Aviatrix," her accomplishment generated a new sense of spectacular race pride. At the same time, airplane pilots had to figure out how to make a living despite the nonexistence of a commercial airline industry, so many, including Coleman, flew in air show productions on Sundays at Chicago's Checkerboard Airdrome.[27]

Coleman's show was located squarely within the context of race pride as 2,000 people gathered to see her perform glides, stalls, and a "figure 8 in honor of the Eighth Illinois infantry," while many black residents were taken up for their first ride in an airplane. Coleman toured the country as a physical spectacle of black modern possibility, flying at various airdromes, county fairs, and especially Juneteenth celebrations. She also developed relationships with filmmakers, including Peter Jones, and was slated to star in the eight-reel picture *Shadow and Sunshine*; however, in the middle of filming,

Coleman quit. Filmmakers argued that she was eccentric, but Coleman countered that she did not want to reinforce dominant images of ignorant migrants. The script called on her to dress in tattered clothing and carry a walking stick in the part of a country girl just arriving to the city. Coleman's response was, "No uncle tom stuff for me," and she walked out.[28]

Coleman continued to set up exhibitions throughout the country, but air shows were costly and dangerous. Therefore Coleman shifted to the lecture platform, encouraging black women to fly and exhibiting 2,000 feet of film from her performances in Europe and the United States. Like other forms of entertainment, these lectures benefited from preexisting black theater networks and were marketed by Thomas through the Theater Owners' Booking Association. At the same time, Thomas and Coleman began correspondence with the white race filmmaker Richard Norman about developing the feature film *Yesterday, Today and Tomorrow* based on Coleman's existing two reels. In letters to Norman, Coleman argued: "I am, and know it, the most known colored person (woman) alive other than the jazz singers. I have my life work that I want to put into pictures. I know I have been a success in every house I have played in Chicago and other cities." Coleman explained, "I am sure my pictures will go big in Colored houses . . . as my two new reels have drawn in house more so than some Colored dramas." Norman wrote back with enthusiasm that Coleman's film "would be a good drawing card in Colored houses." However, before a relationship could materialize, Coleman was killed in 1926 during one of her air shows in Jacksonville, Florida.[29] While Coleman never appeared in a feature film, both she and Jack Johnson serve as examples of the ways in which non-filmic spectacles maintained influence on the production of feature films.

However, even as feature film production eliminated offscreen amusements, race-specific exhibition spaces continued to inform the way in which feature films were received and understood. For example, in 1921, when Chicago's Blue Bird Theater celebrated its reopening under black management, it premiered the latest Lincoln Motion Picture Company film, *A Man's Duty*. The most mainstream films were also reinterpreted within race-specific contexts, particularly through advertising and the cinema orchestras of the silent film era. When the Hollywood Western serial *The Bull's Eye* played at Chicago's Owl Theater, the *Chicago Defender* gave black actor and Lincoln Motion Picture Company partner Noble Johnson top billing, with a full-length picture above the actual star, Eddie Polo. For the movie *Soft Boiled*, the *Defender* ran the standard copy probably sent to every newspaper that highlighted Tom Mix and Tony the Wonder Horse. However, on the right-hand side, the standard ad was contrasted with a proclamation that Tom Mix was assisted by, in bold type, "TOM WILSON the celebrated COLORED MOVIE COMEDIAN."[30] While these moments exhibit a unified race pride, similar extra-filmic strategies became the nexus for class conflict within the race.

During the 1920s, one key element in the creation of the respectable feature film was the musical accompaniment, especially since this was the era of silent moving pictures, which also marked the arrival of the jazz age. Many jazz musicians including "Fats" Waller, Louis Armstrong, and Erskine Tate (who led the Vendome Theater orchestra), found motion picture pit orchestras to be a wonderful way to supplement their income while staying active on the Stroll. However, the clash between the rules of movie accompaniment and the performance styles of jazz musicians in picture house orchestras enacted a struggle between competing cinematic expressions of racial respectability.

Music columnist and bandleader Dave Peyton attempted to maintain old settler musical "standards" through commentary in his *Chicago Defender* column, "The Musical Bunch." Peyton described "standard music, or what is commonly called 'classics,' [as] the genuine goods." He then went on to insert a class hierarchy of aesthetic distinctions by contrasting classics (European orchestral music) with jazz music: "Of course, more noise is made by the jazz fiends and popular music lovers, because that class of music invites noise and frivolity. It is simply harmonic noise, void of theoretical thematic construction." For movie orchestras, Peyton argued, "The classic atmosphere must prevail in the cinema house if that house is to be a continued success."[31] In the tradition of earlier forms of exhibition, the improvisational style and flare that jazz musicians brought to the orchestra disrupted the belief that the story line was ever fully contained within the movie.

Peyton desired to make black metropolis pit orchestras "high art" through a seamless narrative coherency where the "standard" musical accompaniment served as mere backdrop to the visual exhibition. He thought this would control viewing pleasure because classics "paint the musical interpretation" and "bring out the emotional features." He called on music orchestras to "play the screen drama with appropriate classical musical settings" and eliminate the saxophone from "the legitimate orchestra" because "you cannot play jazz music in a tense dramatic setting." Like a moral or industrial reformer, Peyton sought to discipline the performance and reception of movie orchestras toward the goals of old settler respectability. He set standards of work deportment and presentation for performers to the point that talking was discouraged: "Let your talk be in the dressing room." Peyton

Noble Johnson movie ad, *Chicago Defender*, January 18, 1918.

wanted to tame what he called "bad boys" from "ranting and shimmying in the pit" in any way that might distract audiences or alter the meaning of the film text due to what he saw as the secondary theater context. In frustration, he even called the name of a white music director in the Loop to shame musicians of the race: "What would Nathaniel Finaton, the director of Balaban and Katz's orchestras, look like, shaking and ranting over his musicians?"[32] Despite attempts to put improvisation in its place, the persistence of Peyton's column also revealed that the rules of black exhibition resisted a predetermined, self-contained film narrative and movie experience.

His special column, "The Picture House Orchestra," visibly explored how actual leisure and performance habits were competing against his ideas of appropriate silent film accompaniment: "The Race orchestras discolor the atmosphere that should prevail in the picture house by not characterizing the photoplay. . . . During a death scene flashed on the screen, you are likely to hear the orchestra jazzing away on 'Clap Hands, Here Comes Charlie.' I blame the leader for this carelessness. He should watch his pictures more closely and make his settings to harmonize." The disciplining of performers and audiences was as much an issue of control and authority as a question of musical harmony. There were competing visions between Peyton's belief that "what draws people to the amusement place is the 'attraction'" and what he described as the "riff-raff element who loudly clap hands when . . . 'hokum' is played in our Race picture houses."[33] The improvisational musical moments of standing out from and even parodying the "standards" in pit orchestras resonated with the new settler sensibilities of many migrants, workers, and some older residents drudging away as anonymous cogs in the industrial wheels of Chicago's factories and kitchens. Those in the "better class" may have had different notions of race pride, but for others, the musical disruptions offered by jazzing up the movie score were integral parts of an alternative leisure atmosphere of racial respectability.

As this chapter turns to Oscar Micheaux as an individual filmmaker, one must resist holding him up as an autonomous figure and instead locate Micheaux's work in these preexisting black film traditions and innovations. Situating him within race film struggles over production, exhibition, and criticism forces us to reconsider assessments of his political and social desires, technological choices, and marketing strategies. Only through recognition of Micheaux's negotiation and sometimes resistance to Chicago's black film culture can a fuller understanding of his career and film history in general be gained.

PULP FICTIONS AND WESTERN FRONTIERS:
"SENSATIONAL REALISM" IN THE WORK OF OSCAR MICHEAUX

Between 1918 and 1948, Micheaux produced, directed, and wrote at least twenty-seven silent and seventeen sound features. This was a phenomenal feat for any filmmaker but especially so in light of all the technological, economic, and ideological adversity facing a black filmmaker in the 1920s. An analysis of Micheaux could take hold in any one of the many areas of his life that are ripe for study; however, this chapter focuses on the films that he produced and screened in Chicago, on the ways in which the black metropolis continued to shape his vision even when he moved to Harlem, and on how his cinematic spectacles helped black residents reimagine urban living and the larger world. The sheer number and diversity of feature films that Micheaux produced to specifically uplift the race brought filmmaking closest to the cinematic desires of old settler respectability. Yet the specific strategies that he used to balance his particular vision of reform with demands for high box-office returns embroiled him in a series of community controversies. As much as Micheaux used his films for moral reform, he was a shrewd businessman and therefore had to appeal to the new settler sensibilities found within the mass consumer marketplace and in the process created a New Negro film aesthetic.[34]

The Lincoln Motion Picture Company was among the first to embrace the uplift idea that a strict display of middle-class lifestyles and positive values in rural pastoral settings was enough to reform the masses, whereas, in the tradition of the Royal Gardens Motion Picture Company, Micheaux sought to reform social vice and immorality by explicitly exhibiting the downfall of his characters as they struggled directly within dangerous urban settings and amid behavioral temptations. Thrills and attractions within the film brought the audience, while the moral story served as a form of instruction. Like mainstream productions, his films were shaped by the conventional narrative of heroines in distress saved by heroic male figures. However, the films of Micheaux went beyond critiquing the common urban adversities and alluring trappings of vice and decadence. He engaged the race-specific themes of passing for white, racial intermarriage, corrupt black institutions, and even racial violence embodied in lynchings and the KKK.

Micheaux's choice of imagery in the film marketplace brought a number of criticisms from his contemporaries and later film scholars. Some have argued, "Micheaux's films were not designed to uplift or to enlighten. They were meant to entertain, to appeal to his concept of black popular taste, and to make money." Another perspective is that his use of sensational images and controversial themes were "not there as enticement or as entertainment . . . but to educate." Yet, the "sensational realism" of Oscar Micheaux fell somewhere in between these two positions. He utilized the mainstream melodramatic conventions of the male and female protagonist confronting and eventually overcoming a series of adversities and perils but did so through gripping climatic events of action and suspense. Displays of the underworld, fights, and train wrecks and the revelation of a hidden secret were already proven attractions; however, for Micheaux, there was an added twist. The sins(ations) that his characters dealt with were race-specific realities that he sought to reform within black life. At the center of his sensational realist films was the recurring theme of black people confronting various pulp fictions in search of a livable social frontier. For Micheaux, the Western frontier was a "mythic space of moral drama and the site of opportunities seemingly free of the restrictive and discriminatory laws and social arraignments of the rural South and the urban metropolis."[35] Micheaux's critique of any restrictions, whether the dysfunction of urban living or the gothic horror of the South, was heavily informed by his own life experiences and requires a short examination of his personal history.

Micheaux was born in 1884 near Metropolis, Illinois, the son of freed slaves. After some time in school, he migrated to Chicago and worked a series of jobs including shoeshine boy, stockyard worker, and porter on a Pullman car. When Micheaux was a porter, he read about the famous Rosebud Indian Reservation in South Dakota opening for settlement and promptly left Chicago to try his hand at homesteading. In fact, Micheaux was first known to Chicago's black community as an advocate of the Western frontier as a racial promised land.

In *Chicago Defender* articles, Micheaux criticized that the Negro led in the consumption of many products but had no interest in the production of goods. He rhetorically asked, "What is the northern Negro doing as a self-supporter[?]" and warned those banking on southern farm land for economic autonomy to rethink staying where the "white race will run you off your feet." Micheaux recognized social inequalities, but he seemed most dissatisfied with the lack of "personal bravery" and overabundance of "social demagogues" that limited opportunities within black communities.

This political frustration partially stemmed from a personal episode in Micheaux's life when he married Orlean McCraken, the daughter of Chicago minister N. J. McCraken. The *Chicago Defender* reported that after a series of

Oscar Micheaux. From the frontispiece of his novel *The Conquest* (1913).

illnesses, Orlean returned to her father's home in Chicago from South Dakota. Later fictional accounts insinuated that the heavy-handed interference
of Reverend McCraken caused frequent trips to Chicago and hence was a
major influence in the actual foreclosure of Micheaux's farm.[36]

During the downtimes of the farm schedule, Micheaux had cultivated his skills as a writer, eventually penning the novels *The Conquest* and *The Homesteader* based on the people around him and the many frustrations concerning his wife and father-in-law. In fact, much of the information about his early biography has been loosely gathered from the characters and events of these novels. The main character in *The Conquest*, Oscar Devereaux, is a thinly veiled disguise for Micheaux, and Jean Baptiste from *The Homesteader* is perhaps an homage to the first non-Indian settler of Chicago, the Francophone trader Jean Baptiste Point DuSable.

Espousing the "pull yourself up" work ethic, Micheaux went door-to-door establishing his Western Book and Supply Company in Sioux City, Iowa, to promote and distribute his novels. Micheaux dedicated *The Conquest* to Booker T. Washington, reinforcing his affinity with the "Wizard of Tuskegee" and with the idea that industrial training would uplift "the ignorant masses."[37] However, the later works of Micheaux fluctuated between examining larger social inequality and addressing individual responsibility as the primary "race problem." One thing is for certain; the themes of his novels caught the attention of the race.

In 1918, correspondence started between the Lincoln Motion Picture Company and Micheaux about turning *The Homesteader* into a film. However, the Johnson brothers felt that the central romance between the black homesteader and a white neighbor would not encourage "support from white houses." For Micheaux, it was precisely "the litho reading SHALL THE RACES INTERMARRY" that would entice the public. When the two parties could not reach an agreement, Micheaux produced his own movie, setting up Micheaux Picture Company offices in Sioux City and Chicago (8 S. Dearborn Street). He utilized the marketplace networks he had developed selling his books to convince white farmers and businessmen around Sioux City to buy shares in his movie *The Homesteader*.

This eight-reel film "lasting almost three hours" was at the time the longest race film ever produced. The film combined story lines from his novels *The Conquest* and *The Homesteader* to tell the tale of Jean Baptiste, who migrated to South Dakota to claim land under the Homestead Act of 1862. While there, the black protagonist falls in love with his white neighbor, but because of social custom he enters into marriage with the daughter of a prominent Chicago minister. The girl's father makes the marriage miserable, forcing Baptiste back to the Dakotas, where he discovers that he can marry his first love because she has Ethiopian ancestry. The film's premiere at the famous Eighth Regiment Armory—and near repression at the Vendome—in

Chicago showcases Micheaux's savvy for politics, marketing, and promotion within the cinematic sphere of the marketplace intellectual life.[38]

The 1919 half-page advertisement for *The Homesteader* was a showcase of Micheaux the celebrity figure as much as it was an announcement for the film. Six pictures of the film's "stars" border the print, including a photo of "Oscar Micheaux, Author of *The Homesteader*." While the film was described as a "powerful drama of the great American Northwest," more focus was placed on the film ushering in "a new epoch in the achievements of the Darker Races." At the same time, the actual physical space in which Micheaux debuted his first film was a key element in its promotion and meaning. The Eighth Regiment Armory was constructed in honor of Chicago's all-black infantry and had become a site of community pride for important public exhibitions. In addition to the February 20 screening were "the REAL pictures" of the Eighth Regiment infantry just when this all-black unit was returning from Europe. While *The Homesteader* was not a war story, its location within this particular collage of physical and cinematic attractions contributed to the film's wartime community significance. As additional symbols of racial respectability, the film exhibition was framed by George R. Garner Jr., "The Race's Greatest Tenor," and the Byron Brothers' Symphony Orchestra directed by Chicago's own David Peyton. However, not even all of these attractions of old settler respectability could protect the film from controversy.[39]

Right before a scheduled run at the Vendome, three ministers protested *The Homesteader*'s depiction of the reverend character as a villainous cinematic representation of N. J. McCraken, the prominent Chicago minister and the father-in-law of Micheaux. The Chicago censor board responded by having a group of notable black citizens screen the film, including Oscar De Priest, Mr. and Mrs. Robert Abbott, Ida B. Wells, and *Chicago Defender* critic Tony Langston. For many years, black citizens had made appeals to Chicago censor boards on the grounds of a general race interest.[40] However, this controversy exposed the class interests of those involved and raises questions about the use of censorship politics amid competing visions within the race. The strategy of censorship backfired, though, and the unanimous endorsement of the film by this distinguished committee both brought the community together and exposed an ideological fault line within the "better class" while the controversy generated an even wider buzz of curiosity.

Micheaux capitalized on this moment to increase ticket sales and criticize Chicago's orthodox black leadership. The Vendome advertisements an-

The Homesteader ad, *Chicago Defender*, February 22, 1919.

nounced in bold print: "Passed by the Censor Board, Despite the Protests of THREE CHICAGO MINISTERS." Other ads included a reversal of judgment from one of the prominent black reviewers, Bishop Fallows: "I can see no just cause for the personal objection to this play. Every Race has its hypocrites. Frequently they are found in the churches." Micheaux even used this controversy to establish himself as filmmaking expert. In his *Half-Century Magazine* article "The Negro and the Photoplay," Micheaux offered his own commentary that contrasted the mild cuts proposed by the Kansas Board of Censors with the efforts of "certain race men to prevent the showing of 'The Homesteader' before the Chicago Board of Directors." As a film expert who survived controversy, Micheaux now counseled, "Before we expect to see ourselves featured on the silver screen as we live, hope, act and think today, men and women must write original stories of Negro life" and "money must be risked in Negro corporations for this purpose."[41]

Micheaux was deemed a smashing success and considered "the most popular author of the city" in the same breath with "Charles W. Chestnutt [and] James Weldon Johnson." Instead of silencing the controversy, Micheaux used the opportunity to gain status as an honored author and filmmaker as *The Homesteader* traveled on a "Great Southern Tour" that summer, where he benefited from the older vaudeville networks of film distribution. At the same time, he developed his own strategies of traveling from city to city with a print of the film and promotional materials. While at a theater, he talked of future story lines and displayed pictures of potential stars. Micheaux then asked bookers for advanced payment in exchange for exclusive booking rights once the film was completed. In 1920, these independent strategies would prove quite helpful in the face of both black and white resistance toward his second film, *Within Our Gates*.[42]

At first, Chicago's black censor board member Reverend Alonzo Bowling turned down the melodrama *Within Our Gates* due especially to its graphic depiction of southern lynching. In the aftermath of the bloody summer of 1919, ANP editor Claude Barnett reported, "It was claimed the effects on the mind of the spectators would result in another 'race riot.'" The *Chicago Defender* reported: "Every plan possible was exhausted in the efforts of a certain coterie of 'Race leaders,' etc. to head off the showing of this production but without effect. Those in authority at the City Hall were not to be misled and as a consequence the 125,000 Race people in Chicago here have a chance to see" the film. Again the controversy merely generated larger audiences, and the film was advertised as a "Great Lesson," which "required two solid months to get by the Censor Board." At the eventual screening of *Within Our Gates*, the ANP observed, "People are standing in streets for hours waiting for an opportunity to get inside."[43]

When the movie toured the country, it was further billed as the "Race Film Production That Created Sensation in Chicago." Placing an initial ban on images of lynching was a compelling enough draw. However, Micheaux's use of melodramatic conventions, controversial subject matter, and older vaudeville character types to tell a story of racial uplift and protest are what appear most compelling about this film. In many regards, Micheaux's films brought further to life the style of sensational agitation perfected by Abbott and his *Chicago Defender*. More than a simple response to *The Birth of a Nation*, this film was part of the larger "Grand Narrative" of race-specific concerns drawing together the issues of lynching, rape, miscegenation, and migration that were already part of a larger black public sphere of conversation.[44]

Within Our Gates was billed as "8,000 Feet of Sensational Realism" narrating controversial race issues through the conventions of melodrama and was advertised as "the greatest preachment against race prejudice and the glaring injustices that are being practiced upon our people." However, the ads also promised, "It will hold you spellbound—full of details that will make you grit your teeth in deepest indignation." As a direct attack on both white and black nostalgia for the simpler times of the pastoral South, Micheaux offered a melodrama of horror, betrayal, intrigue, and racial and family terror.

Within Our Gates initially tells the story of Boston schoolteacher Sylvia Landry and her love for physician Dr. Vivian. However, this love is potentially compromised when Vivian is told of Sylvia's tumultuous southern past during an innovative flashback sequence. This "backstory" directs the ensuing events and climax. In the flashback, we learn that after Sylvia prepares the books of her stepfather, a black sharecropper named Jasper Landry, she and Jasper realize that he has been taken advantage of, and so he goes to the wealthy white plantation owner Philip Girdlestone for payment due. At the same time, the fire of controversy between the two men is fanned by "a worthless unlikable fellow named Eph."[45] As the confrontation between Landry and Girdlestone takes place, from a distance the black character Eph observes the events. When Eph turns to giggle at the conflict, Girdlestone is shot, but Eph does not see the actual murderer, an angry white farmer. Based on what he does see, Eph runs to tell the town that Jasper has killed Girdlestone.

At this point, the town (including the actual murderer) erupts into a carnivalesque rage of mob violence to hunt down the Landry "family." In the midst of violence, citizens accidentally shoot the actual killer and set fire to Sylvia's parents while Girdlestone's brother Armand corners Sylvia in a nearby house. His attempt to rape Sylvia is an interesting reversal of the "Gus scene" from *The Birth of a Nation*, but there are a series of race-based twists. *Within Our Gates* graphically depicts the lust of a white man for a black woman, but in his pursuit, Armand discovers a birthmark on Sylvia's chest. Within the film, this badge of identity marks her as a product of rape and violence. Armand also realizes that this mark identifies Sylvia as his daughter. But before he can continue the rape, the flashback ends and we are brought to Sylvia's suitor Dr. Vivian. Despite her past, Dr. Vivian accepts Sylvia and encourages her to honor and recognize her truly American legacy of miscegenation and racial violence.[46]

Despite or because of public resistance, *Within Our Gates* was an enormous success due to its sensational realism. For later screenings, Micheaux added promotional controversy by publicly defying censors. At the States Theater, *Within Our Gates* was promised "without the cuts which were made before its initial presentation, so the patrons . . . will see it in its entirety, exactly as the famous producer intended." Moreover, in a letter to the *Chicago Defender*, Willis Huggins expressed appreciation for the film's ability to "constitute a favorable argument against southern mobocracy, peonage and

Within Our Gates ad, *Chicago Defender*, January 31, 1920.

concubinage." Huggins compared Micheaux's film to the work of Frederick Douglass and W. E. B. Du Bois, but unlike the writings of these figures, Huggins saw the power of *Within Our Gates* as far "more dramatically transcendent." The photoplay, much due to the sensational realist approach of Micheaux, was gaining further influence as a medium of New Negro representation and protest. However, Micheaux also understood that he could not bombard audiences with propaganda. He realized, "Our people do not care—nor the other race for that matter for propaganda as much as they do all for story."[47]

It was clear that "Micheaux well understood the mass imagination, and by catering to its wants and needs he was able to survive and become successful" in the face of fiscal constraints. At the same time, Micheaux seemed to be developing a black cinematic aesthetic to fully represent the complexity and contradictions of the black modern experience despite the argument that his "sloppy, 'single-take' aesthetic" was what offset his insufficient financial backing for projects. Therefore, what has been deemed as technical difficulties, arbitrary shot angles, inconsistent and jarring cuts, fade-outs, and lighting choices only appear so in the context of conventional "Hollywood tropes and ways of organizing things." In fact, the consistent inconsistency of Micheaux's technical choices was not a mistake or simply a cost-cutting decision. His seemingly market-driven choices constitute "refusals" of standard conventions within the African American aesthetic framework of "treatment, that is, transforming in some meaningful fashion, given materials" from the vantage point of a different set of experiences. In this context, his later use of music and dance sequences in sound films were not simply tacked on for entertainment but "completely disrupt[ed] the narrative flow" in ways that radically departed from the Hollywood rules of storytelling in the 1920s. Micheaux's alternative marketing strategies, racially provocative subject matter, and use of older black film conventions met head-on material constraints to wholly transform cinematic standards, creating aesthetic alternatives that turned his films literally into cinematic expressions of a black modernity.[48]

For example, *Within Our Gates* continued to play on the typical story line of male heroes saving or accepting heroines, but Micheaux experimented with a number of other aesthetic and social tropes to tell this story. First, his use of flashback to depict "the incendiary lynching sequence" was way ahead of its time. While the shuffling of chronological events is now called innovative and new, Micheaux utilized this technique in the 1920s. Second, the film offered a diversity of black male characters. Dr. Vivian is the northern race man who is conscious of both personal and professional issues. Jasper Landry is the southern sharecropper, both hardworking and abused. In contrast, Girdlestone's servant Eph serves as the inversion of a popular black film type or stereotype. Micheaux places Eph within the minstrel and vaudeville tradition through "his costuming, makeup and antics." In mainstream films, these minstrel antics are usually held up to represent black authenticity. However, *Within Our Gates* offered multiple black characters, so the very same minstrel antics mark a traitor to the race. Finally, the film depicted the realities of lynching and sharecropping from the perspective of black people, many of whom had just left the South from those very lived experiences. The film engaged the theme of both forced and voluntary miscegenation that wed black and white worlds together in a complicated family/national tale. Micheaux saw issues like passing for white, color-caste hierarchies, and weak black institutions as unfortunate consequences of the American national family. Despite resistance and even censorship, he continued to mine this legacy for the subject matter and aesthetic innovations found within his films, setting the basic parameters for a race film expression of the New Negro experience.[49]

After the relative success of his first two films, Micheaux sought to expand his maverick marketing strategies by heading to Europe to set up new distribution networks. Upon his return, Micheaux continued to produce controversial and thought-provoking films. With the headline "TO MAKE A WOMAN LOVE YOU, KNOCK HER DOWN," *The Brute* (1920) criticizes the underworld of gambling and violence against women. *Symbol of the Unconquered* (1920) takes a stand against "passing for white" and contains scenes of black retaliation against the ravages of the KKK. *The Dungeon* (1922) is more generally a mystery but also focuses on a black politician who gains office by voting on a bill that justifies residential segregation. *Birthright* (1924) follows the attempts of a black Harvard graduate to establish a school in the South that is met with resistance by both whites and blacks who fear that education will disrupt the social order. Again, these pulp depictions of corrupt black politicians, retribution against the KKK, and scenes of the underworld brought resistance from white censor boards and members of black leadership all over the country.[50] Micheaux's attempts to shed light on the hypocrisies of American culture and the subsequent resistance to his vision of racial uplift are best exemplified in his film *Body and Soul*.

The 1925 film *Body and Soul* is an explicit critique of the unchecked power afforded religious leaders in black communities. The story line of this film fit well within Micheaux's general frustrations with both racial oppressions and community institutions that held back race progress. *Body and Soul* focuses on the charismatic religious figure Reverend Jenkins, portrayed by Paul Robeson (his first leading role), who lives a life of hypocrisy and deception. While Reverend Jenkins preaches the gospel in the pulpit, the viewer sees him drinking alcohol during sermons, gambling, and even taking a payoff to silence his condemnation of a local nightclub. In the film, the abuses of Jenkins are directly unleashed on the blind faith of Sister Martha Jane and her daughter Isabelle. Micheaux uses Sister Martha Jane's obedience to Jenkins, as he robs her of money and rapes her daughter, to warn audiences against any blind faith in the charisma of black leaders.[51] However, this very same depiction of Sister Martha Jane speaks back to critics who argue that Micheaux only used light-skinned actors for positive roles.

Unfortunately, Sister Martha Jane is depicted as a naive "mammy" figure, complete with dialect and clothing, reinforcing stereotypes about the primitive nature of black southern or folk behaviors. However, her hair is not in a rag but straightened, and she is light-skinned. Moreover, while Micheaux did normally "color-cast" his stars along a Hollywood model, one of Jenkins's underworld cronies is a light-skinned villain named "Yellow Curly," whereas the dark-skinned Robeson plays the complex dual role of the villain Reverend Jenkins and the family's savior, Sylvester, a black inventor whose patent pays off, allowing him to return and marry Isabelle.[52]

This critique of a minister in a small rural town could have easily resonated with many migrants who specifically interpreted northern freedom as the chance to escape the orthodoxy of smaller town life. Micheaux presented himself as a race man, and the opposition here between a preacher and an inventor spoke to his advocacy for a new modern black leadership that rose above privileges of the flesh and individual gain. However, actual black leaders were again upset over such a complex representation of the "better class" that potentially undermined their authority. Protest ranged from the required edits of censor boards to very personal condemnations. In a letter to the *Chicago Defender*, William Henry asked, "Which screen production does our people the most harm, The Klansman, Birth of a Nation or Michoux's [sic] Body and Soul of course?" In the eyes of Henry, Micheaux was guided by profit, had not taken the responsibility to "plant proper seeds," and instead produced "such filth as Body and Soul." However, Micheaux's depiction of black leadership was quite consistent, applying his vision of individual and moral responsibility to all classes. At the same time, his representation of the poor and especially women as weak was also consistent in ignoring very real social inequalities.[53] While some saw Micheaux as a traitor and others were the ambivalent object of his reform, he played on race-specific themes within the existing black film culture to guarantee that his films be seen as community documents to be debated and defended.

Although Micheaux moved his production offices to New York, he continued to use community heroes and the "local actuality" format to generate the lure of celebrity and cinematic excitement for consumer patrons on Chicago's Stroll. Advertisements of his later film *The Millionaire* played on the local actuality format, specifically highlighting that the picture was made in Chicago and provided local viewers "many opportunities of seeing yourself and friends on the screen" alongside location shots of "the Dreamland cabaret, South parkway and many other familiar places." Micheaux also used patrons of the Plantation Café in a cabaret scene alongside small roles for *Chicago Defender* editor Abbott and his wife.[54] This diversity of promotion, distribution, and filmmaking strategies was what allowed Micheaux to be one of the few black producers to barely survive the onslaught of capital-intensive sound technology, the Depression, the creation of big-budget Hollywood black-cast films, and the growing demands of black audiences. Micheaux's sensational realist aesthetic and activities in the marketplace intellectual life produced race film spectacles that captured the imagination and ire of consumer patrons and critics alike while challenging the dominant representation of the race on movie screens. In the process, race films changed the way black people viewed themselves and the world in which they lived.

While Micheaux was able to produce five silent and nine sound films between 1928 and 1935, his themes were quickly becoming "passé" compared to the big-budget Hollywood musicals. As early as 1922, Thomas warned that the novelty of "race films" had worn off, and audiences "have to be shown that it is a good picture." Filmmaker Richard Norman also said to Thomas, "Colored audiences are becoming more critical" and "more money must be spent in production." In addition, exhibitors were "disgusted with the class of Race productions" distributed. The increasing aesthetic demands were combined with growing technological and financial constraints. By 1928, larger theaters were wired for sound, leaving small-town and all-black theaters behind in attendance and profits. This technological shift also paralleled the expansion of national chains, like Baliban and Katz's Regal Theater, onto the southern (and predominantly white-owned) end of the expanding Stroll. The very next year, Hollywood also increased production of black-cast musical shorts while writing small parts for black performers in larger musicals, finally creating black-cast musical features including *Hallelujah* and *Hearts in Dixie*. This pulled black actors away from the race films market, while Chicago filmmaking legends Peter Jones and William Foster also began working behind the scenes for major Hollywood studios. If anything, the consolidation of these multiple forces sounded the hibernation of race films until, arguably and with severe modifications, the "blaxploitation" era of the 1970s.[55]

One could easily, based on conventional evaluations, see the race films era as a moment of makeshift movie entertainments and insurmountable aesthetic failures. However, underneath these surface judgments, we must recognize the limitations, victories, and altogether alternative expectations that a diversity of black consumer patrons placed on their spectacles of amusement. New Negroes including Motts, Bowling, Peyton, Coleman, Langston, and Micheaux were more than entrepreneurs, critics, and filmmakers but part of an intellectual life, struggling over competing visions of race uplift and respectability. At the same time, Micheaux's heavy-handed attempts to instruct and uplift never fully determined how his films raised anxieties for some race leaders and offered mere pleasure for others. The pleasures and politics derived from Chicago's race films world betrayed strict race or class lines, but in turn, black amusements had to stay aware of these fluctuating social positions in order to survive. One thing is for certain: between pure entertainment and strict racial uplift, the black public sphere of film production, distribution, and exhibition offers an important window into the hearts and minds of Chicago's New Negroes.

While black film culture took shape, the very same nighttime distractions and attractions on the Stroll and their various meanings were also absorbed by those responsible for creating Chicago's growing gospel sound. As visually arresting as the scopic arenas of beauty and film were, it was the sonic synthesis of sacred and secular sensibilities found in the "good news" of gospel music that gave spiritual sight to the blind, shaking the old settler foundations of religious respectability.

Chapter Five

Sacred Tastes

THE MIGRANT AESTHETICS AND
AUTHORITY OF GOSPEL MUSIC

The mass of "gospel" hymns which has swept through
American churches and well-nigh ruined our sense of song
consists largely of debased imitations of Negro melodies made
by ears that caught the jingle but not the music, the body but
not the soul, of Jubilee songs.
—W. E. B. Du Bois, *The Souls of Black Folk*, 1903

The popularity of the sermons and gospel songs . . . contested
the ethics and aesthetics of the black middle class . . . and . . .
speak to the existence of multiple and conflicting subcultures
within the black working class.
—Evelyn Brooks Higginbotham, "Rethinking Vernacular
Culture: Black Religion and Race Records in the 1920s
and 1930s," in *The House That Race Built*, edited
by Wahneema Lubiano, 1997

Thomas A. Dorsey . . . was able to take the anxieties, joys
and aspirations of the poor, rejected, and often uneducated
African American population and express them in lyrics.
—Horace Clarence Boyer, conversation with author, 1999

In his landmark 1903 collection of essays, *The Souls of Black Folk*, W. E. B. Du Bois examined the dogged persistence of a color line into the twentieth century. In the most general sense, he argued that this racial demarcation continued to deform the moral and democratic promise of the nation while unintentionally encouraging a "second sight" in the descendants of slaves that could offer America salvation from its sinfully materialistic "Gospel of Wealth." According to Du Bois, America's "brutal dyspeptic blundering" and abuse of power was embodied in the nation's vulgar music, and, to continue the metaphor, he concluded that such immorality could only be remedied with the "determined Negro humility" maintained in the face of slavery and found in the "soul of the Sorrow Songs." He made clear that because the variably termed Negro spirituals, slave songs, or sorrow songs were produced in the bowels of a contradictory American slave democracy, they contained a message of "longing toward a truer world." Du Bois concluded that the redemption found within these songs was "the singular spiritual heritage of the nation and the greatest gift of the Negro people." In fact, the epigraphs to many of the essays in *The Souls of Black Folk* pair a verse of Euro-American poetry with a notated composition of "the articulate message of the slave to the world" found in the "sorrow song."[1]

What is perhaps most striking about this detailed musical discussion is Du Bois's identification of styles of music or derivations from the "sorrow songs," which he pointedly rejected as threats to the critical moral message provided in the "folk" legacy of the American slave. Importantly, he grouped "many of the 'gospel' hymns" together with black "minstrel" and "coon" songs in the category of musical deviance. Du Bois was concerned that with growth and development, these more popular derivations from the sorrow songs had lapsed over into the arena of "debasements and imitations" because they had abandoned the proper high cultural aesthetic qualities in composition, musical training, bodily discipline, and especially mood. He demanded a refined focus on the sorrow of sorrow songs to counter the corruption of Negro spirituals as happy, "plantation darky" anthems and to challenge Booker T. Washington's *Up from Slavery* hold on authentic "folk" blackness represented through manual labor, gradual progress, and contented humility. Du Bois charged that such sonic derivations collectively formed a "mass of music in which the novice may easily lose himself and never find the *real* Negro melodies."[2] For Du Bois, the gospel hymns, with their seeming focus on the rhythmic release of the body and not enough restrained disciplining of the soul, were as much a threat as black minstrel or "coon" songs in debasing the moral message of Negro spirituals and reinforcing stereotypes of racial primitivism.[3]

Yet, the desire for preserving the purity of message found in an authentic "folk" music was as much about reforming the actual folk migrating to urban centers and the dangers of vice they potentially carried north in unregulated and excessive amusements, including sporting venues, dance halls, and gospel music (along with jazz and blues) settings. On one side, an obsessive white focus on gospel music's emotional musicality and "Holy Ghost" dancing confirmed a romantic belief in the invigorating powers inherently found in black bacchanalian decadence while encouraging a wave of sacred slumming. On the other side, Du Bois the reformer felt the gospel setting of religious revivals and storefront churches, alongside nightclubs and sporting dens, was not properly regulated. This allowed for potentially uplifting recreations to devolve into unproductive amusements where self-restraint, decorum, and respectability were overwhelmed by the passion and sensuality of ecstatic worship. In this sense, gospel music signaled a tyranny of the masses, a religious setting Du Bois tellingly described as a release of "pythian madness, a demonic possession" like a "suppressed terror" hanging in the air. Those among the "better classes" were haunted by their lack of control over the possible impressions of their white peers in gospel settings and by their limited cultural authority over black practitioners and patrons of the music.[4]

Gospel music, however, was more than a "pythian madness" that needed to be repressed, or at best reformed. The black modern world represented in the gospel sound was a sacred variant within Chicago's larger marketplace intellectual life. As a sonic practice, it contested the "ethics and aesthetics" of the "better classes" by providing a musical voice and tenor for "the anxieties, joys and aspirations" of the new settler worldview. The rise of gospel music in Chicago provided a counter-response to the supposedly more formalized New Negro spirituals project, highlighting a struggle over competing sacred expressions of black modernity. The music, the worship it inspired, and the spirited responses to its sonic force embody the untold story of Chicago's New Negro experience. The gospel sound combined sacred texts and secular rhythms; it was developed in large 5,000-person churches and storefronts and on radio airwaves and provided a "new" religious philosophy and industry for its primarily migrant consumer patrons. What was seen in 1903 as simply a "terror" haunting musical "preservation" became by the late 1920s an all-out gospel revolt of "good news" against the "sorrow songs" as the dominant musical expression of black religious respectability.[5]

Ideologically, the hybrid form of gospel music emerged at the intersection of old-line Protestant church thought, the Sanctified/Pentecostal movement, and migrant forms of musical expression on sacred and secular race records, on radio, and in music venues within Chicago's urban industrial landscape. The initial old-line black Protestant church resistance against the gospel sound encouraged the creation of a commercial market for the music. Within this commercial context, the individual accomplishments of gospel music performer/composer/publisher Thomas A. Dorsey remain central. However, the more collective and woman-centered sphere of demonstration was much more important than composition in marketing and providing the distinct meaning of the improvisational gospel sound. Therefore, live forms of demonstration and collective consumption practices are more instrumental in chronicling the appeal and power of gospel music than are the traditionally modern indicators of production, like songwriting and composition.

Therefore, this chapter chronicles more than the rise of gospel music by charting the competing circuits of cultural authority within the New Negro moment that would determine sacred music tastes and guide the direction of modern worship practices for most of the twentieth century. The urban desires of church parishioners, race record consumers, and the largely female corps of demonstrators and preachers would forever transform the parameters of religious respectability. By the late 1930s, the gospel sound had gone from "the devil's music" to the most notable indicator of black Protestant church life, with its own exclusionary rules and regulations of musical authority, while Chicago served as the center of gospel music publishing and performance. The distinct power and threat of gospel music cannot be understood, however, without a fuller discussion of the concretized Negro spirituals project it challenged.

"MY SOUL HAS GROWN DEEP LIKE RIVERS": SUNDAY MUSICALES, CONCERT SPIRITUALS, AND RACIAL UPLIFT IN OLD-LINE CHURCHES

By the turn of the twentieth century, Chicago's old-line Protestant churches had become key sites for the construction of the religious variant of old settler respectability, primarily defined by large church size, building ownership, and social welfare programs within an emerging classical music context. Between Presbyterian, Episcopalian, and Catholic parishes and the establishment of Pentecostal/Sanctified storefronts and larger houses of worship stood Chicago's "old-line" Baptist and African Methodist Episcopal churches. Almost all old-line churches in the city had at some time splintered off from Quinn Chapel AME, Chicago's first black church established in 1847. For example, Ebenezer Baptist and Pilgrim Baptist, two churches central to struggles over gospel music, started out as dissident prayer bands or revival factions that by the 1920s had established old settler respectability.[6] With congregations numbering in the thousands, these churches negotiated possible class tensions over "sacred tastes" by offering status through leadership positions in their social welfare programs directed at the poor and uneducated. Many migrants endured social programs on hygiene and domestic arts and sermons on public behavior in order to have access to childcare and job referral networks while also acquiring social status through attendance.[7]

Alongside church building ownership and social outreach programs, urban black Protestant churches also sought to reform worship practices; many argued that up-tempo, demonstrative forms of religion were not respectable but backward and embarrassing. Shortly after emancipation, leaders like AME bishop Daniel Alexander Payne demanded congregants to "sit down and sing in a rational manner" because their worship "was disgraceful to themselves, the Race and the Christian name." In Chicago, W. A. Blackwell at Walters AME added that "singing, shouting and talking" were "the most useless ways of proving Christianity." Another minister hoped that intelligence would "sweep from our worship the last vestige of superstition and ranting." Pulling from the anxieties of Du Bois, black church leaders lumped together both sacred and secular forms of emotional and physical expression as primitive and disgraceful and therefore not modern.[8]

By the early twentieth century, Chicago's old-line Protestant churches seemed successful in their repression of congregational singing, clapping, dancing, and shouting through a strict regimen of European classical music and hymns or what were called "musical numbers of the higher type." Anthems by Mozart and Beethoven, often played by large orchestras, encouraged subdued worship while also imposing "dignity on the patrons."[9] These changes in church music also attracted a nonreligious following by those who could not enjoy classical music in racially restrictive Loop theaters downtown. When patrons of classical music realized that worship time limited the music program to only one movement of a complete classical piece, churches began to organize monthly musicales. The actual structure of the music relegated singing to the choir, usually led by a professional director, and instilled a slow and consistent pace to the service. This approach discouraged call and response practices and eliminated the rhythms needed to inspire ring shouts and other collective behavior; respectability was marked by individual worshipers having conversations with Jesus in the private realm of the mind without public proof of religious sanctification. Some old-line preachers were still known to periodically "shout up and down" a church, but these reforms still established a general religious and class ideology by setting new cultural tastes symbolic of refinement, restraint, and distinction among other black churches. In a sense, all vestiges of black folkways were being eliminated, repressed, or devalued within the old-line racial memory until interest in the redemptive, rejuvenating capacity of "folk" culture became a central issue on the national stage.

During the time of war and imperial expansion at the turn of the twentieth century, the United States was self-conscious about its national identity and cultural role on the world stage. The country witnessed a rise in concern over definitions of "American" art, music, and general culture through support of national museums, conservatories, and centers. Authorities turned to the "folk" cultures of the nation to determine the characteristics and qualities that were unique and distinct to the United States. However, all of the musical traits identified as superior (and hence white) could be traced to European origin. In turn, it was the "darker races" of the nation who developed the folk cultural forms that were arguably distinct to the United States. In fact, Antonín Dvořák, Bohemian-born composer and director of the National Conservatory of Music, announced, "I am now satisfied that the future music of this country must be founded upon what are called the Negro melodies. This must be the real foundation of any serious and original school of composition to be developed in the United States. . . . These are the folk songs of America, and your composers must turn to them." What Dvořák described as "Negro melodies" were the very same Negro spirituals that old-line churches despised "as a vestige of slavery" but Du Bois had already reclaimed as a national moral conscience. However, Dvořák's institutional authority wrapped the spirituals within a cloak of legitimacy that prominently gave the old songs a new value.[10]

A cadre of black composers and cultural critics had long turned to "folk" culture and now tried to capitalize on the larger wartime interest in Negro spirituals. Pulling from the notable Hampton and Fisk Jubilee traditions, "Negro melodies" were in vogue as a symbol of black artistic achievement and through cultivation could force white recognition of black entrance into American and world civilization.[11] Black composers and performers of show music and minstrel entertainment were already using African and black folk–inspired themes in shows like *Abyssinia* and *In Dahomey*. James Weldon Johnson worked in this arena of black musical theater while also advocating the canonization of Negro spirituals through his collections of folk-inspired poems and songs. Under the tutelage of musicians like Dvořák and Azalia Hackey, classically trained black composers, including Harry Burleigh and Robert Nathanial Dett, joined the call to "uplift" the spirituals. Hackey set up a booth at the 1915 Lincoln Jubilee Half-Century Exposition in Chicago specifically to sell the concert spirituals of Burleigh and Dett. The common bond among this cadre of elite cultural producers was their shared belief in the superior value of notated composition above and beyond the original folk source from which the composition drew inspiration. For example, Burleigh did not create the popular spiritual "Deep River," but he could and did claim authorship of the song because he developed a classically composed and arranged version.[12]

Black composers thought they were continuing in the tradition of such directors as Fisk Jubilee Singers' John Wesley Work while at the same time they faced protest from college students who argued that performing spirituals reinforced white romances with black racial primitivism.[13] Advocates of the spirituals believed wrapping black subject matter within European classical conventions was the solution to black cultural progress. In fact, the Negro spirituals that modern listeners have grown familiar with merely contain themes and phrasings *inspired* by the songs of slaves; many even nullify the older and more radical messages of liberation from slavery, advocating the universal virtues of a peaceful Christianity in the hereafter. As the spirituals gained a new prominence, New Negro cultural critics took advantage of compositional accomplishments to continue an argument for the central place of "the Negro spirituals" within the American national identity.[14]

Alain Locke's *New Negro* essay "The Negro Spirituals" consolidated the ideas of Du Bois, Dvořák, and others to proclaim Negro spirituals "the most characteristic product of race genius as yet in America" and "America's folk-song." But unlike Du Bois, he somewhat excised the music's political critique of American democracy to paint a picture of peaceful multiculturalism under the banner of an exceptionally American national "unity in diversity." Locke argued these songs were fundamentally "primitive" and had to be transformed if the black folk song was to become a high art song. As a modernist critic, Locke spent the majority of his essay describing the spirituals as "undeveloped musical resources" that must be expunged from the "folk religion that produced them." He wanted to do for Negro spirituals what had been done to Russian, British, and German folk songs: make them the source of a national music. Locke argued for a tempered innovation, calling for cultivation without a loss of what he considered the "proper idiom," specifically citing Dett, Hall Johnson, and notably Edward Boatner as model musicians who struck a balance between cultivation and preservation. Mentioning Boatner is significant because he was an instrumental figure in bringing about a "renaissance" of spiritual singing in Chicago's concert halls and, most important, in its churches. Boatner serves as an important link between larger New Negro developments and the local transformation of spirituals into a sacred symbol of old settler respectability.[15]

Boatner studied at the Boston Conservatory and was later recruited to lead the choir at Olivet Baptist. Eventually, he was courted with a larger salary by Pilgrim Baptist, a location that placed his training and musical ideology at direct odds with the emergence of gospel music. As the popularity of concert spirituals grew, Boatner was aptly trained to play a significant role in the dissemination of Negro spirituals into the church. In fact, he composed the concert spirituals "Twelve Gates into the City" (1923) and "Trampin'" (1927). With the help of the National Baptist Convention he also published the collection *Spirituals Triumphant Old and New*. The spirituals were racially distinct in content, but their form extolled the same kinds of physical restraint that European classical music demanded. The choirs were reverent ensembles that required a certain kind of vocal and bodily control, importantly distinct from the minstrel usage of spirituals. Choir directors focused on dress, diction, and a chorale sound that demanded round, smooth, blended voices with no moving or improvisation. Hall Johnson, Harlem Renaissance composer of "Give Me Jesus" and "Ain't Got Time to Die," was noted for his comment, "Don't let anyone cutsey up my spirituals." The choir was restricted to the notes on the page and the commands of the director, and the performance was a fixed, self-contained cultural product with little room for response or interpretation by the congregation.

The concert setting of church worship and the Sunday musicales attempted to establish a new standard of musical taste and cultural authority. The concretized spiritual became the old settler expression of a New Negro racial consciousness. The ability of both choir and congregation merely to observe, follow directions, and suppress individual desires within the worship service was an important form of bodily discipline, restraint, and reform. The spirituals survived into the twentieth century but as a status symbol, a historical artifact, documenting the aspirations of an emerging class of black professional cultural critics more than the voice of any "folk."[16]

As the cultural criticism of Du Bois and Locke make clear, attempts to reclaim and preserve slave spirituals in their original form ignored the ways in which the "folk" themselves cultivated and arranged songs and trained and developed musicians to meet their own ideas about progress and modernity. This alternate process of musical growth and development challenged both elite cultivations/preservations of "folk" culture while sometimes creating a series of countercultural elitisms and hierarchies among working-class migrant musicians.[17] To be sure, old-line churches were increasingly not places where worshipers could "sing without appearing strange" or "hear somebody else pray besides themselves." Yet, neither these churches nor cultural critics had the final word on the cultivation, development, and transformation of the black folk song, especially as it circulated within new urban spaces. The cultural elite advocated a particular kind of cultivation for the "sorrow songs." But their definitions of musical authenticity were created in response to an equally important development of black folk song happening in blues clubs and storefronts and on city streets, eventually giving rise to gospel music.[18]

RENT PARTY CIRCUITS AND STREET REVIVALS:
ALTERNATIVE FORMS OF URBAN MIGRANT ADJUSTMENT

One of the most popular and convincing statements about black music is that "all the different forms can be traced back to [the] Negro church." However, it would be a mistake to perceive the black folk church and its musical practices as insulated from the transformations that were affecting its migrant carriers in the move from rural area to small town to southern city and eventually to the urban North. Like its secular progeny, the blues and jazz, sacred folk music adapted to various influences both from within and outside the changing black community. Open fields, small churches, and revivals expanded and relocated to storefronts, street revivals, cathedrals, hymnbooks, and recording studios. In these spaces, performers continued to experiment with rhythmic variations and lyrical content by incorporating everything from old spiritual refrains to popular Tin Pan Alley melodies.[19]

The close relationship between sacred and secular black music found its way into the work of pioneer gospel and blues composers like Charles Tindley and W. C. Handy. Both Tindley and Handy witnessed the stylistic developments affecting black music and brought them all to bear on early prototypes of gospel and blues songs that were distinguishable by lyrical content but musically similar. This more dynamic relationship between black music, composition, and the music marketplace is the lens through which migrants like Dorsey and Arizona Dranes made sense out of the city and developed a music that could adequately express their modern urban experiences and desires. To gain a clearer understanding of how and why a shift in sacred music aesthetics and authority took place, it is important to detail the entanglement of individual musicians, composers, and institution builders with the larger transformations of black music and the parallel migrant remaking of urban centers like Chicago.[20]

For many who ended up in the North, the migration from the rural South to Chicago was not a direct route but included stops in southern cities and towns. Between the family farm in rural Georgia and Chicago's black metropolis, Dorsey lived in Atlanta, where he gained piano instruction. But it was actually on Decatur Street, Atlanta's black leisure district, where Dorsey's interests in the piano began to flourish. In Atlanta, Dorsey worked selling drinks at the Eighty-One, a vaudeville house on Decatur Street. He was not an accomplished-enough player to perform at the club but, during downtime, gained instruction on technique and composition from resident musician Ed Butler. At the dance hall he was also exposed to the "show experience" and performance styles of famous Theater Owners' Booking Association circuit performers including Ma Rainey and Chicago traveling legends Butter Beans and Susie.[21]

Dorsey took his observations under Butler (augmented by classical lessons from a Mrs. Graves) and applied them to his piano-playing jobs at low-profile juke joints, brothels, and rent parties. These events contained an intimate and interactive variety of dancing, drinking, gambling, and prostitution, forcing Dorsey to develop quick improvisational skills catering to the different moods and settings. In these venues, Dorsey had to master an array of trills, embellishments, and changes on standard songs to meet the demands of party-goers and prevent party shutdowns. Unlike ballrooms, the intimacy and sometimes illegality of small house parties left musicians more directly subject to crowd demands and the larger environment. These skills came in handy as Dorsey attempted to make his mark as a professional musician when he moved to Chicago in 1916.[22]

According to Dorsey, he "made a name for" himself his "first night in Chicago" after playing in the wine room of the Kelley Garden cabaret. However, in reality, wine rooms and buffet flats provided employment for pianists who couldn't pass the music union standards to compete for the high-profile vaudeville and dance club jobs. In Chicago, as in most cities, buffet flats were originally spaces of lodging for Pullman porters in between train runs and became less respectable places with a different set of behavioral restrictions that allowed sexual encounters and after-hours drinking. While Dorsey claimed ease in his professional ascendancy, he had only moved from the back rooms and rent parties of Atlanta to the buffet flats and rent party circuits of the South Side. Yet, Dorsey knew how to play music where dancers "could drag there all night, drink to mornin' and wouldn't disturb the neighbors" nor bring the police, and this put him in great demand. The playing style he learned in Atlanta did not provide a union card but was perfect for Chicago's house party circuit. A number of migrants flocked to these more informal settings when they could not afford the dance hall or simply desired a familiar blues over the faster-paced, syncopated jazz music that was taking over the city.[23]

Dorsey and the other migrants at these flats were searching for a collective experience through which to mediate Chicago. Buffet flats and rent parties, with their soul food dinners and small fees, served as alternative sites of cultural production, leisure, and labor on the Stroll. Buffet flats particularly offered "landlady" proprietors and women musicians the kinds of entrepreneurial and employment opportunities they would not have acquired elsewhere. Blueswomen and female dancers could perform and take up lodging at flats, allowing them to both make and save money while on the Theater Owners' Booking Association circuit. Sex workers also provided more private services alongside more public sex shows, all for a price. Madams at these flats even became informal banks, where traveling performers and customers left their money in confidence. At the same time, buffet flats and rent parties provided an alternative arena in which guests could express personal aspirations and desires. Under dim lights, customers engaged in illegal drinking, gambling, taboo sexual (particularly gay and lesbian) encounters, music, dancing, laughing, and playing. Outside the force of labor scrutiny or urban anonymity, these times and spaces offered the chance to voice individual personalities or create new identities within surroundings that were both new and familiar. But, no matter how much these leisure activities helped mediate the city for some, most migrants reserved some part of their lives for God, even as older divisions between sacred and secular were being constantly renegotiated. As full members, ushers, saints, or just periodic visitors, many migrants also utilized the diversity of both foreign and familiar forms of worship to help navigate and remake themselves, the Chicago landscape, and the new sacred gospel sound shaping and being shaped by black urban living.[24]

Gospel pioneers like blind pianist Arizona Dranes, Elder Lucy Smith, Sallie Martin, and Sister Rosetta Tharpe were direct products of Sanctified and Pentecostal/Holiness church networks that emerged alongside old-line

Protestant, ballroom, and rent party life. These networks were partial out-growths of industrial and domestic labor's failure to fully define the migrant navigation of the city but also of the Protestant church's inability to represent migrant desires in urban religious life. The push toward formality and re-finement as symbolic of public virtue in old-line worship practices eventually pushed some migrants to "shop around" from church to church for entirely new religious visions. Many church leaders and social scientific scholars interpreted this dissension from membership as a sign of urban maladjust-ment, whereas sacred experimentation actually represented different modes of adaptation that took into account the sacred desires of migrants that were directly tied to the musical and behavioral settings of different churches.

Moreover, Sanctified religion served as a powerful medium for new settler respectability. Women "saints," with their demonstrative worship in modest white robes and full turn away from the secular, were directly critical of old settlers for being too worldly and denounced religious restraint as both uppity and even ungodly. One woman who joined Olivet Baptist recalled that she left after not being able to "understand the pastor and the words he used." A Louisiana migrant remembered that at Pilgrim Baptist, "Nobody said nothing aloud but there were whispers all over the place." The sense of alienation Atlanta migrant Lucinda Madden felt at Olivet pushed her to move to the smaller Ebenezer Baptist Church and then leave the Baptist faith altogether. She then joined the predominantly white Pentecostal Stone Church on 37th and Indiana and then, under the name Elder Lucy Smith, eventually started her own Church of All Nations that played an instrumen-tal role in the performance and distribution of gospel music. The repeated failures of migrants to "understand" and worship "aloud" within the reform-oriented, "this-worldly" context of growing old-line churches encouraged a turn to other religious faiths where they could engage in a personal, experi-ential Christianity.[25]

Images of the Sanctified faith as simply a resistance against formality and particularly as a repository of older "ring shout" forms of demonstrative worship suggest a religious retention of African and black southern "folk" cultures. In fact, by the late nineteenth and early twentieth centuries, Pen-tecostal parishioners had transformed the "folk" ring shout in cities like Memphis, Newark, and significantly Los Angeles, making the Sanctified church a pronounced expression of black modernity in the urban landscape. The Sanctified church formally took hold in black Chicago as early as 1908 through the Holy Nazarene Tabernacle Apostolic Church and the Church of Redemption of Souls on State Street by 1915. However, the full force of this urban religion wasn't felt until the larger onrush of the Great Migration. By 1919, there were at least twenty documented Sanctified storefront churches, and within the next decade, these houses of worship would hold one-fifth of Chicago's black churchgoing population. Outside of a simple resistance to old-line ideology, Sanctified churches created an independent physical and philosophical religious worldview with a space and soundtrack for both personal and communal transformation.[26]

The Sanctified conversion to the "otherworld" of religious salvation offered a way to voice sacred but also secular and personal aspirations in cities like Chicago. Instead of repressing bodily release, these churches advocated using the body as a medium through which to demonstrate one's faith. After conversion into the faith or "being saved," a "saint" could be empowered with the Holy Spirit, most notably through glossolalia (speaking in tongues), revelations, or even healing powers. Members believed in a living God who filled worshipers with spiritual power. Within the church, Holy Ghost possession and liberation were brought on by communal and bodily expressions of religious shouting, dancing, and singing that required a musical accompaniment to bring about such a spirited conversion. With a focus on Spirit-induced release over learned bodily discipline, the music in Sanctified churches was as important in constructing a modern identity as concert spirituals were to old-line Protestant sites of worship. Moreover, the Sanctified philosophy toward demonstrative, public worship rationalized a use of music in ways that both helped develop the gospel sound and created a space for migrant adjustment through employment and social recognition as singing evangelists in the city.[27]

Ideally, the belief that Holy Ghost possession or being "Spirit filled" armed saints with the blood of Jesus. Believers walked "in" the world among sinners and even appropriated secular musical instruments and sounds in secular settings to save souls while not being "of" that world. For example, members of Sanctified churches did not believe that blues music conventions were inherently secular, and in fact, with the right intentions, upbeat rhythms and improvisations were "instrumental" to giving God public praise where guitars, drums, and horns became essential conduits for bringing on the "Holy Spirit." From the beginning, music and public praise were key factors in an aggressive approach to institution-building that afforded every congregant the right to go out and spread the holy word in churches and tent revivals and even on street corners with the goal of creating the world in God's image. The singing/preaching style of evangelicalism that Church of God in Christ (COGIC) founder Charles Mason perfected from his Memphis headquarters is in fact credited with producing some of the earliest examples of modern gospel music.[28]

The two earliest registered COGIC congregations in Chicago were those of Elder Favor on the west side and Elder (later Bishop) W. Roberts on the south side of the city in the first decade of the twentieth century. The famous traveling evangelist F. W. McGee used the revival platform provided by Roberts to bring his singing/preaching style to the city beginning in 1925. McGee's style grew so popular that he organized his own revivals until he made a complete move from Iowa to Chicago in 1926 and established his own congregation. His ministry was powerful because his preaching/singing style also incorporated a diversity of instruments, including the guitar and trombone, in ways that brought a rhythmic intensity to music and hence to his spiritual message. This revival style of institution-building was critical to the reported explosion from just nine COGIC churches in the whole state of Illinois in 1919 to twenty-four congregations just in the city of Chicago by 1928.[29]

The quasi-populist revival style of music found in the COGIC denomination attracted women like Smith to the Sanctified church. Unlike other churches that may have required a religious education for leadership positions, divine gifts could be possessed by anyone who was a "true believer" or "saint." In the heart of Chicago's impoverished urban realities, salvation provided transcendence of the worldly divisions of race, class, and gender. However, Smith, along with many other women, confronted the standard religious opposition to female leadership that was even mandated in the bylaws of the COGIC. In fact, Smith had to use the populist tradition of the church, pronouncing that she was "raised up pastor by the mighty hands of God," to contest the strong tradition against female leadership from within. She then maintained the aggressive evangelist philosophy of "being in the world but not of it" by organizing prayer meetings with a small group of women in her home, which led to a tent on Langley Avenue called the Langley Avenue All Nations Pentecostal Church. Over the next decade, her church moved from place to place, holding services in the Star and Pekin theaters on the Stroll, in various church basements, and in a Masonic Hall temple. Smith was eventually able to lead "the only church in Chicago built by a woman." The precarious and contradictory nature of Sanctified religious theory in practice exposed very real gendered divisions of leadership that found women struggling for recognition both inside and outside of its social hierarchy. The women evangelists who remained within the COGIC order found a "safer" middle ground. Many used the institutional cover of the COGIC to go out onto city street corners and, with a blues backbeat, serve as primary builders of the Sanctified church, gain provisional spaces of leadership and authority, and in the process become major figures in the development of gospel music.[30]

Women evangelists had "church in the street" in order to remake the world in "God's image," but at the same time they were shaped by secular sites and sounds in the world, which laid the foundation for a gospel music performance style that was intimately tied to the commercial marketplace. The fleeting or floating nature of street congregations required evangelists to get people to stop and take notice of sacred messages by wrapping ministry in an everyday vernacular with anecdotes that could appeal to the predominantly working-class people who passed. Moreover, the use of jazz instruments and blues rhythms surely appealed to so-called sinners on the street. Under the leadership of women evangelists, the abbreviated hour-long street meetings, without chairs or even the protective covering of a tent, packaged singing, preaching, praying, and testimonials about what God had done in someone's life in ways that blurred hard lines between sacred and secular.[31]

Within the context of the traveling revival and street preaching, Dranes became one of the country's most influential performers in Chicago and recorded at the local race records studio at Okeh. Dranes incorporated a barrelhouse blues piano style with her ministry, making embellishments and trills individual expressions of her spiritual voice. The way in which the blind Dranes was known to "sing . . . [and] get up off of that piano and turn all around and sit back down and start" was a dual expression of Holy Spirit–induced religious salvation and self-styled showmanship that demonstrated her individual leadership as a woman evangelist with communal ties to the children of God.[32]

Dranes's style had a significant impact on "guitar evangelists" like Sister Rosetta Tharpe, who started out as a traveling missionary with her mother, Katie Bell Nubin, before they settled in Chicago in the 1920s. Tharpe, unlike Dranes, did not record until the late 1930s, but in churches all around town she was known to "make that guitar talk," with blues inversions and a swinging syncopation that paralleled her vibrato vocal style. The full impact of Tharpe's gospel innovations extend beyond the scope of this study, but she went on to incite serious controversy as she took the Sanctified logic to its fullest extent by performing in theaters and nightclubs and even with Cab Calloway's band. Both Dranes and Tharpe used the institutional power of COGIC affiliation to trek out on their own to establish distinction and in the process to become music ministry innovators.

In between industrial labor and jazz music elitism, the rent party circuit became an important source of status and employment for migrant musicians like Dorsey. In the same way and at the same time, women evangelists in Sanctified churches used the tent revival and street preaching to negotiate a gender hierarchy in both sacred and secular worlds while asserting authority, mobility, and distinction. Sanctified spaces held a position equal to the blues world of Dorsey in offering migrants the opportunity to take their bodies back from the inhumane working conditions in Chicago's factories and elite homes and hotels. However, these musical developments in predominantly working-class life were still on the margins of old settler respectability.[33]

AT THE CROSSROADS OF THE HOLY AND THE PROFANE:
THE COMMERCIAL CONVERGENCE OF THE SACRED AND SECULAR

The official tastemakers in black communities continued to promote the genres of concert spirituals and jazz as parallel symbols of race pride and respectability. The Musicians' Protective Union with syncopated jazz leaders like Dave Peyton and Erskine Tate determined the kind of sound that would be played in the "high class" dance halls and helped decide who got jobs. At the same time, spiritual music composers, including Dett and Boatner, set the tone for an appropriate worship setting. Like other musicians, Dorsey hoped piano playing would allow him to sidestep the inhumane dictates of industrial labor while gaining some personal recognition and economic security as a professional musician. Within the rent party and buffet flat circuit, however, Dorsey did not find the desired control over his life because of the economic and psychological instability that being a professional blues musician inflicted on his pride and pocketbook. Dorsey also began to rethink the power of religious salvation while suffering a debilitating nervous breakdown caused by the disparity between his professional/personal intentions and his actual conditions. By 1930, important events turned the tide and forced sacred/secular musical orthodoxy to engage working-class consumer demands in a way that placed both blues musicians and singing evangelists at the center of black musical developments.[34]

During his recovery from depression, Dorsey attended the National Baptist Convention in 1921, held at Chicago's Eighth Regiment Armory. Although the convention was a stronghold of sacred old settler ideology, an important development within the convention forever affected Dorsey and old-line worship practices. Despite strong advocacy for concert spirituals and European classical music, the National Baptist Convention was concerned over the loss of music that could inspire a spiritual conviction in congregants.

Leaders hoped the new official Baptist songbook, *Gospel Pearls*, would fill this void by transcending denominational distinction to include traditional Isaac Watts Protestant hymns, the composed spirituals of John Wesley Work, and—importantly—the "jubilees" of Charles Tindley. At this convention, singing evangelist "Professor" W. M. Nix also amazed Dorsey with his performance of the song "I Do Don't You."[35]

Nix aesthetically personalized this standard hymn through improvisational techniques that ran counter to old-line notions of musical respectability. He came from behind the pulpit and changed the tempo, allowing him to stray from the text, embellish the melody, and control the musical sentiment of the song. The entire audience was thrilled, and Dorsey was amazed most by how Nix inspired the audience through embellishments similar to those he used to stir up emotions at rent parties. Nix's authority, gained by adding "a touch of the blue note"—along with the collection plate—made Dorsey exclaim, "That's where I oughta be!" As an audience member, Dorsey's own "inner being was thrilled," challenging the old settler sensibility that equated religious respectability with emotional restraint. He claimed immediate conversion and soon published the religious song "If I Don't Get There" (1922).[36]

Dorsey became a religious musical director at the New Hope Baptist Church without removing his improvisational style or silencing the emotive crowd responses he generated with the blues. However, the "like down home" context provided at New Hope offered little in church collection plates. Dorsey soon realized he had merely moved in a linear fashion from a second-tier secular music job to a second-tier sacred music position. He quickly decided to take an offer to join the Whispering Syncopators, learning the more respectable jazz music and finally touring in theaters and dance halls. On the local front, Dorsey received the elusive Musicians' Protective Union pay standard, frequented jazz music haunts like the House of Jazz music store on State Street, and associated with music greats like Handy and Peyton as a respected peer. The *Chicago Defender* even noted that "Dorsey [was] busy" with musical arrangements of jazz compositions. However, as Dorsey left the barrelhouse blues behind, the growing congregational demand for the embellishments and moans of Nix were paralleled by consumer patron demand for a similar style in the secular world of the race music marketplace.[37]

When Mamie Smith's "Crazy Blues" sold 75,000 copies in 1920, it instigated a blues music explosion and radically expanded the race music market. In 1924, Dorsey was brought to Paramount Records by black music impresario and former local football star J. Mayo "Ink" Williams to work in the tour band for Ma Rainey. Dorsey's "down home" blues style attracted Rainey, and he was appointed musical director, requiring him to organize and manage her promotional band, the "Wild Cats Jazz Band."

Dorsey was sought out for his sound, but the description "down home" is a bit misleading. In the same vein as concert spirituals and the emerging gospel style, the blues went through significant changes on the road. Handy, Mamie Smith, and Rainey were all professional vaudeville performers who traveled on the Theater Owners' Booking Association circuit. Even though some scholars argue that "the so-called 'classic' blues" had been "adulterated for public consumption" on race records, they were nonetheless able to resonate with the masses of black Americans. Perhaps what Paul Oliver calls the "conscious artistry" and stylization that vaudeville artists added to the blues are precisely what made the performance style attractive for public consumption. The blues of Bessie Smith or Rainey, with their suggestive lyrics, diversity of musical style, and elegant stage shows, were perhaps an alternative form of race progress and pride for those who felt left out of "high class" jazz and the "pomp and circumstance" of concert spirituals. At the same time, popular musical development symbolized a desired departure away from the older blues style. In Chicago alone, House of Jazz owner Clarence Williams remembered: "Colored people would form a line twice around the block when the latest record of Bessie or Ma or Clara or Mamie come in." A new voice of black modernity was emerging on race records that consolidated sacred and secular developments in ways that undermined the authority of old settler musical uplift and even notions of folk authenticity.[38]

The commercialism of music in the 1920s created a space for both sacred and secular working-class cultural production. The national distribution of race records not only allowed the blues to move past the brothels and rent parties but also brought emotional preaching and religious song out of exile from storefronts and street corners. It was not necessarily through community institutions but again in the marketplace of race records and performance circuits that blues singers and singing evangelists added their soundtrack to the larger public sphere of black musical authority. However, this was not a fully liberatory tale of the rise of a working-class migrant sound. Popular history documents that between 1923 and 1926, black music buyers began to lose interest in the vaudeville blues and demanded the more "authentic" sound of "down home" blues singers and singing preachers. However, evidence for a decline in the popularity of vaudeville women blues singers is not indicated in record sales. In fact, it was partially the record "industry's desire not to confront the image of the slick city black" that encouraged a shift to the marketing and promotion of the down home blues music genre. While the blues explosion of 1920 showcases the ability of the "Negro market" to influence the production decisions of record companies, we also see corporate power's ultimate ability to limit the market to a particular kind of blues image. The rise in down home blues and music ministers complete with "down-south" and even plantation images did not necessarily reflect black marketplace demands as much as it did white interests.[39]

Record company resistance against black modern images accelerated the production shift to down home blues and the popularity of singing evangelists, but there was a sharp incongruence between rural marketing stereotypes and the actually existing urbanity of style within the musical performances. For example, Sanctified singers' and preachers' aggressive missionary style motivated preaching out on the street, but it also rationalized an early embrace of recording technologies as another medium to emit their rhythm-centered theology. Their experiences highlight an alternative black modern musical experience in the city that betrayed images of pure rural innocence and/or urban adulteration. These singing evangelists did not convey the old settler church values of progress through cultivated harmonies, written compositions, and restrained performances, but neither were they the country bumpkin stereotypes seen on their album covers or the mindless "holy rollers" as perceived by many race leaders.

These singing evangelists carried their own critiques, anxieties, and race visions into a conscious engagement with older musical traditions and newer recording technologies. Performers including "The Lady Preacher" R. H. Harris and her Pentecostal Sisters and the Chicago Sanctified Singers spoke back to the dispassionate delivery and classical sound of old-line musical uplift. F. W. McGee's first recording, "Lion of the Tribe of Judah," was a stirring spiritual that included Dranes on ragtime piano. He later added a combination of horn, string, and rhythm instruments to the over forty titles he recorded with Victor between 1927 and 1930, while Dranes accompanied herself on piano in the sixteen singles she recorded during the 1920s. On "God's Mercy to Colonel Lindbergh," Reverend Leora Ross of Chicago's Church of the Living God used current events to engage her listeners. As already discussed, traveling preacher Nix was a prominent figure in the uplift-oriented National Baptist Convention, but his race records were also extremely popular.[40]

The above examples highlight the oversimplification of terms like "folk" and "refined," "down home" and "artificial." These designations also gloss over the ways in which old settler and "down home" musical ideas were allied in race uplift and reform. The messages of "Black Diamond Express to Hell" by Nix and Reverend Burnett's "Downfall of Nebuchadnezzar" were as impassioned in their condemnation of urban vices like alcohol, crime, laziness, and infidelity as old-line reform programs. Instead of general references to moral reform, "Pay Your Honest Debts" (Nix), "Shine-Drinking" (McGee), "Dying Gambler" (Rev. J. M. Gates) and "The Jailhouse Blues" (Emmett Dickinson) spoke with the language and used the melodies of the day to warn migrants about the specific pitfalls of urban living. While Sanctified churches advocated an "otherworldly" theology, they utilized worldly conventions and technologies for disseminating their message to the largest audience possible. In 1926, Burnett's "Downfall of Nebuchadnezzar" sold 80,000 units, which was four times the average sales of Bessie Smith, the leading blues artist that year.[41]

Working-class migrant sacred and secular tastes converged on the dangerous terrain of the race records industry in the late 1920s and early 1930s to offer a challenge to the black modern vision of jazz and concert spirituals. In many regards, the music industry marketplace was an instrumental space where the consolidation of this new sound could take advantage of racist white fascinations with black "primitive" culture and sidestep community standards of respectability to reach the consumer base that would drive it to black cultural prominence. However, musicians and consumers were still faced with navigating the cost-benefit morality of record companies and the racist assumptions used to commodify and market the new sacred/secular sound. This power politics between music industrial control, community standards, and black musical innovation are exemplified in Dorsey's professional tenure at Paramount Records after coming off tour with Rainey.[42]

Paramount had neither the ability nor the desire to deal with black musical development or distribution, but it wanted to benefit from the profitable race market. "Ink" Williams served as the mediator between industry and talent to the point that he became the unofficial director of Paramount's race records. At the same time, he started his own Chicago Music Publishing Company to regain some of the copyright profits lost when he handed talent over to the record companies. The position Williams held and his own company benefited a number of black musicians, talent scouts, and composers, including Dorsey. However, in exchange for employment, they became cogs in the industrial wheel of both black musical appropriation and innovation. As the more improvisational blues style became more commercially popular, distinctions emerged between the composition of a song and the arrangement of a song. Record companies refused to pay royalties by arguing that their singers' arrangements were entirely different compositions. Williams caught wind of this strategy and began bringing artists to Paramount from his publishing company with a complete package of arranged and copyrighted songs.[43]

The Chicago Music Publishing Company became an intermediary between talent and industry. For example, a talent scout would bring to the studio an artist who would demonstrate a song while Dorsey set the arrangement, coached the singer, and secured the copyright. The act of "re-creating" songs was a popular event in black musical traditions, but in the music industry it meant relinquishing ownership and hence money to the Chicago Music Publishing Company and primarily Paramount. The performer was happy to accept compensation for a single oral performance with little or no knowledge of music property rights and royalties or options outside the monopoly of record companies. The irony is that the authority and status that Dorsey received from his work in blues translation and artist development helped create a new urban sound but also robbed black artists of their cultural product. Dorsey himself was a victor in these relations, as a hired composer/arranger, but also a victim when he traded the rights to his own compositions for the security of consistent employment at the Chicago Music Publishing Company.[44]

Black performers like Dorsey turned to the music profession as one way to exert independence and authority over their life and labor choices. However, the commodification of their talent on music sheets and records subjected them to the whims of another urban industrial machine. The adoption of multiple pseudonyms for single performers became another way in which black music was subjected to cost-benefit values. Giving performers a different name allowed competing companies to use the same performer on a different label without violating previous contracts. However, performers began to understand these market strategies and use them to their own benefit. For example, during the late 1920s "revival" for down home blues, Dorsey teamed up with Hudson "Tampa Red" Whitaker in 1928 and recreated himself as "Georgia Tom" to put out the successful double entendre song "It's Tight Like That." He realized that "the more records you made . . . the more money you made." To gain some sense of control over his musical labor, Dorsey played on the rural stereotypes of the moment to come up with pseudonyms like "The Hokum Boys" and "Barrelhouse Tom" to "bootleg . . . from record company to record company."[45] Dorsey was able to create small victories in the recording industry, but the constant struggle for ownership

"Georgia Tom" Dorsey. (Courtesy of Riverside Records and Jim O'Neal)

and the itinerant lifestyle never satisfied his desires for economic stability and artistic autonomy.

Dorsey's experiences in the recording business caused internal conflicts within his personal psyche and spirit. In the late 1920s, he began reconciling this conflict by composing and publishing his "first" distinctly blues-inflected gospel songs, "If You See My Savior" (1926) and later "How About You" (1932), as sheet music. These songs were significant because they did not hark back to an idealized folk vision of musical preservation but continued in the hybrid blues/spiritual styles of Tindley, Handy, Dranes, and Nix. Nix's performance at the National Baptist Convention demonstrated that only a blues-inflected style could get "down into the individual to set him on fire, dig him up or her up way down there 'til they come out with an expression verbally." Dorsey realized that whether it was "Amen in the church" or "Sing it now" in blues, the same feeling was being elicited. He concluded: "The only thing about all the music is the words are different." Clearly, Dorsey did not instigate this sacred/secular convergence. The rhythmic and stylistic connections between bluesmen and singing evangelists on race records point to a mass consumer demand for this sound, while old-line churches remained critical of the music and the emotions it inspired. But Dorsey's days as a blues musician, his desire for personal distinction, and his turn to the church for religious salvation made his life the perfect medium through which this spiritual "expression" would challenge old-line worship practices.[46]

"WE TOOK OUR STRUGGLE TO THE STREETS": THE MASS APPEAL AND MARKETING OF GOSPEL MUSIC

If it had not been for his nervous breakdown earlier, Dorsey may have continued to ride the blues success of "It's Tight Like That." Instead, he decided to open up the expressive possibility within inspirational sacred music by bringing blues (or secular spiritual) techniques to the church. The restrained worship practices supported by concert spirituals at old-line churches had meant to impose a dignity on the patrons, whereas the "bluesing up" of a song with gaps in the seven-note scale, pauses, and a distinct chorus/verse structure built into the song resonated with the desires of migrants for individuality within the anonymity of city life. Like singing evangelists, Dorsey explicitly chose the musical "trills, turns, movements" from rent party blues and storefronts to make his gospel compositions attractive. He thought, "If I could get into the gospel songs the feeling and the pathos and the moans and the blues[,] that [would get] me over." While spirituals restricted singing to the choir, Dorsey's gospel songs structurally made a space for congregational singing, a voice within the composition. He believed these changes offered an opportunity to speak back: "When you don't have a voice, with these expressions and embellishments, you can express yourself." Similar to singing evangelists, the distinction between sacred and secular music was less important for Dorsey than was a spirit of conviction: "Now when I was singing blues I sang 'em with the spirit. Now, I've got gospel songs, I sing 'em with the spirit." Dorsey further combined this change in music theory with a revolution in composed lyrical style.[47]

Dorsey's lyrics especially spoke "to the economy, jobs and how one felt." Instead of the more objective approach of spirituals, like "Listen to the Lambs" and "Ain't That Good News," in his new songs Dorsey proclaimed his religious conviction and directly asked "How About You." One of his earliest gospel songs, "If You See My Savior," takes his own bout with near suicide and converts it into a redemptive tale of personal salvation through religious faith:

> I was standing by the bedside of a neighbor
> Who was just about to cross the swelling tide
> And I asked him if he would do me a favor,
> Kindly take this message to the other side.
> Now if you see my savior, tell him that you saw me
> And when you saw me that I was on my way.
> You may chance to meet my father and my mother,
> Just tell them I'm coming home some day.

The lyrics invited the listener to feel the pain, conversion, and eventual salvation of the performer. The sense of a common experience was created when Bible references were replaced with first person narratives and reinforced by simple melodies, fewer words (and in the language of everyday people), and harmonies that people could anticipate.

As Dorsey moved further into the world of gospel composition, he also replaced a more subdued sound with the same kind of musical beat that he had used with Tampa Red. His blues-oriented syncopated rhythms and driving percussion supported blues trills and common speak to help Dorsey establish distinction within the Protestant sacred music world. He argued that because his gospel songs "had a beat," they were not Du Bois's "sorrow songs" of the past but "good news" of everyday trials and tribulations overcome by faith in God. Dorsey realized that the rhythmic and textual differences in gospel songs could also be used as marketing tools in the church. However, the attempt to stake out a space for a gospel music is precisely what generated conflict over religious doctrine and ministerial authority.[48]

When old-line Protestant ministers heard this music and saw the way parishioners responded, all they thought was "sin music." The message was overlooked because the sound was too reminiscent of "worldly things—like jazz and blues." Respected Pilgrim Baptist choir director and composer Boatner heard Dorsey and replied, "I felt it was degrading. How can something that's jazzy give a religious feeling? If you're in a club downtown, a nightclub, that's all right. That's where it belongs. But how can you associate that with God's word?" For Boatner and others, a religious voice spoke in the subdued tone of concert spirituals, cantatas, and operas. These musical forms represented classical training and therefore religious respectability. The addition of a swinging sound and percussive syncopation was a sign of bringing street music to the church and abandoning musical training.

Clearly the problem was not that Dorsey lacked training but that his musical training was structured around hard-driving rhythms and not "refined," smooth harmonies. The distinction was significantly one of competing sacred tastes. However, church leaders masked their frustrations in reactions ranging from Dorsey being "put out of or barred from churches" to debates on religious ideology. Yet, the challenge to gospel music did not solely rest in the pseudo-religious indictments of it as sinful music. The way in which the music "moved people and drew crowds" also exposed internal struggles of authority between professional musicians and professional ministers in mainstream churches.[49]

Dorsey laid blame for resistance directly at the feet of those he called the "high toned people who thought that God just wants to hear anthems and arias." In interviews, he continually recalled a popular ministerial response: "You can't sing no gospel. You can only preach the gospel." Dorsey quickly challenged this "academic philosophy" with his own: "Man, you don't know what you're talking about. Look up your definition, even in your Bible, the gospel's good news." On the surface, this exchange displays a simple doctrinal difference, but Dorsey identified it as a shift in the balance of power between musicians and pastors who didn't "want anyone encroaching on their territory." The approach of many old-line preachers and composers was to provide respectability through a restrained and controlled worship that eliminated "shaking and wobbling your hips . . . and hollering out." Dorsey was challenging the uplift ideology of the "sorrow songs" with a music that met people where they were through both a popular language and musical style.

Instead of repressing emotion, whether in church or on the job, it was *through* emotional outbursts and individual articulations that congregations were able to reinsert their individuality and demonstrate religious conviction.[50]

Dorsey made a profound breakthrough in musical developments, but his marketing strategies relied too heavily on the musical tastes of ministers as the gatekeepers through which to reach large Protestant church congregations. Dorsey sent out thousands of copies of his first two gospel songs through a mailing list in the National Baptist Convention publication, the *Foreign Mission Herald*. He also demonstrated them locally with Louise Keller at churches and sold songs door-to-door but met with little success. Door-to-door and mail-order sales and song demonstrations in churches were mediated by the musical tastes of ministers and music directors, rarely the majority of the actual congregations. In addition, sheet music could not convey all of the improvisation that Dorsey added to the music: "Give me a song, I stick to the note and play it like it is, you won't pay much attention to it. . . . You got to always have something, a little trick; a little embellishment or something." The freedom to embellish the text was precisely the element that made his gospel music compositions so distinct.[51]

Writing out the entire song, including Dorsey's improvisations, would make it impossible for a trained pianist to actually follow: "If you write too many embellishments and they see too many notes, they won't play it. . . . You can't put all that stuff up there on that paper. They can't read it." The actual demonstration therefore had to sell not only the music sheets but also the new musical sound. Dorsey thought that by hiring "high class" singer Keller to help demonstrate his songs, the music would take on an air of respectability and hence bolster his authority in the old-line church. However, Keller's musical training left her unfamiliar with Dorsey's improvisational demands to perform according to the needs of each church setting. Both of these strategies unintentionally repressed the demonstrative spirituality that his songs were meant to inspire. Dorsey finally realized that his new sacred songs required secular strategies of marketing and promotion to partially sidestep the old-line tradition of the published hymnbook and reach his targeted mass audience.[52]

First, Dorsey began demonstrating his songs with the more "down home" preacher Reverend E. H. Hall. But it was when St. Louis singer Willie Mae Ford Smith was "laying them out in the aisle" with her stirring rendition of Dorsey's "If You See My Savior" at the 1930 National Baptist Convention that everyone demanded "the Dorsey that writes the songs." That Smith made people "hear" the gospel sound was not a surprise, because while she had been a devout Baptist for years, she had grown up singing "everything, [she] could sing blues, reels, you name it, when Mama wasn't around." Smith's demonstration allowed Dorsey to see that he could potentially achieve both economic and spiritual salvation in the sacred world in a way that instigated a turning point in his gospel career.

The convention was an important commercial venue with immense cultural authority, and now Smith demonstrated a gospel song in a way that captured Dorsey's blues style. At that point, his earlier turn to sheet music appeared a stroke of brilliance, because he was the only black sacred composer using this medium of distribution and ownership. Once his songs were sonically recognized, there was no competition. He shrewdly realized the importance of these converging forces and took advantage of this direct access to consumer tastes within the walls of old-line orthodoxy. Dorsey quickly set up a table and demonstrated his songs with a young migrant Baptist singer from New Orleans, Mahalia Jackson, who had also been thrown out of churches because of a "snake hips" style reminiscent of her idol Bessie Smith. By the end of the convention, they had sold approximately 4,000 copies of his music. The sacred institution and the song sheet system that repressed emotion and individual interpretation would now become the mediums through which Dorsey and his new sound gained distinction.[53]

Once the popularity of his songs spread, ironically through the National Baptist Convention, it was up to Dorsey to respond to his new market. Dorsey took on a two-tiered approach, using the old-line church for cultural legitimacy while also extending beyond this institution to begin developing a gospel music industry. The uniting factor was the way in which Dorsey utilized his training as a race records composer, arranger, and voice coach to promote gospel music in old-line churches. In 1931, Dorsey, Magnolia Lewis Butts, and Theodore Roosevelt Frye organized the first gospel chorus at Ebenezer Baptist. This chorus gained such a quick following that even the *Chicago Defender* announced its presence with a photograph. When Junius Austin, pastor of the prominent Pilgrim Baptist, saw the excitement and crowd that the chorus generated at every performance, especially during a time of national depression, he asked Dorsey to organize a chorus for him in 1932. The crowds drawn by gospel performances brought more attention to old-line parishes. In turn, it was only these churches that could provide the music with the religious respectability Dorsey desired.[54]

Popular images of congregations experiencing wild frenzy and uncontrolled spiritual exhortation during gospel music performances suggest that the down home, "old-time religion" had been brought back into the old-line church. However, underneath romances with the folk purity of spontaneous hand clapping, shouting, and driving rhythms were the disciplined musical cues, planned choreography, and histrionics that Dorsey pulled from his days as a blues musician and composer. Dorsey bragged that it was his instruction in blues techniques that created the gospel sound and made Frye a gospel singer. With Rainey, Dorsey recalled that he "stood up and played the piano which was then a great novelty."[55] In the gospel world, Dorsey provided Frye with the musical material to sing and strut across the stage where Dorsey would again "stand up at the piano and pound the beat out to his marching steps." These performers were clear in their use of rehearsed secular elements. As Dorsey recalled, "We had our songs well worked up and knew every cue." Reminiscent of blind evangelist Dranes getting up and turning around in the middle of a song, Dorsey and Frye's pronounced showmanship and skill helped get old-line churches "all worked up" into a legitimately spiritual frenzy.

Furthermore, Dorsey self-consciously brought his training as a vocal coach and musical arranger to the church to develop and cultivate a new and disciplined gospel performance style. Dorsey remembered that at Paramount, he had accented the songs "in a way that . . . will grasp the public and set them up straighter." In the church, he was clear that emotion in the gospel song was "something you got to practice in the throat." Singers must learn "how to say [their] words in a way, in a moanful way and more of a crying way." Folk singers were not simply allowed to step on the stage and let the Spirit move them.[56]

Yet, a description of the constructed nature of gospel music is not meant to suggest that the religious conviction generated was "fake." This discussion merely hopes to challenge cultural studies that over-romanticize folk continuities and underestimate the way in which migrants consciously developed their own notions of style, status, and spiritual respectability. In fact, the above discussion lends context to Dorsey's comments about his most well known demonstrator, Mahalia Jackson. Early on, Jackson was identified as a great singer with a "down home style" popular with revivals and storefronts, and much has been made of her alienation from old-line church traditions. However, in Dorsey's mind, this style did not initially prepare her for the gospel stage. Like he did with Frye, Dorsey claimed to have trained Jackson "how to do my numbers and do them with the beat—shake at the *right* time; shout at the *right* time" (emphasis added).[57]

Migrants were perhaps familiar with vibrant displays of religious conviction, but Dorsey and Frye organized this experience into a disciplined, orchestrated performance. They understood the need to *sell* the gospel sound, in both senses of the word. The demonstration had to establish faith, confidence, and even belief in the music ministry, which then allowed an exchange of song sheets as a product for money. Every performance was an opportunity to reach souls and new markets to the point that these interests became one. Dorsey and his demonstrators brought "indigenous" worship back into the church, but more accurately they offered a new style of sophisticated urban worship that captured the aspirations of many migrants filling up the pews. Even choir members recall having "to be taught everything, even how to march," in order to elicit the proper mood.[58] The "old-time religion" was dressed up with showman performers who orchestrated slow musical buildups and crescendos that brought crowds to a cued up sanctification.

Dorsey's new settler gospel sound was different from the "old-time religion" but was still not universally accepted by old-line churches. The middle ground staked out by both gospel musical performance and audience demands was most evident in Dorsey's 1933 organization of the Thomas A. Dorsey Publishing Company and the National Convention of Gospel Choirs and Choruses (NCGCC).[59] He hired aspiring evangelist Sallie Martin to act as national organizer for the NCGCC. The role of demonstrators like Willie Mae Ford Smith in St. Louis and Martin throughout the South and Midwest was instrumental because their song demonstrations facilitated the organization of gospel choirs and unions.

Martin and Smith's organizing strategies highlight the way in which the gospel music marketplace was an alternative modern expression, deploying newer technologies of distribution combined with older techniques of demonstration. Martin could barely read music, but she would find a piano and someone to read the sheet music. After a while, the musician had to catch on to her vocal instruction. This technique of instruction became so effective that the manuscripts of new songs were tailored to Martin's particular style. While in St. Louis, Smith was best known for her abilities in performance instruction. She took the most standard and staid hymn and with "slurs and note bending" demonstrated how it could be transformed into a new song. Her solos ignited later gospel music conventions, and she traveled across the country to train many of the great singers in gospel music. These styles of demonstration created a communal atmosphere where the musical experience of playing and listening was the method of instruction. In Cincinnati, however, Martin found strong pastoral resistance against gospel music and could not gain church support. She decided to turn away from the church and organize a community gospel chorus. While she faced the displeasure of ministers, her improvisational creation of the community gospel chorus helped extend the reach of the music beyond church control.[60]

The community choir and gospel union bypass of ministerial authority secured a direct link between gospel music and its practitioners while still encouraging contact with church-affiliated music groups. Moreover, both Dorsey-affiliated local unions and yearly national conventions secured a captive audience for the dissemination of gospel song sheets (later called "Dorseys"). The NCGCC, combined with the dissemination technology of music publishing, "helped to create a mass audience of African Americans for gospel music." This institution of instruction and commerce was driven by gospel music's focus on performance over composition and secured Dorsey's status and authority as a successful professional musician.[61]

The exploitative nature of music recording and the uncontrollable interpretation of gospel sheet music made Dorsey realize that his authority was best secured by controlling demonstration practices. In some instances, Dorsey saw that as musical accompanist, it was his "duty to subordinate himself." However, staying behind the scenes was not necessarily an act of deference. Since his days at rent parties, Dorsey represented the piano player as "king of the night." He also heavily overestimated the level of his authority with Rainey. Clearly, Rainey was the headlining draw and the source of his economic stability. However, in one interview, Dorsey recalled her "Jazz Wildcats" as "my band, with Ma Rainey." Throughout his career, Dorsey maintained that performing was an important source of self-empowerment and control. He always understood that performers, with the right training, had the ability to move and control an audience. As attention shifted from band to singer during the era of sound recording, Dorsey began to make distinctions between the performer and the superior authority of himself as a composer, accompanist, and musical director. Even in a religious context, Dorsey maintained, "Whoever is the pianist, is the master. You handle people like you want them. Tell them what you want them to do."[62]

Dorsey would continue to foreground his control over performers when recounting the rise of the NCGCC and of gospel music more generally. Smith and Martin drew interest to gospel not only through their style of singing but also through their marketing and demonstration, which secured the infrastructure for Dorsey's publishing business. In fact, it was Martin who told Dorsey, "You have something here but you don't know what to do with it,"

Thomas A. Dorsey with Sallie Martin. (Courtesy of GTN Pictures)

and proposed, "Let me go travel, carry the music and then sell it when I'm finished singing." For Martin, her role as an organizer and song demonstrator placed her alongside Dorsey as a key figure in the formalization of the gospel sound. In one interview, Dorsey appropriately recognized Martin as a co-organizer but then quickly asserted his authority over her in the all-too-important realm of song demonstration: "She had a lovely voice, but she needed a little roughness knocked off. . . . I trained her." His insistence on the authorial distinction between composer and demonstrator finally encouraged Martin and one of Dorsey's young accompanists, Northwestern University–trained Roberta Martin, to break away from his "control."[63]

Dorsey's self-definition as a trainer of the influential Martin recognized her importance while maintaining a name for himself as the cause of her greatness. Dorsey also claimed he had to "smooth . . . the roughness out of" Mahalia Jackson's singing. However, his later concession that "she wouldn't listen. She said I was trying to make a stereotyped singer out of her" points to the even then tenuous hold Dorsey had on his newly acquired masculine position of authorship. For some, Dorsey's use of female vocalists highlighted a challenge to gender divisions within sacred leadership. However, his patronizing evaluations expose a dogged determination to secure mastery over his female demonstrators, especially in telling the story of gospel music's ascendancy, when their actual significance was equal to his own.[64]

The particular way in which Dorsey remembered the rise of gospel music has reinforced the traditionally modern idea that composition is the primary indicator of authorship. However, the rise of gospel music was located squarely within a black modern context of collective authorship that exceeded the written text. The story of Dorsey reveals that the music was distinct because of its improvisation of standard texts and that the sound did not come into "being" or exist until it was demonstrated. In this sense, authorship must be shared with female demonstrators like Smith and Martin and at the sites of demonstration where consumer patrons equally shared in the creation of the music.

Dorsey's own self-perception and image control until recently have relegated the role of demonstration to footnotes and asides in the aesthetic history of the early years. Moreover, while histories recognize the role of Sanctified churches, the establishment of gospel music as an art form or even as the standard worship sound has been intimately tied to its final acceptance in old-line churches. Old-line churches may have been the last line of defense against Dorsey's professional prominence, but the music was already heard and heralded elsewhere. In the black sacred world of the 1930s, secular radio airwaves were key to the transmission of a music-centered Sanctified church culture. The sacred appropriation of radio technology created a consumer context of support for gospel and, in the processes of reception, a new music that further extended beyond the control of Dorsey.

As Dorsey continued to face strong resistance from old-line leaders and composers, Sanctified churches in the city quickly identified with his compositions of the gospel sound and "began calling for the music." Pentecostal churches, with their particular kind of worship in pews and on radio airwaves, became important safe spaces for musical demonstration and were receptive toward gospel music before it became acceptable in mainstream church life. To Sanctified and Spiritualist churches, radio airwaves were seen in a similar light as race records: not inherently sinful but another means through which to spread the message of God to the larger world. Through radio programming, large Sanctified churches, the even more controversial Spiritualist churches, and local secular radio shows helped create the imagined religious community that would recognize and rejoice in the gospel music transformation of sacred worship.[65]

At the inception of black voices on the airwaves, Sanctified and Spiritualist churches played a key role in ways that changed both religion and radio. Consistent with the aggressive missionary style of those churches, the radio was a logical extension of Sanctified revivals on the street and race records, long before mainstream black churches even considered the power of this relatively new popular technology. Many small independent radio stations began selling time to black churches by the 1930s, with remote broadcasts being the dominant mode of religious programming. The centrality of music performed both by choirs and pastors on radio demonstrated how church broadcasts were principally "gospel" in style and form. Radio broadcasters universally agreed that because studio shows were divorced from the church context, they lacked the power of remote broadcasts, so live sermons and musical performances became the standard format. At the same time, pastors placed a heavy emphasis on song, where programs were dominated by singing preachers and large choirs.[66]

As the new gospel sound was spreading through Chicago's black churches, many first heard the music through the sonic ministry of singing evangelists and Spiritualist preachers on the radio. Because of their gospel-powered ministry, these radio preachers were able to arguably reach "more Americans of both races than any group of Negroes in any communication medium." In Chicago, Clarence Cobbs's First Church of Deliverance began its show in 1930; former railroad porter and founder of the Greater Harvest Baptist Church, Louis Boddie, started to broadcast on WAAF in 1932; Elder Lucy

Smith's Church of All Nations followed suit in 1933; and COGIC pastor Bishop Roberts broadcast on WSBC as early as 1935. Radio was a powerful medium, but again these preachers were also good singers and spoke in a popular or vernacular language. Radio created a space where these "marginal" religious centers showcased their music ministry by transmitting a fascinating blend of old and new, foreign and familiar sounds to a larger listening community in the creation of a modern religious experience.[67]

Even before his radio program, Spiritualist pastor Cobbs and his First Church of Deliverance were both celebrated and berated because of his sacred world flamboyance, open association with politicians and policy gamblers, and quite public expressions of a gay male sexual charisma. While scholar Joseph Washington has called the Spiritualist faith a "house of religious prostitution," as a child he was also captivated lying in his "bed on Sunday nights listening to the fantastic music" on Cobbs's radio program. Whether described as fantastic or fanciful, Cobbs's self-conscious orchestration of contrast between his soft vocal tones and "the well trained but 'swingy' choir" with pianos, organs, electric guitars, and violins was universally deemed "the most famous" aural spectacle in gospel. Many in the Sanctified world from which the music emerged criticized Cobbs's exploits as too worldly, but his radio-driven religious vision drew in black and white listeners throughout the Midwest, saints and sinners alike.[68]

Only three years after Cobbs, Smith's radio ministry became a driving force in generating a large part of the gospel mass consumer base through the musical setting she created at her Pentecostal church outside the authority of old-line leadership. University of Chicago scholar Herbert Smith (no relation) attempted to fit Smith and her Church of All Nations' mass appeal within a sociological model offered by E. Franklin Frazier's *The Negro Family in Chicago*. Herbert Smith argued that All Nations was a "church of the disinherited group" of what Frazier called the "ignorant and impoverished peasant families" unable to fully assimilate into the normative patterns of urban modernization.[69] His study revealed a social scientific fascination with worship at All Nations as something foreign, different, and from another time. He described All Nations as a "primitive Christian church" where the emotionally explosive and frenzied efforts at salvation were accompanied by a "babel of voices" that "shouted unintelligible words" of praise.[70]

Moreover, personal profiles of Smith as "corpulent" and "dark-skinned" reminded people like Herbert Smith of "Aunt Jemima" and promoted an image of the Sanctified faith as a variably urban or rural primitivism. She was further described as "simple, ignorant and untrained" with an "un-schooled" language. Other preachers suggested that Smith's appearance and demeanor are why she reached "a group of people that none of us can get to." Accordingly, worship at All Nations was presented as "a flight from reality" for the "city's socially disinherited." In reality, this Pentecostal "Aunt Je-mima" figure was able to construct two new church buildings, establish a peak congregation of 5,000 members, start a live radio worship show on three stations, and win the approval of both civic and religious leaders across all racial and class lines.[71]

All over the city, "Smith's vernacular speech, preaching style and the church's frenzied worship services struck a responsive chord." However, the main attraction reported over and over again, with both fascination and derision, was the power of music within All Nations' healing services. In one account, Herbert Smith described the songs as of the ordinary "Billy Sunday revival type" but different because they were "syncopated with an ever-increasing tempo" to accompany the increased intensity of praise. Reports argued that "one of the most interesting features about this church is the band."[72] Herbert Smith dismissed the choir's music as "jazz, savage and imperious," but it was precisely this "different" kind of music—essentially the church's promotion of the gospel sound—that catapulted All Nations to a "staple of Chicago nightlife," which in turn helped further propel the music.[73]

All Nations had a 100-voice choir accompanied by the church orchestra, which included an organist, pianist, drummer, and guitarist and sometimes even a French horn and coronet. On occasion, Smith's granddaughter, Little Lucy, was featured vocalist. The mass appeal of the "jazzy hymn playing" at All Nations also powered Smith's pioneering exploits in religious radio pro-gramming. In 1933, Smith debuted her live worship radio program in the city, *The Glorious Church of the Air.* Her tenure on the radio challenged accounts of the wholesale diluting, homogenizing, and demoralizing effects of commodification on black cultural production. In the case of Smith, she appropriated the airwaves of three different stations (including WIND, WCFL, and WGES) to transmit her "live" faith healing and music ministry as far away as Mexico. Smith was also able to utilize the far reach of radio to expand her charitable donations program during the Depression.

The Glorious Church of the Air did not just consolidate the independent authority of Smith's unique ministry; it also became an important space for the demonstration of what Herbert Smith called "syncopated" music, other-

Elder Lucy Smith, ca. 1920s. (Courtesy of the Vivian G. Harsh Research Collection of Afro-American History and Literature, Carter G. Woodson Regional Library, Chicago Public Library)

wise known as the gospel sound. Smith directly promoted the mass-market exploits of Dorsey and his NCGCC. Smith's choir sang original compositions and arrangements of hymns but also instantly embraced Dorsey's songs. Furthermore, local singers and NCGCC demonstrators, including Jackson and Martin, frequently appeared on Smith's radio program with Dorsey on piano.[74]

At the height of her gospel radio prominence, Smith had the respect of both religious and civic leaders, making it decidedly true that if one wanted to find someone "on a Sunday night, go to Elder Lucy Smith's." The significance of this radio program helped make Smith "the most widely known of all women pastors in Chicago" but also provided an important worship context and showcase for Dorsey's gospel songs. Dorsey's ability to demonstrate his songs, not just in old-line churches but in Sanctified parishes and on radio airwaves, is an important component of the music's ascendancy. For different reasons, pastors like Cobbs and Smith and musicians like Dorsey and Martin turned to the mass marketplace to bypass community traditions, strengthen their legitimacy through a consumer patron base, and then delve back into traditional community organizations to establish new standards. The convergence of migrant musical and religious interests on the mass marketplace in the early 1930s marks not just a "religious transformation" but also an important realignment of cultural authority within the black public sphere. However, Dorsey was not entirely enthused with how far gospel music had come. Once gospel music and its openness to improvisational interpretation began to take on a life of its own, Dorsey again grew anxious about his control over the sound in ways that had been foreshadowed by his struggles with both Martin and Jackson.[75]

There is no question that the gospel texts and organizational strategies of Dorsey were a driving force in the emergence of gospel music popularity and legitimacy. However, the mass appeal and marketing of gospel music exposes larger religious struggles and intellectual dialogues among parishioners, consumers, music producers, and preachers within Chicago's sacred world. Shifting focus to the important realm of demonstration strategies forces us to consider the role of (primarily) women singing evangelists and demonstrators who catered to the important sacred tastes of working-class migrant patrons as key figures shaping Chicago's marketplace intellectual life. Alongside Dorsey's "author"-ship, a whole host of actors helped prepare the necessary consumer context for gospel music's reception and ascendancy in ways that frustrated even Dorsey as the gospel sound eclipsed concert spirituals to become the most recognizable New Negro symbol of black sacred modernity. However, this cultural revolution did not stop at the altar call. Gospel music's sonic bumps and grinds, trills and embellishments, and calls for rebellion against bodily restraint physically reverberated out onto for-profit playing fields with their double-time, pivot move, counter-punch politics in the muscularly amazing spectacle of Chicago's black sporting life.

Chapter Six

The Sporting Life

RECREATION, SELF-RELIANCE, AND
COMPETING VISIONS OF RACE MANHOOD

Art and athletics furnish the greatest opportunity
for the American Negro, to demonstrate, that he acts and
re-acts, to all human activities, just as all other people.
—*Baltimore Afro-American*, July 14, 1928

As for Rube Foster, well, if it were in the power of the
colored people to honor him politically or to raise him to the
station to which they believe he is entitled, Booker T. Washington
would have to be content with second place.
—Frederick North Shorey, Indianapolis *Freeman*,
September 7, 1907

Two years after his historic 1910 defeat of Jim Jeffries, Jack Johnson gave an address at a Chicago theater where he seemed to realize the larger significance of the victory. Johnson reflected that he "used to see white folks celebrating on July 4," but his defeat of Jeffries gave members of the race "an equal chance to make merry on that day." More than just a general celebration, the nationwide, unprecedented, collective, and excessive black occupation of public space after the fight matched the frustratingly extravagant ways in which this southern migrant from Galveston, Texas, executed lopsided victories and lived his public life in Chicago. In fact, Chicago's mayor and police chief outlawed a parade upon Johnson's return on July 6, 1910, but Robert Motts and the reception committee still took him on a city tour with "decorated autos" to his home adorned with a picture of Johnson "surrounded by American flags." This informal processional then moved to the Pekin Theatre where "his pathway was strewn with flowers [and] rich and poor alike lost distinction in the crushing throng" while the famous Eighth Regiment Band belted out not "The Star Spangled Banner" but a jazzed-up "There'll Be a Hot Time in the Old Town Tonight."[1]

The case of Johnson makes clear that the larger realm of sport or "physical culture" is an important stage where the dramas of social relations are reinforced, magnified, and sometimes directly challenged. At the outset, black participation in and production of both amateur and commercial recreation events have simultaneously been appeals for racial integration while also "playing out" moments of race pride and distinction. However, studies of race and athletics are rarely spatially and geographically situated, and Chicago was a central place in the rise of a black "sporting life." On the surface, the sporting life ran counter to visions of black and white reformers who believed that a strict work ethic and/or knowledge of the "higher arts" were the sole routes to interracial understanding, self-reliance, and respectability. At best, black and white advocates of recreation and physical culture modernized the relationship between sport and social discipline that, not coincidentally, had been perfected in the era of slavery in larger attempts to produce efficient and sober workers, American citizens, and, within the old settler model, even new "race men."[2]

As recreation moved further into the commercial world, however, "sporting life" displays of the New Negro no longer exclusively relied on Victorian, industrial, or race uplift visions of specifically black manhood. The virile masculinity of Johnson, the "scientific" prowess of baseball's Chicago American Giants, and the efficient speed of the Chicago Blackhawks on the gridiron began to place, according to some, "art and athletics" alongside each other as parallel expressions of the mental and physical power of New Negroes. Some even argued that the success of sports entrepreneurs forced noted individuals, like Booker T. Washington, "to be content with second place" within the circles of race leadership. Events such as the Savoy Big Five and Harlem Globetrotters (from Chicago, never from Harlem) basketball spectacles, with their halftime jazz dances, or the NNL's East-West All-Star baseball game, which was held in Chicago every summer, used the marketplace to express black dignity, distinction, and even defiance of black bodily servitude.

However, this "room to play" with conventional models of race and masculinity also caused problems for the aspiring class of black sports entrepreneurs when the "raucous" acts of consumer patrons and players compromised any pure image of old settler respectability. Moreover, within the sporting life, the term "sport" took on both meanings of the word as much of the startup capital for most sports—athletic enterprises—was generated by sports in the informal economy, and through policy gambling in particular. The "sporting life" public sphere within the larger marketplace intellectual life provided a relative autonomy where athletes, owners, and fans produced competing styles of bodily labor, along with new racial identifications on the field, in the front office, and in the stands. The specter of Johnson is again useful here to begin untangling the convergence of race pride, class conflict, and a muscular masculinity that collided in the name of sport and challenged the conventional "order of things."[3]

DISTINCTION, DEFIANCE, AND DANDYISM: JACK JOHNSON AND THE (RE)CONSTRUCTION OF REPRESENTATIVE RACE MANHOOD

Johnson's victory and those celebrating him represented a very real vocal and physical dissension against the social order, announcing an alternative, but nonetheless overwhelmingly masculine, way of being. The sporting sphere offered New Negro expressions of black ownership over body, behavior, and community through varying ideas about gender. General meanings of power and defiance were expressly "played out" through the gendered metaphors of masculinity as physical virility and athletic aggression, while femininity was athletically marked by competitive passiveness and bodily/playing field penetration. But it is still important to engage the general masculinist space of the black sporting life and, in particular, the varying intellectual positions about Johnson as a representative race figure (including his own). Ideas about

Johnson foretold how shifting meanings of race, class, and community were (and continue to be) worked out at the site of masculine physicality in ways that profoundly shaped the emerging black modern experience.[4]

Johnson and other athletes not nearly as controversial represented a new modern position on race manhood somewhere between the archetypes of Washington's skilled trade laborer and W. E. B. Du Bois's "talented tenth" professional/intellectual. Washington and Du Bois are usually presented as promoting competing visions of masculinity: a Victorian accommodationist orientation toward a privatized economic productivity versus modern public agitation and advocacy for full rights as citizens. However, in many regards, both positions shared a focus on the repression or at least disciplining of the body toward "higher" moral ideals. Whether public humility or rights-based citizenship was the divergent means, moral character and racial uplift remained the shared end. However, the "sporting life" masculinity that Johnson represented did not set up a hierarchy between mind and body, but, in a fashion parallel to demonstrative worship, bodily adornment, and theatergoing behaviors, it exalted personality, sexuality, and the physical exterior as the expression of a new race consciousness. The legacy of slavery legitimized arguments for both bodily repression and expression while also exposing the emerging class-based stances of each position. In many ways, those of the "better class" wanted to distinguish themselves (through restraint) from the slave body as one of inherent promiscuity, laziness, and inferiority. After Johnson's victory, however, many took the white *Chicago Daily Inter Ocean* pronouncement, "Son of a Slave Is Made Master," quite literally.[5]

Particularly, migrants, sharecroppers, and domestics were the physical inheritors of the slave body politic. Therefore, self-mastery and transformation of the ex-slave body into a beautiful, desirable, and self-controlled (but not necessarily restrained) body was key to pragmatic expressions of freedom and agency that defied Victorian/modern distinctions. In testament to this wider spectrum of manhood, some "sporting" men were college-educated but sought the economic advantages and relative labor autonomy provided in the mass culture of play, while others were barely literate but established social mobility through elitist rules of disciplined athletic performance and gentlemanly conduct. Generally, these New Negro athletes were staunch advocates of radical integration but on the grounds of both mental and physical ability. Therefore, Johnson predated both black and white articulations of modern masculinity. As many black observers predicted, images of appropriate race manhood, inside and outside of sports, would be running away from or placed in comparison with the specter of Johnson (that is, how not to act) for decades. But just what was it specifically about Johnson's athletic masculinity that made his influence on black and white lives so profound?[6]

As a physical specimen, Johnson was an ominous being. But in addition, he was conscious of the kind of racial and gendered notions associated with his performance of personhood, and in many ways he played with those very ideas. Yet, Johnson's extremely public self-presentation within the larger racist world gave his personal exploits a politically symbolic meaning. First, as a boxer, his cerebral physicality, as a "ring scientist in a day of ring laborers," solidified Johnson's position within the marketplace intellectual life, according to his 1927 autobiography, both "in the ring and out." In the ring, Johnson exhibited a defensive boxing genius by crafting an elaborate battery of counterpunches, deploying sports psychology, and capitalizing on keen observations of his opponents' tendencies, especially in a racist world where "if he kept order in the ring he was lazy" and "if he damaged his opponents he was a brute."

Second, the white male heavyweight body, as a symbol of supreme virile physicality, represented the apex of manhood in the shift from Victorian to modern America. The fact that Johnson had a comparable—and some say superior—muscular physique but was using it for prizefighting and interracial desire and not for manual labor caused a severe level of anxiety in the racial order.[7]

Third, Johnson consciously played on white stereotypes about black masculinity through, for example, the oft-told act of wrapping his penis in gauze to increase its perceived size. At the same time that his muscular body was draped in multicolored robes and gauze, emanating a black sex appeal, Johnson was equally quick-witted and seemed to fully understand his place in the racial world, challenging and transgressing that very place with a style of arrogance complete with a British accent. He flashed an extravagant smile full of gold teeth at insults that were supposedly effective in making black fighters easily lose mental concentration. Johnson offered quick repartee to both white fighters and fans while defeating his opponents. For example, when Tommy Burns leveled the popular claim that black people were inherently yellow during a fight, Johnson quickly replied, "You're white Tommy— white as the flag of surrender!" For many black people, Johnson was able to do what they could not: talk back to a white man, knock him out, and then take "his woman," all on a world stage and without an automatic reprieve to the lynch rope. The relative protection or at least expression of aggressive black power found on playing fields was instrumental to a sporting life expression of New Negro masculinity.[8]

Jack Johnson, ca. 1901. (Courtesy of the Al-Tony Gilmore Collection)

Probably one of the most antagonistic aspects of Johnson's persona was that he did not leave his arrogance in the ring but carried his excessive performance of black masculinity to the street. Through his attention to self-presentation, embodied in media savvy, quick wit, fast cars, and expensive suits, Johnson took on the persona of a dandy (the 1969 edition of his autobiography was even retitled *Jack Johnson Is a Dandy*). Prosperity also gave Johnson a literal kind of mobility, privilege, and worldliness that was certainly not afforded most African Americans, nor even many white Americans at the time. He bought an expensive roadster only a year after such imports first landed on U.S. shores and proceeded to drive this symbol of modernity with reckless abandon all through what were deemed white public spaces. One time Johnson drove his "big red devil auto" up on the sidewalk of Chicago's Michigan Avenue, receiving a warning from the police but also "admiration from the Negroes of the South Side." This roadster also transported him to his lavish black-and-tan saloon, the Café de Champion, where visitors were awed by wall-size portraits of Cleopatra represented as a black woman and Johnson's acquisition of the ultimate commodity in a racist world—white women. In fact, to balance a more feminized dandyism with traditional images of manhood, Johnson was equally notorious for engaging in domestic violence. He also ironically believed that while finding his own racial freedom and wives in the saloon, the public "activities of the 'new woman'" brought women "down from the pedestal" and out of their "natural place" in the home. Yet, outside of the physical violence against women, Johnson's performance of a hypermasculine dandy persona remained a source of race pride within the spaces of black popular culture, folklore, and politics.[9]

A series of jokes and bits of folklore chronicling Johnson's life stood powerfully alongside the very physical moments of resistance expressed in working-class celebrations of his exploits. Jokes about Johnson allowed the teller (usually a man) to take ownership of victory, mobility, and the metaphorical conquest of white womanhood by literally getting the last word. It was reported that in Indiana, "Open Mouth Johnson" went into a grill and ordered "a cup of coffee as strong and black as Jack Johnson and a steak beat up like Jim Jeffries." In Brooklyn, a black man told his dog "Jeffries" to lie down. A white man then asked why he didn't call the dog Johnson, and the black man responded, "Because Johnson is black and this dog is yellow." Johnson's "possession" of white women, considered "beating the white man at his own game," was also celebrated in another joke. Here, a Jim Crow hotel denied Johnson service because they "didn't serve his kind." He then reportedly laughed, pulled out a roll of money, and said, "Oh, you misunderstand me, I don't want it for myself, I want it for my wife—she's your kind." Becoming Johnson, within the ironic space of the joke and many times within earshot of white listeners, allowed the teller to invert the traditional roles of racial power through parody and laugh at "the ways of white folks" in their very presence. However, Johnson's activities also caused very real repercussions for black communities, where the effects of simply acting like Johnson in public spaces ranged from racial violence to the loss of jobs.[10]

Anxieties within black leadership about Johnson were most directly fed by the condemnations put forth in the white press that, while varied, found harmony in the key of black humility. For example, after the 1910 Johnson-Jeffries fight, the *Los Angeles Times* tellingly sought to discourage aggressive postfight race pride, foreshadowing proscriptions directed at black migrants across the country six years later: "Do not point your nose too high. Do not swell your chest too much. Do not boast too loudly. Do not be puffed up. Let not your ambition be inordinate or take a wrong direction. . . . Your place in the world is just what it was."[11] Moreover, as soon as Johnson defeated and demoralized the white Jeffries, and hence white science and white superiority, some tellingly wondered if even Victorian biologist and social philosopher "Herbert Spencer [could] extract comfort from so dread a situation." There was a rush to reestablish a racial science that justified the social logic of white on top and black on bottom.[12]

Politicians, ministers, and critics attempted to blot out Johnson's public display of black dominance by banning the fight films on the grounds of their immorality; some even proclaimed Johnson may have been "black on the outside," but his boxing skills showed that he was "white in conduct." Finally, most disconnected dominance in the ring from the manly domain of racial superiority, civilization, and virtue altogether. As soon as Johnson won, white commentators scrambled to remind "the Black Man . . . [that] brains count for more than muscle" and that white superiority rested on "brain development that has weighed worlds and charmed the most subtle secrets from the heart of nature."[13] These various pronouncements helped popularize and solidify what I call the *paradox of playfulness*.

This paradox refers to the ongoing and shifting contours of racial science that connected black failure in sport to an inherent biological or cultural inferiority. Yet in the face of black athletic success, the same science simultaneously became a rationale for black physical superiority due to an innate mental deficiency, the ancestral legacy of a "primitive" African past, and/or measurable anatomical differences in black bodies. The true paradox is that racial science has always been unstable, unscientific, and challenged within mainstream science. Yet up to the present, it continues to find legitimacy in the "everyday" or vernacular intellectual discourse of sports analysis and journalism. Present-day beliefs like "white men can't jump" and "black men are physically gifted" find "scientific" roots in turn-of-the-century discourse and directly challenge the notion that sport is an inherently merit-based, color-blind, and "level playing field."[14]

Such white condemnations, dismissals, and reappraisals of race, science, and sport were pervasive and universally threatening to racial uplift, yet there was no uniform response within the circles of black leadership. Community opinions about Johnson, for example, ranged from seeing him as "racial asset" to "failure as a representative of the race" to racial "menace." That there was a debate, especially after Johnson's controversies outside the ring, reveals a backlash to loosening Victorian values but also the rise of a third position on race manhood with the "sporting life" at its center. After Johnson was charged with violating the Mann Act—the trafficking of white women across state lines for "immoral purposes"—most could not understand why he chose a "white prostitute over a Black woman." But many also protested that the immoral abuse of black women at the hands of white men was much more significant and that Johnson was primarily a target of "race prejudice." Most black reformers and leaders spoke in general race terms, but their comments reveal a specific concern for a loss in personal contacts with the "better class" across the color line because of Johnson's actions.[15]

Even before the Mann Act case, those associated with the extremely powerful and prominent "Tuskegee Machine" tried to steer Johnson in the direction of Washington as a male role model. Such prescriptions made clear both Washington's prominence and the threat of the "Negro's Deliverer" to the "Wizard of Tuskegee." Johnson's ideas and actions posed at the very least a symbolic challenge to the prolonged relegation of black people to a Victorian moral system as the country moved into a modern era. Tellingly, the Tuskegee-funded *New York Age* asked Johnson to conduct himself in a "modest manner" and avoid "making a useless, noisy exhibition of himself." An editorial in the same edition put it bluntly: "One Booker Washington is worth millions of Jack Johnsons," continuing that Johnson would do well to become "a large prosperous farmer," while Washington's secretary Emmett J. Scott even wrote Johnson to encourage him to follow Washington's example of "simplicity and humility of bearing."[16]

After the successful prosecution of Johnson in the courts, Washington himself went against his own directive to never personally attack another prominent race figure, proclaiming Johnson was "doing a grave injustice to his race." He went on to say, "Chicago is now witnessing a good example of the result of educating a man to earn money without due attention having been given his mental and spiritual development." Totally out of character, Washington "blame[d] the White men for Johnson's prominence." However, the contradictions embedded within both the over-the-top condemnation of Johnson by the "Tuskegee Machine" and the unfair representation of the Mann Act case in the mainstream white papers galvanized a community-wide backlash. The black professional managerial class then offered a much needed, albeit ambivalent, critique of the white supremacy shaping Johnson's persecution, finally catching up to shifts in the collective race consciousness first found in the streets and jokes after July 4, 1910.[17]

With typical prophetic insight and poignant clarity, Du Bois took a divergent position on the "hysteria" surrounding Johnson's "slaving" charges. In the *Crisis*, Du Bois questioned "mixed" marriages in general but socially defended the right of two adults of any color to marry, because legally documented unions could protect black women from the "lust of white men." However, Du Bois's national voice was not alone in this emerging sentiment of professional race manhood, as black agitation took on positions that were particular to Johnson's Chicago context.[18]

After his victory, Johnson was accused of remarking that he "could get any white woman he wanted . . . with his money" and was summoned before the Appomattox Club, a prominent organization of black professional men, including later sports entrepreneurs Julius Taylor and Beauregard Moseley. In his defense at the meeting, Johnson poignantly replied, "I am not a slave and . . . have the right to choose who my mate shall be without dictation of any man." This professional organization subsequently issued a statement first assuring "white citizens" of black commitment to "moral uplift." They then provided a lukewarm defense of Johnson with the corroboration of a "white man," finally offering a plea for whites to not "indict the entire negro race" for the actions of one. The *Chicago Broad Ax* offered parallel reports of the club meeting and another telling headline: "BOOKER T. WASHINGTON SENT TO THE MAT BY CHAMPION JACK." In the article, Johnson directly responded to Washington's condemnation with the quip, "I never got caught in the wrong flat. I never got beat up because I looked in the wrong key hole." When Washington surprisingly blamed white men for Johnson's popularity, the *Broad Ax* countered that the same finger of white influence could be pointed at the "Wizard," because "from whom did Mr. Washington get his prominence?" In a headline they went on to chide, "Booker T. Washington the

Great Wizard of Tuskegee Does Not Like to Share His Popularity with Jack Johnson." The *Broad Ax* further argued that Washington's targeting "of his only serious rival in popularity with the Colored people of the country" only won applause with white people and helped him retain favor at the White House.[19]

Washington held a significant amount of favor with white leaders, yet Johnson challenged his authority in both deed and word. Johnson explicitly denounced the Wizard's infamous concession to sit in a dining room separate from Theodore Roosevelt and his family just so he could eat at the White House and later added, "White people often point to the writings of Booker T. Washington as the best example of a desirable attitude on the part of the colored population. I have never been able to agree with the point of view of Washington, because he has to my mind not been altogether frank in the statement of the problem or courageous in the formulation in his solutions to them." In the *Chicago Defender*, a Milwaukee woman agreed and scoffed more generally at the "very idea of the best thinking people of the race holding 'indignation meetings'" to denounce Johnson. In her mind, Johnson "represents the race more nearly than the so-called self-respectful ones." In self-imposed exile after the Mann Act controversy and even in death, Johnson remained a central "model . . . of action and emulation for other Black people" in the pronounced "New Negro" era of the 1920s and even in the leftist "Black Popular Front" of the 1930s.[20]

During the Red Summer of 1919, Johnson was in exile in Mexico, but still his earlier "wild escapades" were blamed for spawning "the very beginning of race hatred" in Chicago that sparked the riots. And of course Johnson had a reply from across the border. In an ad for the Jack Johnson Land Company advertised in the leftist IWW periodical *Gale's Magazine* and reprinted in the black radical *Messenger* magazine, Johnson told "Colored People: You are lynched, tortured, mobbed, persecuted and discriminated against in the 'boasted' land of liberty; own a home in Mexico, where one [man] is as good as another, and it is not your color that counts, but simply you." In another speech, an American spy reported that Johnson had told Mexicans that if the United States and Mexico went to war, black people would stand with their Mexican brothers against the gringo invaders.[21]

It took two decades for the next black heavyweight champion, Joe Louis, to emerge, not coincidentally as the "anti-Johnson." However, young black radical thinkers of the 1930s and 1940s reclaimed the symbolic importance of Johnson as a political model, precisely because of his brash masculine arrogance and dandy style. In a memorial column, what Joseph Bibb, co-editor of the radical *Chicago Whip*, remembered most was the way Johnson counseled him *and* "turned wide" in his "flashing car." Essayist George Schuyler added that Johnson drove fast, dressed well, and said "what he pleased, not trying to please either colored or white folks by acting as they thought a prominent man should act" at a time "when white terrorism against Negroes was rampant." Writer Ralph Ellison concluded that Johnson was "rejected by most whites and many respectable Negroes but he was nevertheless . . . one of the most admired underground heroes." As these divergent interpretations show, Johnson established a new model of modern black masculinity. Whether because of fear or of fascination with what he represented, leaders, reformers, and scientists scrambled to redefine race manhood, social respectability, and national belonging.[22]

Interestingly, most white dismissals and rationale for what happened at the Johnson-Jeffries fight were articulated through a language of scientific certainty that continually evaded any suggestion that hard work, discipline, and cultural creativity were black possibilities. Despite the dangerous implications, athletics were such a powerful national spectacle that even under the ominous and immediate shadow of Johnson, moral reformers and race leaders could not afford to fully denounce or abandon sport but had to figure out how to manipulate and struggle within it.[23]

SCOLDS AND SPORTS: THE INDUSTRIOUS (RE)CREATION AND
REFORM OF PHYSICAL CULTURE

Early-twentieth-century strikes, race riots, and popular cultures (including the "Jack Johnson Affair") transformed the urban landscape, and city fathers, their professional managers, and race reformers turned to recreation and play as possible means for social control. The general rationale was that recreation could be a viable field where instructions on citizenship and technologies of cultural assimilation might be worked out. On one side, mainstream theories of "Muscular Christianity" and the "Strenuous Life" sought to counter the perceived prevalence of nervous, hysterical, effeminate white men collectively diagnosed with "neurasthenia" and seemingly unfit for the modern era.[24] These strategies found parallels in the "Playground Movement" and factory leagues, where athletic programs were meant to instill efficiency, sobriety, teamwork, and citizenship in both young white boys and the children of "foreign" workers. On the other side, black educational, civic, and church organizations positioned recreation programs as a physical manifestation of larger bids for respectable New Negro manhood and national inclusion. Both projects attempted to place a high premium on "amateurism," with varying levels of success. This strategy of athletic acculturation was clearly a response to waning white science and the threatening migrant working-class black power that surfaced when the sporting life dangerously veered toward professionalization in 1910.[25]

First, a growing concern over the moral state of white masculinity during urbanization at the turn of the century helped shift the specifically religious discourse around the body from one of dismissive repression to supervisory rejuvenation. The ideology of Muscular Christianity advocated that competitive and especially team sports, physical education, and vigorous recreation now had an ethical basis, where physical activities taught lessons of manliness, morality, health, and even patriotism. The connection between racial masculinity, character development, and physical activity was further strengthened by then colonel Theodore Roosevelt's call for a "Strenuous Life." Here physical conflict, like that on the "natural" frontiers of the Caribbean and Asian Pacific, was thought to impose discipline, endurance, honor, and courage on the white male body while purifying the soul of a multiracial imperial nation. These ideals found institutional legitimacy through YMCA, university, playground, and industrial recreation programs, especially in cities like Chicago where masculine and moral decay seemed most acute.[26]

At the forefront of programs in recreational uplift, Chicago hosted the first convention of the Playground Association of America in 1907, where Roosevelt praised the city's elaborate park system. The YMCA-influenced Playground and Recreation Association, generally known as the Playground Movement, was particularly aimed at white boys considered overly domesticated and at immigrant and migrant youth who required Americanization. Alongside retreats outside of the city organized by groups like the Boy Scouts, playgrounds became "natural" preserves in the middle of urban decay where supervised play could counter the closed-off, diseased, and vice-ridden lure of "foreign" immigrant cultures reportedly found in dance halls, taverns, and moving picture shows.[27]

Black middle-class professionals and intellectuals had their own struggles with urban industrialization and shared a similar desire to use physical training and bodily discipline to build, preserve, and assert their manhood. Physical culture was deployed to contest the onslaught of white racism and of those Du Bois described as the "dangerous class" of black "criminals, gamblers, and loafers" thought to be entering cities among the growing population of migrants. As the process of migration captured the hearts, minds, and bodies of black southerners, black reformers developed a more formalized approach to recreation that resembled but was still distinct from the Muscular Christian philosophy.[28]

Black recreational leaders, also described as "Muscular Assimilationists," emphasized the broader meaning of athletics, not as a safety valve to preserve the past, but as a platform for social change. Masculine performance could protect old settler physical prowess, build character in new settlers, and demonstrate black mental and muscular racial equality—and for some, even superiority—on playing fields. Like mainstream Muscular Christians, New Negro reformers positioned recreation as an amateur endeavor where the demands for victory and lure of "the purse" would not defile the higher ideals of moral purity and racial uplift. Du Bois vigorously campaigned to rescue the promises of play and amusement from the repressive reticence the black church held toward the body. Du Bois shared the opinion of film reformer Jean Voltaire Smith that, especially in urban space, a traditional stance of banning recreation only pushed black youth into the excessive amusements of "dissipation and vice." He continued, "If properly limited and directed . . . between repression and excess," any amusement could "be a positive gain to any society."[29]

Black educators, ministers, social workers, and recreation leaders, like Edwin B. Henderson, William H. Jones, and Emmett J. Scott, echoed the sentiments of Du Bois. In an appeal to the white Playground Movement community for equal facilities, Scott went as far as to specifically highlight Jack Johnson as a symbolic warning of the "lower ideal" that could influence other black people if left to their own devices, especially as "several million colored people are living and will continue to live in close proximity to the rest of the people who reside in America." The institutional presence of parks and YMCAs in cities like Chicago became key physical spaces for articulating black reformers' appeals for equal recreation facilities, regulated amusement, and manly citizenship.[30]

Ideally, Chicago playgrounds were a logical site where the disciplining technologies of Muscular Assimilation could be administered on black men and boys. However, initially, organized recreation became a symbol of racial restriction and violence. As the Great Migration increased the population of Chicago's Black Belt, it was dangerous for residents to go to one of the twenty-nine better-equipped recreation centers, none of which were centrally located in the black neighborhood. Also, while there were fourteen playgrounds within the Black Belt by 1919, residents were heavily discouraged, even by white playground directors, from venturing outside their neighborhood with threat of violence at the hands of white ethnic "athletic clubs." For example, Washington Park touched both black and Irish neighborhoods, but even non-Irish white residents protested black use of baseball diamonds in the park as an infringement on "Irish turf." Indeed, the spark for the race riots of 1919 was a racial contest over recreation space, when young Eugene Williams floated too far into "white" water at 29th Street Beach. In the face of such visceral resistance and the refusal of local YMCAs to integrate, black residents took advantage of sympathetic white philanthropy to build a separate facility. With substantial funds from Sears and Roebuck entrepreneur Julius Rosenwald and additional community donations, the Wabash Avenue YMCA opened in 1913, a symbol of industrial discipline and "rugged individualist" assimilation for some and of a space for race-based pleasure and profit for others.[31]

The Wabash YMCA, like other branches, became an especially acute site of "welfare capitalism," where social programs were developed to secure worker loyalty to Chicago's major manufacturing companies by reforming the way workers related to both superiors and peers. With support from major Chicago companies, the separate all-black Wabash YMCA created an Industrial Department that encouraged a racially stratified program of worker Americanization. Before gymnasium use, old settler leaders, including George Cleveland Hall, chief of surgery at Provident Hospital, gave lectures on "young manhood and proper training." At the same time, black citizens were consistently restricted to all-black teams at the segregated Wabash Y. This in some ways fostered a stronger sense of race pride based on athletic, even professional, competition above and beyond the "higher ideals" of sport as exclusively an expression of amateur character development. The consistently ambiguous rise of semiprofessional basketball on the gymnasium floor of the Wabash Y highlights the ideological struggle over sport as an expression of (amateur) character development or (professionalized) competitive race pride.[32]

In between *Chicago Defender* box scores for cricket, baseball, and basketball and coverage of industrial, Sunday school, post office branch, and veteran leagues, a debate simmered about the merits of a strictly Muscular Assimilationist approach to sport as an expression of amateur character development. In an early essay, sportswriter Frank A. Young was forced to defend the all-inclusive character-building policy of the Wabash YMCA against community appeals for an elite competitive and winning basketball five. In his mind, the preferential treatment afforded a "cracker jack basketball team of five men" bordered on professionalism. The *Defender* went on to republish an article written by Edward Delaporte, assistant supervisor of physical education for Chicago high schools, outlining distinctions between the "amateur" and the "sport" athlete. For Delaporte, the difference was not just a question of payment for play but one of motive as exhibited by behavior. In his mind, "True amateurism stands for a high sense of . . . *temperance*" in behavior and for participation "purely for the pleasure of the game," while "others" play for "victory, the prize or the plaudits of an audience" (emphasis added). Finally, Henry R. Crawford, Wabash Y director of physical education, attacked the development of the semiprofessional category because it gave rise to ambiguously defined athletic clubs that encouraged athletes to leave college teams and/or play on multiple teams in search of higher pay. The idea of competition was especially acute when games were against white opponents. Here, race pride was on the line, and demands for victory seemed to trump pure character development.[33]

When the *Chicago Defender* witnessed the interracial crowds drawn by the elite Forty Club's basketball team, the paper began contributing sponsorship in 1921 (renaming it the Defender Athletic Club) along with an annual tournament between black and white teams thereafter. Most of the community's players had been or were still members of the Wendell Phillips High School basketball team that, sometimes under *Defender* sponsorship or as the Wabash Outlaws, played in a number of intercity games against top black teams across the country. Such brushes with professionalism disqualified Phillips from the 1927 high school playoffs. When the Phillips heavyweight team eventually became city champions in 1930, they were then denied the customary invitation to A. A. Stagg's National Championship at the University of Chicago. Clearly, Stagg's desire for box-office draw from southern states outweighed his Muscular Christian principles of honor, discipline, and courage. Phillips avenged this affront by participating in the next year's tournament after Stagg retired.[34]

Despite the aims of athletic reformers (including Wabash physical education director Crawford) to erect moral walls between amateurism and professionalism, character building and competition, moral progress and pleasure, the actually existing black migrant engagement with the professional sporting life in many ways complicated such divides. Athletes no longer simply wanted to exhibit muscular and mental equality with whites through physical character building. Both black athletes and the larger community sought to demonstrate superiority or at least retribution in an arena where equality, in the minds of many, was a given. Black interest in sporting competition over and above character building was part of America's growing worship of athletic prowess but took on a racially specific importance of achievement when black athletes triumphed over white opponents. Black consumer patron investment in athletics partially demanded victory as a symbolic power over racial restrictions, while athletic participants began to contest the contradictions of the amateur/professional divide as another race and class barrier to urban labor. Moreover, the turn to professional athletics as an alternative to racially stratified industrial labor existed alongside the avenues of beauty culture, filmmaking and performance, and music making within Chicago's New Negro world. The growing U.S. interest in sport during the 1920s helped nationalize the black sporting life consciousness as a site of pleasure, pride, employment, and entrepreneurship.

PROFESSIONAL PLAY: EMPLOYMENT, PROFIT, AND RACE PRIDE IN THE PAGEANT OF SPORT

James Weldon Johnson's 1930 cultural history, *Black Manhattan*, is immediately distinguishable from other studies of the Harlem Renaissance era because it situates actors, intellectuals, *and* athletes alongside each other as cultural producers of the New Negro experience. In many ways it is true that Johnson's chapter on athletics in *Black Manhattan* "adds the story of sports to the pageant of African American culture in ways that had not been elaborated before his time." But at the same time, his fuller reflections were precisely just that, (re)memories of a cultural world that did not make such harsh distinctions between various vocations. In fact, his history recalls the symbolic importance placed on Jack Johnson's defeat of Jim Jeffries, especially for migrants who could not see themselves represented in the world of arts and letters. This more complex sporting life further contextualizes Reverend Reverdy Ransom's comments in 1910 that positioned pugilistic exploits alongside the efforts of black sculptors, writers, and singers as part of a larger challenge to white supremacy. If we take these voices collectively as the call out from black bohemia in Harlem and beyond, Chicago's professional athletic world was a resounding response about the possibilities of adding, literally, a little "body" to an expanded understanding of the brilliance of the New Negro era.[35]

Baseball was the first sport to collectively capture the imagination of Chicago's black residents—and the rest of the country—with the earliest players active in white leagues and on integrated teams. However, with the formalization of the "Gentleman's Agreement" in 1898, barring black baseball players from the "major" leagues, the smaller formations of all-black amateur and variably professional teams quickly became the only sites for athletic participation. There are sporadic reports chronicling the existence of the all-amateur Blue Stockings and Chicago Uniques of the 1870s and early 1880s, while the Chicago Society Baseball League of the 1890s was best known as a space for old settler sociability.

With money from "policy king" Henry "Teenan" Jones and after struggles amid various teams (Columbia Giants, Page Fence Giants, Peter's Union Giants, and so on), the Unions formed in 1881, becoming a leading club in the (Mid)West by 1886. By 1888, they became the Chicago Unions and in 1901 emerged as the Chicago Union Giants, led by Frank Leland. As an old settler businessman and Republican Party politician, Leland managed what became the Leland Giants in 1905 as part of the predominantly white and successful Chicago City League. This move brought on the distinction of interracial sociability and the recreational status of the larger Playground Movement in the city.[36]

To offset overhead costs, in 1907 Leland joined with Appomattox Club members Robert R. Jackson, businessman, and Beauregard Moseley, lawyer/politician, to incorporate the Leland Giants Baseball and Amusement Association (LGBAA). They also developed a sports amusement complex at Auburn Park on 79th and Wentworth targeted at the tastes of the old settler class. Partially marketed within the logic of Playground Movement ideology, this commercial association administered a skating rink, restaurant, baseball team, and summer resort, the Chateau de la Plaisance, as part of a larger assortment of specifically old settler recreation amusements and refuge existing outside the unhealthy confines of black urban living. The location of the park required a relatively pricey "Electric Car ride," while it was advertised as a place where the better class could interact "unmolested or annoyed" by their black social inferiors in confining city spaces. Even with the threat of class mixing, ads promised that the "best of order [is] maintained at all times." Finally, the LGBAA wrapped its enterprise within a distinguished masculinity with a promotional photo package (created by Chicago filmmaker Peter Jones), containing profiles of players and the leading male figures in the association. LGBAA activities clearly sought to display a vision of racial respectability, but their expressions of recreational citizenship and freedom were understood almost exclusively as manhood rights for the "better class."[37]

The LGBAA provided the Leland Giants with more solid financial footing and encouraged black leaders to consider the idea of a National Colored League of Professional Baseball Clubs as further expression of old settler respectable manhood and professional leadership. However, transportation costs proved too high for teams outside the Midwest, so the league never came to fruition. After this failure, Leland forever lost credibility within the larger LGBAA organization, which at the same time opened the door for then Giants player Andrew "Rube" Foster's ascent to race man leadership as a player and manager of the team and eventual organizer of the National Negro League.[38]

As a notable pitcher on a Texas semipro team, Foster initially came to Chicago to play with the Leland Giants, then jumped to a white team in Michigan before pitching for the dominant Cuban X Giants in the East and leading the strong Philadelphia Giants to three consecutive "Colored World Championships" between 1903 and 1906. It was after Foster won a pitching duel against major league Philadelphia Athletics star Rube Wadell that people began to call Foster "the colored Rube Wadell," until his moniker was permanently shortened to "Rube." As a Philadelphia Giant, Foster also played in winter leagues in the southern United States and against the top black and white professional players in the Caribbean. Foster's success provided him the authority to pen the instructional essay "How to Pitch" in Sol White's important 1907 *Official Base Ball Guide.* Foster not only was a successful player but also keenly understood the market forces that shaped Chicago's sporting life.[39]

In 1906, white owners of black teams attempted to organize the National Association of Colored Baseball Clubs of the United States and Cuba. Part of their strategy to secure economic viability for the league was to collectively target and limit player salaries to discourage "player jumping" to the highest bidder. However, one of the central lures of professional baseball to the many agrarian workers and sharecroppers who opted to play ball was the ability to negotiate within a relatively free market. The proposed corporate model for the league system would limit that mobility. Foster specifically understood the value of free labor. He mobilized a number of star players to head to the Midwest as resistance against the emerging corporate league structure. The right to team-jump was a key element within notions of player manhood and autonomy.[40]

As an act of labor resistance, Foster argued that the white owners of black teams were acting in an unfair manner and urged players to unite and join him in Chicago as members of the Leland Giants. With the help of other star players from Philadelphia, Foster was able to meet his own opportunistic desires by jumping for better pay as player/manager, raising the stature of baseball in the Midwest. In a celebrated 1907 Leland victory over Mike

Donlin's All-Stars, made up of many notable white ex—big leaguers, the black community feted the leadership of Foster in ways that instigated a challenge to the color line in baseball and even conventional notions of race leadership. During this six-game series, a number of black "sports" won large sums of money, and crowds soared into the thousands—a larger attendance than at Chicago Cubs games. Black fans boasted athletic superiority among an integrated crowd, and the Giants were celebrated as the "pride of the entire population of Dearborn street." Foster capitalized on such victories and built an image of race pride and team distinction. In the same manner as Madam C. J. Walker, Oscar Micheaux, and Thomas Dorsey, the true power of Foster rested in his media savvy, promotional acumen, and ability to highlight the symbolic capital of events to increase his financial capital.[41]

Through financial support from the larger LGBAA, Foster became an almost mythic figure as he scheduled and reported victorious contests on unprecedented spring training tours south and west on a luxurious private Pullman car, with the team venturing as far as Cuba. After the failed attempts at league formation, combined with Foster's success as player/manager of the Leland Giants, a desire grew within him for complete autonomy. Between the 1909 and 1910 seasons, he broke away to form his own team, which he named the Chicago American Giants by 1911. This act instigated a battle within the city's race leadership waged over competing and shifting means of race pride. LGBAA owner Moseley organized the professional managerial elite into the Leland Giants Booster Club to compete with Foster. The booster club membership of Robert Abbott of the *Chicago Defender* and Julius Taylor of the *Chicago Broad Ax* allowed Moseley to marshal a media attack against Foster and the American Giants organization through an appeal to old settler respectability.[42]

The major point of reported contention among race leaders was Foster's financial partnership with John Schorling, a white saloon keeper and son-in-law of Charles Comiskey, who leased the old White Sox stadium on 39th and Wentworth to the American Giants. Foster was fully exposed as a capitalist businessman not wholly concerned with autonomous race ownership, and the *Chicago Defender* charged him with handing revenue "over to the other race" while not even donating money to black community institutions. However, there were some implicit ways that Foster appealed to black sports fans and working-class patrons in particular while retaining partnership with a white man.[43]

Foster's strategies of entrepreneurship shed light on the solidification of a new settler approach to black baseball. For example, the lease provided by

Schorling placed the American Giants directly within the black community in a much more accessible and affordable location compared to the Leland Giants' Auburn Park. Second, Foster's consistent schedule of weekly play, his celebrations of the team's championship pennant in the California Winter League, and the revival of the desired East-West Colored Championship against New York's Giants engendered confidence in his professional organization. The Foster-Schorling team was also learning the benefits of community relations, and to further engender civic pride, the Giants finally donated funds to community organizations and the use of Schorling Park to community baseball leagues. The growing black demographic of the Great Migration made it clear that race pride not only had to have slogans of uplift and professionalism but also had to actually meet community needs and desires as the class composition of the populace began to change.[44]

For the next decade, Foster's Giants were the most dominant black nine, and some would say baseball team more generally. Foster's disciplining and "scientific" style of speedy play focused on pitching, targeted hitting, base stealing, and signaling. This was matched only by his autocratic demands for "professionalism" of his players, who were awarded with unprecedented pay and luxurious accommodations but penalized with fines for inadequate execution. In an ironic twist, Foster spent his later career seeking to regulate player contracts, including the right of players to team-jump, an action that had brought Foster himself rapid success. As manager/owner, his sense of athletic manhood shifted from player autonomy to league control. From the physical base of Schorling Park, Foster's American Giants defeated strong black teams and white teams, continued to garner pennants in the informal "Colored World Championship," and captured the Chicago League Championship in 1916. While at Schorling Park, interracial crowds numbering as high as 10,000 consistently exceeded the numbers at Comiskey Park or at Cubs games, even on the same day.[45]

By the end of the decade, Foster strengthened his power by booking non-Giants games at Schorling, scheduling games at major league parks, cultivating relationships with Chicago leaders like alderman Oscar De Priest, and placing allies in managerial positions over other black teams to assure unyielding loyalty outside Chicago. These networks provided added financial capital, community legitimacy, and retail space control for Foster as he began to lead the charge for a black league. In April 1919, hundreds of fans and players convened at Schorling Park to watch Foster marshal talent from his own team and among free agents to help build the Detroit Stars as a competitive team. Yet, just three months later, Foster and the American Giants were

Chicago American Giants, ca. 1919. (Courtesy of the National Baseball Hall of Fame Research Library, Cooperstown, N.Y.)

exiled from that very park during the bloody race riots that rocked Chicago. Some thought this racial violence would silence whisperings about a possible league. But as much as the 1919 founding of the militant *Chicago Whip*, the realization of a black league was seen as a direct expression of New Negro resistance against white supremacy and racial violence.[46]

The local media proclaimed Foster "the best known Colored man in the world today" and continued to place their faith in him and in both the financial and symbolic capital of black-owned baseball. The *Chicago Defender* argued, in true race-pride fashion, that it wasn't the Cubs or White Sox but Foster's ability to expand seating in Schorling Park for up to 15,000 spectators that made Chicago "the best baseball city in the world." Community members all along the political spectrum saw in him and in the potential of a league "owned and controlled by Race men" an important manifestation of the New Negro. In October 1919, *Defender* columnist Cary Lewis suggested the possibility of a "circuit of western clubs" for the upcoming season. He argued that the long-awaited community desire for such a project ran parallel to the "dream" of the only man who could make this possible for the "men of his race," Rube Foster. Furthermore, Lewis argued that an independent league would give "a number of our men work" and put money, currently "going daily into the pockets of the other fellows," into the pockets of race men. The very leaders who had bemoaned Foster's controversial partnership with the white Schorling a few years earlier now saw Foster as the conduit to race pride and as a model of relative financial autonomy within the world of baseball. Abbott, one-time critic and *Defender* owner, allowed Foster the opportunity to pen approximately seven essays in the *Defender* under the title "Pitfalls of Baseball." Through these columns, Foster further established racial respectability and his control over black baseball through the position of "expert" as the logical head of a possible independent black league.[47]

In the "Pitfalls" series, Foster first established his authority by showcasing his American Giants as the only black team to show a significant profit and maintain a consistent yearly schedule. Foster also pointed out that the smallest baseball salaries were equal to the respectable professions of "post office carrier clerk or city school teacher." He proclaimed that as a "chief," it was his "intellect and brains of the game" that transformed disorganized black baseball into a league of prosperity. In the middle of this appeal to race pride and solidarity, Foster also offered a veiled defense of his partnership with Schorling as a direct act of race ownership. He argued that it was actually race entrepreneurs' unrealistic insistence on park ownership in the face of racist capital and permit distribution that was "delivering Colored baseball into the control of whites." Avoiding his own player history, Foster suggested that race control of baseball could be secured by a corporate structure (led by Foster) that focused not on park ownership but instead on the relegation of the professional player to "property of the club."[48]

Most commentators agreed that organization was the key, even at the expense of player autonomy. However, some also expressed reservations about Foster's "I am the ship and all else is the sea" autocratic leadership style.[49] In a 1920 *Competitor* series, writer Dave Wyatt directly cautioned that in Foster's proposed system, more financially lucrative urban baseball markets must be regulated in an equitable fashion or it would prove difficult "to induce first-class players to remain in Kansas City, Indianapolis or even St. Louis," especially with the "possibility of the player securing a berth in Chicago." Despite reservations, "the chief" presided over an organizational meeting of "race men" on February 13, 1920, that displayed Foster's ability to heal old wounds and assert his authority. In the meeting, Foster's handpicked owner/manager of the Detroit Stars, John Blount, nominated Foster for president. Then Foster further "dumbfounded" the meeting by revealing an already established "charter incorporated for a National Negro Baseball League." The meeting made clear that no one else had the power to put together or compete with Foster's ability to form a black baseball league. There is no question—and for a variety of reasons—that when the league opened in May 1920, much of its success and failure would extend from Chicago.[50]

The NNL was made up of teams from the Midwest and emerged as a powerful expression of entrepreneurial profit consolidation and race pride. Yet, Foster's various musings on the successes and failures of "blackball" seemed much less general observations than a suppression of rising challenges to his authority, which included manager calls for race umpires who could possibly contest his autocratic control on the field, if not in the front office. In another four-part *Chicago Defender* series, Foster proclaimed that he transformed a game dominated by "the sporting element" into a respectable "profession" as part of his appeal to the dollars and support of the black "better class" for his leadership. To silence challenges from managers, owners, and players, he boasted that their failure rested in a misapplication of his system due to shortsightedness, greed, and power lust. Foster argued that even college-educated players were no match for his practical mastery of the game and were actually considered a more dangerous threat than "players without the advantage of a college education." Within Foster's league system, the best players "play as if they had no mind of their own." Not even umpires had the final word, because in games against Foster, he boasted their rulings could not stand up against his familiarity with the "tricks and technicalities of the rules" nor his superior "system."[51]

The bottom line was that, at least early on, Foster was able to keep dissent at bay because the league was a race enterprise success, even creating smaller subsidiary businesses, including the American Giants (automobile) Garage. However, as grumblings became all-out accusations, the popular understandings of Foster collectively shifted from one of "chief" to "czar." Individual attacks brought to the surface general feelings of suffocation felt under Foster's leadership, which was believed to be softly killing the league. Inside the cover of Abbott's newly formed journal, *Abbott's Monthly*, writer Al Monroe emphatically proclaimed that Foster's main desire for league formation was to "extend his booking agency" by subordinating team autonomy under the structure of "a Race baseball league." The constitutional structure of the league, drawn up by Foster, reinforces this argument. As league president, Foster was given 10 percent of the receipts (5 percent for each team) from each league game for operational costs. At the same time, most teams in the league had to pay a 20 percent leasing fee to play in parks they didn't own while playing around the schedule of the home team. Therefore, most teams were relegated to traveling status to generate revenue and maintain a regular schedule within a league where Foster held leases at the two primary parks available to the NNL (Schorling Park and Mack Park in Detroit). In the face of these problems, Foster simply refused to play league teams at parks in their home region and kept his Giants at home, rationalizing that away teams benefited from Chicago's stronger consumer market. When increased revenue did not materialize for other teams, he continued to collect his leasing and league fees.[52]

NNL teams, according to many, were basically trapped within a booking system passed off as a league to benefit the personal desires of the league president. When managers, owners, or players attempted to protest Foster's "system," in the words of one critic, they had "to file a complaint against Mr. Foster, mail it to secretary Foster, and then President Foster would have to decide." As early as 1920, observers noted, "Fans are tiring of a one-team league" where the president is for his "American Giants, first, last, and always." The *Chicago Defender* suggested, "The president of each league should be someone else than the manager or owner of a team playing in either league," because again, "a one-man czar-like system is not going to succeed." No one denied Foster's athletic and management genius or his organizational skills to display a defiance against white supremacy on the field and in the front office. But as Al Monroe stated, his "vanity to prove" his personal abilities, like many businessmen, above a concern for league stability signaled its downfall. When Foster took ill and eventually died in 1930, no one had been groomed to take over a system so intimately tied to one race man. "Race league baseball" was not effectively revived until the mid-1930s from a direct infusion of capital from one of the few places black entrepreneurs could turn, policy gambling. At the same time, fan frustration with baseball pushed many to other kinds of "commercial" expressions that exhibited New Negro sensibilities of pride, professionalism, and pleasure, including the growing popularity of "winter sports," like basketball and football.[53]

In 1921, Frank Young announced, "Basketball is the next biggest sport to boxing during the winter months." Basketball gradually began to pick up speed in the Midwest by 1917, as the Wabash YMCA and Forty/Defender clubs engaged in amateur contests against eastern powerhouses, including the St.

Christopher five and Will Anthony Madden's "World Famous" Incorporators. Rapidly developing rivalries made basketball popular as local teams became more competitive. However, basketball's fully professional variant did not take full hold in Chicago's black community until the latter part of the decade due to a powerful team from the East. Basketball had always been a journeyman sport organized more by barnstorming trips than league play. But in 1925, white businessmen from the East and Midwest organized the American Basketball League (ABL), including the Original Celtics and football legend George Halas's Chicago Bruins, while decidedly barring the powerful Harlem Renaissance (Rens) five from the league, making it a purposefully white enterprise. League and independent teams loved to capitalize on the gate the Rens drew in nonleague games even while the Rens were excluded from ABL membership. For this reason, when the Rens came to Chicago and many times beat the Chicago Bruins in nonleague play, technically they stood as the away team, but in the black metropolis they were "home."[54]

By 1939, a "world series" of basketball was organized by the *Chicago Herald American* to decide the "real" champions, especially since the Rens were barred from league play. Twelve to sixteen of the country's best teams, regardless of race, were invited to play in this tournament at Chicago Stadium. With crowds occasionally exceeding 20,000, the Rens seized the opportunity and officially became world champions in 1939 to cap off over a decade of basketball dominance. When asked if they would have liked to play in the ABL during that championship year, star player William "Pops" Gates scoffed, "The Renaissance players didn't give a damn about" league membership because "we thought we were their [the white teams'] equal or better." Chicago's black community agreed, as the *Chicago Defender* covered every one of the Rens' tournament victories over "the white boys." The paper could only exclaim, "What a team!" as the Rens were "banqueted at the Hotel Grand" before heading back east. On their way to victory, the Rens also defeated an up-and-coming local team ironically called the Harlem Globetrotters that took third place in that year's tournament en route to taking the world by storm.[55]

The origins of the Harlem Globetrotters is a highly contested narrative, with distinctions falling almost directly upon racial lines, which speaks volumes about questions of masculinity and ownership. The "official" creation myth maintains a narrative of racial patriarchy, where the great white "father" Abe Saperstein enters the scene and turns the black chaotic failure of the Savoy Big Five into an organized success. Alternately, Tom Brookins, a

HARLEM GLOBETROTTERS BASKETBALL TEAM – SEASON OF 1930–31
Left to right: (Standing) Abe Saperstein, Toots Wright, Byron Long, Inman Jackson, William Oliver, Seated: Al Pullins

Harlem Globetrotters, ca. 1930. (Courtesy of the Vivian G. Harsh Research Collection of Afro-American History and Literature, Carter G. Woodson Regional Library, Chicago Public Library)

former Wendell Phillips, Savoy, and Globetrotters player, counters that Saperstein did not engineer Globetrotters success but was managed by black players because they recognized the benefits of his "white face" for booking games. Brookins agrees that Saperstein renamed the team the Harlem Globetrotters to capitalize on the racial consciousness associated with the New York neighborhood and to also benefit from the national reputation of the Harlem Rens. But Brookins adds that while Saperstein was booking this team, first called Tommy Brookins' Globetrotters and then the Original Chicago Globetrotters, Saperstein was simultaneously and secretly touring another team called the Harlem Globetrotters made up of "all the fellows we didn't want." Eventually, many of the best players on the original team were incorporated into the Harlem five as Brookins left to embark on a highly successful vaudeville/theater career.[56]

All agree that the Globetrotters emerged from the world of amateur/

semiprofessional basketball developing in the black metropolis through Wendell Phillips, Wabash YMCA, and Savoy Ballroom teams. The competing stories surely contain some level of embellishment, but they converge at the recognition of basketball as a key element within a larger New Negro sporting life, where a racial consciousness (for different ends) was clearly played out in athletic performance, marketing, and even memory. Moreover, there is no doubt that long before the Globetrotters' signature style of intense dribbling, quick passing, and deceptive shots was simply used to make patrons laugh, these skills were deployed to demoralize opposing teams in "straight ball," clearly indicated by their victory over the Harlem Rens to claim the World Championship Invitational at Chicago Stadium in 1940.

Now if any sport has been collectively erased from the New Negro consciousness, it is undoubtedly football and particularly the way Chicago's black footballers used the gridiron as expertly as a *Half-Century Magazine* essayist crafted the written word. In the early twentieth century, mainstream professional football consistently languished in the shadows of the college game. Therefore, black professional gridiron play is traced primarily through individual players and fleeting all-star conglomerates that were disbanded almost as quickly as they were formed. Yet a notable and vibrant trace remains, with much of its organized history leading back to the black metropolis. To talk about football—the role of football in Chicago's marketplace intellectual life, more specifically—all conversations begin and nearly end with the journeyman experiences of Frederick Douglass "Fritz" Pollard. The younger brother of Ebony Pictures movie producer Luther Pollard, Fritz was a multiple sport all-county star at Albert Lane Technical High School. At the same time and at the same school, Pollard was sporting mates with Virgil Blueitt, who became a basketball star on the Wabash and Defender fives. Later, Blueitt and Pollard occasionally teamed up for basketball and football competitions in Chicago, taking on the name the Pollards or the Lincoln Athletic Club for all-star Thanksgiving games against white teams.[57]

When Pollard graduated from Lane, football players still journeyed from college to college playing for the highest bidder, especially within the esteemed circles of the football powerhouses of the Ivy League. He tramped around from Northwestern to semipro ball in Chicago and Wisconsin (where he passed as an Indian) and back and forth between Brown, Dartmouth, and Harvard before finally settling at Brown University. At Brown, Pollard's classmates included future doctor and scribe of the Harlem Renaissance Rudolph Fischer and later pro teammate and Chicago race music impresario (with gospel music pioneer Thomas Dorsey) Mayo "Ink" Williams. Pollard

SAVOY BIG FIVE BASKETBALL TEAM — 1928. L. to R. Asst. Coach Bobby Anderson, Randolph Ramsey, Inman Jackson, William Watson, Tommy Brookings, Joe Lillard, Wm. Grant, Walter Wright, Lester Johnson, Coach Dick Hudson

Chicago Savoy Big Five, ca. 1928.
(Courtesy of the Harlem Globetrotters International, Inc.)

stood out at Brown amid very real threats of racial violence on the field and academic difficulties, leading the team to the Rose Bowl in 1916. He also became the first African American named to the backfield of Walter Camp's All-American team, converting this status into a coaching position at Lincoln University (Pennsylvania). While coaching, Pollard began his professional career with the Akron (Ohio) Indians of the American Professional Football Association, precursor to the National Football League (NFL). Pollard raised crowd interest in the professional game, especially as he lined up against and outperformed Jim Thorpe and Harold "Red" Grange as player/manager of various teams throughout the Midwest and East. While Pollard did not devote enough time to his later coaching position at Wendell Phillips High School, he recruited college friend and Rutgers All-American Paul Robeson to play with him at Akron in 1921 before they both went to lead the Milwaukee Badgers and also made arrangements for his college roommate "Ink" Williams to play with the Hammond Pros.[58]

Frederick Douglass "Fritz" Pollard at Brown University's Andrews Field, 1916.
(Courtesy of the Brown University Library)

At the end of the 1922 season, Pollard began a strategy that had long been used by black baseball players to demonstrate black equality, inclusion, and even athletic superiority: he organized an all-star exhibition team. The Fritz Pollard All-Stars included Robeson, Williams, and Fred "Duke" Slater, who later completed his law degree and opened a practice in the black metropolis. In addition, the team also brought together future Savoy Big Five owner and NFL player Dick Hudson, track and basketball standout Sol Butler, and basketball star and former schoolmate Virgil Blueitt. This truly all-star cast defeated a team of former white collegians in a game held at the Chicago American Giants' Schorling Park, which also signaled the particular configuration of race consciousness that football continued to exhibit in the New Negro era.

For figures including Pollard, Robeson, and Williams, this "sporting life" race consciousness spilled over into other cultural and political arenas. African Americans who early on were needed as attractions faced serious difficulty by the late 1920s and early 1930s in finding work in football's professional ranks. In this period, Williams and Butler played with the Hammond Pros and Slater held on with the Chicago Cardinals. Local fans grew excited when University of Oregon star Joseph Lillard joined the Chicago Cardinals in 1932, the only African American in the NFL. After Lillard's final season in 1933, there was a decade-long bar against all African Americans from professional football. Lillard went on to play basketball for the Savoy Big Five and pitch with the American Giants before starting his own basketball team, the Chicago Hottentots, in 1934. While black players were certainly dealt a serious blow, they continued to fight, using the all-star model Pollard had devised based on Negro baseball.[59]

As early as 1928, Pollard organized the Chicago Blackhawks as another all-star eleven with the goal of demonstrating black athletic prowess against white professional and semiprofessional teams in the Chicago area. Again Pollard assembled many of the old faithful while providing opportunities for young talent who never saw the NFL. The Blackhawks began barnstorming, with a tour as far away as California, but disbanded because of poor attendance and poor competition.

By 1935, Pollard was in Harlem where he started his own tabloid newspaper, the *Independent News*, to compete with the *Amsterdam News* for black readership. In this paper, the politically conservative Pollard offered the most extensive coverage of African American sports and even offered support for the local variant of the radical "Don't Spend Your Money Where You Can't Work" campaign. That same year he accepted the coaching position of a football team named the Brown Bombers in honor of boxer Joe Louis and was determined to schedule games with local white professional teams but to no avail. But the Bombers had a number of successful years playing against teams with white ex All-Americans, while professional teams intentionally dodged Pollard's eleven, which of course hurt the team financially. Under his direction, the Bombers eventually instituted a number of deceptive formations and reversal plays to generate excitement. The team would even "truck" (dance) from the huddle to the scrimmage line singing Negro spirituals to appeal to a stingy and competitive black commercial amusement marketplace. Yet the Bombers resisted the barnstorming clown tactics that many sports teams deployed in appealing to the white imagination of black entertainment.[60]

However, the travails of the Bombers within both the black and white commercial marketplace raise important and more general questions about the meaning of black athletic "style." Just as an example, how did the Bombers' resistance against, but possible crowd requests for, singing and dancing at games reveal contested athletic expressions of blackness or "New Negro-ness"? What do struggles over black athletic style say about definitions of politics and commercial pleasure within a marketplace intellectual life?

PARKS, COURTS, AND COLISEUMS: PLAYING FIELDS AS SITES OF RACIAL CONFLICT AND COMMUNITY IN THE BLACK METROPOLIS

In most areas, society has progressed beyond Social Darwinist notions that particular racial groups are biologically suited to certain mental or physical abilities. However, the culture has not left behind the pluralist or environmental ideals that identify "standard" execution on the playing field as "white" and the disruptive or excessive as "black." To put it plainly, once a black athlete becomes a restrained boxer, controlled pitcher, pocket quarterback, or unselfish point guard, there are still suggestions that he or she has adopted a culturally "standard" or even "white" style of play (hence the new and racialist distinction between being the "most athletic" as opposed to the "best skilled" at a particular position). These seemingly logical assessments for extremely complex developments of athletic performance and performative choice, these racial shorthands of "black" and "white" style, must be historicized. This last section locates what has become an ahistorical discussion about style as simply cultural tradition or solely a response to oppression within a useful sociocultural frame and situates the emergence of distinctively "black" athletic styles within the contexts of the particular spaces of play, the desires for commercial success, and the larger struggles over racial politics (inside and outside the community). This section also discusses the important technological, tactical, and organizational innovations developed in black play spaces like the black metropolis that were later appropriated by mainstream leagues.

To initiate any discussion about black style, one has to examine the social experiences where games were played. Particularly at interracial contests during times when black athletes were excluded from or underrepresented in mainstream events, black playing fields were a combination gambling refuge, religious revival, political rally, and rave party informed by both a policy of race first and performative excellence. For example, the celebrated Leland Giants' defeat of the white Donlin's All-Stars in 1907 was a site of expressed racial antagonism and race pride in ways that preceded the "Johnson Affair" and complicated the dominant old settler vision of sport in the pre-migration era. When the Indianapolis *Freeman* rhetorically asked, "Booker T. Washington or the Fifteenth Amendment?" after the game, it quickly answered by noting the absence of the traditional "color line" in the stands. The paper also reported on the antagonistic exchanges between black and white "sports" in the stands where black people defiantly spoke back. When one white gambler called out twenty dollars against "the chocolate," a "flashily dressed colored man" responded, "I'll take $5 of that money white man." When a white fan attempted to coach the Lelands in "Negro dialect," a black fan shot back, "Befo' you try to imitate someone else you ought to learn the English language." So it was clear that this was a space where black people were not going to be intimidated or stoop in front of a white presence. When the Lelands won, black fans fully appropriated the space "with all kinds of noise-producing apparatus" where "every man was waving a roll of bills."[61]

However, playing fields were not just sites of cohesion between black players and fans; they also became sites of class conflict over competing visions of racial respectability and pride. As baseball became a profession, its black entrepreneurs consistently tried to divorce the sport from its "rowdy" past to attract a more respectable clientele and express a particular vision of respectable race pride. In walking the race pride tightrope between civic professionalism and consumer pleasure, owners found it difficult to maintain order on the field and in the stands, particularly with white game officials. During an interracial contest against Niesen's Pyotts, the American Giants' catcher was accused of letting a throw hit the white umpire. A Pyott outfielder attempted to attack the Giants' catcher, and to the dismay of respectable patrons, a near race riot ensued when both benches were cleared and fans stormed the field.

Another site of race pride and class conflict ensued during the black college football Thanksgiving classics that were, by the mid-1920s, played at Soldier Field in Chicago. Traditionally, the halftime pageantry of respectable society figures mixed with but was distinct from the more informal black students dancing on the field with instruments performing a "wild snake dance" during "rabbles." The rabble was a marked racial contrast to the measured and methodical marching band routines at white universities but also exposed competing visions of pageantry within the black community. It was explicitly noted that at the rain-soaked 1921 Howard-Lincoln game, the muddy field prevented the "fur coat parade" of the society elite from their usual promenade, leaving center stage to the dance and music of the unruly "rabble."[62]

With the rabble in mind, the very meaning of early basketball on ballroom floors was profoundly shaped by important black musical contexts, making the event more one of community sociability than athletic in purpose. The way beauty, film, and gospel music "texts" were given meaning through the larger context of early women's adornment practices, film exhibition behaviors, and music demonstration spaces found parallels in the musical form of basketball. Jazz bands and dancing at halftimes and after parties were the primary drawing card, especially when basketball was an unknown commodity. In 1929, Louis Armstrong played in the jazz band that followed Savoy Big Five games. John J. O'Brien of the white Brooklyn Visitations remembered that black fans came dressed "in tuxedos" and "loved to get the game over for dancing." Harlem Ren Eyre Saitch explained, "We had to have a dance afterwards or nobody would come to the damn thing." However, few note that within this moment of racial community, strategies were also deployed to counter the jazz enticement with alternative musical and social contexts. For example, the Quinn Chapel Athletic Association hosted a basketball game with a more classical concert musicale accompaniment that was similar to the old settler Sunday musicales in old-line churches. The use of "refined" music instead of jazz during basketball games displays the common use of a black musical context while also making a clear statement about class distinctions within black sporting life exhibitions.[63]

Even with subtle points of contestation, it is still important to note how playing fields were continually spaces of solidarity and technological innovation and exchange, especially among athletes of color. For example, in Cuba, black athletes played as relative equals against their white counterparts.

Black baseball league teams also forged cross-racial solidarity, hosting Japanese teams in the United States and traveling to play in the Asian Pacific, while teams like All Nations consciously boasted a multicultural roster composed of black, white, Asian, Cuban, and Mexican players and even one woman. The NNL was also the first to introduce night baseball and field lighting long before it took hold in the majors by 1935. The first exhibition of lighting, at a night game in Chicago, was showcased over the field contest as "the most spectacular event in all baseball history." All of these displays of interracial solidarity and black technological innovation were illuminating, but even they paled next to the East-West All-Star game spectaculars of the 1930s.[64]

Described by black writer Sam Lacy as "a holiday for 48 hours," the East-West All-Star game was a spectacle where the racial order was almost flipped upside down. Started in 1933, the game was played at the centrally located Comiskey Park in Chicago. More than a game, the All-Star event was a physical manifestation of race pride. The Illinois Central Railroad added special train cars to accommodate all the spectators that joined the ride between New Orleans and Chicago. The crowd sometimes swelled to 50,000, exceeding the attendance at the major league version. Unlike mainstream teams that were picked by sportswriters, NNL players were selected by fans through cutout ballots in the *Chicago Defender* and *Pittsburgh Courier*, where the power to vote, even if on a sporting event, took on a very particular significance.

Once in Chicago, patrons dressed in their finest clothes and flooded the black metropolis, staying at the Vincennes and Grand Hotels, patronizing the Regal nightclub, and placing bets at the policy wheels. At Comiskey Park, fans were able to witness some of the best players in all of baseball, where the game was as much an exhibition of black social equality as anything else. This weekend grew so popular and profitable that many argue the East-West All-Star event was the primary catalyst for the integration of major league baseball. Eventually, white spectators entered a world where they observed black celebration and style alongside white modesty and irrelevance both on and off the field.[65]

Collectively, these important social contexts off the field must inform any conversation about a black style of play. More than an ancestral legacy, the variably combined revisions of Afro-diasporic cultural traditions, desires for commercial appeal, and racially uneven application of rules and sportsmanship are what have created a black style of athletic performance. This style emerged as a playing field expression of the migration experience and more general desires for equitable urban spaces of recreation and labor. A perfect example of the Afro-diasporic cultural context is the musical accompaniment at black sporting events. Some have suggested that the black "shimmy" or the appropriately named "jukin'" running style on the gridiron is directly informed by the "rabbles" at halftimes and musical rhythms during the games. Others assert that the transition of basketball from primarily a set shot to jump shot game was heavily influenced by the after-party jazz music contexts with their "air walking" lindy hop dancers. Tellingly, the jazz parlance "hot playing" was used as early as 1919 to describe the sped-up "race horse" style of basketball performed by Virgil Blueitt and the Wabash Outlaws, while in 1924, Lincoln University's running back Harold Byrd developed an elusive and improvisational style described as bucking "the rules" using "his own resources and wit," fittingly earning him the nickname "Jazz." These references to cultural tradition are compelling on their own, but black style, especially professional athletic style, must be further situated within its commercial contexts.[66]

Such an extremely competitive black commercial amusement marketplace, where proportionately more people struggled over fewer resources, required that sports "stars" develop signature markers and styles that set them apart. As a commercial entertainment, basketball in the black metropolis was competitively marketed as advertising more "thrills . . . than the combined movie corporations would be able to release in five years." Black basketball teams also advertised themselves through provocative and descriptive team names, including the speed and efficiency of the Flashes or Cheetahs, the "race" consciousness of the Chicago Hottentots, the sophistication of the Chicago Collegians, or the race-based cosmopolitanism of the Harlem Globetrotters. Yet, these names were almost benign in racial or ethnic identification compared to the Buffalo Germans, Original Celtics, Cleveland Rosenblums, or Olson's Terrible Swedes of the day. But these "black" names were also matched by a distinct style of performance, including the Brown Bomber "trucking" and Negro spiritual singing from huddle to scrimmage. The Globetrotters' "Magic Circle" at least partially came from this commercial impulse as an innovative midcourt exhibition of fancy ball handling, behind the back and no-look passes, and various slight of hand and foot moves with the ball that can now be seen on any court. In the early 1930s, Wendell Phillips alum and Globetrotter Inman Jackson was known to put such a fierce backspin on the ball during a bounce pass that it deceptively returned back to him when it hit the floor. Clowning and trickery on the court also became a way to slow up the game during Globetrotters lopsided victories so fans would remain interested. Moreover, Globetrotters hoped paying white fans, frustrated with such over-the-top displays of race pride and athletic domination, would laugh instead of retaliate with racial violence.[67]

Such commercial influences on the development of "racial" styles was rarely discussed because most ballplayers and reporters were heavily invested in marketing sport as a profession and "science," that is, that what happened on the field was a project of mental and rational application and control over the body. From the outset, a precarious relationship existed between commercial showmanship and civic sportsmanship within professional athletics. On one side, to maintain professional status—that is, pay for play—athletes had to market and entertain their audiences like the Globetrotters did. However, once "professional" status was achieved, showmanship was incorporated in a muted form yet simultaneously dismissed as a thing of the past or a sign of inferior play. Within black contexts, where showmanship often meant minstrelsy, the repression of clownlike entertaining was important. Yet, the rarefied space of professional sportsmanship wasn't possible without the existence of at least a general display of showmanship that even black patrons required, especially for unknown athletic commodities.

Moreover, in a black sporting world, again where capital was sparse and victory both a racial and economic necessity, showmanship was always incorporated into strategies for success. Rube Foster overtly credited the skilled play and gentlemanly conduct of black athletes for moving baseball away from a barnstorming "farce comedy" toward a scientific profession. But he also integrated many of those commercial "antics," including secret signals, trick plays, and directed hitting, into his disciplined "system" of professional play. Bringing together both cultural tradition and commercial intentions also forces a consideration of the black sporting life as both mental and manual labor within a racial capitalism that distributed resources unevenly. Black athletic style must therefore be understood metaphorically as a military struggle over equitable labor relations waged on racialized fields of play. A labor conceptualization of commercialized leisure places sport alongside the film, beauty, and gospel music industries as central to a mass consumer marketplace understanding of the New Negro experience.[68]

The overarching disciplinary and educational function of athletics lies in its rules and codes for measuring and evaluating performance. Ideally, the objective application of these rules and regulations preserves the myth of athletics as a level playing field, subordinating all ethnic, class, and even gender identities under an equalizing apparatus of measurement. But especially in the context of a New Negro sporting life, the added layer of white supremacy further governs and dictates the sporting order. The unequal application of rules and regulations by officials, the insecure guarantee of sportsmanship by both white opponents and teammates, and the expressed relegation of equal or superior athletes to "reserve" leagues and teams, all along racial lines, reveal a racialized division of athletic labor. Looking at the playing field literally as a militarized zone of labor relations highlights that black players did not control what could be considered the *playing fields of production* in terms of strategic white officiating, or the actions of racist opponents and teammates. Many black accounts exist about the application of expanding and contracting strike zones, phantom fouls, missed blocks, and flagrant tackles that existed along racial lines. White supremacy reigned over the racialized playing field and its rules. Yet, within this dominated grid of contestation, black athletes mastered the "standard" and improvised based on given situations by finding tactical loopholes, moving in the gaps, speeding up the tempo, and making new rules within the announced rules that didn't consistently apply to them.[69]

The sporting styles designated as white or "standard" tend to focus on methodical and linear movements and are aggressively offensive in their approach to fields of contestation. This sporting style is purposely modeled on a modern industrial, scientific, and especially military approach to social interaction from the vantage point of those in power. The home run orientation of baseball; the dribble, pass, and shoot method of basketball; the territorial aggression of boxing; and the linear, forward engagement in football all express the "standard" style and govern "legitimate" sporting possibilities in the early twentieth century. Therefore, it is not a coincidence that in the major sports, athletic behaviors that are identified as distinctly "black" are reactionary and premised on defense, speed, adaptation, and adjustment. The slap-fist defense and counterpunch style of Jack Johnson; the elusive, deceptive misdirection football moves of Fritz Pollard and college standout Ossie Simmons; the fast-paced, defensive, base-stealing, pitching-oriented "thinking-man's" tactics of Rube Foster; and the speedy dribble, fake-pass play of the Harlem Globetrotters all denote "black" style.[70]

To succeed, black players engaged on the same field of play but also on a different field of cognitive understanding, a different epistemological plane, during the same game as their opponents and even racist teammates. The workplace notion of "wigging"—where workers "steal" company time and materials for personal use and resist general labor standardization—is directly applicable here. Within sports, the black speeding up of the tempo becomes an act of wigging, where a black athlete is a laborer stealing the owner's material and time but also taking back space and time from a white supremacist application of regulation and order on the playing field. Speeding up the tempo was a tactic used by black athletic teams to pile up points before white officials could practice the well-known strategy of "giv[ing] the opposing team a victory." The speed tempo tactic made it more difficult for opponents or officials to predict and therefore regulate and contain black athletic labor. The power of this black temporal shift is also noted in the ensuing official recognition and re-regulation of playing time.[71]

One *Chicago Defender* article reported on the 1927 rule that would restrict the dribble from multiple bounces to a single bounce by any one player to "eliminate roughness and [to] encourage team play." However, basketball legend Blueitt observed that the bigger effect of the "one bounce rule" would be to eliminate "trick plays." He continued, "The fake shot and pass can no longer be used by the fast and clever player. No longer can a player pretend he will shoot, entice the guard to leave his feet in an attempt to block the shot and then circle around him for a close shot." Most important, regulating the playing "time" allowed a "slow guard" to "halt a fast forward." The playing field became a racialized struggle between strategies and tactics. Strategies are the efforts of the powerful who seek to create places in deliberate conformity with abstract models. Strategies are able to produce, tabulate, and impose on spaces and regulate time, whereas tactical maneuvers are based on "poaching," on "deception," and on "surprises" by "pulling tricks" and by "a clever utilization of time," like a rapidity of movement that changes the organization of space. Different forms of athletic "wigging" are precisely the same tactics that were paramount to black style genius and its appropriation of white time and space, making the black sporting life an original site of "situationist" theory.[72]

Foster constantly boasted about knowing the "tricks and technicalities of the rules." When pitching contests were primarily about the challenge of manly batters standing in to defy the fast ball, Foster instructed pitchers how to "deceive the other fellows" by appearing "jolly and unconcerned" and throwing "what I think he can't hit, sometimes a curve, sometimes a straight ball." While trickery was a means of victory for Foster, deception was a tactic of bodily survival for college football player Ossie Simmons. Before he became the head football coach at Wendell Phillips, Simmons had been a star halfback, drawing black Chicagoans all the way to the University of Iowa to witness his dazzling moves. With white opponents targeting him and teammates conveniently "missing" blocks and tackles, Simmons relied on his own genius by holding the ball in one hand "right out in front" of an approaching tackler and then breaking "to the right or left at incredible speed" or pivoting "like a basketball player," turning his back on the tackler. Reading these awkward fumbling descriptions of what would now effortlessly be named "change up" pitches and "spin" moves displays the visionary advance of twentieth-century black athletes where New Negroes were prophetically "theorizing through behavior."[73]

Whether black expressive traditions, barnstorming showmanship, or recreational racism, black athletic style consistently incorporated the larger social context into on-field play that included innovations within the black metropolis and exclusions from the larger world. By the late 1930s, the black sporting life surely fell on hard times as one of the last black all-star contingents of football players lost 51–0 against the Chicago Bears at Soldier Field in 1938, the Globetrotters went from a world-class championship team to a world-renowned comedy team, and semipro baseball was more generally phased out in preference for the major (white) league. While great, benevolent "white fathers" are credited with the eventual opening of the gates of heaven to "promising" young athletes like Jackie Robinson, it was actually the other way around. "Good ol' boys" networks were pushed, kicking and screaming, into the twentieth century. The New Negro sporting life continually agitated for inclusion and excelled in "racial" exile until both the pleasures and profits of black play could no longer be repressed or denied in the radical, yet uneven and incomplete, transformation of the American cultural landscape.[74]

The "sporting life" primarily associated race pride with muscular masculinity, but its general approach to creating leisure-based forms of labor most expertly drew from the larger demands of a consumer patron base to build a new race enterprise and ideology. This sphere within Chicago's marketplace intellectual life encompassed a much broader and collective approach to the modern world. It was integrationist and nationalist, elitist and democratic, bringing together both mind and body to place farm and factory workers, gamblers, and entrepreneurs in conversation with moral reformers, scientists, and even presidents. The "sporting life," with its policy gambling capital, self-promotion as a "first class attraction," explicit focus on bodily release and adornment, alternate routes of diasporic travel, and stylistic influences from the nighttime Stroll, literally embodied Chicago's New Negro contribution and challenge to the world.[75]

The Crisis of the Black Bourgeoisie, Or, What If Harold Cruse Had Lived in Chicago?

Many Negro professional men and women
take more seriously their recreation than their professions.
—E. Franklin Frazier, *Black Bourgeoisie*, 1957

In Negro life the cultural spheres appear to many
as being rather remote, intangible and hardly related to what
is called the more practical aspect of race relations. However . . . it
is only through a cultural analysis of the Negro approach to group
"politics" that the errors, weaknesses and goal-failures can
cogently be analyzed and positively worked out.
—Harold Cruse, *Crisis of the Negro Intellectual*, 1967

In Alain Locke's period shaping, landmark anthology, *The New Negro: Voices of the Harlem Renaissance*, Chicago sociologist E. Franklin Frazier celebrates, "No longer can men say that the Negro is lazy and shiftless and a *consumer*. . . . He is a producer. He is respectable." Accordingly, the shift from consumer to producer frees the race from "the Negroes' native love of leisure and enjoyment of life." At first glance, it seems odd that such a bold endorsement for enterprise over culture appeared in a cultural anthology like *The New Negro*. However, Frazier and members of the cultural elite, which included Locke, found common ground in their suspicion of mass consumer cultural experiences as artificially manufactured by profit-driven capital interests with neither black artists nor artisans in "productive" control. Where Locke wanted to elevate black life through the discipline of high art and cultural criticism, Frazier sought to reform black life through a discipline of thrift and productive labor. Both scholars represent the prevalent thought of the day, which denied any recognition of the intellectual potential within the mass consumer marketplace. Frazier's essay in Locke's anthology was buried amid a range of poems, stories, and artwork. Yet the link here between respectability and production became a central theme in Frazier's academic career while helping to establish a false divide between New Negro intellectual life and social movements and its mass consumer marketplace. In effect, Frazier's approach was instrumental in shaping our understandings of the period and in limiting possible strategies for social transformation up to the present.[1]

Four years later, Frazier turned his eye back to Chicago, praising its lack of "culture" and lauding the city's focus on enterprise, or what he called more "practical accomplishments." During the 1930s, however, W. E. B. Du Bois suggested that black citizens take another look at the intersection of culture, commerce, and politics to take advantage of an already existing segregation under white supremacy by creating a race conscious cooperative economic system built on consumption strategies. Heavily influenced by Chicago's metropolis model, he hoped that strategic consumption could become a "new instrument of democratic control," specifically securing a level of autonomy for black cultural production by wresting some power away from white media houses and culture industries. Frazier soundly denounced this program as a shortsighted and regressive black nationalism. By 1957, Frazier's polemic *Black Bourgeoisie* waged an all-out assault on the mass consumer marketplace. He specifically marked the decline of the black middle class at the point of the New Negro era, when they turned from the "canons of respectability"—with appropriate focus on "industry and thrift"—and toward a "world of make-believe" that associated racial respectability with conspicuous consumption. Within this framework, Frazier uncritically dismissed the Harlem Renaissance for avoiding economic concerns and also the national black consumer boycott program, "Don't Spend Your Money Where You Can't Work," for fostering a black nationalist "anti-Semitism." He understood the economic and political power of policy gambling as simply a "threat to the respectable ways of life" instigated by a " 'sporting' and criminal element." Frazier also made sharp distinctions between black middle-class interests in athletic contests as opposed to real "culture."[2]

It is still easy to be awed by Frazier's prophetic vision because there is much to be retained, examined, and expanded on from the ideas that led up to his *Black Bourgeoisie*. This is particularly so in light of the current effects of global capitalism on local black communities and of the larger myths that conflate free market commercialism with freedom or assume that black entrepreneurial success will "trickle down" into working-class homes. Yet here I am less concerned with the accuracy of Frazier's conclusions than with how his history of black consumerism and middle-class respectability limits our understandings of the possible relationships between the cultural, political, and economic spheres of existence when constructing more comprehensive visions of black possibility.[3] Has the turn away from the "premodern" genteel virtues of piety, restraint, and thrift been such a central component to racial injustice and economic inequality? What would Frazier's genealogy of the black middle class look like if the "respectable" virtues of the black genteel tradition were seen as actually preventing political and social advance? Frazier's tempered dismissal of Chicago's "Don't Spend" campaign, its sporting life, and the broader New Negro Renaissance places sites of collective consumerism in opposition to productivity and hence not as key spaces toward building moments of productive social change.

Approximately ten years after the publication of *Black Bourgeoisie*, political theorist and cultural critic Harold Cruse added another voice to this conversation with his compelling and equally polemical tome, *The Crisis of the Negro Intellectual*. Taking up the question of the "appropriate" relationship between culture, commerce, and politics, Cruse revisits black cultural production in the 1920s. Like Frazier, Cruse finds "failure" in the disjuncture between the black middle class, its intelligentsia, and the cultural resources of the masses. He agrees that the black bourgeoisie, as a class, did not have the capital, foresight, or desire to provide a strong institutional foundation for a black intelligentsia. But according to Cruse, Harlem's New Negro Renaissance of the 1920s failed not because of the black bourgeoisie's reliance on an insular or provincial black nationalism; Cruse counters that the crisis emerged precisely because this class did not provide a strong enough economic foundation built on the specific consumer needs or interests of the Negro community. Accordingly, economic and political control must first be achieved within communities based on a "broad cultural conditioning." In many ways, it is this very cultural conditioning that Frazier specifically dismissed as a "world of make-believe." Unlike Frazier, Cruse reclaims the insights of Du Bois's cooperative commonwealth model, combined with progressive sociologist C. Wright Mills's notion of the cultural apparatus, to argue that it is precisely within the mass consumer marketplace that a new political economic model could be created.[4]

For Cruse, the 1920s gave rise to the development of the mass cultural communications media, or (to quote Mills) the "cultural apparatus," as much as it gave rise to the New Negro renaissance. He contends that part of the reason culture, politics, and economics are not discussed synthetically derives from a critical analysis overburdened by a "dull fusion of black bourgeois sentiments and leftwing ideology." Cruse charges that radicals extending on up to Frazier himself adopt a "neo-Victorian, pseudo revolutionary" Western Marxism where "economics and politics take precedence over culture." Moreover, critics (both liberal and leftist) understand real "culture" as something unfettered by the demands of the consumer marketplace, and hence mass culture is deemed irrelevant within "grounded" political strategies and invalid according to "authentic" cultural tastes. Cruse, on the contrary, rationalizes that if for Marx the growth of capitalism creates its antithetical source of revolutionary agency (the working class), then the twentieth-century growth of the all-encompassing culture industries (radio, film, and recording industries) creates its opposite—a potentially radical class of intellectual workers. Therefore, if we are to continue using the New Negro renaissance as a case study of the pitfalls and possibilities toward radical social change, we must come to terms with the actually existing economic, political, *and* cultural relations of the period.[5]

In the end, Cruse argued that the failure of the 1920s rested on an inability to see the relationship between the cultural revolution of the New Negro Renaissance and the emerging mass communication media of the era. He observed that the idea of the transcendent intellectual or the pure culture of the grounded community is unrealistic in an age when the mass media has permeated nearly every aspect of human existence. Instead of a turn away from these institutions, or creating harsh distinctions between social movements, the life of the mind, and the marketplace, Cruse demanded that all cultural institutions (theaters, halls, club sites, movie houses, and media production facilities) be "*owned and administered* by the people" (emphasis in original). Ownership would take place within a mixed economy where the exploitative free enterprise and predatory laissez-faire impulses of private black businesses were tempered by cooperative institutional control and state funding. Furthermore, this kind of ownership of the cultural apparatus, "from the *bottom up*," could happen only by bridging the cultural gap between black middle-class patronage, the leadership of the black intelligentsia, and the tastes and "artistic capital" of the black masses.[6]

Black Bourgeoisie and the *Crisis* offer sound critiques of the failures made by the black "middle stratum" of the 1920s, which could easily be leveled against both the political and personal choices made by the marketplace intellectuals within this study. But Cruse's analysis (via Du Bois and Mills) of the actually existing relationship between cultural tastes and the cultural apparatus significantly resonates with the story of Chicago's New Negroes. In the end, Frazier's pessimistic vision of black Chicago's consumer culture became the dominant approach for evaluating the relationship between culture and politics more broadly. At the same time, Cruse makes the limited claim, "The way Harlem goes (or does not go) so goes all black America." As a form of imaginary reconstruction, I want to end with a response to these two oversights by asking: What would happen to our intellectual memory of the crisis of the black bourgeoisie if Harold Cruse had lived in Chicago? To begin, I want to revisit the "Don't Spend" campaign that Frazier dismissed as simply anti-Semitic and also the National Negro Congress (NNC) that Cruse derided as "the working-class sellout of the black ghettos—by the Negro left." Within their black metropolis contexts, these two episodes exemplify the visionary brilliance of Chicago's New Negro intellectual life in ways that serve as seeds of dissent and social organization for future political and cultural movements.[7]

Race and class consciousness came together most expertly in the 1929–30 "Don't Spend Your Money Where You Can't Work" campaign. The "Don't Spend" movement was an important mass protest and boycott strategy that started on Chicago's Stroll and was later successfully used in cities across the country. "Don't Spend" brought together local institutions with various political orientations, including the *Chicago Whip*, the NAACP, and even the Jones brothers' policy gambling family. In fact, Egyptian mystic and black nationalist Sufi Abdul Hamid and his Negro Industrial Clerical Alliance are reported to have actually started the campaign, with the *Whip* taking more prominence when many feared that Hamid's street corner style and anti-white and black separatist positions would alienate residents. These campaigns were instrumental in securing over 2,000 jobs for black workers in Chicago. "Don't Spend" initiatives were repeated with varying levels of success all over the country and instigated the community appeal for a Ben Franklin franchise within the black metropolis that was opened by the Jones brothers in 1937.[8]

What is rarely noted, outside of the structural significance of the campaign, however, was its theoretical impact on black intellectuals like Oliver Cromwell Cox. Cox was a University of Chicago–trained sociologist who criticized leftist scholars like Frazier for offering too wide a definition of class to include status-oriented "lifestyles" instead of limiting it to "purely" economic "life choices." Cox made his name as one of black sociology's most pronounced Marxist and accomplished theorists. In *Caste, Class and Race*, Cox offered a direct challenge to the prevailing perspective on race relations of his "Chicago School" mentors. In this study, he attacked what he called Robert Park's "Caste School" orthodoxy in race relations for describing the phenomena of racial discrimination as a cultural or moral condition instead of an economic condition. In many respects, Cox was an orthodox Marxist who could see race and racism only as derivative of the capitalist world system. But during Chicago's "Don't Spend" campaign, he wrote the notes for his infrequently discussed "Origins of Direct-Action Protest among Negroes [in Chicago], 1932–1933," which seemed to alter his vision of the economic world system.[9]

Like Frazier, Cox exhibited clear worries about nationalist impulses in the campaign but was also noticeably inspired by the "Don't Spend" program and what he described as "something of unusual importance developing in American race relations" where "traditional Negro protest" was being transformed "into direct group action." The "Don't Spend" campaign consolidated a number of relevant issues. According to Cox, the boycott strategy was encouraged by the Socialists but discouraged by the *Chicago Defender* and the Communist Party of the United States of America because the Negro had no control over the white-owned "raw materials" or "basic industries" and because the "petty bourgeoisie orientation" of a boycott could not transform the substantial "coal, iron, steel, automobile, and packing industries." Many of these critiques make sense within an orthodox Marxist frame, but "direct action" conditions in 1929 Chicago had created powerful changes, enough for Cox to reluctantly recognize a growing "economic race consciousness." Cox found in "Don't Spend" a response to racial exclusions from the apprenticeship systems of industrial capitalism and to the union strategies of a racially exclusive closed-shop policy to "limit the supply of labor" and therefore drive up the value of white wages.[10]

Within a Depression-era world where black people could not rely on capital, labor, or the New Deal, the "Don't Spend" campaign succeeded as a comprehensive policy of community development with boycott tactics attending to a range of local issues. Cox noted the movement's importance for challenging long-held racial stereotypes about "lazy and incompetent" black labor that were used to justify policies of exclusion. It also reenergized local black consumer patronage in the face of the chain store onslaught of the late 1920s and generated a demand for political accountability through local voters' leagues. The power of the campaign clearly rested in its direct acts of letter writing petitions and boycott picketing within preexisting networks, where Cox argued that "Don't Spend" both appealed to the masses and made mass action "respectable."[11]

Direct action became so respectable within black communities across the country that Cox noted that many times it failed elsewhere because activists ignored the situated and particular nature of Chicago conditions and strategies. Community acceptance of direct action became so benign that many went on to associate the famed Montgomery bus boycott tactics with the nonviolent philosophy of Gandhi instead of tracing its roots to 1929 Chicago. Cox suggested that a fuller understanding of larger civil rights movement philosophies, including the 1942 Chicago founding of the Congress on Racial Equality and the national acceptance of black boycott politics, must begin with an examination of the New Negro world surrounding the first "Don't Spend" campaign.[12]

Only six years later at a conference on Howard University's campus, another group continued the call to synthesize race and class concerns, and from this emerged the NNC. A national NNC meeting was held in Chicago in 1936 to address directly the general discriminatory treatment black people faced in the New Deal era; the organization maintained strength until its 1940 demise. Its first annual convention, fittingly held at Chicago's famous Eighth Regiment Armory, is universally noted as groundbreaking in cross-class political and occupational coalition building that included black leftist, nationalist, and liberal outlooks. According to the program, those in attendance spanned the full spectrum of the black metropolis model, including political scientist Ralph Bunche, cultural critic Locke, F. B. Ransom of the Madam C. J. Walker Company, Communist Harry Haywood, founder of

Chicago's Institutional Church and Society Settlement Bishop Reverdy Ransom, Reverend J. C. Austin of Pilgrim Baptist Church, the Metropolitan Community Choir, and fellow traveling writers Richard Wright and Langston Hughes. At the end of the meeting, the convention fittingly voted A. Philip Randolph, cofounder of the *Messenger* and Brotherhood of Sleeping Car Porters, as president of the NNC.[13]

The national body was subsequently mired in controversy over whether its leadership had shifted to white leftists or if control remained in black hands. However, the local Chicago Council remained strong and diverse with leadership including organized labor, the Communist Party, and the Brotherhood of Sleeping Car Porters Citizens' Committee, and so on, making successful demands for racial inclusion from regional mainstream capital industries and labor organizations. The NNC also brought together the Steel Workers Organizing Committee with the Congress of Industrial Organizations. Such collaborations were built on preexisting community networks in the black metropolis and included the tactics of direct action organizing that continued to bring the black bourgeoisie over to a politics of mass action in support of, for example, a domestic workers' union and an antilynching bill.

The black metropolis as an ideal and place also directly informed Wright's discussion of American racial fascism and its parallels with conditions in Germany, which served as an introduction to St. Clair Drake and Horace R. Cayton's important and appropriately titled 1945 social scientific volume, *Black Metropolis*. Such a vision of "black worldliness" also found mass expression through the *Chicago Defender*'s and *Pittsburgh Courier*'s "Double V" campaign (victory against fascism abroad, victory against racism at home) during World War II. These political positions and styles of protest helped set the stage for the important NAACP Legal Defense and Education Fund during the civil rights era. After Randolph left the NNC, he formed the March on Washington Committee in 1941, demanding integration in the armed forces and an end to job discrimination. We remember the 1963 March on Washington and its soundtrack accompaniment by another Chicago New Negro, Mahalia Jackson, as part of Martin Luther King's legacy. Yet we forget that this social movement derived both direct symbolic and economic capital from the black metropolis.[14]

If Cruse had lived in Chicago, perhaps he would have identified with the black metropolis model for his desired "broad cultural conditioning" that could cultivate a radical class of culture workers. In the end, the black metropolis model of community consumption and production did not just create a public sphere of intellectual life. The story of Chicago's New Negroes also provides a necessary bridge over the gap between the supposedly disparate "renaissance" 1920s and "radical" 1930s. Moreover, the "Don't Spend" and NNC campaigns that emerged from this New Negro world provided early blueprints that reconnect the racial uplifters of the early twentieth century with the mid- to late-twentieth-century civil righters and black power activists. This historical moment serves as a warning to "intellectuals" and activists that they must take the possible intersections between consumer culture, the cerebral, and community seriously if they ever hope to engage and mobilize people in any way that effectively matches the complexities of their multiracial urban, national, and/or international existence.

More broadly, this book offers a deeper exploration of how knowledge is produced, an expanded world of ideas, and the building of political cultures in unlikely places, particularly the mass consumer marketplace. We must continue to work through very important theories of "everyday life" but also further investigate how actors of the everyday theorize themselves in ways that complicate both academic analysis and public policy. Here, I wanted to showcase and highlight the self-conscious level of artistry, anxiety, desire, pride, guilt, and struggle and the thought and debate that were articulated within the black consumer marketplace. Once we recognize that mass-produced culture and the culture of traditional and community intellectuals are part of larger modes of production and consumption, a revised call and response can be explored. This examination has, I hope, historicized, documented, and talked through the popular theoretical assertion that race is partially a social construction while challenging the idea that racial signifiers have been handed out primarily from the top down. In between the myth of autonomous intellectual genius and the innate authenticity of the folk community stand the popular arts, the cultural apparatus, and the many producers, critics, and consumers who sustain this important sphere of social, political, and material engagement.

At one point, "natural" black "folk" genres of adornment, film, music, and recreation were used to discipline and police black labor and leisure habits toward older notions of race uplift and respectability. However, the powers of consumer tastes in this particular moment were able to overturn, or at least challenge, community gatekeepers to see different ways of being "black" that set the stage for mass action and a second national reconstruction. The realm of mass consumer culture symbolized the push and pull of contestation and integration that marked the potential realities of democratic freedom. People continue to articulate personal and group visions, anxieties, fears, and desires through their consumption habits. The mass consumer marketplace is one arena where we unevenly play out gender, class, sexual, regional, and national exclusions, inclusions, hierarchies, and changes. This resiliently takes place through the varying levels at which we buy or buy into different styles, tastes, forms, and locations of cultural production. Therefore, we must continue to interrogate the lines between "folk" institutions, academic ideas, political platforms, and mass culture. This multilayered history of Chicago's New Negroes in the early twentieth century provides insights for our highly stratified information age of the early twenty-first century. Here again, different and competing forms of marketplace discipline and desire offer equally important insights toward theorizing, challenging, and building a New Negro world.

Notes

INTRODUCTION

1. *New York Times*, July 5, 1910; *NYA*, July 7, 1910; *Boston Globe*, July 5, 1910; *Omaha World Daily*, July 5, 1910; Goodwin, *It's Good to Be Black*, 74–79; *Pittsburgh Courier*, June 22, 1946.

2. *Chicago Daily Inter Ocean*, July 5, 1910; Indianapolis *Freeman*, July 9, 1910; Farr, *Black Champion*, 115; *Chicago Tribune*, July 5, 1910.

3. Phrases "Great White Hope" and "Negro's Deliverer" could be found in all the papers; for example, see *Chicago Tribune*, July 2, 1910, and *Current Literature* 48 (Jan. 1910). See also Jack Johnson, *Jack Johnson Is a Dandy*, 155; "Is Prize-Fighting Knocked Out?," *Literary Digest* 41 (July 16, 1910): 85; Farr, *Black Champion*, 72; and *Boston Globe*, July 5, 1910.

4. It's interesting that the white *Boston Globe* estimated a white economic loss of $3 million, while the *New York Age* offered a more realistic number of between $150,000 and $300,000. See *Boston Globe*, July 5, 1910, 5, and *NYA*, July 7, 1910. Reports of black aggression were in every major white newspaper that carried multiple reports from various locations, but for examples, see *Atlanta Constitution*, July 5, 1910; *Boston Globe*, July 5, 1910; and *Chicago Tribune*, July 5, 1910.

5. *NYA*, July 14, 1910; *Atlanta Journal*, July 5, 1910; *Chicago Tribune*, Oct. 20, 1912; *Chicago Daily News*, Oct. 19, 1912. On calls for black modesty, see *NYA*, July 14, 1910; *Chicago Broad Ax*, Nov. 1, 1912; *Chicago Tribune*, Oct. 21, Nov. 9, 1912; and *Los Angeles Times*, Dec. 5, 1912. Sparks controversy comes from *Broad Ax*, Nov. 9, 1912, and *NYA*, Nov. 14, 1912. See also Gilmore, "Jack Johnson and White Women," and Cary B. Lewis, *Freeman*, Oct. 26, 1912.

6. See *Cleveland Gazette*, July 9, 1910; Killens, *Black Man's Burden*, 114–15; and Sammons, *Beyond the Ring*, 46. The general "Jack Johnson" scholarship includes Jack Johnson, *Jack Johnson—In the Ring—And Out*, reprinted as *Jack Johnson Is a Dandy*; Batchelor, *Jack Johnson and His Times*; Farr, *Black Champion*; Gilmore, *Bad Nigger!*; Roberts, *Papa Jack*; and Hietala, *Fight of the Century*. Texts that critically examine Johnson and look at the Social Darwinism logic of the Progressive Era include Bederman, *Manliness and Civilization*; and Mumford, *Interzones*. Studies that directly engage Johnson as a source of race consciousness include Levine, *Black Culture and Black Consciousness*; Sammons, *Beyond the Ring*; and Early, "Black Intellectual." See also Ransom, "The Negro and the Roped Area," *NYA*, Dec. 30, 1909; and Spear, *Black Chicago*, 63, 95–96.

7. The limited understanding of the Harlem or New Negro Renaissance as a project of literary and visual art most prominently begins with Locke's *New Negro*, 3–4. While the term is most associated with the cultural vanguard of the petty bourgeoisie in 1920s Harlem, varying definitions of the term "New Negro" go back to the slave trade. See also Foley, *Spectres of 1919*; Levine, "Concept of the New Negro"; Gates, "Trope of a New Negro"; and Moses, "Lost World of the Negro." Krasner finds use of the term New Negro in black theatrical parodies of racist

stereotypes; see *Resistance, Parody, and Double Consciousness* and his important *Beautiful Pageant.* Moreover, Carby has accurately observed: "Definitions of the Harlem Renaissance are notoriously elusive; descriptions of it as a moment of intense literary and artistic production, or as an intellectual awakening, or as the period of the self-proclaimed 'New Negro' are concepts that are not applicable only to Harlem or to the twenties." See Carby, *Reconstructing Womanhood*, 163. Hine argues that we look beyond Harlem and specifically at cities in the Midwest for New Negro Culture; see *Hine Sight*, 97. B. Edwards makes the same claim but asks that the renaissance be located within a discourse of black internationalism; see his *Practice of Diaspora.*

8. On constructions of "folk" authenticity during the era, see P. Anderson, *Deep River*; Nicholls, *Conjuring the Folk*; Lemke, *Primitive Modernism*; Favor, *Authentic Blackness*; and Kelley, "Notes on Deconstructing the 'Folk.'" See also Locke, *New Negro*, xxv, 3, 201, 224.

9. Levine's work remains the preeminent history of ideas using black folk and popular culture as its site of analysis, yet it is rarely discussed in intellectual history circles. See *Black Culture and Black Consciousness*, x. Projects that continue to focus on Harlem but engage mass culture as at least a parallel formation include P. Anderson, *Deep River*; Marks and Edkins, *Stylemakers and Rulebreakers*; Davis, *Blues Legacies*; Powell, *Rhapsodies in Black*; Spencer, *New Negroes*; and Floyd, *Black Music in the Harlem Renaissance.*

10. Therefore, the production of knowledge and the study of that process has been inappropriately driven by a desire to transcend social realities, understood as a set of limiting constraints on objectivity instead of as engaging in the act of descendence, through a literal *descent* into the material conditions that shape, form, and give life to intellectual possibilities.

11. Cohen's study of Chicago's industrial workers insightfully discusses the black consumer marketplace but doesn't fully examine the diversity of opinion found within that market, examining one black public sphere instead of multiple and overlapping spheres. See Cohen, *Making a New Deal.* This wider understanding of the production of knowledge is influenced by Canclini, *Consumers and Citizens*; Farred, *What's My Name*; Hall, "Notes on Deconstructing the 'Popular'"; and Levine, *Black Culture and Black Consciousness.* Jack Johnson will be covered more thoroughly in chapter 6.

12. Frazier, "Chicago," 73; Johnson, "These 'Colored' United States," 933.

13. On the relationship between consumerism and the racial community in Chicago, see A. Green, "Selling the Race"; and Cohen, "Encountering Mass Culture." The larger black urban cultural studies field includes James Weldon Johnson, *Black Manhattan*; S. Hall et al., *Policing the Crisis*; Lipsitz, *Class and Culture*; Carby, *Reconstructing Womanhood*; Gilroy, *There Ain't No Black in the Union Jack*; E. Lewis, *In Their Own Interests*; Rose, *Black Noise*; Kelley, *Race Rebels*; White and White, *Stylin'*; S. Smith, *Dancing in the Streets*; Mullins, *Race and Affluence*; and Wolcott, *Remaking Respectability.*

14. See "The Old and the New," *Chicago Defender*, Jan. 3, 1920; "The Cause of the New Negro," *Chicago Whip*, Jan. 17, 1920; and "The New Negro" in Robb, *Negro in Chicago*, 16. See also "The Passing of Uncle Tom," *Whip*, Aug. 9, 1919, and "Radicals and Raids," *Whip*, Jan. 10, 1920.

The volumes of work on black Chicago include the CCRR, *Negro in Chicago*; E. Davis, *Illinois Federation*; Robb, *Negro in Chicago*; Frazier, *Negro Family in Chicago*; Herbst, *Negro in the Slaughtering and Meatpacking Industry*; Drake, "Churches and Voluntary Associations"; Drake and Cayton, *Black Metropolis*; Duncan and Duncan, *Negro Population of Chicago*; Strickland, *History of the Chicago Urban League*; Gosnell, *Negro Politicians*; Spear, *Black Chicago*; Tuttle, *Race Riot*; Travis, *Autobiography of Black Chicago*; Grossman, *Land of Hope*; Philpott, *Slum and the Ghetto*; Grimshaw, *Bitter Fruit*; Kenney, *Chicago Jazz*; Capetti, *Writing Chicago*; Weems, *Black Business*; C. Reed, *Chicago NAACP*; Mumford, *Interzones*; Knupfer, *Toward a Tenderer Humanity*; Hendricks, *Gender, Race and Politics*; Stewart, *Migrating to the Movies*; Best, *Passionately Human*; A. Green, "Selling the Race"; Blair, "Vicious Commerce"; and Lerner, "Visions of a Sporting City."

15. Phelps, "Negro Life in Chicago," *HCM*, May 1919, 12; "Colored Chicago," *Crisis* (Sept. 1915), 234. Information about "the metropolis" comes from Commission on Chicago Historical and Architectural Landmarks, "Black Metropolis Historic District," Chicago Historical Society; Drake and Cayton, *Black Metropolis*; Jackson and Wylie, *Movin' On Up*, 46; and Frazier, "Chicago," 73.

Spear and Tuttle included the black radical/nationalists associated with the *Whip* and the climate set by soldiers returning from World War I in their respective conceptualizations of the "New Negro." But challenging conceptual parameters of the New Negro was not the primary concern of their studies; see Spear, *Black Chicago*, and Tuttle, *Race Riot*. Bone was the first to contemplate a Chicago Renaissance in comparison with Harlem, but because he used the Harlem model of visual and literary art, he purposefully dated it in the 1930s era of Richard Wright and "Chicago School" black sociology. See Bone, "Richard Wright and the Chicago Renaissance." Samuel Floyd wonderfully extends Bone's model to include musicians of the 1920s and 1930s but maintains a distinction between "high" and "vernacular" forms. This is evident in Floyd's claim that Chicago lacked "coherence, as a culture building movement" because it had no "black string quartets and no black composed operas . . . but . . . the vernacular genres grew powerfully in influence." See Floyd, *Power of Black Music*, 131, and *Black Music in the Harlem Renaissance*.

16. See Denning, *Mechanic Accents*; and Trachtenberg, *Incorporation of America*.

17. Drawing on the debates between Jurgen Habermas and Oskar Negt and Alexander Kluge, public spheres are generally defined as arenas or realms of social life where people come together for critical debate and public opinion is formed. I am extending this idea to include debates over public representations and political visions of "the race" in the first few decades of twentieth-century Chicago. See Habermas, *Structural Transformation*, and the important response by Negt and

Kluge, *Public Sphere and Experience*. M. Hansen applies theories of the public sphere to ethnic film exhibition; see her *Babel and Babylon*. Black scholars have also made important contributions to public sphere debates, including the Black Public Sphere Collective, *Black Public Sphere*; Higginbotham, *Righteous Discontent*; and Gilroy, *Black Atlantic*.

18. See *Defender* and *Whip* quoted in Grossman, *Land of Hope*, 152, 155, respectively. See also *Defender*, Mar. 24, 1917, May 25, July 6, Sept. 14, 1918, and *Whip*, June 24, Sept. 20, 1919.

19. An American modernity can generally be understood as spanning the time from Reconstruction (1865) to the start of de-industrialization in northern urban centers. Discussing a black modernity highlights the simultaneous exclusion and centrality of black people to the world-system formations of industrial capitalism, scientific rationality, rights-based national belonging, mass cultural production and consumption, and hierarchically experienced heterosocial contact. Here I focus on the uneven shift from property to personhood, from enslavement to relative freedom (or what Gilroy calls from slave ship to citizenship). This is followed by the black politically resistant decision to shift battlefronts from the Jim Crow South to the northern and western cities and their impersonal neglect after the failure of Reconstruction and the resurgence of racial terror. Here the management practices of racial reasoning shift from the religious tales of Ham to the biocultural social sciences, alongside the more intimate forces of housing and labor restrictions enforced by racial violence and legal mandates. At the same time, this exile from national belonging ignited black internationalisms that exceeded the nation-state. Black people simultaneously manipulated international mass cultural networks to labor in both the high (and rapidly middling) forms of theater, literature, and visual art and the popular realms of moving pictures, radio and records, advertising, and athletics.

Much of my discussion of a black modernity centers on internal struggles over the link between the social realities of racial respectability and various aesthetic approaches to identity representation. In a blunt and general way, on one hand we have the modernist critique of racist overindustrialization found in cultural and political radicals and on the other hand bohemians romanticizing the transcendent, individualized, isolated auteur, the folk spirit, and a disciplined adherence to the intention of the cultural text. The quest for cultural coherency, linearity, and textual discipline served as both a morally prescriptive and socially liberating alternative to the urban industrial and mechanical chaos of a uncultured nouveaux riches from above and racial, class, and sexual deviants from below. However, most of my discussion focuses on a new black modern paradigm of expression and meaning situated directly within the seeming chaos of the urban industrial marketplace, making visible (not evading) the cracks, ruptures, breaks, and racial unevenness of the modern experience. Many of these elements have been discussed elsewhere, but not in relation to the New Negro cultural forms covered in this study. This black modern social aesthetic includes the constitution and improvisation of standard texts within demonstration and exhibition contexts, the "treatment" or the making do with given materials and their transformation in some meaningful fashion from the vantage point of a particular set of experiences, and finally the bodily re-coding of time and space through the tactical maneuvers of defense and adaptation on both city streets and playing fields of contestation. See E. Thompson, *Soundscapes of Modernity*; Dinerstein, *Swinging the Machine*; Stansell, *American Moderns*; Poole, *Vision, Race, and Modernity*; S. Hall et al., *Modernity*; Hanchard, "Afro-Modernity"; Mignolo, *Darker Side of the Renaissance* and "Darker Side of the Renaissance"; Gilroy, *Black Atlantic*; Kalaidjian, *American Culture*; Jameson, *Postmodernism*; D. Harvey, *Condition of Post-modernity*; Berman, *All That Is Solid*; and C. Robinson, *Black Marxism*.

20. For early expressions of the New Negro, see Adams, "Rough Sketches"; and Washington, Wood, and Williams, *New Negro for a New Century*. See also Levine, "Concept of the New Negro"; Moses, "Lost World of the Negro"; Gates, "Trope of a New Negro"; and Meier, *Negro Thought in America*.

21. On the migration to Chicago, see Hine, "Black Migration"; Drake and Cayton, *Black Metropolis*; Spear, *Black Chicago*; and Grossman, *Land of Hope*. A sampling of the larger literature includes Griffin, *"Who Set You Flowin'?"*; Trotter, *Great Migration*; C. Marks, *Farewell*; and Henri, *Black Migration*.

22. See Du Bois, "African Roots of War"; and Harrison's important *When Africa Awakes*. On Frazier, see J. S. Holloway, *Confronting the Veil*, and A. Platt, *E. Franklin Frazier Reconsidered*. Also see Moses, *Golden Age of Black Nationalism*; Esebede, *Pan-Africanism*; and Du Bois, *On the Importance of Africa in World History*.

23. See Contee, "Du Bois, the NAACP, and the Pan-African Congress." Other groups are covered in Skinner, *African Americans*.

24. On the larger moment of rebellion, resistance, and race consciousness, see Foley, *Spectres of 1919*; Patterson and Kelley, "Unfinished Migrations"; Mishkin, *Harlem and Irish Renaissance*; Gallichio, *African American Encounter*; E. Allen, "When Japan Was 'Champion of the Darker Races'"; Moses, *Golden Age of Black Nationalism*; Goggins, *Carter G. Woodson*; and Conyers, "Biographical Sketch." On the Bolshevik Revolution as a "slave movement," see Graham, *Soul of John Brown*, 266–67. On Lenin's remarks and the larger question of African Americans as an oppressed nation, see his "Of Capitalism and Agriculture"; and Kelley, *Race Rebels*, 107. On white nativist angst, see Lee, *At America's Gates*; Jacobson, *Barbarian Virtues*; Michaels, *Our America*; and Frederickson, *Black Image*. Also look at Eliot's "Waste Land," 38.

25. A. Platt, *E. Franklin Frazier Reconsidered*; Bond and Gibbs, "Social Portrait"; Wolters, *New Negro on Campus*; and Du Bois, "Returning Soldiers." It was also printed in the *Broad Ax* and *Defender*, both May 24, 1919. See also Tuttle, *Race Riot*, 209; Hartt, "New Negro"; and CCRR, *Negro in Chicago*, 481. For more on the diasporic consciousness of soldiers, artists, sailors, and so on, see, among many, B. Ed-

wards, *Practice of Diaspora*, 3; Stovall, *Paris Noir*; E. Lewis, "To Turn as on a Pivot"; and Gilroy, *Black Atlantic*.

26. See Foglesong, *America's Secret War*, 42; Kornweibel, *"Seeing Red"*; Du Bois, "Returning Soldiers." See also James Weldon Johnson, *Along This Way*, 341; Sandburg, *Chicago Race Riots*; Tuttle, *Race Riot*; de Quattro, "Popular Music"; McKay, "If We Must Die"; and Maxwell, *New Negro*. The poem was reprinted in the *Messenger: New Opinion of the Negro* (Sept. 1919, July 1921), and in the *Crusader*, Sept. 1919, May 1920, and Jan. 1921.

27. In two 1919 cartoons, the *Messenger* criticized the "Old Crowd" Negro leadership for supporting black military patriotism during the war yet asking for nonviolence in the face of white aggression during the riots, whereas the "New Crowd" Negro was represented as a collection of gun-toting black men seeking retribution for racial violence. See "Following the Advice of the 'Old Crowd' Negro," *Messenger* (June 1919), and "The 'New Crowd' Negro Making America Safe for Himself," *Messenger* (July 1919). See also "The New Negro—What Is He?" *Messenger* (Aug. 1920), 73; and revisit the articles about the New Negro in the *Whip* cited at the beginning of this introduction. The diasporic diversity of journals and organizations is discussed in, for example, B. Edwards, *Practice of Diaspora*; Brock and Castenada, *Between Race and Empire*; Egonu, "Les Continents"; and R. Moore, *Nationalizing Blackness*. On U.S. organizations, see C. Reed, *Chicago NAACP*; Solomon, *Cry Was Unity*; C. Hughes, "Negro Sanhedrin Movement"; and Ferris, "Negro Renaissance," *Negro World*, Feb. 11, 1922. The rest of the organizations will be discussed in more documented detail in chapter 1.

28. Hartt, "New Negro"; *Call* quoted in Foner, *American Socialism*, 28; Gerold Robinson, "The New Negro," *Freeman*, June 2, 1920, quoted in Arneson, *Black Protest*, 117. On white primitivism and race pride, see Osofsky, *Harlem*; Huggins, *Harlem Renaissance*; D. Lewis, *When Harlem Was in Vogue*; Hutchinson, *Harlem Renaissance*; Douglas, *Terrible Honesty*; Kenney, *Chicago Jazz*; Filene, *Romancing the Folk* and "'Our Singing Country'"; Bendix, *In Search of Authenticity*; J. Lomax, *Cowboy Songs*; Baldwin, "Black Belts and Ivory Towers"; di Leonardo, *Exotics at Home*; and V. Williams, "Franz Boaz's Paradox," and *Rethinking Race*. On racialized slumming in Chicago, see Heap, "'Slumming'"; and Mumford, *Interzones*.

29. Cronon, *Nature's Metropolis*; H. Platt, *Electric City*.

30. Cronon, *Nature's Metropolis*. See Deegan, *Race, Hull House, and the University of Chicago* and *Jane Addams*. Literature on the University of Chicago is discussed in more detail in chapter 1.

31. Grossman, *Land of Hope*, 4. See also Drake and Cayton, *Black Metropolis*; Duncan and Duncan, *Negro Population of Chicago*; and Spear, *Black Chicago*. On Abbott, see Ottley, *Lonely Warrior*. See also R. Johnson, "Sweet Home Chicago." On Johnson's song, see Best, *Passionately Human*, 21–22.

32. Sandburg, *Chicago Race Riots*; Tuttle, *Race Riot*; Drake and Cayton, *Black Metropolis*; CCRR, *Negro in Chicago*. See also Grossman, *Land of Hope*, especially

the chapter "The White Man's Union"; W. Foster, *American Trade*; and Randolph and Owen, "The Cause of and Remedy for Race Riots," *Messenger* 2 (Sept. 1919).

33. Du Bois, "Let Us Reason Together"; *Messenger* 2 (Sept. 1919); "Our Far-Flung Challenge," editorial, *Crusader*, Sept. 1919. While the racial line of demarcation was evidently quite real, the "imaginary line" quote is from Drake and Cayton, *Black Metropolis*, 66.

34. Chandler Owen, "The Cabaret—A Useful Social Institution," *Messenger* 4 (Aug. 1922); and Grossman, *Land of Hope*, 95.

35. Binder, *Chicago and the New Negro*, 3.

36. Ibid., 4, 11, 13, 15, 24.

37. The idea of "makeover" here responds to Urban League attempts to turn migrants into efficient, ambitious workers. See Sayre, "Making Over Poor Workers."

38. Locke, *New Negro*, 7.

CHAPTER ONE

1. Phelps, "Negro Life in Chicago," *HCM*, May 1919, 12; advertisement for "The Map of Colored Chicago" (The Progressive Book Company), *HCM*, Apr. 1922; Ellington, *Music Is My Mistress*, 131.

2. Of course we could examine the Stroll from a much wider array of cultural mapping possibilities. These three vantage points are the most useful for this study.

3. See Grossman, *Land of Hope*, 127.

4. On restrictive covenants and racial violence, see Bachin, *Building the South Side*; Drake and Cayton, *Black Metropolis*, 178–221; Grossman, *Land of Hope*, 135; Spear, *Black Chicago*, 20–21; Philpott, *Slum and the Ghetto*, 146–200; Tuttle, *Race Riot*, 157–83; and CCRR, *Negro in Chicago*, 117–26. For more on housing stock, see Grossman, *Land of Hope*, 135–38; and Drake and Cayton, *Black Metropolis*, 573–77.

5. "The Bohemia of Colored Folk," *Whip*, Aug. 15, 1919; White and White, *Stylin'*; Travis, *Autobiography of Black Jazz*, 30; Spivey, *Union and the Black Musician*, 38–39; "State Street, 'The Great White Way,'" *Defender*, May 11, 1912; "31st and State Streets," *Defender*, Feb. 12, 1910; *Whip*, Apr. 24, 1920. See also "Colored Citizens Alarmed Over Social Evil Coming into Their Residence District," *Freeman*, Mar. 11, 1916; *Defender*, June 18, Apr. 9, 1910. Depictions of the Stroll can be found in Du Bois, *Dark Princess*, 126–27; R. Wright, *Lawd Today!*; L. Hughes, *Big Sea*; Armstrong, *Louis Armstrong*; Dunham, *Touch of Innocence*; A. Hunter, *Alberta Hunter*; Dance, *World of Earl Hines*; Mezzrow and Wolfe, *Really the Blues*; W. Smith, *Music on My Mind*; and Ellington, *Music Is My Mistress*, among others.

6. *Chicago Tribune*, May 15, 1917; CCRR, *Negro in Chicago*, 524, 529–30, 532.

7. CCRR, *Negro in Chicago*, 323; Ogren, *Jazz Revolution*; *Variety*, Dec. 2, 1925, Apr. 21, 1926; *Chicago Tribune*, Mar. 5, May 5, 1917; *Daily News*, Mar. 14, 1917. For the linking of the Great Migration to reportage of black community vice, see *Tribune*, Mar. 16, Jan. 18, 1917, Nov. 20, Oct. 14, 16, 17, 19, 1916, Jan. 19, 20, 22, 30, 1917;

and *Daily News*, Jan. 18, 19, 1917. See also Heap, " 'Slumming' "; and Mumford, *Interzones*.

8. Vice Commission of Chicago, *Social Evil*, 38. For more on the relegation of particularly women reformers to the School of Social Work, see Bachin, *Building the South Side*; and Deegan, *Race, Hull House, and the University of Chicago* and *Jane Addams*.

9. For just a sample of the extensive "Chicago School" scholarship, see Abbott, *Department and Discipline*; D. Smith, *Chicago School*; Lindner, *Reportage of Urban Culture*; Lal, *Romance of Culture*; Rochberg-Halton, "Life, Literature and Sociology"; L. Harvey, *Myths of the Chicago School of Sociology*; Bulmer, *Chicago School of Sociology*; Kurtz, *Evaluating Chicago Sociology*; Wacker, *Ethnicity, Pluralism, and Race*, and "American Dilemma"; Lewis and Smith, *American Sociology and Pragmatism*; Raushenbush, *Robert E. Park*; Matthews, *Quest for an American Sociology*; and Madge, *Origins of Scientific Sociology*.

10. Persons points out that the distinction between "race" and "ethnicity" is quite recent. The Chicago sociologists under discussion often used "race" where we would now use "ethnicity." Persons prefers to use "ethnicity" as the comprehensive term, whereas the subject of this book encourages me to use "race." I will be using race in the same way that it was deployed by Chicago School social scientists, which exposes both the conceptual instability and social resiliency of the term; see Persons, *Ethnic Studies at Chicago*. See also Park and Burgess, *Introduction to the Science of Sociology*, 138–39; and Park, *Race and Culture*, 208, 262–64, 282. While the urban ecology framework is synonymous with Park, it both includes and precedes him at the University of Chicago; see Small and Vincent, *Introduction to the Study of Society*; W. Thomas, "Race Psychology" and "Psychology of Race Prejudice"; Thomas and Znaniecki, *Polish Peasants*; and Hinkle and Hinkle, *Development of Modern Sociology*, 18–21.

11. Park, Burgess, and McKenzie, *City*, 54–57. In *Race and Culture*, Park goes so far as to argue that the only true route to black cultural assimilation was through both social incorporation and biological miscegenation of white blood; see 387–89. A critical view of the "Chicago School" in relationship to the racial communities in Chicago and abroad exists in Stanfield, "The 'Negro Problem' "; Mumford, *Interzones*; L. Baker, *From Savage to Negro*; Yu, *Thinking Orientals*; and Baldwin, "Black Belts and Ivory Towers."

12. See Carby, "Policing the Black Woman's Body," 754. "Old settler" is a term that goes back to a Chicago club founded in 1902. However, for even a speculative association of the term with a specific time period, I'm using Drake and Cayton's more general idea that "old settler" refers to anyone "who lived in Chicago prior to the First World War." See *Black Metropolis*, 66–67; and "History of Chicago Old Settler Club, 1902–1923," 4, pamphlet in Dunmore Collection, DuSable Museum of African American History. Secondary works examining these class/cultural hierarchies include Spear, *Black Chicago*; and Grossman, *Land of Hope*.

13. See K. Gaines, *Uplifting the Race*, 13.

14. Wolcott's work pays special attention to the highly contested meaning of respectability between the classes; see her *Remaking Respectability*. For particular work on Wells, see McMurray, *To Keep the Waters Troubled*; Schechter, *Ida B. Wells-Barnett and American Reform*; and Wells-Barnett, *Crusade for Justice*.

15. Quotes are from important "Old Settlers" in Chicago, including George Cleveland Hall speech at Frederick Douglass Center reprinted in *Broad Ax*, Dec. 31, 1904; clubwoman Fannie Barrier Williams, "Social Bonds"; theater and film critic Sylvester Russell, "Musical and Dramatic," *Defender*, Apr. 9, 23, 1910; and Frazier, *Negro Family in Chicago*, 112. See also Booker T. Washington's important 1900 speech at Chicago's Bethel AME church, "Booker T. Washington," *Broad Ax*, Jan. 20, 1900.

16. See Bordieu, *Distinction*.

17. M. Ryan discusses in more detail the symbolic representation of women in the public sphere as badges of domestic virtue and as nurturers of future citizens. See "Gender and Public Access." Discussions of race, gender, and respectability can be found in Summers, *Manliness and Its Discontents*; Wolcott, *Remaking Respectability*; Hine, *Speaking Truth to Power*; and Shaw, *What a Woman Ought to Be and Do*. Simmons makes the powerful observation that notions of Victorian morality persisted well into the twentieth century, especially as black citizens continued to combat stereotypes of their inherent promiscuity, laziness, and immorality. See "African Americans and Sexual Victorianism."

18. Wolcott, *Remaking Respectability*, 4. On the turn to racial uplift, see K. Gaines, *Uplifting the Race*; and Higginbotham, *Righteous Discontent*. On Fannie Barrier Williams, see Deegan, *New Woman of Color*; and F. Williams, "Social Bonds," "Colored Girl," "Woman's Part," and "Club Movement."

19. Wells-Barnett, *Crusade for Justice*, 303. See also "Negro Fellowship League," *Defender*, June 11, 1910; the pamphlet *Phillis Wheatley Home for Girls* in Phillis Wheatley Association Papers, University of Illinois at Chicago; Hendricks, *Gender, Race and Politics*; Lasch-Quinn, *Black Neighbors*; Knupfer, *Toward a Tenderer Humanity*; Meyerowitz, *Women Adrift*; E. Davis, *Illinois Federation*; and Bowen, *Colored People of Chicago*.

20. Best, *Passionately Human*; Frazier, *Negro Church in America*; Spear, *Black Chicago*; Daniel, "Ritual and Stratification in Chicago Negro Churches" and "Ritual in Chicago's South Side Churches for Negroes"; Drake, "Churches and Voluntary Associations"; Fisher, "History of Olivet Baptist Church of Chicago." On Ransom and the Social Gospel, see Goddard, "Black Social Gospel"; Luker, *Social Gospel*; C. Morris, *Reverdy C. Ransom*; and R. White, *Liberty and Justice for All*. For conservative views of "migrant" worship by "old line" pastors, see *Defender*, May 27, 1922; Bradden, *Under Three Banners*, 249; and Payne, *Recollections*, 253–54. For information on employment agencies in the churches, see *Fact and Figures* (Chicago, 1920), 4, in folder 6 of Papers of the Chicago Commission on Race Relations; and Wood, *Negro in Chicago*, 9.

21. *Defender*, Jan. 7, 28, Feb. 4, 11, 18, 25, Mar. 25, Oct. 11, 1911; *Whip*, Mar. 13, 1920; and Wells-Barnett, *Crusade for Justice*, 332, 372–73. For information on efficiency clubs and lectures, see Arthur, *Life on the Negro Frontier*, 17, 186; "Young Men's Christian Association Movement among Negroes," *Defender*, Apr. 27, June 15, 1918; and Mjagkij, *Light in the Darkness*. More study should analyze the relationship between the YMCA's "Muscular Christianity" ethos and the reform of black migrants. NAACP quote from "Chicago, Great City," Aug. 1, 1923, box 6-48, group 1, NAACP Papers, Library of Congress, Washington, D.C., quoted in Grossman, *Land of Hope*, 318n46; C. Reed, *Chicago NAACP*.

22. *Defender*, Nov. 23, 1918. Chicago Urban League, *First Annual Report* (1917), 11; Annual Report of the National Urban League (1919); *Bulletin of the National Urban League*, 9, no. 1 (Jan. 1920), 20–21; *Bulletin of the National Urban League* (1920), 21, all quoted in Grossman, *Land of Hope*, 145. See also C. Johnson, "Flight from Persecution"; and Strickland, *History of the Chicago Urban League*. Urban League leaflet in Special Collections, University Library, University of Illinois at Chicago.

23. CCRR, *Negro in Chicago*; Frazier, *Negro Family in Chicago*; Bulmer, "Research Methods of the Chicago Commission on Race Relations."

24. J. S. Holloway, *Confronting the Veil*; Teele, *E. Franklin Frazier and Black Bourgeoisie*; and A. Platt, *E. Franklin Frazier Reconsidered*.

25. See Woodson, "Fifty Years of Negro Citizenship," *Negro in Our History*, and *Negro Professional Man*; Woodson and Green, *Negro Wage Earner*; and Woodson, Harmon, and Lindsey, *Negro as Businessman*. See also Greene, *Selling Black History for Carter G. Woodson*; Goggins, *Carter G. Woodson*; and Conyers, *Carter G. Woodson*. For more on the Washington Intercollegiate Club, see A. Green, "Rising Ride of Youth" and a review of this book by Dewey Jones in *Defender*, Oct. 1, 1927, part 2, 2.

26. For general accounts of Chicago's black journalistic landscape, see Kreiling, "Making of Racial Identities"; R. Davis, "Negro Newspaper in Chicago"; and Detweiler, *Negro Press in the United States*. On the larger context, see Kornweibel, *No Crystal Stair*; Vincent, *Voices of a Black Nation*; and Johnson and Johnson, *Propaganda and Aesthetics*.

27. Kreiling, "Rise of the Black Press."

28. See "Chicago is the embodiment of the dream of Booker T. Washington" in *Defender*, Aug. 23, 1924. For an account of the changing racial ideologies in Negro leadership, see Meier, *Negro Thought in America* and "Negro Class Structure"; and Spear, *Black Chicago*.

29. *The Chicago Black Chamber of Commerce* pamphlet in the Vivian G. Harsh Research Collection of Afro-American History and Literature.

30. Provident Hospital symbolized interracial cooperation, as white philanthropists/industrialists, including Philip Armour, Marshall Fields, and George Pullman, helped fund this medical facility to become the first hospital in the country to provide integrated health care to patients and the only one to offer medical educa-

tion and employment for black nurses, dentists, and doctors. See Gamble, *Making a Place for Ourselves*; Spear, *Black Chicago*, 52–53; and Buckler, *Doctor Dan*. The Eighth Regiment Armory was constructed in honor of Chicago's all-black infantry and had become a site of community pride for important public exhibitions. See Tuttle, *Race Riot*. The Appomattox Club was one of the many networking organizations for those among the professional managerial class who were excluded from socializing with Chicago's black elite. See Spear, *Black Chicago*, 107–8. See also Canty, "Jesse Binga"; McKinley, "Anthony Overton"; and "Some Chicagoans of Note," *Crisis* (Sept. 1915); Ottley, *Lonely Warrior*; L. Evans, "Claude A. Barnett"; and L. Hogan, *Black National News Service*. On the Your Cab Company, see "Announcement Extraordinary," *Defender*, Feb. 28, 1925. General celebrations of black business can be seen in Commission on Chicago Historical and Architectural Landmarks, "Black Metropolis Historic District," Chicago Historical Society; "Business" file, IWP; and "The Chicago Black Chamber of Commerce," Vivian G. Harsh Research Collection of Afro-American History and Literature. For work on insurance companies, see Weems, *Black Business*; Puth, *Supreme Life*; Bryant, "Negro Insurance Companies"; and Woodson, "Insurance Business."

31. See *HCM*, Aug. 1924; and *Whip*, June 26, 1920. Emerging from the race riots of 1919, "college-trained" Joseph Bibb, William Linton, and A. C. MacNeal organized the *Whip* as a unique organ of race pride, political agitation, and economic radicalism. These self-proclaimed "New Negroes" shared a similar vision of economic radicalism with the patrons of Harlem's *Messenger*, but there is no evidence that they were in contact with each other. While the "Don't Spend" campaign began in Chicago, it opened up jobs for black workers all over the country. See Spear, *Black Chicago*, 197–200, and IWP, box 41–47. There is a run of the *Whip* at the Wisconsin Historical Society, Madison, Wisc.

32. Kreiling, "Commercialization of the Black Press," 187; Drake and Cayton, *Black Metropolis*, 412; Ottley, *Lonely Warrior*.

33. For "mass appeal" quote, see Kreiling, "Commercialization of the Black Press," 187. He also cites representative headlines like "State Street a Breeding Spot for Evil," "Influx of Southern Bullies Brings Disgrace to Chicago," " 'Greater Love' Leads Woman to Murder," and "Kills Wife Because She Disobeyed." Sensational *Defender* headlines are also discussed in R. Davis, "Negro Newspaper in Chicago," 60–61. For behavioral prescriptions, see note 21 above and "Some Dont's," *Defender*, May 17, 1919.

34. Grossman, *Land of Hope*, 74; Ottley, *Lonely Warrior*.

35. The notion of "in-betweenness" is drawn from Griffin, *"Who Set You Flowin'?"*

36. C. Marks, *Farewell*, 37; CCRR, *Negro in Chicago*, 95; Henri, *Black Migration*. In fact, every major figure in this study lived in at least one other city or town before settling in the Chicago area. Madam C. J. Walker had spent time in St. Louis and Denver, Oscar Micheaux had experienced various cities as a Pullman porter, and Thomas Dorsey lived in Atlanta. When Jack Johnson and Rube Foster finally settled

in Chicago, they had already been there for short stints as journeymen athletes along complicated routes of travel taking them from coast to coast and back again.

37. Ottley, *Lonely Warrior*, 87–88; Detweiler, *Negro Press in the United States*, 6. Black southerners bought automobiles and radios, and many had visited Chicago in 1893 for the World's Columbian Exposition and challenged Jim Crow shopping limitations with purchases from Chicago-based stores like Sears and Roebuck and Montgomery Ward. See Ownby, *American Dreams in Mississippi*; Kirby, *Rural Worlds Lost*; and C. Reed, *All the World Is Here!* Sampling of black migration literature includes Henri, *Black Migration*; C. Marks, *Farewell*; Grossman, *Land of Hope*; Trotter, *Great Migration*; and Griffin, *"Who Set You Flowin'?"*

38. Southern, *Biographical Dictionary*, 316–17; Peterson, *Only the Ball Was White*, 112. See also Handy, *Blues* and *Father of the Blues*.

39. See CCRR, *Negro in Chicago*; *U.S. Fourteenth Census*, 4:1076–77; and Barnett, "We Win a Place in Industry." See also Hammond, *White Collar Profession*; Barrett, *Work and Community*; Herbst, *Negro in the Slaughtering and Meat-Packing Industry*; Tuttle, *Race Riot*; Brody, *Steelworkers in America*; and Cayton and Mitchell, *Black Workers*.

40. *U.S. Fourteenth Census*, 4:1076–79. See also U. Taylor, "From White Kitchens to White Factories"; J. Jones, *Labor of Love*; and Spear, *Black Chicago*, 151–55. On unions, see Barrett, *Work and Community*; and Grossman, *Land of Hope*. For general work on labor discipline and black resistance, see E. P. Thompson, *Making of the English Working Class*; and Gutman, *Work, Culture and Society*.

41. Wolcott, *Remaking Respectability*, 102; Vice Commission of Chicago, *Social Evil*, 45; Drake and Cayton, *Black Metropolis*, 598 (emphasis in original); and CCRR, *Negro in Chicago*, 387. Critical readings of prostitution that confirm this woman's position include Peiss, *Cheap Amusements*; Rosen, *Lost Sisterhood*; Stansell, *City of Women*; and Gilfoyle, *City of Eros*.

42. There is not enough space to draw special attention to the term "popular arts." But C. L. R. James was a pioneer in cultural studies, and his analysis of consumer culture as a power base for the working class heavily informs this study. See C. L. R. James, *American Civilization* and *Beyond a Boundary*.

43. See Grossman, *Land of Hope*, especially " 'What Work Can I Get if I Go through School?' " and Homel, *Down from Equality*. For general information on Provident, see Buckler, *Doctor Dan*; and Spear, *Black Chicago*. See also Gems, "Blocked Shot."

44. Estimates of the UNIA's strength in Chicago range from 5,000 to 9,000 members. See Drake and Cayton, *Black Metropolis*, 752; Gosnell, *Negro Politicians*, 113; Drake, "Churches and Voluntary Associations," 235, 238–39; Bontemps and Conroy, *They Seek a City*, 171; and Haywood, *Black Bolshevik*, 103–4. On Palmer, Johnson, and the UNIA, see *Negro World*, July 14, 1923, Feb. 19, 1927; *Whip*, Nov. 13, 1921; and Vincent, *Keep Cool*, 73. The connections between Garvey and Walker are from *New York Amsterdam News*, July 6, 1940, in Watkins-Owens, *Blood Relations*.

See also Martin, *Literary Garveyism*. On Noble Drew Ali and the Moorish Science Temple, see Nance, "Respectability" and "Mystery of the Moorish Science Temple"; and E. Allen, "Identity and Destiny." On the early role of the Nation of Islam in Chicago, see Clegg, *Original Man*; Essien-Udom, *Black Nationalism*; and Lincoln, *Black Muslims*.

45. On Haywood and Fort-Whiteman and the Communist Party of the United States of America, see "Lovett Forte Whiteman Home from Russia," *Defender*, Feb. 28, 1925; Kelley, *Race Rebels*; Haywood, *Black Bolshevik*; and Mullen, *Popular Fronts*. On the Local 208, see Spivey, *Union and the Black Musician*. On the *Whip*, see Mullen, *Popular Fronts*; and Spear, *Black Chicago*. For comments on the *Whip* as a cabaret advertising weekly, see Vincent, *Keep Cool*, 73–74. African Blood Brotherhood scholarship includes Makalani, "For the Liberation of Black People Everywhere"; Mullen, *Popular Fronts*; Kelley, *Race Rebels*; Beekman, "This Judas Iscariot"; and T. Taylor, "Cyril Briggs." On the "Don't Spend" campaign, see Mullen, *Popular Fronts*; Greenberg, *"Or Does It Explode?"*; and J. Hunter, " 'Don't Buy from Where You Can't Work." While they had no direct ties to the mass consumer marketplace, another notable example of a combined race and class consciousness is the Brotherhood of Sleeping Car Porters and Maids. See Bates, *Pullman Porters*; and LeRoy, "Founding Heart."

46. For a cultural and historical contextualization of Motley's work, see Robinson and Greenhouse, *Art of Archibald Motley Jr.*; and Mooney, "Representing Race." On literature, see L. Hughes, *Not without Laughter*; R. Wright, *Lawd Today!*; and Flynn and Stricklin, *Frye Street*. Discussions of these works as black versions of the "ghetto pastoral"—stories of working-class communities that reside somewhere between the romantic pastoral and sociologically naturalist realms—can be found in Denning, *Cultural Front*. The Chicago works of Hughes, Wright, and Bonner foreshadow and parallel Gwendolyn Brooks's detailed mapping of Bronzeville life. See G. Brooks, *Maud Martha*. Also look at Mullen, *Popular Fronts*; Capetti, *Writing Chicago*; and Bone, "Richard Wright and the Chicago Renaissance."

47. Vaillant, *Sounds of Reform*, 24; Barlow, *Voice Over*, 50. See also Vaillant, "Sounds of Whiteness." On Amos 'n' Andy, see Ely, *Adventures of Amos 'n' Andy*; and Weinrott, "Chicago Radio." Studies of race radio include Barlow, *Voice Over*; Newman, *Entrepreneurs of Profit and Pride*; MacDonald, *Don't Touch That Dial*; Spaulding, "History of Black Oriented Radio in Chicago"; and JCP.

48. W. H. A. Moore, "In a Black Belt," 3–4, copy in Dunmore Collection, quoted in James Grossman, *Land of Hope*, 140; Locke, *New Negro*, 4; Spear, *Black Chicago*, 156. See also Carby, "Policing the Black Woman's Body."

49. White and White, *Stylin'*, 224; Kenney, *Chicago Jazz*, 13; L. Hughes, *Big Sea*, 33; Spivey, *Union and the Black Musician*, 38–39; Ellington, *Music Is My Mistress*, 131.

50. On the act of strolling, see Stewart, *Migrating to the Movies*, 10–11, 132–38; and White and White, *Stylin'*, 228–34.

51. In Chicago, policy gambling generally describes a lottery game where twelve numbers between 1 and 78 are drawn daily. Participants bet on one or more numbers with the common bet consisting of three numbers, commonly referred to as a "gig." The odds that three numbers bet on were among the twelve drawn was about 100 to 1, making policy an attractive game for the growing number of wage-laboring migrants. See Haller, "Policy Gambling." He also discusses the southern tradition of gambling. Studies that examine the relationship between policy gambling and the structural foundations of the black metropolis include Gosnell, *Negro Politicians*; Travis, *Autobiography of Black Chicago*; and N. Thompson, *Kings*. See also Light, "Immigrant and Ethnic Enterprise in North America"; Watkins-Owens, *Blood Relations*; and Schatzberg and Kelley, *African American Organized Crime*. The best analysis of this specific material and policy in general remains Drake and Cayton, *Black Metropolis*, 470–94.

52. Travis, *Autobiography of Black Jazz*, 26; N. Thompson, *Kings*; IWP, box 35-11, 35-15, 35-17.

53. Travis, *Autobiography of Black Jazz*, 14; IWP, box 35-11, 35-15, 35-17. For more on the Pekin, see Samuelson, "From Ragtime to Real Estate," 201; Knupfer, *Toward a Tenderer Humanity*, 87; "The Colored Press Association of Chicago Organized and News Bureau Established," *Defender*, Feb. 17, 1912; Kenney, *Chicago Jazz*, 5, 6, 11; and Bontemps, *Anyplace but Here*, 119. Douglass Center controversy is discussed in Knupfer, *Toward a Tenderer Humanity*, 293; and Duster, *Crusade for Justice*, 293. N. Thompson offers another account of the Motts inheritance of Johnson money; reportedly when "Mushmouth" died, he had no money to give. See *Kings*, 24. However, the more popular inheritance story is confirmed in Drake and Cayton, *Black Metropolis*, 465, 485.

54. See Kenney, *Chicago Jazz*, 17–18; Travis, *Autobiography of Black Jazz*, 28; *Chicago Daily News*, Dec. 14, 1916. On Dan Jackson, see Weems, *Black Business*. For more on the *Bronzeman*, see Johnson and Johnson, *Propaganda and Aesthetics*, 109. On the Kelley brothers, see N. Thompson, *Kings*, 33.

55. Albertson, *Bessie*, 74; Taylor and Cook, *Alberta Hunter*, 36, 48. For general information, see Vincent, *Keep Cool* and "Community That Gave Jazz to Chicago," 17–20; and C. Hansen, "Social Influences on Jazz Style." See also Ogren, *Jazz Revolution*; Ostransky, *Jazz City*. Black-and-tan cabarets were located in black neighborhoods featuring black performers catering to black and white audiences. These cabarets became points of contact for more intimate interracial relations based both on genuine interest and racist voyeurism. See Kenney, *Chicago Jazz*, 16–17.

56. See N. Thompson, *Kings*, 21–22; Spear, *Black Chicago*, 77; Kenney, *Chicago Jazz*, 9–10; Tuttle, *Race Riot*, 165; Gosnell, *Negro Politicians*, 128–30; "Henry 'Teenan' Jones, Owner of the Elite Café No. 2," *Broad Ax*, Dec. 7, 1918, Aug. 28, 1915; *Defender*, Jan. 23, 1915; and "New Star Theater," *Defender*, Nov. 22, 1913. On Foster, see *Defender*, Dec. 22, Nov. 3, Oct. 20, Oct. 13, 1917, July 1, 1916; and Sampson, *Blacks in Black and White*, 172.

57. *Broad Ax*, June 5, Dec. 25, 1920; *Defender*, Feb. 21, 1920; *Whip*, Dec. 23, 1922. See also N. Thompson, *Kings*, 25; Kenney, *Chicago Jazz*, 19–20; Vincent, *Keep Cool*, 69–77, and "The Community That Gave Jazz to Chicago"; C. Hansen, "Social Influences on Jazz Style"; Ogren, *Jazz Revolution*; and Ostransky, *Jazz City*. See also Grossman, *Land of Hope*, 95; Hennessey, "Black Chicago Establishment"; Calt, "Paramount, Part 2"; Oliver, *Songsters and Saints*, 1–17; Foreman, "Jazz and Race Records"; and Oscar Hunter, "Negro Music in Chicago," Aug. 23, 1940, IWP.

58. *Broad Ax*, July 9, 1910, July 9, 16, 1921, May 6, 1922. See also Kenney, *Chicago Jazz*, 27, 23; Travis, *Autobiography of Black Jazz*, 33; *Defender*, July 2, Sept. 17, 1927; Rogosin, *Invisible Men*, 14–17, 103–14; and Haller, "Policy Gambling," 731.

59. While Cole was not a "policy" leader, his expertise in blackjack and poker allowed him to diversify Metropolitan's holdings and invest in the Chicago American Giants, fund the early black magazine the *Bronzeman*, and sponsor the first black radio program in the United States, Jack Cooper's *All Negro Hour*. See Weems, *Black Business*.

60. On Thompson, see Bukowski, *Big Bill Thompson*; and Wendt and Kogan, *Big Bill of Chicago*. For an understanding of policy and politics, see Gosnell, *Negro Politicians*; and C. Reed, "Study of Black Politics." On Jackson, see Weems, *Black Business*; and Haller, "Policy Gambling," 725. Understandings of community ambivalence and the like are found in interviews, maps, and narratives in IWP, box 35-11, 35-15, 35-17.

61. See Drake and Cayton, *Black Metropolis*, 492, 645. On mediums, see Wolcott, "Culture of the Informal Economy" and "Mediums, Messages, and Lucky Numbers."

62. See Drake and Cayton, *Black Metropolis*, 488; and N. Thompson, *Kings*, 114, 117, 152.

63. See Travis, *Autobiography of Black Jazz*, 25–37.

64. Drake and Cayton, *Black Metropolis*, 487.

CHAPTER TWO

1. For Walker speech, see 1912 NNBL report, 154–55. See also "Side Lights on the Meeting of the National Negro Business League," *Broad Ax*, Aug. 31, 1912. Larger criticisms of black adornment as false consciousness and as treasonous white emulation include Chandler Owens, "Good Looks Supremacy," *Messenger* 6 (Mar. 1924), 80. Booker T. Washington's comments are from a letter dated December 8, 1911, in Harlan and Smock, *Booker T. Washington Papers*, 420. For fictional critiques of black beauty culture, see Schuyler, *Black No More*; and R. Wright, *Lawd Today!*

2. Popular belief was that Washington's hesitations about beauty culture rested on its promotion of white physical emulation. However, Chicago beauty culturist Anthony Overton gave an address at the very same meeting, and women beauty culturists with white clientele had addressed the convention in 1901 and 1905. See Harlan and Smock, *Booker T. Washington Papers*, 385; Anthony Overton, "The Largest

Negro Manufacturing Enterprise in the United States," 1912 NNBL report, 120; and "The 13th Annual Meeting of the NNBL," *Broad Ax*, Aug. 24, 1912. On the two black women culturists, see 1901 NNBL report, 29, LC; and Carrie W. Clifford, "The Story of the Business Career of Mrs. M. E. Williams" in 1905 NNBL report, 119–20.

3. This reference combines a black vernacular phrase for hair and the insights of cultural critic Michel de Certeau. In the black vernacular, the term "hairdo" is popularly shortened to "do." De Certeau uses the term "making do" to suggest that while members of mass culture do not control its production, they do control the way it is used—how it is consumed in everyday life. I am applying de Certeau's phrase to this study of migrant women's production and consumption of beauty culture while keeping in mind the black vernacular resonances of the phrase. See de Certeau, *Practice of Everyday Life*, 29–42.

4. On the union letter, see "Hair Culturists' First Convention," *NYA*, Sept. 6, 1917; and 1917 Hair Culturists' Union Meeting, 2–3, MWC. For general works on black beauty culture and adornment, see Blackwelder, *Styling Jim Crow*; Bundles, *On Her Own Ground* and *Madam C. J. Walker*; Willett, *Permanent Waves*; Peiss, *Hope in a Jar*; White and White, *Stylin'*; Rooks, *Hair Raising*; Starke, *African American Dress*; G. Robinson, "Race, Class and Gender"; and Morrow, *400 Years without a Comb*.

5. In the U.S. context, Social Darwinists argued that racial and sexual inequalities were not social but the result of biological processes where Anglo-Saxons were morally and intellectually superior to descendants of Africa because of genetic differences. Of the volumes of Social Darwinist scholarship, see Rosenberg, *Darwinism in Philosophy*; Bannister, *Social Darwinism*; Tobach, *Four Horsemen*; and Hofstadter, *Social Darwinism in American Thought*. In fact, Rooks points out how Charles Hamilton Smith's *Natural History of the Human Species*, among respected texts, specifically argued for the intellectual and cultural inferiority of the "woolly-haired" race. See the manifestation of this logic in Rooks's analysis and discussion of beauty advertisements in black newspapers in Rooks, *Hair Raising*, 26–40. Also look at "Kink-No-More" ad, *Freeman*, Feb. 18, 1911; "Nelson's Straightine" ad, *St. Louis Palladium*, Oct. 10, 1903; and "Original Ozonized Ox Marrow" ad, *St. Louis Palladium*, Jan. 10, 1903. Many of these ads could be found in papers all over the country, including the *Defender*.

6. F. Williams, "Colored Girl"; Burroughs, "Not Color but Character"; Williams, "The Timely Message of the Simple Life," *Voice of the Negro* (Mar. 1905).

7. Adams, "Rough Sketches." Peiss offers an insightful discussion of the "Rough Sketches" essay in *Hope in a Jar*.

Hackley, music scholar and later proponent of "uplifted" forms of Negro spirituals, mixed African pride with Victorian reform by expressing pride in African features but also by hoping that through care, the texture of black hair could be "improved" in such a way that could be inherited. See Hackley, *Colored Girl Beautiful*, and a similar editorial in *Voice of the Negro* 1 (Aug. 1904). The challenge and maintenance of Victorian values can be seen in an essay by Tillman, who argues that colored "hair dressers" offer an important source of employment outside the home for black women but also provide "good hair" for these women through artificial methods. See her "Paying Professions for Colored Girls." As a contemporary correlative, after a period of struggle and contestation, dreadlocks and cornrows became popular within black bohemian circles, with attendant hair care products and salons in the early 1990s, and were eventually accepted by the entire black mainstream. At the same time, within more working-class circles, excessively adorned straightened hairstyles, with coloring, streaks, rhinestones, etc., became popular. The distinction within both circles was rarely one of natural versus straight but a pronounced modesty versus a pronounced artifice.

8. Adams, "Rough Sketches."

9. Patterson, Ross, and Atkins, *History and Formative Years of the Church of God in Christ*; Synan, *Holiness-Pentecostal Movement*; Sanders, *Saints in Exile*.

10. There was also a specifically religious-based resistance to cosmetics like lipstick, rouge, or face powder because of their association with prostitution or the sexually seductive powers of the biblical figure Jezebel. In the Bible, Jezebel's painting of her face became the embodiment of women's ability to seduce and induce sexual desire by altering the appearance, which in the Bible resulted in destruction and death. See Lange, *Commentary on the Holy Scriptures*, II Kings 9:30–37, Ezekiel 23:40–49; and Peiss, *Hope in a Jar*, 26.

11. Smith-Rosenberg and Rosenberg, "Female Animal." See also Ortner, *Making Gender*; and Ortner and Whitehead, *Sexual Meanings*.

12. See Brown, "Negotiating and Transforming the Public Sphere." See also L. George, "Beauty Culture." In contemporary debates, cultural critic Mercer argues a similar point regarding the "unnatural" aspects of black hairstyling. See "Black Hair/Style Politics."

13. Peiss discusses Madam Rumford's fashion column in the elite *Colored American Magazine* and the short-lived *African American Journal of Fashion*. See Peiss, *Hope in a Jar*, 214. See also *Colored American Magazine* (July 1901); the *Afro-American Journal of Fashion* (May–June 1893); Bullock, *Afro-American Periodical Press*; E. Green, *National Capital Code of Etiquette*; and Woods, *Negro in Etiquette*.

14. G. Robinson, "Race, Class and Gender," 83. Madam C. J. Walker's childhood friend Celeste Hawkins and Walker's Chicago disciple Marjorie Stewart Joyner recall the "wropping" process in Bundles, *On Her Own Ground*, 14, and "Madam C. J. Walker—Cosmetics Tycoon," 92. Historical scholarship and folklore has shown that African men and women treated their hair with earth, lime, vegetable oil, and dyes. Moreover, wigs, tresses, and extensions were part of a long history of African adornment. See Morrow, *400 Years without a Comb*, 35; and Seiber and Herreman's fascinating exhibit and companion booklet, *Hair in African Art and Culture*. The exhibit was on tour between 2000 and 2002. See also N. Jones, *Born a Child of Freedom*; White and White, *Stylin'*; and Walker, *Textbook*.

15. Morrow, *400 Years without a Comb*.

16. CCRR, *Negro in Chicago*, 367, 370, 380–83, 391–92. See also Henri, *Black Migration*, 52; and U. Taylor, "From White Kitchens to White Factories."

17. Fields, *Lemon Swamp*, 187–89; P. Edwards, *Southern Urban Negro as Consumer*, 251. See also White and White, *Stylin'*, 188–90.

18. See Sarah Armstrong to MW, Apr. 29, 1918; Marie Alexander Sykes to MW, Apr. 27, 1918; Annie Dervin to MW, May 4, 1918; Bessie Brown to MW, June 28, 1918, MWC. Also, some made distinctions between hairdressers that gave scalp treatments and "hair straighteners" while considering both as viable employment options. See Tillman, "Paying Professions for Colored Girls." L. George highlighted hairdressing, manicuring, and facial massaging as important employment opportunities. See L. George, "Beauty Culture," 26. Drake and Cayton point out that many Chicago restaurants and stores preferred lighter-skinned girls, with "good" hair, to work in their establishments. See *Black Metropolis*, 499, 501, 503. On skin tones and hair texture hierarchies, see Gatewood, *Aristocrats of Color*. Peiss notes the marketing of Walker products to white immigrants in journals like the *Jewish Daily Forward* as well as the patronage of black hair shops by Jewish women. See Peiss, *Hope in a Jar*, 224; and *HCM* 12 (Feb. 1922). This information also comes from informal conversations with colleagues regarding this "dirty secret" in Jewish women's consumption practices. On image of distinction from subservient labor, see P. Edwards, *Southern Urban Negro as Consumer*; and White and White, *Stylin'*. On "freedom bags," see Clark-Lewis, " 'This Work Had a End.' "

19. Report of Pittsburgh agents meeting, July 25, 1916, MWC.

20. For information on Gray and Stanley, see "The Promised Land: Business," box 20, and Mathilde Bunton interview with Grace Garnett-Abney, Chicago, June 23, 1984, IWP.

21. McKinley, "Anthony Overton"; "Some Chicagoans of Note," *Crisis* (Sept. 1915). For more on black beauty companies as a source of race pride, see "Betrayers of the Race," *HCM*, Feb. 1920. Overton reminded the black public that he was the one to present high-class, refined light-skinned women in his ads to challenge the stereotypes prevalent in white beauty interests. See Overton Hygienic Company, *Encyclopedia of Colored People*.

22. Giddings argues that *HCM* "was probably the most 'bourgeois' and glamour conscious of all the publications of this era." See Giddings, *When and Where I Enter*, 186–87. For more evidence of such distinctions, see Rooks, *Hair Raising*, 101–5; McAdoo Baker "Making a Businessman of the Negro," *HCM*, Sept. 1917; and "Etiquette in the Theater," *HCM*, Nov. 1918. Kreiling calls attention to the conservative middle-class nature of *HCM* and its 1925 transformation into the weekly *Chicago Bee*. He particularly points out *HCM*'s ambivalence about encouraging the Great Migration of southern migrants. See Kreiling, "Making of Racial Identities." Also look at Kathryn Johnson's call for the better classes to take an interest in migrants "socially and otherwise, and by so doing, help to preserve our own liberties." See Johnson, "Immigration and Segregation," *HCM*. D. Brooks argues that the most

important function of *HCM* was to "adjust" migrants to the northern black "Old Settler Society." See D. Brooks, "Consumer Markets," 81–98. For a full discussion of African American periodicals as a method of reform, see Johnson and Johnson, *Propaganda and Aesthetics*.

23. For specific information on Overton's buildings, see "Overton Hygienic/ Douglass National Bank Building" in Commission on Chicago Historical and Architectural Landmarks, "Black Metropolis Historic District," Chicago Historical Society.

24. "The Story of Poro: Forty-Fifth Anniversary," box 262, folder 3, CABP. For pictures and descriptions of Poro's buildings, see ibid. For a general overview of Malone's life and career, see Mongold, "Annie Minerva Turnbo Malone."

25. "Poro in Pictures" (n.d.), CABP. In an interview, Thomas Andrew Dorsey confirmed that the song "Precious Lord" was developed in the Poro music room. See "Thomas A. Dorsey: The Chicago School of Gospel" in *Wade in the Water*. For more on the orchestra, see "Mixing Business and Music to Produce Harmony," Associated Negro Press News Release, Apr. 30, 1925, CABP. Carby's analysis of black lodging houses as instruments of maternal surveillance over migrant women's lives provides me with the framework to discuss Malone; see Carby, "Policing the Black Woman's Body."

26. On the Malone marriage controversy, see "Woman Says Poro College Is Hers to the Last Penny," *St. Louis Post-Dispatch*, Jan. 14, 1927; and Albert Anderson, "The Amazing Inside Story of the Malone Case," *The Light and Heebie Jeebies*, Feb. 19, 1927, CABP. Anderson, "The Amazing Inside Story," CABP; "Woman Says Poro College Is Hers," "Says Husband Was Poro Figurehead," *St. Louis Globe-Democrat*, Jan. 15, 1927; "Chicago Heebie Jeebies Stirs Poro Mess Again," *Standard News* (May 25, 1927). While Malone portrayed herself as a victimized race woman, her economic power and savvy sense of media spin were evident in her correspondence with Barnett. See "Letter to Barnett," folder 5 (Jan. 26, 1927). All in box 262, CABP.

27. "Forty-Fifth Anniversary," CABP; *Help the Orphan's Home*, pamphlet, box 262, folder 5, CABP; "Poro College Head Makes $25,000 Gift to YMCA," box 262, folder 5, CABP; Harold Keith, "Annie M. Turnbo Malone: America's Original Beauty Queen," part 2, *Pittsburgh Courier* (Aug. 3, 1957).

28. "Queen of Gotham's Colored 400," *Literary Digest* 55 (Oct. 13, 1917): 76.

29. Bundles, *Madam C. J. Walker*, 67; Overton Hygienic Company, *Encyclopedia of Colored People*, 8.

30. *Madam C. J. Walker Beauty Manual*, 24, MWC. The advertisement began running in 1914. See *NYA*, Nov. 12, 1914. The ad "Makes Short Hair Long and Cures Dandruff" begins to appear in 1905. See *Indianapolis Ledger*, May 2, 1906; and *Freeman*, Apr. 16, 1910. "Learn to Grow Hair and Make Money" begins to appear in 1913. See *Freeman*, Apr. 12, 1913; and *Defender*, Oct. 21, 1916. See also Rooks, *Hair Raising*, 65–70.

31. See "1920 Walker Agents Convention Speech," 3, MWC. Walker's agrarian metaphors can be found in *Walker Manufacturing Co.* (Indianapolis: Walker Manufacturing Company, 1911), 6, in Special Correspondence (MW file), BTWP.

32. "Instructions to Agents before 1919," MWC. See also R. W. Thompson, "The Negro Woman in Business," *Freeman*, Sept. 20, 1913; Bundles, *On Her Own Ground*, 174n25; and G. Robinson, "Class, Race and Gender," 382. The idea of Walker and other women being a threat at these male-dominated conventions was very real. After her talk at the 1913 NNBL convention, Washington warned, "You talk about what the men are doing in a business way; why if we don't watch out, the women will excel us." See 1913 NNBL report, 212, LC; and Bundles, *On Her Own Ground*, 177.

33. MW to Lynch, June 10 or 11, 1918, MWC. In fact, Walker appropriately named her National Baptist Convention speech "From the Kitchen to the Mansion"; see "Mme. C. J. Walker's Lecture Tour," *Atlanta Independent*, Oct. 7, 1916.

34. MW to FBR, July 31, 1915, MWC.

35. Ibid., Feb. 16, 1916.

36. Bundles, *On Her Own Ground*, 162; *NYT Sunday Magazine*, Nov. 4, 1917.

37. "Madam Walker Who Subscribed $1,000 to the YMCA Building Fund," *Freeman*, Oct. 28, 1911; 1912 NACW Meeting, 40, LC; Mary Talbert, "The Frederick Douglass Home," *Crisis* (Feb. 1917), 174; Harlan, *Booker T. Washington*, 267–68; MW to Booker T. Washington, Mar. 13, 1914, box 746, 1914 Donation File, BTWP.

38. See *Walker Company Booklet*, 1919, 12, MWC; R. W. Thompson, "The Negro Woman in Business," *Freeman*, Sept. 20, 1913; 1914 NNBL report, 152–53, LC.

39. "Thousands Hear Madame Walker Tell Story of Her Rise to Fame and Riches," *Defender*, Mar. 16, 1918. A later account was recorded in the *Defender* that noted this previous speech in light of an upcoming one. See "Mme. CJ Walker to Speak Next Sunday," *Defender*, July 27, 1918.

40. FBR to A. C. Burnett, Sept. 10, 1918, Walker Manufacturing General Correspondence, MWC; Rooks, *Hair Raising*, 66, fig. 6.

41. 1913 NNBL report, 211, and 1914 NNBL report, 150, LC; R. W. Thompson, "Negro Woman in Business"; 1912 NNBL report, 154, LC.

42. See "Mme. CJ Walker's Preparations for the Hair/Supreme in Reputation" ad, *Messenger 2*, no. 1 (Jan. 1918); and R. W. Thompson, "Negro Woman in Business." Ad quoted in Rooks, *Hair Raising*, 65. See also "Over 10,000 in Her Employ," *NYA*, 1916, quoted in Bundles, *On Her Own Ground*, 138.

43. CCRR, *Negro in Chicago*, 387; G. Robinson, "Class, Race and Gender," 385; Bundles, "Madam C. J. Walker—Cosmetics Tycoon," 93, and *Madam C. J. Walker*, 64. "Passport to prosperity" comes from the ad "Learn to Grow Hair and Make Money." This is discussed in Rooks, *Hair Raising*, 66, fig. 6.

44. Rooks notes Walker's class ambivalence regarding preexisting class distinctions; see *Hair Raising*, 89. See also MW to FBR, Dec. 15, 1916, MWC; and National Association of Colored Women, *National Association of Colored Women's Clubs Records, 1895–1992*, July 8–13, 1918, microfilm, 38, LC.

45. MW to FBR, Apr. 10, Oct. 30, 1916, MWC.

46. Chicago agents to MW, Apr. 22, 1918; MW to Smith, Aug. 31, 1917, MWC. See

also "Notice to the Agents of the Madam C. J. Walker Manufacturing Company," undated; and FBR to MW, July 26, 1918, MWC.

47. Samuel Grodson to FBR, Mar. 28, 1918; A'Lelia Walker Robinson to FBR, July 19, 1918, all in MWC. See also "Mme. Walker Holds Second Annual Convention," *Defender*, Aug. 10, 1918.

48. Bundles, *On Her Own Ground*, 262; *NYA*, Sept. 6, 1917. Early discussions about the magazine are found in MW to FBR, Apr. 10, June 18, 1916, MWC. Rooks is the first and only scholar to my knowledge to place *HCM* and *Woman's Voice* within a comparative analysis of "Race Womanhood." See Rooks, *Ladies Pages* and *Hair Raising*, 105–14; and sporadic copies of *Woman's Voice*, Dec. 1919, Dec. 1921, and Mar. 1922, in Moorland-Spingarn Research Center, Howard University, Washington, D.C.

49. Walker's patronage of Washington and Tuskegee was discussed earlier, but we must include Benevolent Association's donation to the Booker T. Washington Memorial Fund. See MW to FBR, Apr. 10, 1916, MWC. Walker's support for the NAACP included $100 to their first antilynching campaign and ads in the *Crisis*. See Bundles, *On Her Own Ground*, 220; and "Madam Walker's Preparations," *Crisis* (Jan., Feb. 1912). Walker hosted William Monroe Trotter, the radical agitator and editor of the *Boston Guardian*, on his midwestern tour in 1915. See "Locals and Personals," *Indianapolis Recorder*, Apr. 3, 1915. Walker went on to consistently attend the annual conventions of Trotter's National Equal Rights League. See "National Equal Rights League Tenth Annual Meeting," *Colorado Statesman*, Oct. 6, 1917. On the *Messenger*, see J. Anderson, *A. Philip Randolph*, 82. Walker also donated money to and even spoke at a meeting in support of the marginally Socialist candidate Frazier Miller for Congress. See MW to FBR, Nov. 4, 1918, MWC; and Bundles, *On Her Own Ground*, 266.

50. "City and Vicinity," *Freeman*, Nov. 8, 1913; "Oruba on Nov. 8," *Freeman*, Nov. 22, 1913; "Madam Walker Sails for Cuba," *Defender*, Nov. 29, 1913; "Madam C. J. Walker of Indianapolis Seeing the Islands of the Southern Seas," *Freeman*, Jan. 17, 1914; "Good News from Madam Walker," *Broad Ax*, Jan. 24, 1914; "Mme. C. J. Walker's Return Home," *Freeman*, Feb. 7, 1914. "A Million Eyes Turned Upon it Daily" begins with the solidification of Walker's international approach. See *Crisis* (1919) and *NYA*, Feb. 18, 1919. Rooks engages in an insightful conversation concerning the evolving focus of Walker's advertising campaign. See Rooks, *Hair Raising*, 65–70. On the wartime context, see Bundles, *On Her Own Ground*, 180–83, 270–72; Contee, "Du Bois, the NAACP, and the Pan-African Congress"; and Skinner, *African Americans*. On Walker and the NERL, see FBR to MW, Nov. 27, 1918; W. Stephenson Holder to MW, Dec. 12, 1918; MW to FBR, Dec. 19, 1918; FBR to MW, Dec. 24, 1918; FBR to MW, Jan. 6, 1919 (mislabeled Jan. 6, 1918); and FBR to MW, Jan. 11, 1919, MWC.

51. On the ILDP, see Bundles, *On Her Own Ground*, 327–29; and Hill, *Marcus Garvey*, 345. See also FBR to MW, Jan. 25, 1919, Dec. 24, 1918, Jan. 6, 1919, MWC; and Walter H. Loving report to Director of Military Intelligence on National Race Congress.

52. FBR to MW, Jan. 1919, Jan. 23, 1919, MWC.

53. Peiss, *Hope in a Jar*, 90.

54. *U.S. Census: Negro Population*; Black, *Black's Blue Book: Business and Professional Directory* and *Black's Blue Book: Directory of Chicago's Active Colored People*.

55. See L. Evans, "Claude A. Barnett," 44–56.

56. See Claude Barnett's manuscript "Fly Out of Darkness," 6, 8, and "Nile Queen Booklet," box 262, folder 2, 4, CABP.

57. "Nile Queen Booklet," box 262, folder 2, 9, CABP. See also "The Royal Way," Kashmir Press Package, box 262, folder 2, 9, CABP. As stated earlier, Barnett was the key figure in disseminating propaganda in support of Annie Malone during her divorce. In addition to this event, there are a number of letters between F. B. Ransom, Malone, and Barnett regarding his innovative ad techniques and the circulation of beauty ads through his ANP network of newspapers, box 262, folders 2 and 3, CABP.

58. See ads in *Crisis* (1918) and *Defender*, Feb. 22, 1919, and World War I ad from G. Robinson, "Class, Race and Gender," 290.

59. "Poro College: School of Beauty Culture," booklet, box 262, folder 3, 3–4, CABP. For a contextualization of this historic shift in race pride regarding Africa after the Italian invasion, see W. Scott, *Sons of Sheba's Race*; J. Scott, "Black Nationalism"; and Kelley, "This Ain't Ethiopia but It'll Do: African Americans and the Spanish Civil War," in *Race Rebels*.

60. See *Chicago Negro Chamber of Commerce*, pamphlet (n.d., a little earlier than 1940), Vertical File, Vivian G. Harsh Research Collection of Afro-American History and Literature; J. E. McBrady & Co., *The Great Central Market* (1915), Chicago Historical Society; and Peiss, *Hope in a Jar*, 110.

61. See "Arroway" ad, box 262, folder 3, CABP; and G. Robinson, "Class, Race and Gender," 292–93. Marguerita Ward's Cosmetics was showcased as a symbol of race pride because it was one of the first companies to specialize in face powders that covered a wide array of colors, catering to both black and white women. However, in her hierarchy of colors, Ward had a Flesh color that was closest to white within her spectrum and far away from her Chocolate and Dark Brown lines. See Ardis Harris, "Marguerita Ward Company, Inc. Cosmetic Company," Nov. 4, 1937, IWP.

62. Adam Langer, "You Know, I'm 95 and I Know What I'm Talking About," *Reader*, Sept. 11, 1992, 22.

63. See Toni Costonie, "Memories of an Early Salon," *Shoptalk* (Spring 1984), and Oral History, MSJP. A wonderful discussion of Joyner is also found in Blackwelder, *Styling Jim Crow*.

64. A. M. Townsend University to MW, Jan. 26, 1917; Wiley University to MW, Mar. 6, 1917; Arkansas Baptist College to MW, Mar. 9, 1917; Utica Normal and Industrial Institute to MW, Mar. 15, 1917; Guadaluce College to MW, Mar. 20, 1917; Florida Baptist Academy to MW, Mar. 23, 1917; MW to Normal Industrial and Agricultural College, Mar. 27, 1917; Mound Bayou Industrial College to MW, Aug. 25, 1917, MWC.

65. Mary McCleod Bethune to MW, Apr. 5, 1917; Flug, "Marjorie Stewart Joyner," 368.

66. *Shampoo* (Apr. 1983), MWC. The MSJP contain a wealth of information on this great figure. An analysis of interviews and correspondence can be wonderfully supplemented with the many photographs and scrapbooks to get a sense of the Chicago school and its ethos.

67. See Langer, "You Know, I'm 95 and I Know What I'm Talking About," 9. There is a copy of Joyner's patent for the permanent wave machine in the MSJP. For information regarding her legislation, see Flug, "Marjorie Stewart Joyner," 368; and MSJP.

68. See Haskell, *Authority of Experts*; Gouldner, *Future of Intellectuals*; and F. Taylor, *Principles of Scientific Management*.

69. Sengstacke recalled that he learned more on that train ride than he had in all his years of formal education. See Flug, "Marjorie Stewart Joyner."

70. For information on the Depression numbers, see MSJP and IWP.

CHAPTER THREE

1. See Juli Jones, "Moving Pictures Offer the Greatest Opportunity to the American Negro in History of Race from Every Point of View," *Freeman*, Oct. 9, 1915. "Photo play," like "moving pictures," is one of the original terms for cinema and also exposes this technology's transitional period within preexisting cultural/mechanical realities. Other terms that highlight these kind of moments range from horseless carriage (car) to talking machine (radio).

2. See Jean Voltaire Smith, "Our Need for More Films," *HCM*, Apr. 1922, 8; and Bogle, *Toms*. For a reconsideration of these very images as inherently negative, see Jacqueline Stewart's important dissertation, "Migrating to the Movies." On the larger culture of black film criticism, see Everett, *Returning the Gaze*. Various criticisms of moving pictures come from Duster, *Crusade for Justice*, 293; Sylvester Russell, "Musical and Dramatic," *Defender*, Feb. 12, 1910; Vice Commission of Chicago, *Social Evil*, 247–48; and Knupfer, *Toward a Tenderer Humanity*, 103, 125–26.

3. See "Loud Talking at the Pekin," *Defender*, Apr. 23, 1910. In a general essay attacking black public deportment, there was a specific attack of "newcomers," calling on the black public to "stop the young miss who chatters like a parrot during a lecture or a program." See Betsey Lane, "War Declared on Aprons and Caps in Street Cars," *Defender*, May 25, 1918.

4. See Stewart's important *Migrating to the Movies*.

5. On film as a social phenomenon, see Rabinowitz, *For the Love of Pleasure*, 1; and Altman, "Silence of the Silents." My notion of a black film culture is heavily informed by Stewart's notion of "reconstructive spectatorship" in particular. However, this project is driven by an examination of Chicago's larger New Negro intellectual life that situates film and exhibition within this larger world and also extends

beyond the period of her study. See Stewart, *Migrating to the Movies*; and on "black film culture," see Bowser and Spence, *Writing Himself into History*, xxi. Also look at the introduction of Bowser, Gaines, and Musser, *Oscar Micheaux and His Circle*.

6. Bowser and Thomas, *Midnight Ramble*. The Civil Rights Act of 1885 covered nondiscrimination in public accommodations. See CCRR, *Negro in Chicago*, 232–34; and *Defender*, June 11, 1910.

7. *Defender*, Jan. 6, 1912; Travis, *Autobiography of Black Jazz*, 16.

8. *Defender*, Sept. 6, 1913. These policies continued well into the 1920s. In 1925, a dentist was awarded $2,000 when an usher at the Tivoli tried to take him to an inferior seat instead of the one he purchased. However, the judge refused to charge the Tivoli with racial discrimination. See *Variety*, Feb. 18, 1925.

9. CCRR, *Negro in Chicago*, 317–20.

10. For information on the early Levee vice district and its relocation into the Black Belt, see Lindberg, *Chicago by Gaslight*. The migration of the vice district into the South Side between 1910 and 1930 is covered by Mumford, *Interzones*, and Carby, "Policing the Black Woman's Body." The response to black leisure behaviors by clubwomen like Mrs. Booker T. Washington, Mary Church Terrell, and Nannie Helen Burroughs and male ministers are discussed by Christina Simmons. See Simmons, "African Americans and Sexual Victorianism." Again, Ida B. Wells challenged the focus on moral talk and lack of social assistance by leaders. See Nimmons, "Social Reform and Moral Uplift." On uplift ideology, see K. Gaines, *Uplifting the Race*.

11. See Sampson's extremely useful work, *Blacks in Black and White*, 24; and Waller, "Another Audience."

12. McCarthy, "Nickel Vice and Virtue," 51–52.

13. This study owes a great deal to the pathbreaking insights of Carbine's seminal essay. Carbine examines exhibition spaces in black Chicago to uncover the importance of context in early black film culture. I build on this project to further assert that these exhibition spaces were an important black public sphere where visions of the race were debated and decided, making black film culture an integral part of the New Negro movement. See Carbine, " 'The Finest outside the Loop,' " 11.

14. Carbine, " 'The Finest outside the Loop,' " 11 and its appendix of Stroll theaters. For a discussion of South Side nickelodeons, see Lindstrom, " 'Getting a Hold Deeper in the Life of the City,' " 254–56. For work on other local film reception contexts, see Griffiths and Latham, "Film and Ethnic Identity in Harlem"; Fuller, *At the Picture Show*; Waller, *Main Street Amusements*; Streible, "Harlem Theatre"; and Gomery, *Shared Pleasures*. There were attempts to break the monopoly that the Theater Owners' Booking Association had on black performers. The Grand Vaudeville Circuit of Chicago was one such attempt to represent the "colored houses throughout the Middle West." See *Freeman*, Feb. 4, 1911.

15. Merritt, "Nickelodeon Theaters"; Gomery, "Movie Audiences"; Havig, "Commercial Amusement Audience"; Musser, "Nickels Count."

16. *Defender*, June 17, 1911, Mar. 8, 1913; *Freeman*, Feb. 6, 1915, June 17, 1911, Aug. 14, 1915. The *Defender* announced that Cincinnati was the "next city to take the Pekin Fever" by opening a theater with the Pekin name. Right below this was an announcement for the New Pekin in Norfolk, Virginia; see "The New Pekin, Norfolk, VA," *Defender*, Jan. 30, 1909. See also Sylvester Russell, "Robert T. Motts Dead," *Freeman*, July 15, 1911; and "Colored Manager Dies," *Variety*, July 15, 1911. On the New Grand, see *Defender*, Mar. 18, 1911. Discussions of the Pekin's fame is also covered in Streible, "Jack Johnson Fight Films," 179.

17. Minnie Adams, "In Union Is Strength," *Defender*, Feb. 4, 1912.

18. Gunning, "Cinema of Attraction[s]"; Sampson, *Blacks in Black and White*, 2.

19. "Tuskegee in Moving Pictures," *Defender*, Dec. 31, 1910.

20. *Defender*, Apr. 9, 1910, Mar. 8, 1913; *Freeman*, Feb. 6, 1915, June 17, 1911, Aug. 14, 1915.

21. "Incidental Music with Pictures at the Phoenix," *Defender*, June 17, 1911. An illustrated song usually consisted of a hired singer with the words to the song projected on either a screen or the wall (sometimes accompanied with pictures) for the purpose of a sing-along. See "Grand Changes Policy," *Defender*, July 25, 1927; "A Great Variety of Vaudeville at the Pekin," *Freeman*, May 20, 1911; "The Test at the Pekin," *Defender*, Mar. 18, 1911; and *Freeman*, Feb. 6, 1915.

22. M. Hansen, *Babel and Babylon*, 61; Rosenzweig, *Eight Hours for What We Will*.

23. M. Hansen, *Babel and Babylon*, 108. On the Chateau de la Plaisance, see *Defender*, Apr. 1910, Mar. 3, 1911. See also ad for a combination merry-go-round/skating rink at 36th and State in *Freeman*, Aug. 14, 1915.

24. Bennett, "Thousand and One Troubles"; Kasson, *Amusing the Millions*; Rabinowitz, *For the Love of Pleasure*, 135–43. M. Hansen and her use of Michel Foucault's notion of the heterotopia inform this conversation about places absolutely different from the sites they reflect. See Foucault, "Of Other Spaces," 22–27; and M. Hansen, *Babel and Babylon*, 107–8.

25. M. Adams, "In Union Is Strength."

26. See *Defender*, June 13, 1911; "Theater," IWP; "The Pekin Opening at Chicago," *Freeman*, Mar. 13, 1909; and "Ilea Vincent at the Pekin," *Freeman*, Feb. 4, 1911.

27. Sylvester Russell, "Musical and Dramatic," *Defender*, Apr. 9, 1910; *Defender*, Apr. 23, 1910; "Loud Talking at the Pekin," *Defender*, Apr. 23, 1910.

28. "Hats Off!" *Defender*, July 9, 1921; "Lip Slobbering in Theaters Is Given the Razz," *Defender*, Sept. 16, 1922; D. Ireland Thomas, "Motion Picture News," *Defender*, Sept. 30, 1922.

29. For information on the relationship between blueswomen, carnival, and vaudeville conventions, see Carby, " 'It Jus' Be's Dat Way Sometime' "; and A. Davis, *Blues Legacies*.

30. "A Letter," *Defender*, July 25, 1927; "Kill the Cause and Remove the Effect," *Defender*, Dec. 2, 1922. Thomas's title can be found on his column, "Motion Picture

News"; for example, see *Defender*, May 1925. See also Thomas, "Motion Picture News," *Defender*, Aug. 9, 1924, Apr. 11, 1925, July 25, 1927. For a powerful survey of black film criticism, see Everett, *Returning the Gaze*.

31. Streible, "Jack Johnson Fight Films." See also Gilmore, *Bad Nigger!*; Roberts, *Papa Jack*; Farr, *Black Champion*; and Bederman, *Manliness and Civilization*.

32. "Fight Fans See Pictures," and the cartoon "'Twas Ever Thus," *Chicago Tribune*, Mar. 22, 1909. See also "Burns Would Like to Be Slaughtered by Johnson," *Freeman*, Jan. 9, 1909, 7; and "Burns-Johnson Films," *Freeman*, Feb. 20, 1909.

33. "As the Fight Pictures Told the Story," *Freeman*, May 1, 1909; "Back Jack Johnson Heavily," *Freeman*, Jan. 23, 1909; Juli Jones, "Dehomey in Peace," *Freeman*, Oct. 23, 1909.

34. Uncle Rad Kees, "Johnson Shows Physical Prowess of the Negro," *Freeman*, Nov. 27, 1909; Sylvester Russell, "Musical and Dramatic," *Defender*, Apr. 30, 1910. The circulation of the films is covered in Streible, "Jack Johnson Fight Films," 179.

35. "Review of the World," *Current Literature* 48 (Jan. 1910): 606. In the films, the Jack Johnson character was played by whites in blackface, making comedy out of white fears of Johnson while controlling that same image. Both *The Night I Fought Jack Johnson* (Vitagraph, 1913) and *Some White Hope* (Vitagraph, 1915) are at the British Film Institute. Cripps notes that the white fighter in the second film was named Bam Langford, a play on the black boxer Sam Langford (ironically, the real Langford would later star in the Oscar Micheaux race film *The Brute*). See Cripps, *Slow Fade to Black*; and Roberts, *Papa Jack*, 114.

36. Gilmore, *Bad Nigger!*, 75–93. See also *Defender*, July 30, 1910; and Mildred Miller, "The Nigger Unmolested," *Defender*, Dec. 10, 1910. The Johnson-Jeffries film was advertised to be screened by "electricity" on the day of the fight at the Coliseum by the Northern Amusement Company. See "Fight Shown in Chicago," *Defender*, July 2, 1910.

37. Johnson was convicted under the Mann Act. This prohibited the transportation of women across state lines for "immoral sexual relations." Authorities charged that Johnson traveled across state lines for the purpose of prostitution with his former girlfriend, Bell Schreiber. Black papers responded that if Johnson were a white man, his relations with a white prostitute would have never come under legal scrutiny. See Mumford, *Interzones*, 8–14; and Jack Johnson, *Jack Johnson—In the Ring—and Out*, 83. These comments were commensurate with the thoughts of other race leaders like Adam Clayton Powell Sr. See Gilmore, *Bad Nigger!*, 89.

38. Brown and Kimball, "Mapping the Terrain of Black Richmond," 312. The opening events are covered in *Defender*, Aug. 17, 1912.

39. *Defender*, Aug. 17, 1912. See White and White, *Stylin'*, 181.

40. White and White, *Stylin'*, 128, 125–52. See also Stuckey, *Slave Culture*; Southern, *Music of Black Americans*; and Gatewood, *Aristocrats of Color*, 51–52. For discussions of the meaning of black parades, marching, and celebrations, particularly Mardi Gras, see Malone, *Steppin' on the Blues*; R. Mitchell, *All on Mardi*

Gras Day; Kinser, *Carnival, American Style*; Lipsitz, "Mardi Gras Indians"; and DeCaro and Ireland, "Every Man a King."

41. Rabinowitz, *For the Love of Pleasure*, 47–67. General scholarship on the exposition includes Gilbert, *Perfect Cities*; N. Harris, "Great American Fairs"; Rydell, *All the World's a Fair*; and Trachtenberg, *Incorporation of America*. See also the pamphlet by Wells and Douglass, *The Reason Why the Colored American Is Not in the World's Columbian Exposition*, and discussed in Bederman, "Civilization."

42. *Defender*, Aug. 10, 1912. The Eighth Regiment band had extreme community significance. The Illinois "Fighting Eighth" was Chicago's own all-black military regiment that fought on the Mexican border in 1916 and in World War I. This infantry was one of the most decorated outfits during the war. In fact, a local armory was named in their honor for community events, including film screenings that seated 8,000. See Tuttle, *Race Riot*, 217–19. On the opening speech, see *Defender*, Aug. 31, 1912. The recuperation of positive African themes, within theatrical entertainments, was not entirely new. The blackface musical *In Dahomey* incorporated the vaudeville conventions of double entendre and parody to create many of the same meanings. Songs like "Colored Aristocracy" and "On Emancipation Day" bear this point out. This musical starred the famous team of George Walker and local hero Bert Williams and played a week, December 14–20, 1902, at the Great Northern Theatre in Chicago. See Riis, *More Than Just Minstrel Shows*; Sotiropoulos, "Staging Race"; and James Weldon Johnson, *Black Manhattan*.

43. *Defender*, Sept. 7, 1912.

44. Ibid., Aug. 10, 1912.

45. "Difficult Photographic Feat," *Defender*, Jan. 20, 1912. For a general overview of Jones's career, see Sampson, *Blacks in Black and White*, 183–85; "Pictures by Electric Light" ad, *Defender*, Mar. 26, 1910; and "Peter P. Jones, the Photographer, Retries," *Defender*, Aug. 31, 1912.

46. "Peter P. Jones Taking Moving Pictures of Shriners," *Defender*, May 23, 1914.

47. "Peter P. Jones Heads Moving Picture Company," *Defender*, June 13, 1914.

48. Sampson, *Blacks in Black and White*, 183–84. *For the Honor of the Eighth* was later incorporated into Jones's multifilm exhibit, *The Dawn of Truth*. This exhibit will be discussed later in full, but a description of *For the Honor of the Eighth* can be found in a review of the larger project. See *Freeman*, Apr. 1, 1916. For a wonderful discussion of this film and of Jones as a pioneering black documentary filmmaker, see Bowser, "Pioneers of Black Documentary Film."

49. Sampson, *Blacks in Black and White*, 172; "Funeral of Robert T. Motts," *Defender*, July 15, 1911. For more on Foster, see "Jack Johnson Buttons" ad, *NYA*, May 26, 1910; "For Sale, Entire Theatre Equipment," *Freeman*, Oct. 23, 1909; "Sheet Music" ad, *Freeman*, June 17, 1911; and "Enterprising Mr. Wm. Foster," *Defender*, Aug. 5, 1911.

50. Sampson, *Blacks in Black and White*, 172–76; "Foster's Movies Make Big Hit," *Defender*, July 26, 1913; "The States Theater," *Defender*, Aug. 9, 1913. See also

"Stroll," *Defender*, Aug. 30, 1913; and "At the All-Picture Houses," *Freeman*, Oct. 4, 1913. For critiques of Foster films, see Leab, *From Sambo to Superspade*; and Cripps, *Slow Fade to Black*, 80.

51. For counteranalysis of Foster, see Reid, *Redefining Black Film*, 8; and "Foster's Movies Make Big Hit." See also "The States Theater."

52. Sampson, *Blacks in Black and White*, 172–76, 581, 587; Juli Jones, "Dehomey in Peace"; "Negro Theaters," *Freeman*, Mar. 13, 1909. See also Stewart, *Migrating to the Movies*, 194–96.

53. "Foster Photo Play Co. Licensed in Florida," *Defender*, Apr. 11, 1914; Sampson, *Blacks in Black and White*, 175; "Jim Europe's Jazz" ad, *Defender*, May 31, 1919; Juli Jones, "Moving Pictures Offer the Greatest Opportunity," *Freeman*, Oct. 9, 1915.

CHAPTER FOUR

1. C. Taylor, "Re-birth of the Aesthetic in Cinema," 19; Cripps, *Slow Fade to Black*, 42. For film histories that focus on *Birth*'s aesthetics as separate from its racism, see Jacobs, *Rise of American Film*; Mast, *Short History of the Movies*; Agee, *Agee on Film*; and M. Williams, *Griffith*. See also Lang, *Birth of a Nation*.

2. C. Taylor, "Re-birth of the Aesthetic in Cinema," 19. See also Griffith, *Birth of a Nation*; and Cripps, *Slow Fade to Black*, 53.

3. See Rogin, *Ronald Reagan*; and May, "Apocalyptic Cinema."

4. Willis N. Huggins, "The Editor's Mailbox," *Defender*, Jan. 17, 1920. See also Lanier-Seward, "Film Portrait."

5. IWP, box 50-1; Edward Sheldon, "Two Plays in Town—The Clansman—The Nigger," *Chicago Daily Inter Ocean*, Jan. 14, 1912; Logsdon, "Reverend A. J. Carey," 23–50; Gosnell, *Negro Politicians*, 49–51. See also *Crisis* 10 (June 1915); *Chicago Tribune*, Apr. 26, 1915; and Wendt and Kogan, *Big Bill Thompson*, 162–68. For information on the Chicago ban within the context of larger protests, see Cripps, "Reaction of the Negro."

6. "Facts about the Birth of a Nation Play at the Colonial," *Defender*, Sept. 11, 1915; " 'Birth of a Nation' Assailed by Leading White Pastor," *Defender*, Oct. 9, 1915; "Contentment of Race Leaders Favored 'Birth of a Nation,'" *Defender*, Feb. 19, 1916; "States Theatre Displays Vile Race Pictures," *Defender*, May 30, 1914. On Alonzo Bowling, see "On the Board," *Defender*, July 30, 1921.

7. "Johnson and Jeffries Pictures to Be Shown," *Defender*, Sept. 4, 1915.

8. See ads "50 Years Freedom, 50 Years Freedom," *Defender*, Oct. 2, 1915; "Leading Characters in the Dawn of Truth," *Freeman*, Mar. 25, 1916; and review, "Featuring Negro Progress in Moving Pictures," *Freeman*, Apr. 11, 1916. Also look at Bowser, "Pioneers of Black Documentary Film," 13.

9. Cripps, "Birth of a Race: An Early Stride toward a Black Cinema" and "Two Early Strides toward a Black Cinema" in *Slow Fade to Black*, and "The Making of *The Birth of a Race*." See also Sampson, *Blacks in Black and White*, 208–9.

10. An incomplete print of *The Birth of a Race* can be seen at the Library of Congress. See also *Moving Picture World*, May 10, 1919, and *Variety*, Dec. 6, 1918.

11. Much of the information that we have today about the "race films" industry exists because of the exhaustive clippings file that Lincoln maintained. The original archive exists as the GPJC but is also available on microfilm at libraries like the University of Indiana. See Bowser and Spence, *Writing Himself into History*, 90. On the *The Trooper of Troop K*, see *California Eagle*, Oct. 14, 1916.

12. Tony Langston to GPJ, Aug. 10, 1916, GPJC; Sampson, *Blacks in Black and White*, 138. See also Langston to GPJ, Nov. 24, Oct. 23, 1916, May 24, 1917, GPJC; and *Defender*, July 14, 1917. See also Cripps, *Slow Fade to Black*, 80–81.

13. "Does Well," *Defender*, July 9, 1921; Langston to GPJ, Aug. 10, 1916, GPJC; "Endorsed," *Defender*, May 7, 1917. See also Sampson, *Blacks in Black and White*, 132; and "Satisfaction Guaranteed," *Defender*, Aug. 18, 1917.

14. Reid, *Redefining Black Film*, 10.

15. See Unique promotional material for "Shadowed by the Devil," GPJC. Synopsis of *Shadowed by the Devil* from Sampson, *Blacks in Black and White*, 270. See also *Champion Magazine*, Sept. 1916; Howe Alexander, "Shadowed by the Devil," *HCM*, Mar. 1919; D. Ireland Thomas, "Musical and Dramatic," *Defender*, Oct. 27, 1923; and "Colored Motion Picture Drama," *HCM*, Mar. 1919.

16. "Darky Humor on the Screen," *Moving Picture World*, July 19, 1918; Luther J. Pollard to GPJ, June 12, 1918, GPJC; *Moving Picture World*, Aug. 10, 1918. See also Sampson, *Blacks in Black and White*, 201–4; and Cripps, *Slow Fade to Black*, 80.

17. "Ebony Films," *Defender*, July 1, 1916.

18. "Ebony Film Cancelled," *Defender*, May 12, 1917; Langston to GPJ, Oct. 23, Nov. 24, 1916, GPJC. This controversy is also discussed in Butler, *Black Manhood on the Silent Screen*, 182–85.

19. "Ebony Film Cancelled," *Defender*, May 12, 1917.

20. See D. Ireland Thomas, "Musical and Dramatic," *Defender*, Oct. 27, 1923; and M. Hansen, *Babel and Babylon*, 84.

21. "Wanted for Colored Motion Pictures," Gate City ad, *Whip*, Oct. 22, 1921; "Millions in Movies," Klimax ad, *Whip*, May 7, 27, 1921. Two articles appear regarding the Railroad Association. See "Studio to Open Soon" and "New $300,000 Movie Co. Will Feature Race Actors and Actresses Exclusively," both in *Defender*, May 19, 1917; "Demand for Race Film Actors and Actresses Increasing," *Pittsburgh Courier*, Dec. 23, 1924; Bowser and Spence, *Writing Himself into History*, 76; and *Defender*, May 27, 1922.

22. R. Allen, "Contra the Chaser Theory," 4–11. See also "Picture Exhibition" and "At Last Something New! For Chicago and Its Citizens" ad, *Defender*, Sept. 22, 1923.

23. See *Whip* ad, Apr. 9, 1921; *Cincinnati Union*, May 21, 1921. On Poro College, see box 262, folder 3, CABP.

24. "Something New in Movies," *Defender*, Apr. 27, 1918; "The Moving Picture," *HCM*, June 1919; "The Colored Boys over There," *Defender*, July 30, 1921; "Right

Now, Moving Pictures of the Fighting 8th," *Defender*, Mar. 1, 1919; Sampson, *Blacks in Black and White*, 6–7.

25. See "The Royal Gardens Motion Picture Company: Producers and Instructors" ad, *Defender*, Jan. 17, 1920; and "Lincoln League," *Defender*, Mar. 13, 1920. See also reviews, "Big Feature" and "Great Feature" in *Defender*, Oct. 25, Nov. 13, 1920; and "In the Depths of Our Hearts," *Whip*, Nov. 13, 1920.

26. See "Jack Johnson's Road Show," *Defender*, Apr. 22, 1922. It was made clear that the Burton Holmes Company of Chicago made the prints. See also "As the World Rolls On," *Defender*, Aug. 20, 1921.

27. "Miss Bessie Coleman," *Defender*, Sept. 22, 1923; "Bessie Coleman" ad, *Defender*, Oct. 7, 14, 1922. Throughout the years, Coleman developed contacts with a number of race leaders in Chicago, including Oscar De Priest, Anthony Overton, and Marjorie Stewart Joyner, and was rumored to be romantically involved with Jesse Binga. See Rich, *Queen Bess*, 20–22.

28. "Miss Bessie Coleman Entertained," *Defender*, Sept. 30, 1922; "Miss 'Queen Bess' to Try Air October 15," *Defender*, Oct. 7, 1922; "Bessie Coleman Makes Initial Aerial Flight," *Defender*, Oct. 21, 1922; *Defender*, Sept. 8, 1923. The debate between Jackson, Jones, and Coleman can be found in "Walking Out on Film," "Jackson Returned Bessie's Blast," and "In an Interview with Jackson," *Baltimore Afro-American Ledger*, Nov. 10, Dec. 1, 1922; and Sampson, *Blacks in Black and White*, 185.

29. See promotional materials; Thomas to Norman, Jan. 15, 1926; and Coleman to Norman, Feb. 3, 23, 1926; all in RENC, box 1. Also see Rich, *Queen Bess*, 97; and Gibson-Hudson, "Norman Film Manufacturing Company."

30. "Blue Bird Theater Re-opens," *Whip*, Aug. 27, 1921; "Colored Movie Star," *Whip*, Oct. 11, 1919; "Race's Daredevil Movie Star" ad, *Defender*, Jan. 19, 1918; *Defender*, June 6, 1925.

31. Carbine, " 'The Finest outside the Loop,' " 26; Shapiro and Hentoff, *Hear Me Talkin' to Ya*. While my discussion of the struggle between "standard" and improvisational music accompaniment to movies focuses on Chicago, this battle was waged throughout the country. See Dave Peyton, "Standard Music," *Defender*, June 5, 1926. Peyton's opinions were consistent with the film industry's opinions about musical accompaniment. See Zinn, Frank, and Kelley, *Three Strikes*; M. Marks, *Music and the Silent Film*; Sabneev, *Music for the Films*; Lang and West, *Musical Accompaniment*; and Frelinger, *Motion Picture Piano Music*.

32. Dave Peyton, "The Musical Bunch," *Defender*, May 15, 1926; "Standard Music," *Defender*, June 5, 1926; Peyton, "Playing on the Job," *Defender*, Jan. 22, 1926; "Things in General," *Defender*, Oct. 9, 1926.

33. Dave Peyton, "Picture House Orchestra," *Defender*, Sept. 23, 1926; "Orchestras as Theater Assets," *Defender*, Oct. 16, 1926; "Things in General," *Defender*, Oct. 9, 1926.

34. Louise Spence argues, "I'm not going to claim that Micheaux was akin to the

Harlem Renaissance. . . . But I certainly think anyone studying black cultural life of the 1920's who gets beyond the Harlem Renaissance should definitely include Micheaux." Quoted in Scott Heller, "A Pioneering Black Film Maker," *Chronicle of Higher Education*, Mar. 3, 1995. Cripps, *Black Film as Genre*, 81; interview with Pearl Bowser by Jeremy Geltzer for Turner Classic Movies' Separate Cinema Series in 1999, <www.tcm.turner.com/MONTH_SPOTS/9807/seperateCINEMA/Bowser.htm.

35. Cripps, *Black Film as Genre*, 81; interview with Pearl Bowser by Jeremy Geltzer. However, Bowser and Spence revise this position to argue that Micheaux's use of sensation was a way "of building expectations in his customers and developing a following that expected sensations." See Bowser and Spence, *Writing Himself into History*, 184. *Within Our Gates* was described in an ad as "8,000 Feet of Sensational Realism," *Defender*, Jan. 31, 1920. See also J. Green, " 'Twoness' in the Style of Oscar Micheaux"; J. Gaines, "Fire and Desire"; and J. Brown, "Pulp Fiction of Oscar Micheaux." On Micheaux's frontier ideology, see Bowser and Spence, "Identity and Betrayal," 61; Elder, "Oscar Micheaux"; Fontenot, "Oscar Micheaux"; and Herbert, "Oscar Micheaux."

36. Martin J. Keenan, "Quiet Motion Picture Legend Buried in Great Bend," <www.greatbend.net/gbcc/history/micheaux/micheaux.htm; and Van Epps-Taylor, *Oscar Micheaux*. A general frontier thesis is found in Q. Taylor, *In Search of the Racial Frontier*; Painter, *Exodusters*; and Griggs, *Imperium in Imperio*. See also Micheaux, "Colored Americans Too Slow," *Defender*, Oct. 28, 1911; "Mr. Micheaux in City," *Defender*, Apr. 29, 1911; J. Green, *Straight Lick*, xiii; Bowser and Spence, *Writing Himself into History*, 4; and Micheaux, *Homesteader*, 400.

37. Micheaux, *Conquest*, 252–53; Bowser and Spence, *Writing Himself into History*, 9.

38. Noble Johnson to George Johnson (no date); Micheaux to Lincoln, June 25, 1918, GPJC; and Phelps, "Negro Life in Chicago," *HCM*, May 1919.

39. For *The Homesteader* ad and a complimentary review article, see *Defender*, Feb. 22, 1919. See also Bowser and Spence, *Writing Himself into History*, 113.

40. "The Homesteader," *Defender*, Mar. 1, 1919.

41. Bowser and Spence, *Writing Himself into History*, 13; Micheaux, "The Negro and the Photoplay," *HCM*, May 1919.

42. O. C. Hammond to Micheaux, Mar. 1919, GPJC; Phelps, "Negro Life in Chicago"; Juli Jones, "Moving Pictures and Inside Facts," *HCM*, July 1919. See also "Great Southern Tour of Oscar Micheaux's Mammoth Photoplay" ad, *Defender*, May 31, 1919.

43. "Within Our Gates," *Defender*, Jan. 10, 1920; "Great Lesson," *Defender*, Jan. 17, 1920. Quotes are from ANP press release, Feb. 20, 1920, GPJC.

44. See "Race Problem Play Comes to Omaha" (no date or paper affiliation), GPJC. The idea that *Within Our Gates* is a direct response to *Birth of a Nation* is made in J. Gaines, "*The Birth of a Nation* and *Within Our Gates*," and suggested in

J. Green, "Micheaux vs. Griffith." Bowser and Spence however, convincingly respond that *Within Our Gates* was merely part of a much larger "Grand Narrative" of race-specific issues. See *Writing Himself into History*, 125–29.

45. "Within Our Gates" ad, *Defender*, Jan. 31, 1920; "Within Our Gates," *Defender*, Jan. 10, 1920.

46. Micheaux, *Within Our Gates*.

47. "Within Our Gates," *Defender*, Feb. 21, 1920; Willis N. Huggins, "The Editor's Mailbox," *Defender*, Jan. 17, 1920; Micheaux to GPJ, Aug. 14, 1920, GPJC.

48. Snead, "Images of Blacks in Black Independent Cinema," 20; Bogle, *Toms*, 110; Jafa, "Notion of Treatment," 12–15. Also look at Hoberman, "Bad Movies"; and "Oscar Micheaux Writes on Growth of Race and Movie Field," *Pittsburgh Courier*, Dec. 13, 1924.

49. Charles Musser quoted in Heller, "Pioneering Black Film Maker"; Bowser and Spence, *Writing Himself into History*, 147.

50. "Going Abroad," *Defender*, Jan. 31, 1920; "Producer Returns," *Defender*, May 29, 1920; "Great Picture," *Defender*, Aug. 25, 1920; "The Brute," *Defender*, Sept. 25, 1920. See also *Defender* ads, Aug. 14, Sept. 4, 18, 1920. There is also a detailed ad in GPJC. Perhaps the first criticism of Micheaux's use of underworld scenes appears in Lester Walton, "Sam Langford's Wallop Makes 'The Brute' a Screen Success," *NYA*, Sept. 18, 1920. On Micheaux's other films, see "Motion Picture News," *Defender*, July 8, 1922; D. Ireland Thomas, "Motion Picture News," *Defender*, Feb. 14, 1925, Mar. 15, 1924; B. Peterson, "Filmography of Oscar Micheaux"; and J. Green, *Straight Lick*. On censorship, see Regester, "Black Films, White Censors."

51. See Micheaux, *Body and Soul*; Cripps, "Paul Robeson and Black Identity in the Movies"; and Regester, "Oscar Micheaux's *Body and Soul*."

52. Micheaux, *Body and Soul*; Regester, "Oscar Micheaux's *Body and Soul*."

53. William Henry, "Correcting Oscar Micheaux," *Defender*, Jan. 22, 1927. See also Bowser, "Sexual Imagery"; and Donaldson, *Representation of Afro-American Women in Hollywood*.

54. See ad for the fight at the Royal Gardens, *Defender*, July 10, 1920; Jack Cooper, "Colored Film at the 'Met' Monday, Tuesday and Wednesday," *Chicago Bee* (no date), and "Cabaret Patrons in Micheaux Film," July 1927, both in GPJC; and "Editor Abbott and Wife Star in Movies," *Defender*, Nov. 19, 1927.

55. Romeo L. Daugherty, *Amsterdam News*, Dec. 23, 1925; D. Ireland Thomas, "Musical and Dramatic," *Defender*, Apr. 1, 1922; Norman to Thomas, Jan. 19, 1926, RENC; Thomas, "Musical and Dramatic," *Defender*, May 27, 1922. See also Carbine, " 'The Finest outside the Loop' "; Travis, *Autobiography of Black Jazz*; J. A. Jackson, "Peter Jones Follows the Rainbow," *Billboard*, Apr. 1, 1922; and Lester Walton, "Fortune Smiles on Negro in Hollywood," *New York World*, June 6, 1929. A discussion of the continuities and distinctions between the "race film" and "blaxploitation" eras can be found in Diakite, *Culture and the Black Filmmaker*.

1. See the epigraphs to many of its essays and the particular essay "On the Sorrow Songs" in Du Bois, *Souls of Black Folk*, 12, 205–9. See also P. Anderson's important chapter " 'Unvoiced Longings': Du Bois and the Sorrow Songs" in *Deep River*; Radano, "Soul Texts"; D. Lewis, *Biography of a Race*, 281, 71–95; Fishkin, "Borderlands of Culture"; and Rampersand, *Art and Imagination*.

2. Du Bois's political project of even renaming the Negro spirituals "sorrow songs" was meant to counter such debasements. See Radano, "Soul Texts"; and P. Anderson, *Deep River*.

3. Du Bois, *Souls of Black Folk*, 209. See also P. Anderson, *Deep River*.

4. Du Bois, *Souls of Black Folk*, 155–57. For Du Bois's critique of white fascination with musical primitivism, see "Our Music," *Crisis* (July 1933), in Huggins, *W. E. B. Du Bois*, 1239; and Du Bois, "Religion of the American Negro," 216. His ambivalence about "folk" culture or at least his desire to discipline it within high art forms is discussed in Rampersand, *Art and Imagination*, 74; West, *American Evasion of Philosophy*, 143; and Bell, "Du Bois's Struggle to Reconcile Folk and High Art." For more on Harlem Renaissance–era development of Negro spirituals and questions of "folk music" as a site of racial/national memory, see Cruz, *Culture on the Margins*; Spencer, *New Negroes*; Radano and Bohlman, *Music and the Racial Imagination*; Radano, "Denoting Difference"; Floyd, *Black Music in the Harlem Renaissance*; Favor, *Authentic Blackness*; Nicholls, *Conjuring the Folk*; and Kelley, "Notes on Deconstructing the 'Folk.' "

5. Higginbotham, "Rethinking Vernacular Culture," 158–59; H. Boyer, " 'Take My Hand,' " 143; M. Fisher, "Organized Religion." Many shared the sentiments of writer and anthropologist Zora Neale Hurston, who offered an attack on the concretized Negro spirituals for "squeezing all of the rich black juice out of the songs and presenting a sort of musical octoroon to the public," which amounted to "some more 'passing for white.' " See Hurston, "Concert," appendix to *Dust Tracks on a Road*, 805; "Spirituals and Neo-Spirituals," in *Folklore, Memoirs, and Other Writings*, 873; and *Sanctified Church*. L. Hughes's more noted critique of "high art" through secular music can be found in "Negro Artist." General studies of gospel music include Darden, *People Get Ready*; Reagon, *If You Don't Go* and *We'll Understand It Better By and By*; H. Boyer, *Golden Age of Gospel*; and Heilbut, *Gospel Sound*.

6. Williams and Jennings, "Churches and Voluntary Associations in Chicago: Earliest Baptist Negro Community," in *Historical Letters and Records of the Hall Branch of the Chicago Public Library*, Microfilm No. 2, 4–5, Vivian G. Harsh Research Collection of Afro-American History and Literature; Stackhouse, *Chicago and the Baptists*, 49; Drake, "Churches and Voluntary Associations"; Fisher, "History of Olivet Baptist Church of Chicago"; Spear, *Black Chicago*, 91–97.

7. L. Hughes, "Negro Speaks of Rivers"; Harry Burleigh's concert arrangement

of the spiritual "Deep River" in *Deep River: The Songs and Spirituals of Harry Burleigh.*

8. Payne, *Recollections*, 253–54, quoted in Grossman, *Land of Hope*, 157; Penn and Bowen, *United Negro*, 69.

9. These insights are taken from a conversation between the author, Michael Harris, and Horace Clarence Boyer, at the "Thomas A. Dorsey, the Father of Black Gospel: His Life, His Lyrics and Music, and His Legacy" symposium at the Schomburg Center for Research in Black Culture, New York, New York, July 10, 1999. See also Frazier, *Negro Church in America*, chaps. 3 and 5; and M. Harris, *Rise of Gospel Blues*, 107–13.

10. "Real Value of Negro Melodies," *New York Herald*, May 21, 1893. See also "Dvořák's Theory of Negro Music," *New York Herald*, May 28, 1893; James Creelman, "Dvořák's Symphony a Historic Event," *New York Herald*, Dec. 17, 1893; Beckerman, *New Worlds of Dvořák*; Makdisi *Romantic Imperialism*; Hamm, "Dvorak in America"; Abrams, "Phantoms of Romantic Nationalism"; Zuck, *History of Musical Americanism*; Southern, *Music of Black Americans*, 266–68; and Dvořák, "Music in America". Radano makes the insightful point that Dvořák was hardly the first white music enthusiast to make such observations; see his "Magical Writing" chapter in *Lying Up a Nation.*

11. Graham, "Fisk Jubilee Singers"; Marsh, *Story of the Jubilee Singers*; Pike, *Jubilee Singers.*

12. M. Harris, *Rise of Gospel Blues*, 113–15. See also James Weldon Johnson, *Book of American Negro Poems*; and Johnson, Johnson, and Brown, *Book of American Negro Spirituals*. The second volume from Viking appeared in 1926. For more on Burleigh and Dett, see Simpson, *Follow Me*; Simpson, *Hard Trials*; Floyd, *Black Music in the Harlem Renaissance*, chaps. 3 and 4; Keck and Martin, *Feel the Spirit*; and Southern, *Music of Black Americans*, 268–79.

13. Du Bois, "John Work: Martyr and Singer," *Crisis* (May 1926); John W. Work, "Negro Folk Song," *Opportunity* (Oct. 1923); J. Work, *Folk Song of the American Negro*. Student protests are covered in Wolters, *New Negro on Campus.*

14. Levine, *Black Culture and Black Consciousness*. This point is taken from Johnson, Johnson, and Brown, *Book of American Negro Spirituals*, preface.

15. Locke, "The Negro Spirituals" in *New Negro*, 199–210. This important essay is followed by two equally important works by Locke that give a complete picture of his views on Negro spirituals. See Locke, "Our Little Renaissance" and *Negro and His Music.*

16. M. Harris, *Rise of Gospel Blues*, 107. See also Boatner and Townsend, *Spirituals Triumphant Old and New*; and "African American Musical Sacred Traditions" and "The Concert Spirituals Tradition" in *Wade in the Water.*

17. Levine, *Black Culture and Black Consciousness*, 206–7, 107–13. We must be careful to not replace the notion of a "denatured" or compromised spiritual with *real* folk music to produce a mode of anti-elitist elitism and authoritarian populism. In

the process, we ignore the constructed nature of "folk" music. M. Harris's negative evaluation of what he calls anthem spirituals seems to help cohere his tale of Thomas Dorsey's struggle and eventual rise to old-line legitimacy. Harris's reading of concert spirituals is necessarily tempered within the larger black musical context provided by Levine. See *Rise of Gospel Blues*, 117. Yet, in what is otherwise a pathbreaking examination of the "cross-fertilization in Afro-American music, dating back to the interaction of African and Euro-American musical styles in the colonial period," Levine is uncharacteristically critical of the "denatured" concert spirituals as well. Within his own framework, concert spirituals would seem to serve as one more example of the cultural syncretism that took place in the United States with their own particular social context and currency. See Levine, *Black Culture and Black Consciousness*, 166. Also look at Radano, "Hot Fantasies."

18. J. Work, "Changing Patterns"; Grossman, *Land of Hope*, 157. See also Favor, *Authentic Blackness*; Nicholls, *Conjuring the Folk*; and Kelley, "Notes on Deconstructing the 'Folk.'"

19. W. Smith, *Music on My Mind*, 3; Levine, *Black Culture and Black Consciousness*, 238; Southern, *Music of Black Americans*, 453–56; J. Work, "Changing Patterns," 286; Epstein, *Sinful Tunes and Spirituals*, 294.

20. Tindley's "Stand By Me," "What Are They Doing in Heaven," and "I'll Overcome Someday" and Handy's "Memphis Blues" and "St. Louis Blues" had been copyrighted as early as 1901. See Reagon, *We'll Understand It Better By and By*; H. Boyer, "Charles A. Tindley"; Southern, *Biographical Dictionary*, 316–17; Handy, *Blues* and *Father of the Blues*.

21. O'Neal and O'Neal, "Living Blues Interview," 22. For a thorough cultural biography of Dorsey's life in music, see M. Harris, *Rise of Gospel Blues*. See also Garrett, *Atlanta and Its Environs*; Alan Rogers, "True Stories of Atlanta: Decatur Street's Ghetto," *Atlanta Constitution*, Jan. 22, 1906, 4; Gordon N. Hurtel, "Down in the Dance Halls of Decatur Street," *Atlanta Constitution*, July 13, 1902, sec. 4, 1; Roell, *Piano in America*; and M. Harrison, "Boogie-Woogie."

22. M. Harris, *Rise of Gospel Blues*, 26–46.

23. "The Thomas Andrew Dorsey Story: From Blues-Jazz to Gospel Song" (Chicago, 1961), 23, quoted in M. Harris, *Rise of Gospel Blues*, 51; O'Neal and O'Neal, "Living Blues Interview," 26.

24. Albertson, *Bessie*, 122–24; B. Smith, "Soft Pedal Blues"; Ira De A. Reid, "Mrs. Bailey Pays the Rent," in Davis and Peplow, *New Negro Renaissance*. General discussion about buffet flats as "social centers" is covered in Wolcott, *Remaking Respectability*, 98, 106–9; Mumford, *Interzones*, 73–92; Chauncey, *Gay New York*, 244–67; and Heap, "'Slumming.'"

25. Drake and Cayton, *Black Metropolis*, 634; Grossman, *Land of Hope*, 157. See also "The Biography of Lucy Smith," LCP. Another version of her biography appears as "From the Farm to the Pulpit" in the index of Strong, "Social Types." Many black churches combined preexisting concerns about their parishioner's needs beyond the

religious with the Progressive Era Social Gospel movement that sought to reform the social vices of poverty and public immorality. See Higginbotham, *Righteous Discontent*; Curtis, *Consuming Faith*; Luker, *Social Gospel*; C. Morris, *Reverdy C. Ransom*; and R. White, *Liberty and Justice for All.*

26. On the "ring shout" tradition, see McLoughlin, *Revivals, Awakenings and Reform*; Lincoln and Mamiya, *Black Church*; and Frazier, *Negro Church in America.* See also Rabateau, *Slave Religion*; Stuckey, *Slave Culture*; and Synan, *Holiness-Pentecostal Movement.* Primary documents that chronicle the rise of this urban religion include "Weird Babel of Tongues," *Los Angeles Times*, Apr. 18, Apr. 19, 1906; St. Clair Drake, "Churches and Voluntary Associations in the Chicago Negro Community," IWP; and *Defender*, May 17, July 12, 1913, Aug. 28, 1915. For a general picture of race and racism in Holiness-Pentecostal congregations, see Sanders, *Saints in Exile*; Baer, *Black Spiritual Movement*; and Paris, *Black Pentecostalism.* While Sanctified worship is described as the purest example of both African and black southern retentions, it was an urban religion that went through important transformations and distinctions within each sub-denomination. See MacRobert, *Black Roots of White Racism*; and Patterson, Ross, and Atkins, *History and Formative Years of the Church of God in Christ.*

27. Sanders, *Saints in Exile*; Paris, *Black Pentecostalism*; R. Anderson, *Vision of the Disinherited*; Shopshire, "Socio-historical Characterization of the Black Pentecostal Movement"; Synan, *Holiness-Pentecostal Movement.*

28. Sanders, *Saints in Exile*; Paris, *Black Pentecostalism.* On the relationship between Mason and gospel music, see C. Boyer, "Gospel Blues," 120–21. See also T. Reed, *Holy Profane.*

29. J. Jackson, "Testifying at the Cross"; Cornelius, *Pioneer History of the Church of God in Christ*; Patterson, Ross, and Atkins, *History and Formative Years of the Church of God in Christ*; Pleas, *Fifty Years of Achievement*; and Wells, "Historical Overview."

30. H. Smith, "Three Negro Preachers," 16. For the best critical accounts of Elder Lucy Smith, see Best, "A Woman's Work, an Urban World" in *Passionately Human, No Less Divine* and "Lucy Madden Smith." The genesis story of Bishop Roberts's church testifies to the contradictory practices of gender inclusion and inequality within the COGIC specifically. In a similar fashion as Smith, Lillian Brooks Coffey and Anna Davis actually started the first COGIC congregation in Chicago from a small fellowship of thirteen women. However, as the church began to grow, the Memphis headquarters brought in William Roberts to "pastor" or lead the church. See Elder A. A. Childs, ed., *Eighteenth Annual Convocation: Churches of God in Christ Illinois, convening at 4019–21 S. State Chicago, Friday, Aug. 13–22, Inclusive 1937*, referenced in J. Jackson, "Testifying at the Cross."

31. Interview with Agnes Campbell in Oliver, *Songsters and Saints*, 200.

32. On Arizona Dranes, see Ray Funk, liner notes for *Preachin' the Gospel*; Heilbut, *Gospel Sound*, 26, 191; Oliver, *Songsters and Saints*, 188–91; Shaw, "Arizona

Dranes and Okeh"; liner notes for *Arizona Dranes, 1926–1928*; Southern, "Arizona Dranes," *Biographical Dictionary of Afro-American and African Musicians*, 115; and "Arizona Juanita Dranes."

33. J. Jackson, *Singing in My Soul*, 40; George D. Lewis, "Spirituals of Today," IWP; Rosetta Reitz, liner notes for Tharpe, *Sincerely Sister Rosetta Tharpe*; Heilbut, *Gospel Sound*, 191–96; Oliver, *Songsters and Saints*, 180–83.

34. O'Neal and O'Neal, "Living Blues Interview," 18, 20; Thomas A. Dorsey, interview with Michael Harris, Feb. 2, 1976, in M. Harris, *Rise of Gospel Blues*, 8; H. Boyer, "Analysis of His Contributions"; Dorsey, "From Bawdy Songs to Hymns," and "Gospel Music"; M. Harris, *Rise of Gospel Blues*, 75, 220–21; O'Neal and O'Neal, "Living Blues Interview," 28–29; R. Smith, *Thomas Andrew Dorsey*, 17.

35. Thomas A. Dorsey, interview with Michael Harris, Jan. 18, 1977, in M. Harris, *Rise of Gospel Blues*, 23; "Baptist End Most Remarkable Meeting," *Defender*, Sept. 17, 1921; Music of the Sunday School Publishing Board, *Gospel Pearls*, 1–2; M. Harris, *Rise of Gospel Blues*, 64–68.

36. O'Neal and O'Neal, "Living Blues Interview," 28–29; J. Jackson, "Testifying at the Cross," 95–102. M. Harris supplies a detailed textual analysis of the way in which Nix embellished the hymn. See M. Harris, *Rise of Gospel Blues*, 69–75; and Thomas A. Dorsey, interview with Michael Harris, Jan. 21, 1977, 68.

37. Thomas A. Dorsey, interview with Michael Harris, Jan. 19, 1977, in M. Harris, *Rise of Gospel Blues*, 75–76; O'Neal and O'Neal, "Living Blues Interview," 21; "Dorsey Busy," *Defender*, Mar. 1, 1924.

38. Mamie Smith's debut was celebrated in *Defender*, Mar. 13, 1921. For the larger context of race records, see Foreman, "Jazz and Race Records," 57; Bradford, *Born with the Blues*; and Dixon and Goodrich, *Recording the Blues*. On Dorsey and the vaudeville circuit, see M. Harris, *Rise of Gospel Blues*, 64–68; Oliver, *Bessie Smith*, 3–5; Southern, *Biographical Dictionary*, 316–17; Clarence Williams, quoted in Levine, *Black Culture and Black Consciousness*, 226; and Stearns, *Story of Jazz*, 167–68.

39. Higginbotham, "Rethinking Vernacular Culture"; Titon, *Early Downhome Blues*, 243; Levine, *Black Culture and Black Consciousness*, 228. See also Barlow, *Looking Up at Down*; Dixon and Goodrich, *Recording the Blues*, 22–27; and Charters, *Country Blues*, 46–48. Carby adds that the anxiety was also bound by the gendered and racial desires of possibly both record companies and black men to rid the black public sphere of strong women blues singers. See Carby, " 'It Jus' Be's Dat Way Sometime.' "

40. Titon, *Early Downhome Blues*, 254; Oliver, *Songsters and Saints*, 176–77.

41. Oliver, *Songsters and Saints*, 179–80; Dixon and Goodrich, *Recording the Blues*, 56–57.

42. "Thomas Andrew Dorsey Story" in M. Harris, *Rise of Gospel Blues*, 47–51.

43. See Calt, "Anatomy of a 'Race' Label—Part II."

44. Ibid.; O'Neal and O'Neal, "Living Blues Interview," 23; M. Harris, *Rise of Gospel Blues*, 78–81; Dixon and Goodrich, *Recording the Blues*, 20–22.

45. Dixon and Goodrich, *Recording the Blues*, 30, 54; O'Neal and O'Neal, "Living Blues Interview," 27. Dorsey's various musical identities are chronicled in J. Jackson, "Testifying at the Cross," 120; and Dixon and Goodrich, *Blues and Gospel Records*, 207–8.

46. Tom, *Complete Recorded Works in Chronological Order*; Dorsey, *Professional Thomas Andrew Dorsey, The Maestro Sings*; "The Thomas A. Dorsey Story," 42, and Thomas A. Dorsey, interview with Michael Harris, Jan. 19, 1977, in M. Harris, *Rise of Gospel Blues*, 91–101.

47. Thomas A. Dorsey, interview with Michael Harris, Jan. 19, 1977, in M. Harris, *Rise of Gospel Blues*, 91–101, 75–78; O'Neal and O'Neal, "Living Blues Interview," 30.

48. Transcribed from audio recording "Thomas A. Dorsey" in *Wade in the Water*. See also Duckett, "Interview with Thomas A. Dorsey," 5; and J. Jackson, "Testifying at the Cross," 211.

49. J. Jackson, "Testifying at the Cross," 211; Thomas A. Dorsey, interview with Michael Harris, Sept. 26, 1977, in M. Harris, *Rise of Gospel Blues*, 192–206. On his experiences in resistant churches, see O'Neal and O'Neal, "Living Blues Interview."

50. O'Neal and O'Neal, "Living Blues Interview," 31; Duckett, "Interview with Thomas A. Dorsey," 5; Thomas A. Dorsey, interview with Michael Harris, Dec. 3, 1977, in M. Harris, *Rise of Gospel Blues*, 192.

51. M. Harris, *Rise of Gospel Blues*, 123–34; R. Smith, *Thomas Andrew Dorsey*, 17–18; Thomas A. Dorsey, interview with Michael Harris, Jan. 29, 1976, in M. Harris, *Rise of Gospel Blues*, 91–101. See also Dixon and Goodrich, *Blues and Gospel Records*.

52. Thomas A. Dorsey, interview with Michael Harris, Feb. 2, 1976, in M. Harris, *Rise of Gospel Blues*, 52; "Thomas Andrew Dorsey Story" in M. Harris, *Rise of Gospel Blues*, 13–149; Thorson, "History of Music Publishing." This reading of Dorsey's initial inability to apply secular marketing practices to his sacred songs is heavily influenced by J. Jackson, "Testifying at the Cross," 131–32.

53. Thomas A. Dorsey, interview with Michael Harris, Dec. 3, 1977, in M. Harris, *Rise of Gospel Blues*, 176–77; "Baptists Inc., Gather for Golden Jubilee in Chicago," *Defender*, Aug. 16, 1930; Dorsey, "Gospel Music," 192; Goreau, *Just Mahalia, Baby*, 63; M. Harris, *Rise of Gospel Blues*, 178; H. Boyer, "Analysis of His Contributions," 22; Heilbut, *Gospel Sound*, 197.

54. "Ebenezer Boasts Largest Gospel Chorus," *Defender*, Feb. 6, 1932.

55. "Thomas Andrew Dorsey Story," 49–51, and Thomas A. Dorsey, interviews with Michael Harris, Dec. 3, Jan. 18, 19, 1977, Mar. 29, 1976, in M. Harris, *Rise of Gospel Blues*, 87, 175–87.

56. "Thomas Andrew Dorsey Story," 73, and Thomas A. Dorsey, interviews with Michael Harris, Jan. 18, 19, 1977, Mar. 29, 1976, in M. Harris, *Rise of Gospel Blues*, 87, 175–87, 259.

57. M. Harris, *Rise of Gospel Blues*, 259.

58. June Levell, interview with Michael Harris, Dec. 8, 1977, in M. Harris, *Rise of Gospel Blues*, 195.

59. M. Harris, *Rise of Gospel Blues*, 215. See also R. Smith, *Thomas Andrew Dorsey*, 38.

60. Heilbut, *Gospel Sound*, 198, 3–19. See also "Sallie Martin," *Ebony* (Mar. 1986); "Thomas A. Dorsey," *Wade in the Water*; National Convention of Gospel Choirs and Choruses Inc., *Welcome to NCGCC: We're Fulfilling the Dorsey Dream*, in J. Jackson, "Testifying at the Cross," 223–24.

61. Boyer's comments at "Thomas Dorsey, The Father of Black Gospel" symposium at the Schomburg Center for Research in Black Culture, New York, New York, July 10, 1999; J. Jackson, "Testifying at the Cross," 230.

62. M. Harris, *Rise of Gospel Blues*, 173; Thomas A. Dorsey, interviews with Michael Harris, Jan. 18, Jan. 19, 1977, in M. Harris, *Rise of Gospel Blues*, 51–63, 76; O'Neal and O'Neal, "Living Blues Interview," 21.

63. Heilbut, *Gospel Sound*, 44; Dorsey observations in Dorsey, "Gospel Music," 192–93; J. Jackson, "Testifying at the Cross," 247. See also Heilbut, *Gospel Sound*, 45–47; and H. Boyer, "Contemporary Gospel Music," 22–24.

64. Heilbut, *Gospel Sound*, 95.

65. George Lewis, "Spirituals of Today," 15, IWP. While not about black evangelists, see the important Hangen, *Redeeming the Dial*. For general studies of radio, see Barlow, *Voice Over*; Newman, *Entrepreneurs of Profit and Pride*; Spaulding, "History of Black Oriented Radio in Chicago"; and Edmerson, "Descriptive Study of the American Negro."

66. Spaulding, "History of Black Oriented Radio in Chicago," 101–4.

67. *Ebony* 5 (July 1949), 58; Spaulding, "History of Black Oriented Radio in Chicago," 101–4; Drake and Cayton, *Black Metropolis*, 643–46.

68. J. Washington, *Black Sects and Cults*, 114–15; Heilbut, *Gospel Sound*, 46–47. On Cobb, see also Best, *Passionately Human, No Less Divine*.

69. Frazier, *Negro Family in Chicago*, 101.

70. H. Smith, "Three Negro Preachers," 12–15.

71. Drake and Cayton, *Black Metropolis*, 643; H. Smith, "Three Negro Preachers," 11, 12; Strong, "Social Types," 270, 274,

72. Best, "Passionately Human, No Less Divine," 273; H. Smith, "Three Negro Preachers," 12; "The Langley Avenue All Nations Pentecostal Church," Federal Writers' Project Records, box 182, folder 36, Illinois State Historical Library.

73. H. Smith, "Three Negro Preachers," 12; Best, "Passionately Human, No Less Divine," 233.

74. H. Smith, "Three Negro Preachers," 12; "All Nations Pentecostal Church" and "Interview with Elder Lucy Smith," Federal Writers' Project Records, Illinois State Historical Library; Best, "Lucy Smith and Pentecostal Worship in Chicago."

75. M. Fisher, "Organized Religion"; Federal Writers' Project Records, box 187,

"Negro Materials" folder, Illinois State Historical Library; Best, "Passionately Human, No Less Divine," 282.

CHAPTER SIX

1. *Pittsburgh Courier*, June 7, 1912; Farr, *Black Champion*, 123; *Freeman*, July 16, 1910.

2. The greatest meditation on the relationship between race, culture, politics, and sport remains C. L. R. James, *Beyond a Boundary*, which heavily influences the conceptual framework of this chapter. See also Sammons, " 'Race' and Sport."

3. *Baltimore Afro-American Ledger*, July 14, 1928; Frederick North Shorey, *Freeman*, Sept. 7, 1907.

4. This metaphorical gender dialogue on playing fields was further supervised by athletic codes of homosocial sports(man)ship. Even black "sporting life" challenges to the dominant racial and economic order confined this public sphere to a dynamic reworking of the language and logic of the rights and/or "rites" of man at best. See Burstyn, *Rites of Men*. See also Amarillo, "Mexican American Baseball"; and Jarvie, *Sport, Racism, and Ethnicity*. General race and masculinity scholarship includes Summers, *Manliness and Its Discontents*; Wallace, *Constructing the Black Masculine*; Booker, *"I Will Wear No Chain!"*; Hine and Jenkins, *Question of Manhood*; Carby, *Race Men*; Stecopoulos and Uebel, *Race and the Subject of Masculinities*; Harper, *Are We Not Men?*; Wiegeman, *American Anatomies*; Bederman, *Manliness and Civilization*; Mercer, *Welcome to the Jungle*; and hooks, "Reconstructing Black Masculinity."

5. Summers, *Manliness and Its Discontents*; Bederman, *Manliness and Civilization*. See also "Son of Slave Is Made Master of the World's Fighting Men by Conquering the Undefeated White Champion," *Chicago Daily Inter Ocean*, July 5, 1910, 1.

6. Pendegrast, *Creating the Modern Man*; Gorn, *Manly Art*; Rotundo, *American Manhood*; and Carnes and Griffen, *Meanings for Manhood*.

7. Jack Johnson, *Jack Johnson Is a Dandy*. Also look at its original publication under the title *Jack Johnson—In the Ring—and Out*. See Farr, *Black Champion*, 68. Theories about masculine body types are in Bederman, *Manliness and Civilization*, 8. My notion of "cerebral physicality" is heavily influenced by Farred's brilliant discussion of Muhammad Ali as a vernacular intellectual in *What's My Name?*, 8, 69–72.

8. Farr, *Black Champion*, 60. On the larger symbolic meaning of Johnson, see also Farr, *Black Champion*; Gilmore, *Bad Nigger!*; Roberts, *Papa Jack*; and Hietala, *Fight of the Century*.

9. *Freeman*, Mar. 20, 1910; Farr, *Black Champion*, 31; Jack Johnson, *Jack Johnson Is a Dandy*, 67–68. The dandy figure has historically been characterized by his or her worldliness, attention to dressing the body, self-conscious presentation of the body as a public spectacle, and mobilization of that "artificial" body through the public in ways that trouble conventional race, class, and/or sexualized social positions. With

this definition in mind, Jack Johnson powerfully embodied the dandy persona. For a history of the dandy, style, and body politics, see Powell, "Sartor Africanus"; White and White, "Dandies and Dandizettes" in *Stylin'*; and Garelick, *Rising Star*. See also Hendrickson, *Clothing and Difference*; Hollander; *Sex and Suits*; E. Wilson, *Adorned in Dreams*; and Hebdige, *Subculture*.

10. Drake and Cayton, *Black Metropolis*, 391. On jokes, see Neal, "Uncle Rufus Raps on the Squared Circle," 46; Farr, *Black Champion*, 116; W. Wiggins, "Jack Johnson as Bad Nigger," 46; and Levine, *Black Culture and Black Consciousness*, 432–33.

11. *Chicago Tribune*, July 6, 1910. The *New York Times* lamented that if Johnson won, "thousands and thousands of his ignorant brothers will misinterpret his victory as justifying claims to much more than physical equality with their white neighbors." See *New York Times*, July 2, 1910. See also *Los Angeles Times*, July 6, 1910; and *Freeman*, Nov. 9, 1912.

12. *Chicago Daily News*, July 2, 1910. Just as a point of fact, Spencer is recognized as coining the famous phrase "Survival of the Fittest." For white responses to the fight, see *Chicago Daily Inter Ocean*, July 3, 4, 1910; "The Psychology of the Prize Fight," *Current Literature* 49 (July 1910): 57–58; *Chicago Daily News*, July 3, 4, 1910; *Chicago Tribune*, July 3, 4, 1910; and Hendricks and Shepard, *Jack London Reports*, 266–68.

13. Streible, "Jack Johnson Fight Films." For attempts to turn Johnson "white," see *New York World*, quoted in *NYA*, July 14, 1910, and "Psychology of the Prize Fight." White responses that shift civilization from "muscle" to "mind" include *Los Angeles Times*, July 6, 1910; *Kansas City Star*, July 5, 1910; *Chicago Tribune*, July 6, 1910; and reprint of speech of Archbishop Glennon of St. Louis in *Washington Bee*, July 9, 1910.

14. P. Miller, "Anatomy of Scientific Racism," 125; D. Wiggins, " 'Great Speed but Little Stamina' "; E. Mitchell, "Racial Traits in Athletics," was a three-part series in *American Physical Education Review*, Mar. 1922, 93–95, Apr. 1922, 151–52, and May 1922. See also Hoffman, *Race Traits and Tendencies*.

15. *Freeman*, Dec. 14, 1912; Gilmore, "Jack Johnson and White Women."

16. *NYA*, July 14, 1910; *Baltimore Afro-American Ledger*, Oct. 26, 1912; Scott to Johnson, July 11, 1910, 407, BTWP.

17. *Broad Ax*, Nov. 16, 1912. See also *Defender*, Oct. 26, 1912, Jan. 4, 1913; and *Indianapolis Ledger*, Oct. 2, 1912.

18. *Crisis* (Feb. 1913), 180.

19. *Freeman*, Nov. 9, 1912; Cary B. Lewis, "Johnson Denies Guilt!" *Freeman*, Nov. 2, 1912; *Defender*, Nov. 2, 1912; *Broad Ax*, Nov. 2, 1912. For Johnson response, see Cary B. Lewis, "JACK JOHNSON IS BAD!," *Defender*, Oct. 26, Nov. 2, 1912; *Chicago Tribune*, Oct. 24, 1912; and "John Arthur Johnson, Heavy Weight Prize Fighter of the World," *Broad Ax*, Oct. 26, 1912. His comments referred to a 1911 controversy when white New Yorker Henry Ulrich falsely accused and subsequently beat up Washington for peering into a keyhole to look at his wife. See Gatewood, "Booker T.

Washington and the Ulrich Affair"; and Gilmore, "Jack Johnson and White Women." See also "Booker T. Washington the Great Wizard of Tuskegee Does Not Like to Share His Popularity with Jack Johnson," *Broad Ax*, Jan. 4, 1913.

20. It's interesting that Johnson's critique of Washington's lack of courage resonates with Du Bois's gendered placement of Washington on the low end of "race man" examples in history again because of his lack of virility and courage. See Jack Johnson, *Jack Johnson Is a Dandy*, 239; and Du Bois, *Souls of Black Folk*; and for analysis, Carby, *Race Men*. On the larger backlash against Washington, see *Freeman*, Oct. 26, 1912; and *Defender*, Nov. 16, 1912. See also Levine, *Black Culture and Black Consciousness*, 421.

21. Charles Marshall, *Freeman*, Feb. 7, 1920; IWW and Mexico speech quoted in Roberts, *Papa Jack*, 211–13. This ad also appeared in *Messenger* (1919).

22. Louis, *Joe Louis*, 50–51; JBC; and Hietala, *Fight of the Century*. See also *Pittsburgh Courier*, June 22, 1946; and Ellison, *Going to the Territory*, 215.

23. Frederick Lewis Allen, "Breaking World's Records," *Harper's*, Aug. 1926, 308; Holloman, "On the Supremacy of the Negro Athlete"; Cromwell and Wesson, *Championship Techniques in Track and Field*, 6; Metheny, "Some Differences in Bodily Proportions," 51–52. A fuller discussion of this literature can be found in Oriard, *King Football*; P. Miller, "Anatomy of Scientific Racism"; and D. Wiggins, " 'Great Speed but Little Stamina.' "

24. Almost collectively, white middle-class men were diagnosed with the new disease "neurasthenia," where chronic physical and mental fatigue were the medical results of an effeminate overrefinement that was leading to a (white) racial death. See Lutz, *American Nervousness*; and Gosling, *Before Freud*.

25. See Kimmel, *Manhood in America*; Bederman, *Manliness and Civilization*; Rotundo, *American Manhood*; Douglas, *Feminization of American Culture*; Kimmel, "Men's Responses to Feminism"; Mangan and Walvin, *Manliness and Morality*; and Lears, *No Place of Grace*. See also Lutz, *American Nervousness*; and Gosling, *Before Freud*.

26. Putney, *Muscular Christianity*; Ladd and Mathisen, *Muscular Christianity*; D. Hall, *Muscular Christianity*. See also Overman, *Influence of the Protestant Ethic*; Swanson, "Acceptance and Influence"; Higgs, *God in the Stadium*; H. Green, *Fit for America*; and Whorton, *Crusaders for Fitness*. On Roosevelt, the strenuous life, and the racial frontier, see Bederman, *Manliness and Civilization*; Slotkin, *Gunfighter Nation*; Hoganson, *Fighting for American Manhood*; Haraway, "Teddy Bear Patriarchy"; Ninkovich, "Theodore Roosevelt"; Dyer, *Theodore Roosevelt*; and Roosevelt, "Strenuous Life.".

27. Getz, *MBI*; Pollock, *Moody*; Hopkins, *History of the YMCA*. On Billy Sunday, see Bruns, *Billy Sunday*; and Dorsett, *Billy Sunday*. On the Muscular Christianity of Stagg and Naismith, see Ellis, *Mr. Football*; Guttman, *Whole New Ball Game*; Webb, *Basketball Man*; and Naismith, *YMCA as Basketball*. For more on the development of both white and immigrant boys through playgrounds, see Reiss, *City Games*;

W. Wilson, *City Beautiful Movement*; Macleod, *Building Character*; and Cavallo, *Muscles and Morals*. On Chicago and the "Playground Movement," see G. Taylor, "Public Recreations Facilities."

28. Mjagkij, "True Manhood," 144–45; Du Bois, *Black North*, 28.

29. Wiggins and Miller, *Unlevel Playing Field*, 3–4; Du Bois, "Problem of Amusement," 226. See also P. Miller, "To 'Bring the Race along Rapidly' "; and Captain, "Enter Ladies and Gentleman of Color." For more on Du Bois's philosophy on the body, see P. Anderson, *Deep River*, 48; and Tate, *Psychoanalysis and Black Novels*, 47–85.

30. E. Scott, "Leisure Time"; W. Jones, *Recreation and Amusement*. More attention must be paid to Edwin B. Henderson's series of articles on "Athletics" in the *Messenger* (Mar. 1925), 132–33, (Feb. 1926), 51, (Apr. 1926), 117, (May 1926), 149, (Feb. 1927), 52, 61, and his book *The Negro in Sports*, sponsored by Carter G. Woodson's Association for the Study of Negro Life and History (ASNLH). Many of these primary documents are included in the important collection by Wiggins and Miller, *Unlevel Playing Field*.

31. Robert Abbott, "Ruffianism in the Parks," *Defender*, July 12, 1919; CCRR, *Negro in Chicago*, 272–97; Drake and Cayton, *Black Metropolis*; Grossman, *Land of Hope*; Vaillant, *Sounds of Reform*, 173–81. See also Reiss, *City Games*, 146–49; Tuttle, *Race Riot*, chap. 2; and Spear, *Black Chicago*, 205–6. On the Wabash YMCA, see Mjagkij, "True Manhood" and *Light in the Darkness*.

32. Companies that offered funding included Pullman, International Harvester, Corn Products Refining, and five packinghouses. Team names included the Swift's Premiums, Armour Star Lambs and Ovals, and International Harvester Industrial Tractors. On the Wabash YMCA and industrial programs, see Reiss, *City Games*, 82–86; Cohen, "Contested Loyalty at the Workplace" in *Making a New Deal*; and Grossman, *Land of Hope*, 200–203. See also Gems, *Windy City Wars*. For a report of the industrial league, see "Industrial Baseball League Meets," *Defender*, Mar. 26, 1921, June 12, 1926. For George Cleveland Hall Lecture, see "Sporting," *Defender*, Dec. 6, 1913.

33. On the church league, see *Defender*, Oct. 14, Nov. 15, Dec. 13, 1919, Jan. 17, 1920, Dec. 17, 1921, Jan. 12, 19, 1924, Feb. 14, 1925; and on the post office league, see *Defender*, Feb. 2, 1924. See also Frank Young, "The Y.M.C.A. Spirit," *Defender*, Feb. 25, 1922; Frank Young, "FAY SAYS," *Defender*, Nov. 4, 1922; "Supervisor of High School Athletics Defines 'Amateurism,' " *Defender*, Feb. 25, 1925; and Henry R. Crawford, "Amateur Athletics vs. Professional," *Defender*, Feb. 25, Apr. 7, 1928. On commendation of a team for taking non-amateur teams off their schedules, see "Commends St. Christopher's Stand in New York and Points Way for Other Clubs to Follow," *Defender*, Dec. 18, 1920.

34. Gems, "Blocked Shot." On Wabash Outlaws, see *Defender*, Feb. 14, Mar. 7, 1914, Dec. 2, 1916. On Lincoln, see *Defender*, Oct. 30, Nov. 6, 13, Dec. 18, 1915, Nov. 12, 1912. On Forty Club, see *Defender*, Apr. 2, 1921, Nov. 6, 20, Dec. 4, 25, 1920, Jan. 8, Feb. 26,

Mar. 5, 22, 1921. On Chicago Defenders team, see *Defender*, Dec. 17, 24, 1921. On Eighth Regiment, see *Defender*, Apr. 2, 1921. The name change is noted in "Defender A.C. Takes Opener from Evanston," *Defender*, Nov. 14, 1921. The Defender Tournament is covered in "Basketball Championship," *Defender*, Mar. 18, 1922; "Stage Set for Defender's Basketball Championships," *Defender*, Mar. 25, 1922; and "Championship to Be Decided in Basketball," *Defender*, Apr. 1, 1922. On Wabash versus the New York City Incorporators, see *Defender*, Mar. 24, Apr. 7, 1917. On Wabash eastern tour, see *Defender*, Dec. 27, 1919, Mar. 6, 1920. On Phillips High School rivalries, see *Defender*, Apr. 5, 26, 1924, Feb. 21, 12, 28, 1925, Jan. 2, 9, 1926. On disqualification, see *Defender*, Feb. 12, 1927. See also "Color Made a Difference," *Defender*, Mar. 18, 1922; "City's Finest—Mr. Stagg, Will You Take 'Em?," *Defender*, Mar. 22, 1930; "Wendell Phillips, City High School Champions, Fail to Get 'Invitation' to Tourney," *Defender*, Mar. 29, 1930; "Passing of Stagg Is Good News for Race," *Defender*, Feb. 11, 1933; and Gems, "Blocked Shot."

35. Wiggins and Miller, *Unlevel Playing Field*, 145; James Weldon Johnson, *Black Manhattan*.

36. On Unions and Leland, see promotional packet *Frank Leland's Chicago Giants Base Ball Club* (Chicago, 1910), BHFL; "The Chicago Giants Show Class," *Defender*, Oct. 26, 1910; "Frank Leland Laid to Rest," *Defender*, Nov. 21, 1914; S. White, *History of Colored Base Ball*; Gosnell, *Negro Politicians*, 67–68; Peterson, *Only the Ball Was White*, 63–64; Riley, *Biographical Encyclopedia of the Negro Baseball Leagues*, 474–75; and M. Lomax, *Black Baseball Entrepreneurs*, 123–31, 149–52, "Black Baseball," 188–98, and "Black Entrepreneurship." See also the wonderful pictorial book by Lester, Miller, and Clark, *Black America Series*. On the Columbia Giants, see Powers, "Page Fence Giants Play Ball"; S. White, *History of Colored Base Ball*, 28–31, 38–40; and Dixon and Hannigan, *Negro Baseball Leagues*. For information on shift to Leland Giants and membership in the Chicago league, see S. White, *History of Colored Base Ball*, 28–31, 38–40; Ziemer, "Chicago's Negro Leagues," 37; and M. Lomax, "Black Entrepreneurship," 50.

37. Notably Jackson and Moseley were presented to the public in the *Broad Ax* with the manly and gentlemanly military distinctions of major and colonel respectively. With no evidence of military service, it appears they were "soldiers" in the army of race entrepreneurs. See "Major General R. R. Jackson, Assistant Supt. Armour Station Financial Secretary Appomattox Club," *Broad Ax*, Dec. 27, 1902; "Col. B. F. Moseley," *Broad Ax*, Mar. 30, 1901; and "Col. Beauregard F. Moseley, Lawyer, Orator, and Property Holder," *Broad Ax*, Dec. 29, 1906. See also "Opening of the Chateau de Plaisance," *Broad Ax*, Nov. 2, 1907; and "The Chateau de Plaisance," *Broad Ax*, Nov. 16, 1907. Ads to stockholders can be found throughout the *Broad Ax* from January 4, 1908, through April 25, 1908. See also *Broad Ax*, Sept. 27 1907; *Defender*, May 13, 1911; "Auburn Ball Park," *Broad Ax*, July, 20, 1907; and *Frank Leland's Chicago Giants Base Ball Club*, BHFL. The Leland Giants Playlot Park currently exists on Chicago's South Side at 7526 W. Lowe Ave.

38. "A National League of Professional Negro Clubs for Next Season," *Freeman*, Nov. 9, 1907, 6; "Growing Interest Taken in Proposed League," *Freeman*, Nov. 16, 1907; "To Organize Colored League," *Freeman*, Nov. 23, 1907; "A Successful Meeting Is Sighted," *Freeman*, Jan. 25, 1908; "League Does Not Fear Outlaws," *Freeman*, Dec. 28, 1907; "An Understanding about the League," *Freeman*, Feb. 15, 1908. On Rube Foster, see George Mason, "Rube Foster Chats about His Career," *Defender*, Feb. 20, 1915; John Holloway, *Blackball Stars*, 9–10; Whitehead, *Man and His Diamonds*, 3, 18–23; Peterson, *Only the Ball Was White*, 104–8; and Cottrell, *Best Pitcher in Baseball*.

39. See "The Philadelphia Giants, Colored Champions of the World," *Philadelphia Item*, Sept. 21, 1904; "Base Ball," *Philadelphia Item*, Oct. 28, 1905; John L. Footslug, "In the World of Sports," *Freeman*, Nov. 18, 1905; Frederick North Shorey, "A Historical Account of a Great Game of Ball: How Rube Foster Cleaned Up with One of the Best Teams in the Country," *Freeman*, Sept. 14, 1907; and "Baseball's Greatest Figure Dead," *Defender*, Dec. 13, 1930. See also A. Foster, "How to Pitch."

40. On league formation and resistance, see "A Meeting Held Monday Afternoon," *Philadelphia Item*, Oct. 29, 1906, 7. See also "The International League Has Made More Changes . . . ," *Philadelphia Item*, July 24, 1906; "International League Standing," *Philadelphia Item*, Aug. 19, 1906; Peterson, *Only the Ball Was White*; and Cottrell, *Best Pitcher in Baseball*.

41. Mason, "Rube Foster Chats about His Career"; Peterson, *Only the Ball Was White*, 107; Dave Phillips, "Boxing Baseball and Athletics," *Freeman*, Aug. 31, 1907; "Pride of Dearborn" and Shorey, "A Historical Account of a Great Game of Ball," *Freeman*, Sept. 7, 1907. See also David Wyatt, "Baseball: Booker T. Washington or the Fifteenth Amendment," *Freeman*, Sept. 21, 1907.

42. "Champion Leland Giants to Go South for Spring Training," *Freeman*, Feb. 20, 1909; "Leland Giants Complete a Successful Southern Trip," *Freeman*, May 15, 1909; "Leland Giants to Play Baseball in Cuba," *Defender*, Oct. 8, 1910; Lester Walton, "Baseball Flourishing in Cuba," *NYA*, Dec. 8, 1910; "Growing Interest in Proposed League," *Freeman*, Nov. 16, 1907; "Nothing but Success in Sight for League Meeting," *Freeman*, Dec. 7, 1907. See also "League Meeting a Successful One," *Freeman*, Dec. 7, 1907; "Attorney B. F. Moseley Favors the Formation of National Negro Baseball League," *Broad Ax*, Nov. 26, 1910; "Call for a Conference of Persons Interested in the Formation of a National Negro Baseball League," *Broad Ax*, Dec. 17, 1910; "Play Ball" ad, *Defender*, May 6, 1911; and "A Baseball Appeal of a Worthy Undertaking by a Worthy Man to Worthy Men; Read and Respond," *Broad Ax*, Jan. 21, 1911. On booster activities, see "Diamond Dust," *Defender*, May 20, June 3, 10, 24, 1911; " 'Boosters' Ukase from the President," *Defender*, May 27, 1911; and "Moseley's Leland Giants to Have New Park," *Defender*, Mar. 12, 1910.

43. On black leadership frustration with Foster, see "Here and There," *Defender*, July 12, 1913; and "Sporting," *Defender*, Aug. 2, 1913.

44. "Rube Foster's Review on Baseball," *Freeman*, Dec. 28, 1912; Frank Young,

"Local Sports," *Defender*, Mar. 22, 1913; "American Giants Lose," *Defender*, July 5, 1913; "Sporting," *Defender*, Aug. 9, 1913; "Benefit for the Old Folks Home," *Defender*, Aug. 16, 1913; Mason, "Foster Chats about His Career," 10; M. Lomax, "Black Baseball," 274–76.

45. Julius Avendorph, "Rube Foster and His American Giants," *Defender*, Apr. 5, 1913; David Malarcher notes from tape, David Malarcher File, Ashland Collection, BHFL; John Holloway, *Blackball Stars*, 18, 26; Gardner and Shorelle, *Forgotten Players*, 2, 28–29; Peterson, *Only the Ball Was White*, 109–10. For attendance information, see Frank Young, "More about Foster's Baseball Team," *HCM*, June 1, 1919; "American Giants Beat City Champions," *Defender*, Sept. 16, 1916; and "10,000 Frenzied Fans Witness Greatest 12-Inning Game of the Season," *Defender*, Aug. 24, 1918. Even from the start, not everyone was happy with Foster's leadership, as revealed in a heated controversy over the Colored Championship between Foster and Indianapolis ABC's leader C. I. Taylor in 1916. See "Andrew 'Rube' Foster," *Freeman*, Oct. 21, 1916; Mr. Fan, "Mr. Foster Tells a Few Things of Interest," *Defender*, Nov. 11, 1916; "Rube Foster Speaks," *Defender*, Nov. 18, 1916; A. Foster, "Rube Foster Wants Championship without Fighting for It," *Freeman*, Nov. 11, 1916; and J. R. Warren cartoon, "An Attempted Hold-Up," *Freeman*, Dec. 2, 1916.

46. "Havana Cubans a New Chicago Nine," *Defender*, Mar. 29, 1917; Peterson, *Only the Ball Was White*, 82; "Rube Foster Leads His Team to Indianapolis," *Defender*, Aug. 18, 1917; "American Giants in Detroit for Sunday and Labor Day Games," *Defender*, Sept. 1, 1917; "Detroit Stars Ready for Next Season," *Defender*, Feb. 19, 1920; "Detroit Stars Open at Mack's Park April 20," *Defender*, Apr. 19, 1919; Bak, *Turkey Stearnes*. On the reconciliation between Foster and the political elite, see Mr. Fan, "American Giants Beat City Champions," *Defender*, Sept. 16, 1916; Mr. Fan, "American Giants Begin Local Season," *Defender*, Apr. 21, 1917; Mr. Fan, "American Giants Take Opening Game 5 to 3," *Defender*, Apr. 28, 1917; "Guest of Alderman," *Defender*, Apr. 28, 1917; "Foster Asks Patience," *Defender*, Apr. 19, 1919; and M. Lomax, "Black Baseball," 298–303.

47. Quote about Foster as "best known" from Phelps, "Andre 'Rube' Foster," *HCM*, Mar. 1, 1919. On seating, see "Foster Asks Patience," *Defender*, Apr. 19, 1919; and "Giants Seating Capacity Enlarged," *Defender*, June 7, 1919. For "owned and controlled" quotes, see Phelps, "Andrew 'Rube' Foster." See also Cary Lewis, "Baseball Circuit for Next Season," *Defender*, Oct. 4, 1919.

48. "Pitfalls of Baseball" series, *Defender*, Nov. 29, Dec. 13, 20, 27, 1919, Jan. 3, 10, 17, 1920.

49. C. I. Taylor, "The Future of Colored Baseball," *Competitor* (Feb. 1920), 76–79.

50. Charles D. Marshall, "Rube Foster Wants 'Get Together' Meet of All Baseball Owners," *Freeman*, Jan. 17, 1920; "The 'Stove League': Smoking 'Em Across with the Winning Run on the Sacks," *Competitor* (Jan. 1920); "Call for National League Issued: Kansas City Selected for Meeting of Baseball Magnates," *Defender*, Feb. 7, 1920; "Baseball Magnates Hold Conference" *Defender*, Feb. 14, 1920. See also "Negro

Base Ball League Assured," *Freeman*, Feb. 21, 1920; "Baseball Men Write League Constitution," *Defender*, Feb. 21, 1920; Ira F. Lewis, "Athletics: National Baseball League Formed," *Competitor* (Mar. 1920); and Dave Wyatt, "Athletics: National League of Colored Clubs Prepare for Season's Opening," *Competitor* (Apr. 1920).

51. "Rube Foster Tells What Baseball Needs to Succeed" and "Many Shortcomings and Suggests Way to Permanent Success," *Defender*, Dec. 10, 1921; "Why Managers and Owners Have Been a Rank Failure," *Defender*, Dec. 17, 1921; "Players Prove Serious Drawback to Baseball," *Defender*, Dec. 24, 1921; A. Foster, "Future of Race Umpires Depends on Men of Today," *Defender*, Dec. 31, 1921. See also "Demand for Umpires of Color Is Growing among the Fans," *Defender*, Oct. 9, 1920.

52. See "The American Giants Garage" ad, *Defender*, Feb. 7, 1925. On controversies between Foster and the predominately white-owned Eastern Colored League, see "East's Baseball Teams Organize," *Whip*, Dec. 9, 1922; "Easterners Organize a New League," *Whip*, Dec. 23, 1922; and " 'Rube' Foster Launches Out against Easterners," *New York Amsterdam News*, Jan. 17, 1923. On East-West World Series, see Frank Young, "Entirely Up to Eastern League Whether Wishes of Fans Will Be Ignored," *Defender*, Aug. 30, 1924; "Bolden and Foster Also Move for Peace between Eastern and Western Clubs," *Defender*, Sept. 6, 1924; "Colored World Series Is Arranged between Clubs of East And West," *NYA*, Sept. 13, 1924; "Hilldale and Chicago Get the World Series Apple; We Get the Core—If There Is One!" *Kansas City Call*, Sept. 12, 1924; and "Change in Dates Made for Fandom," *Defender*, Sept. 20, 1924. See also "Rube Foster Has a Word to Say to the Baseball Fans," *Defender*, Jan. 9, 1924; Edward Bolden, "Association of Eastern Clubs Replies to Andrew Foster," *New York Amsterdam News*, Jan. 17, 1923; "League Too Big for Newspapers, Can't Grasp Idea—Rube," *Whip*, Oct. 28, 1922; Al Monroe, "What Is the Matter with Baseball?" *Abbott's Monthly* (Apr. 1932); and Rogosin, *Invisible Men*, 27.

53. W. S. Ferrance, "Says Foster Got $11,000 Out of League," *Baltimore Afro-American Ledger*, Feb. 2, 1923; "Demand for Umpires of Color Is Growing among the Fans," *Defender*, Oct. 9, 1920; Dave Wyatt, "Marcos Lose to the Giants," *Defender*, July 24, 1920; "Rube Foster's 'Sportsmanship,' " *Kansas City Call*, July 11, 1924. On fans' interest in other "commercial amusements," see Frank Young, "Entirely Up to Eastern League Whether Wishes of Fans Will Be Ignored," *Defender*, Aug. 30, 1924. On "winter sports," see "League Too Big for Newspapers, Can't Grasp Idea—Rube," *Whip*, Oct. 28, 1922. See also Frank Young, "Rube Foster—Master Mind of Baseball," *Abbott's Monthly* (Nov. 1930); "Rube Foster Dead," *Defender*, Dec. 13, 1930; and "Thousands Attend Last Rites for Rube Foster," *Defender*, Dec. 20, 1930.

54. Frank Andrew Young, "Sport Editorial," *Defender*, Jan. 8, 1921; "First Time in History: Chicago vs. New York" ad, *Defender*, Mar. 24, 1917; "Incorporators Beat Wabash YMCA Five," *Defender*, Apr. 7, 1917; "Basket-Ball! East vs. West," *Defender*, Dec. 27, 1919; "Forty Club Victors over Fast Gotham Five," *Defender*, Jan. 8, 1921; "Forty Club Defeats St. Christopher Five," *Defender*, Mar. 5, 1921; "Defender A. C.—

Evanston Arrow Game Opens Basketball Season," *Defender*, Nov. 12, 1921; "Interest Grows in Coming Basket Ball Game in City," *Defender*, Oct. 16, 1921. See also Gems, "Blocked Shot," 146; N. George, *Elevating the Game*; Peterson, *From Cages to Jump Shots*; the pioneering Ashe series *Hard Road to Glory*; Chalk, *Pioneers of Black Sport*; and Henderson, *Negro in Sports*.

55. Peterson, *From Cages to Jump Shots*, 101. On the 1939 season, see "To Return for Game Jan. 23," *Defender*, Jan. 14, 1939; "Rens, Globe Trotters Eye World's Pro Title," *Defender*, Mar. 25, 1939; and "New York Rens Five Wins World Pro Title," *Defender*, Apr. 1, 1939.

56. "Real Founder of Globe Trotters: Tom Brookins Not Saperstein Dreamed Up Team in 20s," *Bronzeville Press* (not dated but confirmed by N. George's account in *Elevating the Game*). See also Gems, "Blocked Shot"; N. George, *Elevating the Game*, 41–45; Peterson, *From Cages to Jump Shots*, 105–7; Jim Bowman, "Basketball Hoopla: The Globetrotters' Legend Begins on Chicago's South Side," *Chicago Tribune Magazine* (Dec. 18, 1983). See also Chalk, *Pioneers of Black Sport*, 96–103. A selection of Savoy Big Five articles include *Defender*, Mar. 3, 10, 17, Dec. 14, 1928, Dec. 21, 1929. For the Savoy Big Five as the Zenith Five, see *Defender*, Nov. 3, Dec. 7, 1929, and as Globetrotters, *Defender*, Mar. 14, 1931; "Former Phillips Stars Make Good," *Defender*, Feb. 6, 1932; and "Globe Trotters Have Yet to Lose Game on Its Tour," *Defender*, Jan. 21, 1933. On Globe Trotter's 1940 Championship, see "Globe Trotter '5' in National Pro Cage Tournament," *Defender*, Mar. 9, 1940; "Win Title in Last 5 Minutes," *Defender*, Mar. 23, 1940; and "Trotters Harlem Globe Crowned Pro Champs," *Defender*, Jan. 4, 1941.

57. Carroll, *Fritz Pollard*, 12, 28, 33; Gems, "Blocked Shot"; *Defender*, Oct. 30, Nov. 6, 13, Dec. 18, 1915. On Lincoln Athletic Club, see Julius Avendorph, "Thanksgiving Day Football Games," *Defender*, Dec. 7, 1912; and "Chicago Team Faces Strong Test Sunday," *Defender*, Nov. 11, 1922.

58. Carroll, *Fritz Pollard*, 109; Ashe, *Hard Road to Glory*, 102–3; Al Harvin, "Pollard, at 84, Reflects on His Days of Glory," *New York Times*, Feb. 7, 1978; Ron Rapoport, "A Star 60 Years Ago: Prejudice in Sports: It's Old as Fritz Pollard, 82," *Los Angeles Times*, July 6, 1976.

59. "Pollard, Slater, Robeson and Co. Here Saturday," *Defender*, Dec. 9, 1922; "Pollard & Co. Win 6–0 Game from All Stars," *Defender*, Dec. 16, 1922. See also Carroll, *Fritz Pollard*; T. Smith, "Outside the Pale"; Al Harvin, "Pollard, at 84," *New York Times*, Feb. 7, 1978; Rapoport, "A Star 60 Years Ago"; Chalk, "The Early Struggles and the Emerging Black Stars of Football" in *Pioneers of Black Sport*. On Lillard, see Al Monroe, "What Say," *Defender*, Oct. 15, 1932; "Baseball Too Clean?" *Defender*, Oct. 29, 1932; "Joe Lillard Joins Savoy Cagers for Coming Season," *Defender*, Nov. 12, 1932; Al Monroe, "What Say," *Defender*, Dec. 3, 1932; and "Says Cardinals Would Whip Any College 11," *Defender*, Nov. 11, 1933.

60. On Blackhawks, see *Defender*, Oct. 27, 1928; "Professional Football to Hit Chicago," *Defender*, Sept. 26, 1931; "Pro Gridders Show Well in Early Drills," *De-*

fender, Oct. 10, 1931; "Pro Grid Crew to Play Coast Eleven Dec. 20," *Defender*, Oct. 17,
Nov. 14, 1931; "Godfrey Is Off Stride in Comeback," *Defender*, Nov. 21, 1931; "All Stars
to Play Coast Charity Go," *Defender*, Dec. 5, 1931; "All-Stars Leave for Coast Short,
but Rather Hopeful," *Defender*, Dec. 19, 1931; "Chicago Grid 11 Wins Coast Tilt,"
Defender, Jan. 2, 1932; "All-Stars, Like Money Loaned Out, Return Home in Drib-
bles," *Defender*, Jan. 16, 1932; and "Chicago 11 Wins Coast Grid Fest," *Defender*,
Jan. 23, Aug. 27, 1932. On the Brown Bombers, see "With the Bombers," *New York
Amsterdam News*, Sept. 28, 1935; "Local Gridders Best Seen Here," *Amsterdam
News*, Oct. 19, 1935; "Bombers Blast Cliff's Eleven," *Amsterdam News*, Oct. 26, 1935;
"Bombers Bomb Another Victim," *Amsterdam News*, Nov. 2, 1935; "Yellow Jackets
Beaten at Oval," *Amsterdam News*, Nov. 9, 1935; "Bombers Hard at Work at Oval,"
Amsterdam News, Sept. 21, 1936; "Lillard Stars for the Bombers," *Amsterdam News*,
Nov. 16, 1935; "Bombers Will Close Season This Sunday," *Amsterdam News*, Nov. 23,
1935; and "Winners to Take All on Sunday," *Amsterdam News*, Dec. 7, 1935. See also
"Brown Bombers Win Another Game," *NYA*, Oct. 26, 1935. On Howard's shimmy
shift, see "Coach Young Calls Byrd Best Broken Field Runner, Says Game Was
'Clean,'" *Baltimore Afro-American Ledger*, Dec. 6, 1924.

61. Shorey, "A Historical Account of a Great Game of Ball"; Wyatt, "Baseball:
Booker T. Washington or the Fifteenth Amendment."

62. "Game End in Near Race Riot," *Defender*, June 15, 1918; "Near Riot Breaks
Up Giants-Pyotts Game," *Defender*, Oct. 20, 1923. On rabbles, see P. Miller, "To
'Bring the Race along Rapidly,'" 119; *Howard University Record*, Dec. 16, 1921, 126;
W. Jones, *Recreation and Amusement*, 75; Hurd and Spence, "Halftime," 123–29; and
Malone, *Steppin' on the Blues*.

63. Armstrong, *Louis Armstrong, In His Own Words*, 100; Peterson, *From Cages to
Jump Shots*, 98; N. George, *Elevating the Game*, 36. For examples of musical accom-
paniment to games, see ads "Dance—Basketball—Dance," Apr. 5, 1919, "Everybody
Is Going," Nov. 21, 1921, and "Championship Game," Dec. 17, 1921, and articles
"Musicale and Basketball Game of Unusual Interest," Dec. 17, 1921, "Howard Five
Scheduled to Play Jan 3d.," all in *Defender*. However, in the annual Phillips-
Armstrong (Washington, D.C.) basketball "Winter Classic," box seats and young
women ushers in evening gowns helped set a mood of distinction, adding a respectable "coloring to the setting." See "Armstrong-Phillips Game Ushers," *Defender*,
Feb. 7, 1925; "Society Watches Phillips Hi Win Winter Classic," *Defender*, Feb. 21,
1925; and "The Armstrong High vs. Wendell Phillips Game," *Defender*, Feb. 28,
1925.

64. Burgos, "Playing Ball"; Ruck, *Tropic of Baseball*. On Japanese exhibition
games, see "All Star Baseball Club May Go to Japan," *Defender*, Feb. 5, 1921, Mar. 19,
1927; and *Pittsburgh Courier*, Aug. 22, 1936. See also Pascoe, "Seasons in the Sun,"
65. For information on Wilkinson, his All Nations team, and lighting technology, see
Bruce, *Kansas City Monarchs*, 17–18, 68–70; and Pascoe, "Seasons in the Sun," 63–
64. More general reports of night games include "Twilight Ball," *Defender*, July 13,

1918, May 24, 1930; Alvin F. Harlow, "Unrecognized Stars," *Esquire* 10 (Sept. 1938), 119; and *Defender*, June 14, 1930.

65. The All-Star game was extensively covered yearly in the summer editions of both the *Defender* and the *Pittsburgh Courier*. See also the important Lester, *Black Baseball's National Showcase.*

66. For "hot playing" reference, see "Winters' Costly Foul Defeats Home Boys at End of Game," *Defender*, Mar. 1, 1919. On Byrd, see "Howard's New Plays Gave Crowd a Thrill," *Baltimore Afro-American Ledger*, Dec. 6, 1924, and "Eleven Second Legs!" *Baltimore Afro-American Ledger*, Nov. 24, 1928. For powerful exceptions to the ahistorical approach to black style, see Kusner, *Beautiful Pageant*, 46–52; Benston, *Performing Blackness*; "Black Style?" section in Oriard, *King Football*, 319–27; Caponi-Tabery, "Jump for Joy"; and Caponi, *Signifyin(g).*

67. "Wabash Y Defeated in Indiana and Ohio," *Defender*, Mar. 3, 1917; Gems, "Blocked Shots"; N. George, *Elevating the Game*; Peterson, *From Cages to Jump Shots*; Chalk, *Pioneers of Black Sport*, 96–103. See also "Collegians Win Windy City League 1st Half," *Defender*, Feb. 3, 1940.

68. "Success of the Negro as a Ball Player," *Freeman Supplement*, Apr. 16, 1910; Cottrell, *Best Pitcher in Baseball*, 55.

69. Oriard, *King Football*, 319–27; Caponi-Tabery, "Jump for Joy"; Caponi, *Signifyin(g).* On officials stealing games, etc., see "A Few Words to the Sporting Editor of Chicago American," *Defender*, Feb. 9, 1924; "Chicago Bruins Defeat New York Rens with Ref's Help," *Defender*, Jan. 18, 1930.

70. "Rube Foster's" brand of baseball was explicitly described as a "fast paced, thinking-man's brand of baseball." See Cottrell, *Best Pitcher in Baseball*, 63.

71. "A Few Words to the Sporting Editor of Chicago American *Defender*." Discussion of "wigging" is found in Kelley, *Race Rebels*, 20; and de Certeau, *Practice of Everyday Life*, 25–27.

72. "Change Basketball Rules to Eliminate Rough Play," *Defender*, Apr. 16, 1927. See also de Certeau, *Practice of Everyday Life*, 37–39.

73. A. Foster, "How to Pitch"; "Success of the Negro as a Ball Player"; Shorey, "A Historical Account of a Great Game of Ball"; A. Foster, "Future of Race Umpires Depends on Men of Today." On Simmons, see Schmidt and Fitzgerald, "New Open Game." See also Oriard, *King Football.*

74. George Strickler, "Bears Bolster Attack; Point for Negro Team," *Chicago Tribune*, Sept. 21, 1938; "Ray Kemp to Do Double Duty against Bears," *Chicago Tribune*, Sept. 22, 1938; "Bears Battle Colored Star Eleven Tonight," *Chicago Tribune*, Sept. 23, 1938; "51 Points and Stars Get None," *Chicago Tribune*, Sept. 24, 1938; "All-Star Negro Grid Team to Battle Chicago Bears at Soldier's Field September 23," *Pittsburgh Courier*, Aug. 6, 1938; "Bears, All-Star Interest Soars as Votes Pile In," *Pittsburgh Courier*, Sept. 3, 1938; " 'Pros' Too Strong So All-Stars Lose, 51–o," William G. Nunn, "All-Stars Fall before Battering Chicago Bears," *Pittsburgh Courier*, Oct. 1, 1938; Frank Young, "All Stars Unable to Halt Bears, Lose 51–o,"

and John Lake, "All Star Players Complain about Division of Money," *Defender*, Oct. 1, 1938.

75. C. Lewis, "Baseball Circuit for Next Season." See also description of basketball as a first-class attraction and thrill comparable to the movies in "Wabash Y Defeated in Indiana and Ohio."

EPILOGUE

1. Frazier's essay gives solid context to his larger materialist distinction between culture and enterprise. His notion of an entrepreneurial middle class is directly linked to the Protestant ethic of frugality, thrift, and productivity that continues to guide American morality to the present. Furthermore, Frazier's quasi-Marxist influences lead him to see ideas within the marketplace as artificially manufactured by capital with no "productive" control. See Frazier, "Durham," 333. See also Weber, *Protestant Ethic*.

2. On Du Bois and the "cooperative commonwealth," see early insights in *Crisis* (Jan. 1926), 81; Chicago speech/essay, "Criteria of Negro Art," *Crisis* (Oct. 1926); Aptheker, *Selections from the Crisis*; and Du Bois, *Dusk of Dawn*, 198, 209. See also D. Lewis, "A New Racial Philosophy" in *Fight for Equality*. On Frazier, see editorial, *Opportunity* (Mar. 1929), 69; and Frazier, *Black Bourgeoisie*, 56, 27–28, 104, 109–10. Frazier's bourgeoisie insights were foreshadowed in his essay "La Bourgeoisie Noire," which appears in Calverton's anthology. This anthology served as a more materialist response to Locke's *New Negro*.

3. For more detailed assessments of Frazier and his work, see J. S. Holloway, *Confronting the Veil*; Teele, *E. Franklin Frazier and Black Bourgeoisie*; and A. Platt, *E. Franklin Frazier Reconsidered*.

4. Cruse, *Crisis of the Negro Intellectual*, 24–26. For his comments on Du Bois and Mills, see 39–40, 331–34, 467–69.

5. Ibid., 64–65, 236, 41, 92.

6. Ibid., 80–81, 83–84, 88–89. See also E. Allen, "Cultural Methodology of Harold Cruse."

7. Cruse, *Crisis of the Negro Intellectual*, 12, 177.

8. Mullen, *Popular Fronts*; Greenberg, *"Or Does It Explode?"*; J. Hunter, "'Don't Buy from Where You Can't Work'"; Cox, "Origins of Direct-Action Protest among Negroes [in Chicago], 1932–1933," 1963 (microfiche copy at Kent State University Libraries).

9. Bond and Gibbs, "Social Portrait." See Cox, "Origins of Direct-Action Protest," *Caste, Class and Race*, "Race, and Caste," and "Racial Theories." See also H. Hunter, *Sociology of Oliver C. Cox* and "Life and Work of Oliver C. Cox"; Abraham and Hunter, *Race, Class and the World System*; Klarlund, "Origins of Racism"; and Denning, *Cultural Front*, 445–54.

10. Cox, " Origins of Direct-Action Protest among Negroes," 6, 143, 145, 122, 158, 5.

11. Ibid., 151, 7.

12. Ibid., 5, 157, 7.

13. *Fight for Negro Rights!*, Convention Proceedings, official program, 1936, Northwestern University Library, Evanston, Ill.

14. On varying perspectives on NNC leadership, see "Toward Negro Unity," *Nation*, Mar. 11, 1936, 302; and Cruse, *Crisis of the Negro Intellectual*, 175. On larger studies of the NNC, see Bates, "New Crowd"; Wittner, "National Negro Congress"; and Granger, "National Negro Congress." On "black worldliness" and "Double V" politics during World War II, see Singh, "Culture/Wars"; Kelley, "Riddle of the Zoot"; Marable, *Race, Reform, and Rebellion*; Lott, "Double V, Double-Time"; Korstad and Lichtenstein, "Opportunities Found and Lost"; Kellogg, "Civil Rights Consciousness"; Wynn, *Afro-American and the Second World War*; Sitkoff, "Racial Militancy"; Dalfume, *Desegregation of the U.S. Armed Forces* and "'Forgotten Years'"; and Garfinkel, *When Negroes March*.

Bibliography

MANUSCRIPT COLLECTIONS

Black Film Center/Archive, Indiana University, Bloomington, Indiana

Chicago Historical Society, Chicago, Illinois

    Claude A. Barnett Papers

    Commission on Chicago Historical and Architectural Landmarks, "Black Metropolis Historic District"

    Jack Cooper Papers

DuSable Museum of African American History, Chicago, Illinois

    Dunmore Collection

Vivian G. Harsh Research Collection of Afro-American History and Literature, Carter G. Woodson Regional Library, Chicago Public Library, Chicago, Illinois

    Lucy Collier Papers

    Historical Letters and Records of the Hall Branch of the Chicago Public Library

    Illinois Writers Project, "The Negro in Illinois"

    Marjorie Stewart Joyner Papers

Hatch-Billops Collection, New York, N.Y.

Illinois State Archives, Springfield, Illinois

    Papers of the Chicago Commission on Race Relations, 1919–20 (microfilm)

Illinois State Historical Library, Springfield, Illinois

    Federal Writers' Project Records

Indiana Historical Society, Indianapolis, Indiana

    Madam C. J. Walker Collection

George P. Johnson Negro Film Collection, Department of Special Collections, University of California at Los Angeles, Los Angeles, California

Library of Congress, Washington, D.C.

    Motion Picture Broadcast and Recorded Sound Division, Film Division

    Booker T. Washington Papers, Manuscripts Division

Lilly Library of Rare Books and Manuscripts, Indiana University, Bloomington, Indiana

    Richard E. Norman Collection

Moorland-Spingarn Research Center, Howard University, Washington, D.C.

National Baseball Hall of Fame Research Library, Cooperstown, N.Y.
Northwestern University Library, Evanston, Illinois

Fight for Negro Rights! National Negro Congress, Chicago, Convention Proceedings, official program, 1936

Schomburg Center for Research in Black Culture, New York Public Library, New York, N.Y.

Smithsonian Institution, National Museum of American History, Washington, D.C.

Julian Black Collection

Special Collections, University Library, University of Illinois at Chicago

Phillis Wheatley Association Papers

CONVENTION PROCEEDINGS

Madam Walker Hair Culturists' Union. *Minutes of the First National Convention of the Mme. C. J. Walker Hair Culturists' Union of America, Philadelphia, PA*. August 30–31, 1917.

National Association of Colored Women. *National Association of Colored Women's Clubs Records, 1895–1992*, microfilm. Bethesda: University of America, 1993, Library of Congress, Washington, D.C.

National Negro Business League. *Report of the Second Annual Convention of the National Negro Business League at Chicago, Illinois*. August 21–23, 1901. R. S. Abbott Publishing Company, 1901.

——. *Report of the Sixth Annual Convention of the National Negro Business League, New York City*. August 16–18, 1905.

——. *Report of the 13th Annual Convention of the National Negro Business League Held at Chicago, Illinois*. August 21–23, 1912. N.p.

——. *Report of the 14th Annual Convention of the National Negro Business League, Philadelphia, PA*. August 20–22, 1913. Washington, D.C.: William H. Davis, Official Stenographer.

——. *Annual Report of the 15th Annual Convention of the National Negro Business League, Muskogee, Oklahoma*. August 19–21, 1914. Nashville: AME Sunday School Union, 1914.

——. *National Negro Business League Annual Report of the Sixteenth Session and the Fifteenth Anniversary Convention*, microfilm. August 19–20, 1915. Library of Congress, Washington, D.C.

——. *National Negro Business League Report of the Seventeenth Annual Session, Kansas City, Missouri*. August 16–18, 1916. Washington, D.C.: William H. Davis, 1916.

——. *National Negro Business League Report of the Eighteenth and Nineteenth Annual Sessions, Chattanooga, Tennessee, 1917 and Atlantic City, N.J., 1918*. Washington, D.C.: William H. Davis, 1918.

GOVERNMENT DOCUMENTS

Loving, Walter H. Report to Director of Military Intelligence on National Race Congress, Dec. 20, 1918, RG 165, File 10218-302, Records of the War Department, General and Special Staffs, Correspondence of the Military Intelligence Divisions, Correspondence relating to "Negro Subversion," microfilm M1440, National Archives, Washington, D.C.

U.S. Census Office. *U.S. Census: Negro Population, 1790–1925*. Washington, D.C.: GPO/Department of Commerce, U.S. Bureau of the Census, 1918.

———. *U.S. Fourteenth Census of the United States Taken in the Year 1920*. Vol. 4, *Population, Occupations*. Washington, D.C.: GPO, 1922.

NEWSPAPERS AND PERIODICALS

Abbott's Monthly
Afro-American Journal of Fashion
Amsterdam News
Atlanta Constitution
Atlanta Independent
Atlanta Journal
Baltimore Afro-American Ledger
Billboard
Boston Globe
California Eagle
Champion Magazine
Charities
Chicago Bee
Chicago Broad Ax
Chicago Daily Inter Ocean
Chicago Daily News
Chicago Defender
Chicago Tribune
Chicago Tribune Magazine
Chicago Whip
Chronicle of Higher Education
Cincinnati Union
Cleveland Gazette
Colorado Statesman
Colored American Magazine
Competitor
Crisis
Current Literature

Ebony
Esquire
Half-Century Magazine
Harper's
Indianapolis *Freeman*
Indianapolis *Freeman Supplement*
Indianapolis Ledger
Indianapolis Recorder
Kansas City Call
Kansas City Star
Literary Digest
Los Angeles Times
Messenger: New Opinion of the Negro
Moving Picture World
Nation
Negro World
New York Age
New York Amsterdam News
New York Herald
New York Times
New York World
Omaha World Daily
Opportunity
Philadelphia Item
Pittsburgh Courier
Reader
Reflexus
St. Louis Palladium
St. Louis Post-Dispatch
Standard News
Talking Machine World
Variety
Voice of the Negro
Washington Bee
Woman's Voice

BOOKS

Abbott, Andrew. *Department and Discipline: Chicago Sociology at One Hundred.* Chicago: University of Chicago Press, 1999.

Abraham, Sameer, and Herbert Hunter. *Race, Class and the World System: The Sociology of Oliver C. Cox.* New York: Monthly Review Press, 1987.

Adero, Malaika, ed. *Up South: Stories, Studies and Letters of This Century's African-American Migrations.* New York: New Press, 1993.

Agee, James. *Agee on Film.* Boston: Beacon Press, 1958.

Albertson, Chris. *Bessie.* New York: Stein and Day, 1972.

Anderson, Jervis. *A. Philip Randolph: A Biographical Portrait.* New York: Harcourt Brace, 1973.

———. *This Was Harlem: A Cultural Portrait, 1900–1950.* New York: Farrar, Straus and Giroux, 1982.

Anderson, Paul. *Deep River: Music and Memory in Harlem Renaissance Thought.* Durham: Duke University Press, 2001.

Anderson, Robert. *Vision of the Disinherited: The Making of American Pentecostalism.* New York: Oxford University Press, 1979.

Aptheker, Herbert, ed. *Selections from the Crisis.* Millwood, N.Y.: Kraus-Thompson, 1983.

Armstrong, Louis. *Louis Armstrong—A Self Portrait.* New York: Eakins Press, 1971.

———. *Louis Armstrong, In His Own Words.* New York: Oxford University Press, 1999.

Arneson, Eric. *Black Protest and the Great Migration: A Brief History with Documents.* Boston: Bedford's Press, 2003.

Arthur, George. *Life on the Negro Frontier.* 1908. Reprint, New York: Harper and Row, 1964.

Ashe, Arthur. *A Hard Road to Glory.* Vol. 1 of *A History of the African-American Athlete, 1619–1918.* New York: Warner Books, 1988.

Audree. *Explorations in the City of Light: African-American Artists in Paris, 1945–1965.* New York: Studio Museum in Harlem, 1997.

Bachin, Robin. *Building the South Side: Urban Space and Civic Culture in Chicago, 1890–1919.* Chicago: University of Chicago Press, 2003.

Baer, Hans A. *The Black Spiritual Movement: A Religious Response to Racism.* Knoxville: University of Tennessee Press, 1984.

Bak, Richard. *Turkey Stearnes and the Detroit Stars: The Negro Leagues in Detroit, 1919–1933.* Detroit: Wayne State University Press, 1994.

Baker, Danny. *A Life in Jazz.* Edited by Alyn Shipton. New York: Oxford University Press, 1986.

Baker, Houston. *Modernism and the Harlem Renaissance.* Chicago: University of Chicago Press, 1987.

Baker, Lee. *From Savage to Negro: Anthropology and the Construction of Race, 1896–1954.* Berkeley: University of California Press, 1998.

Balshaw, Maria. *Looking for Harlem: Urban Aesthetics in African American Literature.* London: Sterling; Virginia: Pluto Press, 2000.

Banner, Lois. *American Beauty.* Chicago: University of Chicago Press, 1983.

Bannister, Robert. *Social Darwinism: Science and Myth in Anglo-American Social Thought.* Philadelphia: Temple University Press, 1979.

Barlow, William. *Looking Up at Down: The Emergence of Blues Culture.* Philadelphia: Temple University Press, 1989.

———. *Voice Over: The Making of Black Radio.* Philadelphia: Temple University Press, 1999.

Barrett, James R. *Work and Community in the Jungle: Chicago Packing House Workers, 1894–1922.* Urbana: University of Illinois Press, 1987.

Bassett, John Earl. *Harlem in Review: Critical Reactions to Black American Writers, 1917–1939.* Selinsgrove, Penn.: Susquehanna University Press, 1992.

Batchelor, Denzil. *Jack Johnson and His Times.* London: Phoenix Sports Books, 1956.

Bates, Beth Tompkins. *Pullman Porters and the Rise of Protest Politics in Black America, 1925–1945.* Chapel Hill: University of North Carolina Press, 2001.

Baudrillard, Jean. *For a Critique of the Political Economy of the Sign.* Paris: Telos, 1981.

Beckerman, Michael. *New Worlds of Dvořák: Searching in America for the Composer's Inner Life.* New York: Norton, 2003.

Bederman, Gail. *Manliness and Civilization: A Cultural History of Gender and Race in the United States, 1880–1917.* Chicago: University of Chicago Press, 1995.

Bendix, Regina. *In Search of Authenticity: The Formation of Folklore Studies.* Madison: University of Wisconsin Press, 1997.

Benson, Susan Porter. *Counter Culture: Saleswomen, Managers and Customers in American Department Stores, 1890–1940.* Urbana: University of Illinois Press, 1995.

Benston, Kimberly. *Performing Blackness: Enactments of African American Modernism.* London: Routledge, 2000.

Berman, Marshall. *All That Is Solid Melts into the Air: The Experience of Modernity.* New York: Penguin Books, 1988.

Bernardi, Daniel, ed. *The Birth of Whiteness: Race and the Emergence of U.S. Cinema.* New Brunswick, N.J.: Rutgers University Press, 1996.

Best, Wallace. *Passionately Human, No Less Divine: Religion and Culture in Black Chicago, 1915–1952.* Princeton: Princeton University Press, 2005.

Binder, Carroll. *Chicago and the New Negro.* Chicago: Chicago Daily News, 1927.

Black, Ford. *Black's Blue Book: Business and Professional Directory.* Chicago: Ford S. Black, 1917.

———. *Black's Blue Book: Directory of Chicago's Active Colored People and Guide to Their Activities.* Chicago: Ford S. Black, 1921.

The Black Public Sphere Collective, ed. *The Black Public Sphere.* Chicago: University of Chicago Press, 1995.

Blackwelder, Julia Kirk. *Styling Jim Crow: African American Beauty Training during Segregation.* College Station: Texas A&M University Press, 2003.

Blackwell, James, and Morris Janowitz. *Black Sociologists: Historical and Contemporary Perspectives.* Chicago: University of Chicago Press, 1974.

Boatner, Edward, and Willa A. Townsend. *Spirituals Triumphant Old and New.* Nashville: Sunday School Publishing Board, National Baptist Convention, 1927.

Bogle, Donald. *Toms, Coons, Mulattoes, Mammies and Bucks: An Interpretive History of Blacks in American Films.* New York: Viking Press, 1973.

Bontemps, Arna. *Anyplace But Here.* 1945. Reprint, Columbia: University of Missouri Press, 1966.

——. *The Harlem Renaissance Remembered.* New York: Dodd, Mead, 1972.

Bontemps, Arna, and Jack Conroy. *They Seek a City.* New York: Doubleday, Doran, 1945.

Booker, Christopher. *"I Will Wear No Chain!" A Social History of African American Males.* Westport, Conn.: Praeger, 2000.

Borchert, James. *Alley Life in Washington: Family, Community, Religion and Folklife in the City, 1850–1970.* Urbana: University of Illinois Press, 1980.

Bordieu, Pierre. *Distinction: A Social Critique of the Judgment of Taste.* London: Routledge, 1984.

Bottomley, Gillian. *From Another Place: Migration and the Politics of Culture.* Cambridge: Cambridge University Press, 1992.

Bowen, Louise DeKoven. *The Colored People of Chicago: An Investigation Made for the Juvenile Protective Association.* Chicago: Press of Rogers and Hall, 1913.

Bowser, Pearl, Jane Gaines, and Charles Musser. *Oscar Micheaux and His Circle: African-American Filmmaking and Race Cinema of the Silent Era.* Bloomington: Indiana University Press, 2001.

Bowser, Pearl, and Valerie Harris. *Independent Black American Cinema.* New York: Theater Program of Third World Newsreel, 1981.

Bowser, Pearl, and Louise Spence. *Writing Himself into History: Oscar Micheaux, His Silent Films and His Audiences.* New Brunswick, N.J.: Rutgers University Press, 2000.

Boyer, Horace Clarence. *The Golden Age of Gospel.* Urbana: University of Illinois Press, 2000.

Bradden, William S. *Under Three Banners: An Autobiography.* Nashville: National Baptist Publishing Board, 1940.

Bradford, Perry. *Born with the Blues: The Salty and Uninhibited Autobiography of One of the Greatest of the Old-Time Jazz Pioneers.* New York: Oak Publications, 1965.

Bragdon, Henry. *Woodrow Wilson: The Academic Years.* Cambridge: Harvard University Press, 1967.

Brock, Lisa, and Digna Castenada. *Between Race and Empire: African-Americans and Cubans before the Cuban Revolution.* Philadelphia: Temple University Press, 1998.

Brody, David. *Steelworkers in America: The Nonunion Era.* Urbana: University of Illinois Press, 1998.

Brooks, Gwendolyn. *Maud Martha.* New York: AMS Press, 1953.

Bruce, Janet. *The Kansas City Monarchs: Champions of Black Baseball.* Lawrence: University Press of Kansas, 1987.

Bruns, Roger. *Billy Sunday and Big Time American Evangelism*. New York: Norton, 1992.

Buckler, Helen. *Doctor Dan*. Boston: Little, Brown, 1954.

Bukowski, Douglas. *Big Bill Thompson, Chicago, and the Politics of Image*. Urbana: University of Illinois Press, 1998.

Bullock, Penelope L. *The Afro-American Periodical Press, 1838–1909*. Baton Rouge: Louisiana State University Press, 1981.

Bulmer, Martin. *The Chicago School of Sociology: Institutionalization, Diversity and the Rise of Sociological Research*. Chicago: University of Chicago Press, 1984.

Bundles, A'Lelia Perry. *Madam C. J. Walker, Entrepreneur*. New York: Chelsea House Publishers, 1991.

———. *On Her Own Ground: The Life and Times of Madam C. J. Walker*. New York: Scribners, 2001.

Burgess, Stanley, and Gary McGhee. *Dictionary of Pentecostal and Charismatic Movements*. Grand Rapids, Mich.: Zondervan, 1988.

Burkett, Randall, and Richard Newman. *Black Apostles*. Boston: G. K. Hall, 1978.

Burns, Ben. *Nitty Gritty: A White Editor in Black Journalism*. Amherst: University of Massachusetts Press, 1996.

Burstyn, Vada. *The Rites of Men: Manhood, Politics and the Culture of Sport*. Toronto: University of Toronto Press, 1999.

Butcher, Margaret Just. *The Negro in American Culture*. New York: New American Library, 1971.

Butler, Gerald, Jr. *Black Manhood on the Silent Screen*. Lawrence: University of Kansas Press, 2002.

Calverton, V. F., ed. *Anthology of American Negro Literature*. New York: Modern Library, 1929.

Campbell, Collin. *The Romantic Ethic and the Spirit of Modern Consumption*. Oxford: Blackwell Press, 1987.

Campbell, Daniel M., and Rex Johnson. *Black Migration in America: A Social Demographic History*. Durham: Duke University Press, 1981.

Canclini, Nestor Garcia. *Consumers and Citizens: Globalization and Multicultural Conflicts*. Minneapolis: University of Minnesota Press, 2001.

Capetti, Carla. *Writing Chicago: Modernism, Ethnography and the Novel*. New York: Columbia University Press, 1993.

Caponi, Gena Dagel, ed. *Signifyin(g), Sanctifyin,' and Slam Dunking: A Reader in African American Expressive Culture*. Amherst: University of Massachusetts Press, 1999.

Carby, Hazel. *Race Men*. Cambridge: Harvard University Press, 1998.

———. *Reconstructing Womanhood: The Emergence of the Afro-American Woman Novelist*. New York: Oxford University Press, 1987.

Carnes, Mark, and Clyde Griffen, eds. *Meanings for Manhood: Constructions of Masculinity in Victorian America*. Chicago: University of Chicago Press, 1990.

Carroll, John. *Fritz Pollard: Pioneer in Racial Advancement.* Urbana: University of Illinois Press, 1992.

Cavallo, Dominick. *Muscles and Morals: Organized Playgrounds and Urban Reform, 1880–1920.* Philadelphia: University of Pennsylvania Press, 1981.

Cayton, Horace R., and George S. Mitchell. *Black Workers and the New Unions.* Chapel Hill: University of North Carolina Press, 1939.

Chalk, Ocania. *Pioneers of Black Sport: The Early Days of the Black Professional Athlete in Baseball, Basketball, Boxing and Football.* New York: Dodd, 1975.

Cham, Mbye, and Claire Andre-Watkins. *Blackframes: Critical Perspectives on Black Independent Cinema.* Cambridge: MIT Press, 1988.

Chapkis, Wendy. *Beauty Secrets.* Boston: South End Press, 1986.

Charters, Samuel. *The Country Blues.* New York: Holt, Rinehart and Winston, 1959.

Chauncey, George. *Gay New York: Gender, Urban Culture, and the Making of the Gay Male World, 1890–1940.* New York: Basic Books, 1994.

Chestnutt, Charles. *The House behind the Cedars.* Boston: Houghton Mifflin, 1990.

Chicago Commission on Race Relations [Charles Johnson]. *The Negro in Chicago: A Study of Race Relations and a Race Riot.* Chicago: University of Chicago Press, 1922.

Clarke, Graham, ed. *The American City: Literary and Cultural Perspectives.* New York: St. Martin's Press, 1988.

Clegg, Claude. *An Original Man: The Life and Times of Elijah Muhammad.* New York: St. Martin's Press, 1997.

Cohen, Lizabeth. *Making a New Deal: Industrial Workers in Chicago, 1919–1939.* New York: Cambridge University Press, 1990.

Coleman, Leon. *Carl Van Vechten and the Harlem Renaissance: A Critical Assessment.* New York: Garland Publishing, 1998.

Conyers, James. *Carter G. Woodson: A Historical Reader.* New York: Taylor and Francis, 2000.

Cooper, Anna Julia. *Voices from the South.* New York: Oxford University Press, 1988.

Cornelius, Lucille J. *The Pioneer History of the Church of God in Christ.* Memphis: Church of God in Christ Publishing, 1975.

Cottrell, Robert. *The Best Pitcher in Baseball: The Life of Rube Foster, Negro League Giant.* New York: New York University Press, 2001.

Couvares, Francis. *The Remaking of Pittsburgh: Class and Culture in an Industrializing City, 1877–1919.* Albany: State University of New York Press, 1975.

Cox, Oliver Cromwell. *Caste, Class and Race.* New York: Modern Reader Paperbacks, 1948.

Crew, Spencer. *Field to Factory: Afro-American Migration 1915–1940.* Washington, D.C.: Smithsonian Institution Press, 1987.

Cripps, Thomas. *Black Film as Genre.* Bloomington: Indiana University Press, 1978.

——. *Slow Fade to Black: The Negro in American Film, 1900–1942.* New York: Oxford University Press, 1977.

Cromwell, Dean, and Al Wesson. *Championship Techniques in Track and Field: A Book for Athletes, Coaches, and Spectators.* New York: McGraw-Hill, 1941.

Cronon, William. *Nature's Metropolis: Chicago and the Great West.* New York: Norton, 1991.

Cruse, Harold. *Crisis of the Negro Intellectual.* New York: William Morrow, 1967.

Cruz, Jon. *Culture on the Margins: The Black Spiritual and the Rise of American Cultural Interpretation.* Princeton: Princeton University Press, 1999.

Curtis, Susan. *A Consuming Faith: The Social Gospel and Modern American Culture.* Baltimore: Johns Hopkins University Press, 1991.

Dalfume, Richard. *Desegregation of the U.S. Armed Forces: Fighting on Two Fronts, 1929–1953.* Columbia: University of Missouri Press, 1969.

Dance, Stanley. *The World of Earl Hines.* New York: Scribners, 1977.

Darden, Robert. *People Get Ready: A New History of Black Gospel Music.* New York: Continuum International Publishing Group, 2004.

Davis, Allison, Burleigh Gardener, and Mary Gardener. *Deep South: A Social Anthropological Study of Caste and Class.* Chicago: University of Chicago Press, 1941.

Davis, Angela. *Blues Legacies and Black Feminisms: Gertrude "Ma" Rainey, Bessie Smith, and Billy Holiday.* New York: Pantheon Books, 1998.

Davis, Arthur P., and Michael Peplow. *The New Negro Renaissance: An Anthology.* New York: Holt, Rinehart and Winston, 1975.

Davis, Elizabeth Lindsay. *The Story of the Illinois Federation of Colored Women's Clubs.* 1921. Reprint, London: Prentice Hall, 1997.

de Certeau, Michel. *The Practice of Everyday Life.* Berkeley: University of California Press, 1984.

Deegan, Mary Jo. *Jane Addams and the Men of the Chicago School, 1892–1918.* New Brunswick, N.J.: Rutgers University Press, 1998.

———. *Race, Hull House, and the University of Chicago: A New Conscience against Ancient Evils.* Westport, Conn.: Praeger, 2002.

———, ed. *The New Woman of Color: The Collected Works of Fannie Barrier Williams, 1893–1918.* Dekalb: Northern Illinois University Press, 2002.

Denning, Michael. *The Cultural Front: The Laboring of American Culture in the Twentieth Century.* London: Verso Press, 1997.

———. *Mechanic Accents: Dime Novels and Working-Class Culture in America.* London: Verso, 1987.

Dent, Gina, ed. *Black Popular Culture.* Seattle: Bay Press, 1992.

Detweiler, Frederick. *The Negro Press in the United States.* Chicago: University of Chicago Press, 1922.

Diakite, Madubuko. *Culture and the Black Filmmaker: A Study of Functional Relationships and Parallel Developments.* New York: Arno Press, 1980.

Diawara, Manthia, ed. *Black American Cinema.* New York: Routledge, 1993.

di Leonardo, Micaela. *Exotics at Home: Anthropologists, Others, American Modernity.* Chicago: University of Chicago Press, 1998.

Dinerstein, Joel. *Swinging the Machine: Modernity, Technology, and African American Culture between the World Wars*. Amherst: University of Massachusetts Press, 2003.

Dixon, Phil, with Patrick J. Hannigan. *The Negro Baseball Leagues, 1867–1955: A Photographic History*. Mattituck, N.Y.: Amereon House, 1992.

Dixon, Robert, and John Goodrich. *Blues and Gospel Records, 1902–1943*. 3rd ed. London: Storyville Publications, 1982.

———. *Recording the Blues*. New York: Stein and Day, 1970.

Donaldson, Melvin. *The Representation of Afro-American Women in Hollywood, 1915–1949*. Ann Arbor: University Microfilms, 1984.

Dorsett, Lyle. *Billy Sunday and the Redemption of Urban America*. Grand Rapids, Mich.: William B. Eerdmans, 1991.

Douglas, Ann. *The Feminization of American Culture*. New York: Doubleday, 1988.

———. *Terrible Honesty: Mongrel Manhattan in the 1920s*. New York: 1995.

Drake, St. Clair, and Horace R. Cayton. *Black Metropolis: A Study of Negro Life in a Northern City*. 2 vols. New York: Harcourt, Brace, 1945.

Du Bois, W. E. B. *The Black North: A Social Study*. 1901. Reprint, New York: Arno Press, 1969.

———. *Dark Princess: A Romance*. 1928. Reprint, Jackson: University of Mississippi Press, 1995.

———. *Dusk of Dawn: An Autobiography of the Race Concept*. 1940. Reprint, New Brunswick, N.J.: Transaction, 1984.

———. *On the Importance of Africa in World History*. New York: Black Liberation Press, 1978.

———. *Philadelphia Negro: A Social Study*. 1899. Reprint, Philadelphia: University of Pennsylvania Press, 1996.

———. *The Souls of Black Folk*. 1903. Reprint, New York: Penguin Books, 1989.

DuCille, Ann. *Skin Trade*. Cambridge: Harvard University Press, 1996.

du Gay, Paul. *Consumption and Identity at Work*. London: Sage Press, 1996.

Duncan, Otis D., and Beverly Duncan. *The Negro Population of Chicago: A Study of Residential Succession*. Chicago: University of Chicago Press, 1957.

Dunham, Katherine. *A Touch of Innocence: Memoirs of Innocence*. New York: Harcourt Brace, 1959.

Durkheim, Emile. *The Division of Labor*. New York: Free Press, 1997.

Duster, Alfreda, ed. *Crusade for Justice: The Autobiography of Ida B. Wells*. Chicago: University of Chicago Press, 1988.

Dyer, Thomas G. *Theodore Roosevelt and the Ideal of Race*. Baton Rouge: Louisiana State University Press, 1980.

Edwards, Brent. *The Practice of Diaspora: Literature, Translation, and the Rise of Black Internationalism*. Cambridge: Harvard University Press, 2003.

Edwards, Paul. *The Southern Urban Negro as Consumer*. 1932. Reprint, New York: Negro Universities Press, 1969.

Ehrenreich, Barbara, and John Ehrenreich. *Between Labor and Capital*. Boston: South End Press, 1979.

Ellington, Edward Kennedy. *Music Is My Mistress*. Garden City, N.Y.: Doubleday, 1973.

Ellis, Lucia. *Mr. Football: Amos Alonzo Stagg*. South Brunswick, N.Y.: A. S. Barnes, 1970.

Ellison, Ralph. *Going to the Territory*. New York: Random House, 1986.

Ely, Melvin Patrick. *The Adventures of Amos 'n' Andy: A Social History of an American Phenomenon*. New York: Free Press, 1991.

Epstein, Dena J. *Sinful Tunes and Spirituals: Black Folk Music to the Civil War*. Urbana: University of Illinois, 1977.

Erenburg, Lewis A. *Steppin' Out: New York Nightlife and the Transformation of American Culture, 1890–1930*. Chicago: University of Chicago Press, 1981.

Esebede, P. O. *Pan-Africanism: The Idea and Movement 1776–1963*. Washington, D.C.: Howard University Press, 1982.

Essien-Udom, E. U. *Black Nationalism: A Search for Identity in America*. Chicago: University of Chicago Press, 1962.

Everett, Anna. *Returning the Gaze: A Genealogy of Black Film Criticism, 1909–1949*. Durham: Duke University Press, 2001.

Ewan, Stuart. *Captains of Consciousness: Advertising and the Social Roots of Consumer Culture*. New York: McGraw Hill, 1976.

Fabre, Michel. *From Harlem to Paris: Black American Writers in France, 1840–1980*. Urbana: University of Illinois Press, 1991.

Farr, Finnis. *Black Champion: The Life and Times of Jack Johnson*. London: Macmillan, 1964.

Farred, Grant. *What's My Name: Black Vernacular Intellectuals*. Minneapolis: University of Minnesota Press, 2003.

Fausett, Arthur Huff. *Black Gods of the Metropolis: Negro Religious Cults in the Urban North*. Philadelphia: University of Philadelphia Press, 1944.

Favor, Martin J. *Authentic Blackness: The Folk in the New Negro Renaissance*. Durham: Duke University Press, 1999.

Fields, Mamie Garvin. *Lemon Swamp and Other Places: A Carolina Memoir*. New York: Free Press, 1983.

Filene, Benjamin. *Romancing the Folk: Memory and American Roots Music*. Chapel Hill: University of North Carolina Press, 2000.

Floyd, Samuel. *Black Music in the Harlem Renaissance: A Collection of Essays*. New York: Greenwood Press, 1990.

———. *The Power of Black Music*. New York: Oxford University Press, 1995.

Flynn, Joyce, and Joyce Stricklin. *Frye Street and Environs: The Collected Works of Marita Bonner*. Boston: Beacon Press, 1987.

Foglesong, David. *America's Secret War against Bolshevism*. Chapel Hill: University of North Carolina Press, 1995.

Foley, Barbara. *Spectres of 1919: Class and Nation in the Making of the New Negro.* Urbana: University of Illinois Press, 2003.

Foner, Phillip S. *American Socialism and Black Americans: From the Age of Jackson to World War II.* Westport, Conn.: Greenwood Press, 1977.

——. *The Voice of Black America: Major Speeches by Negroes in the United States, 1797–1971.* New York: Simon and Schuster, 1972.

Foster, William Z. *American Trade Unionism: Principles and Organization, Strategies and Tactics.* New York: International, 1947.

Fox, Richard Wightman, and T. Jackson Lears, eds. *The Culture of Consumption: Critical Essays in American History, 1880–1980.* New York: Pantheon Books, 1983.

Franklin, John Hope. *Three Negro Classics.* New York: Avon Books, 1965.

Franklin, V. P. *Black Self-Determination: A Cultural History of the Faith of Our Fathers.* Westport, Conn.: Greenwood Press, 1984.

Frazier, E. Franklin. *Black Bourgeoisie: The Rise of New Middle Class.* Glencoe, Ill.: Free Press, 1957.

——. *The Negro Church in America.* New York: Schocken Books, 1964.

——. *The Negro Family in Chicago.* Chicago: University of Chicago Press, 1932.

Frederickson, George. *The Black Image in the White Mind: The Debate on Afro-American Character and Destiny, 1817–1940.* New York: Harper and Row, 1971.

Frelinger, Gregg. *Motion Picture Piano Music: Descriptive Music to Fit the Action, Character or Scene of Moving Pictures.* Lafayette, Ind.: Gregg A. Frelinger, 1909.

Fuller, Kathryn H. *At the Picture Show: Small-Town Audiences and the Creation of Movie Fan Culture.* Washington, D.C.: Smithsonian Institution Press, 1996.

Gaebner, William. *The Engineering of Consent: Democracy and Authority in 20th Century America.* Madison: University of Wisconsin Press, 1987.

Gaines, Jane. *Fire and Desire: Mixed-Race Movies in the Silent Era.* Chicago: University of Chicago Press, 2002.

Gaines, Kevin. *Uplifting the Race: Black Leadership, Politics, and Culture in the Twentieth Century.* Chapel Hill: University of North Carolina Press, 1996.

Gallichio, Marc. *The African American Encounter with Japan and China: Black Internationalism in Asia, 1895–1945.* Chapel Hill: University of North Carolina Press, 2000.

Gamble, Vanessa Northington. *Making a Place for Ourselves: The Black Hospital Movement, 1920–1945.* New York: Oxford University Press, 1995.

Gans, Herbert J. *Popular Culture and High Culture: An Analysis and Evaluation of Taste.* New York: Basic Books, 1974.

Gardner, Robert, and Dennis Shorelle. *The Forgotten Players: The Story of Black Baseball in America.* New York: Walker and Co., 1993.

Garelick, Rhonda. *Rising Star: Dandyism, Gender, and Performance in the Fin de Siècle.* Princeton: Princeton University Press, 1998.

Garfinkel, Herbert. *When Negroes March: The March on Washington Movement in the Organizational Politics for FEPC.* Glencoe, Ill.: Free Press, 1959.

Garrett, Franklin. *Atlanta and Its Environs: A Chronicle of Its People and Events.* Vol. 2. Athens: University of Georgia Press, 1969.

Gatewood, William B. *Aristocrats of Color: The Black Elite, 1880–1920.* Bloomington: University of Indiana Press, 1990.

Gems, Gerald. *Windy City Wars: Labor, Leisure and Sport in the Making of Chicago.* Lanham, Md.: Scarecrow, 1997.

George, Nelson. *Elevating the Game: Black Men and Basketball.* New York: Harper Collins, 1992.

Getz, Gene A. *MBI: The Story of Moody Bible Institute.* Chicago: Moody Press, 1969.

Giddings, Paula. *When and Where I Enter: The Impact of Black Women on Race and Sex in America.* New York: Pantheon, 1984.

Gilbert, James. *Perfect Cities: Chicago's Utopias of 1893.* Chicago: University of Chicago Press, 1991.

Gilfoyle, Timothy. *City of Eros: New York City, Prostitution, and the Commercialization of Sex.* New York: W. W. Norton and Company, 1992.

Gilmore, Al-Tony. *Bad Nigger! The National Impact of Jack Johnson.* Port Washington, N.Y.: Kennikat Press, 1975.

Gilroy, Paul. *The Black Atlantic: Modernity and Double Consciousness.* Cambridge: Harvard University Press, 1993.

——. *There Ain't No Black in the Union Jack: The Cultural Politics of Race and Nation.* London: Hutchinson, 1987.

Goggins, Jaqueline. *Carter G. Woodson: A Life in Black History.* Baton Rouge: Louisiana State University Press, 1993.

Gold, Howard R., and Byron Armstrong. *A Preliminary Study of Inter-Racial Conditions in Chicago.* New York: Home Missions Council, 1920.

Gomery, Douglas. *Shared Pleasures: A History of Movie Presentation in the United States.* Madison: University of Wisconsin Press, 1992.

Goodwin, Ruby Berkley. *It's Good to Be Black.* Garden City, N.Y.: Doubleday, 1953.

Goreau, Laurraine. *Just Mahalia, Baby: The Mahalia Jackson Story.* Waco, Tex.: Word Books, 1975.

Gorn, Elliot. *The Manly Art: Bare-Knuckle Prize Fighting in America.* Ithaca: Cornell University Press, 1986.

Gosling, F. G. *Before Freud: Neurasthenia and the American Medical Community, 1870–1910.* Urbana: University of Illinois Press, 1987.

Gosnell, Harold F. *Negro Politicians: The Rise of Negro Politics in Chicago.* Chicago: University of Chicago Press, 1935.

Gottlieb, Peter. *Making Their Own Way: Southern Blacks' Migration to Pittsburgh, 1916–1930.* Urbana: University of Illinois Press, 1987.

Gouldner, Alvin W. *The Future of Intellectuals and the Rise of the New Class.* New York: Seabury, 1979.

Graham, Stephen. *The Soul of John Brown.* New York: Macmillan, 1920.

Green, Edward S. *National Capital Code of Etiquette*. Washington, D.C.: Austin Jenkins, 1920.

Green, Harvey. *Fit for America: Health, Fitness, Sport, and American Society*. Baltimore: Johns Hopkins University Press, 1986.

Green, J. Ronald. *Straight Lick: The Cinema of Oscar Micheaux*. Bloomington: Indiana University Press, 2000.

Greenberg, Cheryl. *"Or Does It Explode?" Black Harlem in the Great Depression*. New York: Oxford University Press, 1991.

Greene, Lorenzo. *Selling Black History for Carter G. Woodson: A Diary*. Columbia: University of Missouri Press, 1996.

Greenhouse, Wendy, and Jantyle Theresa Robinson. *The Art of Archibald Motley Jr.* Chicago: Chicago Historical Society, 1991.

Griffin, Farah Jasmine. *"Who Set You Flowin'?" The African-American Migration Narrative*. New York: Oxford University Press, 1995.

Griggs, Sutton. *Imperium in Imperio*. 1899. Reprint, New York: Arno Press, 1969.

Grimshaw, William. *Bitter Fruit: Black Politics and the Chicago Machine, 1931–1991*. Chicago: University of Chicago Press, 1992.

Gronow, Jukka. *The Sociology of Taste*. London: Routledge, 1997.

Grossman, James R. *Land of Hope: Chicago, Black Southerners and the Great Migration*. Chicago: University of Chicago Press, 1989.

Gurrero, Ed. *Framing Blackness: The African American Image in Film*. Philadelphia: Temple University Press, 1993.

Gutman, Herbert. *Work, Culture and Society in Industrializing America: Essays in American Working-Class and Social History*. New York: Random House, 1977.

Guttman, Allen. *A Whole New Ball Game: An Interpretation of American Sports*. Chapel Hill: University of North Carolina Press, 1988.

Habermas, Jurgen. *The Structural Transformation of the Public Sphere*. Cambridge: MIT Press, 1989.

Hackley, E. Azalia. *The Colored Girl Beautiful*. Kansas City: Burton Publishing, 1916.

Hall, Donald E., ed. *Muscular Christianity: Embodying the Victorian Age*. New York: Cambridge University Press, 1994.

Hall, Stuart, et al. *Modernity: An Introduction to Modern Societies*. London: Blackwell, 1996.

——. *Policing the Crisis: Mugging, the State, and Law and Order*. London: Macmillan, 1978.

Hammond, Theresa A. *A White Collar Profession: African American Certified Public Accountants since 1921*. Chapel Hill: University of North Carolina Press, 2002.

Handy, W. C. *Father of the Blues: An Autobiography by W. C. Handy*. Edited by Arna Bontemps. New York: Macmillan, 1941.

——, ed. *Blues: An Anthology*. New York: Albert and Charles Boni, 1926.

Hangen, Tona. *Redeeming the Dial: Radio, Religion, and Popular Culture in America*. Chapel Hill: University of North Carolina Press, 2002.

Hansen, Miriam. *Babel and Babylon: Spectatorship in American Silent Film*. Cambridge: Harvard University Press, 1991.

Harlan, Louis. *Booker T. Washington: The Wizard of Tuskegee, 1901–1915*. New York: Oxford University Press, 1983.

Harlan, Louis, and Raymond Smock. *The Booker T. Washington Papers*. Vol. 2, *1911–1912*. Urbana: University of Illinois Press, 1981.

Harmon, J. H., Arnett Lindsay, and Carter G. Woodson. *The Negro as a Business Man*. 1929. Reprint, College Park, Md.: McGrath Publishing, 1969.

Harper, Philip Brian. *Are We Not Men? Masculine Anxiety and the Problem of African-American Identity*. New York: Oxford University Press, 1996.

Harris, Abram. *The Negro as Capitalist: A Study of Banking and Business among American Negroes*. Philadelphia: American Academy of Political and Social Sciences, 1936.

Harris, Leonard. *The Philosophy of Alain Locke: Harlem Renaissance and Beyond*. Philadelphia: Temple University Press, 1989.

Harris, Michael. *The Rise of Gospel Blues: The Music of Thomas Andrew Dorsey in the Urban Church*. New York: Oxford University Press, 1922.

Harrison, Daphne Duval. *Blues Queens of the 1920s: Black Pearls*. New Brunswick, N.J.: Rutgers University Press, 1988.

Harrison, Hubert. *When Africa Awakes: The "Inside Story" of the Stirrings and Strivings of the New Negro in the Western World*. 1920. Reprint, Baltimore: Black Classic Press, 1997.

Harvey, David. *The Condition of Post-Modernity: An Enquiry into the Origins of Cultural Change*. Oxford: Blackwell Press, 1989.

Harvey, Lee. *Myths of the Chicago School of Sociology*. Aldershot, England: Gower, 1987.

Haskell, Thomas. *The Authority of Experts*. Urbana: University of Illinois Press, 1984.

Haywood, Harry. *Black Bolshevik: Autobiography of an Afro-American Communist*. Chicago: Liberator Press, 1978.

Hazzard-Gordon, Katrina. *Jookin': The Rise of Social Dance Formations in African-American Culture*. Philadelphia: Temple University Press, 1990.

Hebdige, Dick. *Subculture: The Meaning of Style*. New York: Methuen, 1979.

Heilbut, Anthony. *The Gospel Sound: Goods News and Bad Times*. New York: Harper and Row, 1985.

Helbling, Mark Irving. *The Harlem Renaissance: The One and the Many*. Westport, Conn.: Greenwood Press, 1999.

Henderson, Edwin B. *The Negro in Sports*. Washington, D.C.: ASNLH, 1939.

Hendricks, King, and Irving Shepard, eds. *Jack London Reports: War Correspondence, Sports Articles and Miscellaneous Writings*. Garden City, N.Y.: Doubleday, 1970.

Hendricks, Wanda A. *Gender, Race and Politics in the Midwest: Black Club Women in Illinois*. Bloomington: Indiana University Press, 1998.

Hendrickson, Hildi. *Clothing and Difference: Embodied Identities in Colonial and Post-Colonial Africa*. Durham: Duke University Press, 1996.

Henri, Florette. *Black Migration: Movement North, 1900–1920: The Road from Myth to Man*. New York: Anchor Press, 1975.

Henry, Charles P. *African-American Culture and Politics*. Bloomington: Indiana University Press, 1990.

Hentoff, Nat, and Albert J. McCarthy. *Jazz: New Perspectives on the History of Jazz*. New York: Da Capo Press, 1974.

Herbst, Alma. *The Negro in the Slaughtering and Meat-Packing Industry in Chicago*. Boston: Houghton Mifflin, 1932.

Herreman, Frank. *Hair in African Art and Culture*. New York: Museum of African Art, 2000.

Hietala, Thomas. *The Fight of the Century: Jack Johnson, Joe Louis and the Struggle for Racial Equality*. Armonk, N.Y.: M. E. Sharpe, 2002.

Higginbotham, Evelyn Brooks. *Righteous Discontent: The Woman's Movement in the Black Baptist Church, 1880–1920*. Cambridge: Harvard University Press, 1993.

Higgs, Robert. *God in the Stadium: Sports and Religion in America*. Lexington: University Press of Kentucky, 1995.

Hill, Robert A., ed. *The Marcus Garvey and Universal Negro Improvement Association Papers*. Vol. 1, *1826–August 1919*. Berkeley: University of California Press, 1983.

Hine, Darlene Clark. *Hine Sight: Black Women and the Re-construction of American History*. Brooklyn: Carlson, 1994.

———. *Speaking Truth to Power: Black Professional Class in the United States*. Brooklyn: Carlson, 1996.

Hine, Darlene Clark, and Earnestine Jenkins. *A Question of Manhood: A Reader in U.S. Black Men's History and Masculinity*. Bloomington: Indiana University Press, 1999.

Hinkle, Roscoe C., and Gisela Hinkle. *The Development of Modern Sociology: Its Nature and Growth in the United States*. New York: Random House, 1954.

Hirsch, Arnold. *Making the Second Ghetto: Race and Housing in Chicago, 1940–1960*. New York: Cambridge University Press, 1983.

Hoffman, Frederick. *Race Traits and Tendencies of the American Negro*. New York: Macmillan, 1896.

Hofstadter, Richard. *Social Darwinism in American Thought*. Boston: Beacon Press, 1944.

Hogan, David J. *Class and Reform: School and Society in Chicago, 1880–1930*. Philadelphia: University of Pennsylvania Press, 1985.

Hogan, Lawrence. *A Black National News Service: The Associated Negro Press and Claude Barnett, 1919–1945*. London: Associated University Presses, 1984.

Hoganson, Kristin. *Fighting for American Manhood: How Gender Politics Provoked the Spanish-American and Philippine-American Wars*. New Haven: Yale University Press, 1998.

Hollander, Anne. *Sex and Suits: The Evolution of Modern Dress*. New York: Kodansha, 1995.

Holli, Melvin, and Peter d'A. Jones. *The Ethnic Frontier: Essays in the History of Group Survival in Chicago and the Midwest*. Grand Rapids, Mich.: William B. Eerdmans, 1977.

Holloway, John. *Blackball Stars: Negro League Pioneers*. New York: Carroll and Graf, 1988.

———. *Voices from the Great Black Baseball Leagues*. New York: Dodd, Mead, 1975.

Holloway, Jonathon Scott. *Confronting the Veil: Abram Harris Jr., E. Franklin Frazier and Ralph Bunche*. Chapel Hill: University of North Carolina Press, 2002.

Holway, John. *Black Diamonds: Life in the Negro Leagues from the Men Who Lived It*. Westport, Conn.: Meckler, 1989.

Homel, Michael. *Down from Equality: Black Chicagoans and the Public Schools, 1920–1941*. Urbana: University of Illinois Press, 1984.

Hopkins, C. Howard. *History of the YMCA in North America*. New York: Association Press, 1951.

Huggins, Nathan. *The Harlem Renaissance*. New York: Oxford University Press, 1971.

———, ed. *W. E. B. Du Bois: Writings*. New York: Library of America, 1986.

Hughes, Langston. *The Big Sea: An Autobiography*. New York: Alfred A. Knopf, 1945.

———. *Not without Laughter*. 1930. Reprint, New York: Collier Books, 1969.

Hunter, Alberta. *Alberta Hunter: A Celebration in Blues*. New York: McGraw Hill, 1987.

Hunter, Herbert, ed. *The Sociology of Oliver C. Cox: New Perspectives*. Stamford, Conn.: JAI Press, 2001.

Hurston, Zora Neale. *Dust Tracks on a Road: An Autobiography*. Philadelphia: J. B. Lippincott, 1942.

———. *Folklore, Memoirs, and Other Writings*. Edited by Cheryl A. Wall. New York: Library of America, 1995.

———. *The Sanctified Church*. Edited by Toni Cade Bambara. Berkeley: University of California Press, 1983.

Hutchinson, George. *The Harlem Renaissance in Black and White*. Cambridge: Harvard University Press, 1995.

Jackson, Jerma. *Singing in My Soul: Black Gospel Music in a Secular Age*. Chapel Hill: University of North Carolina Press, 2004.

Jackson, Mahalia, with Even Wylie. *Movin' On Up*. New York: Hawthorn Books, 1996.

Jacobs, Lewis. *The Rise of American Film: A Critical History*. New York: Teachers College Press, 1939.

Jacobson, Matthew Frye. *Barbarian Virtues: The United States Encounters Foreign Peoples at Home and Abroad, 1876–1917*. New York: Hill and Wang, 2001.

James, C. L. R. *American Civilization*. Edited by Anna Grimshaw and Keith Hart. Oxford: Blackwell Press, 1993.

———. *Beyond a Boundary*. 1963. Reprint, Durham: Duke University Press, 1983.

James, Joy. *Transcending the Talented Tenth*. New York: Routledge, 1997.

Jameson, Frederic. *Postmodernism, or, The Cultural Logic of Late Capitalism*. Durham: Duke University Press, 1991.

Jarvie, Grant. *Sport, Racism, and Ethnicity*. London: Falmer Press, 1991.

Jhally, Sut. *The Codes of Advertising: Fetishism and the Political Economy of Meaning in the Consumer Society*. New York: Routledge, 1990.

Johnson, Abby, and Ronald Johnson. *Propaganda and Aesthetics: The Literary Politics of Afro-American Magazines in the Twentieth Century*. Boston: University of Massachusetts Press, 1979.

Johnson, Charles. *Shadow of the Plantation*. Chicago: University of Chicago Press, 1934.

———, ed. *Ebony and Topaz: A Collectanea*. New York: Opportunity, National Urban League, 1927.

Johnson, Daniel, and Rex Campbell. *Black Migration in America: A Social and Demographic History*. Durham: Duke University Press, 1981.

Johnson, Eloise E. *Rediscovering the Harlem Renaissance: The Politics of Exclusion*. New York: Garland Publishing, 1997.

Johnson, Jack. *Jack Johnson—In the Ring—and Out*. Chicago: National Sports, 1927.

———. *Jack Johnson Is a Dandy: An Autobiography*. New York: Chelsea House Publishers, 1969.

Johnson, James Weldon. *Along This Way: The Autobiography of James Weldon Johnson*. New York: Viking Press, 1933.

———. *Black Manhattan*. 1930. Reprint, New York: Antheum, 1977.

———. *The Book of American Negro Poems*. 1922. Reprint, New York: Harcourt, Brace and World, 1959.

Johnson, James Weldon, J. Rosamond Johnson, and Lawrence Brown, eds. *The Book of American Negro Spirituals*. New York: Viking Press, 1925.

Jones, George William. *Black Cinema Treasures: Lost and Found*. Denton: University of North Texas, 1991.

Jones, Jacqueline. *Labor of Love, Labor of Sorrow: Black Women, Work and the Family from Slavery to the Present*. New York: Basic Books, 1985.

Jones, Leroi. *Blues People: The Negro Experience in White America and the Music That Developed from It*. New York: William Morrow, 1968.

Jones, Norrece T. *Born a Child of Freedom, Yet a Slave: Mechanisms of Control and Strategies of Resistance in Antebellum South Carolina*. Middletown, Conn.: Wesleyan University Press, 1989.

Jones, William. *Recreation and Amusement among Negroes in Washington D.C.* 1927. Reprint, Westport, Conn.: Negro Universities Press, 1970.

Kalaidjian, Walter. *American Culture between the Wars: Revisionary Modernism and Postmodern Critique*. New York: Columbia University Press, 1993.

Kasson, John. *Amusing the Millions: Coney Island at the Turn of the Century*. New York: Hill and Wang, 1978.

Katznelson, Ira. *Black Men, White Cities*. Chicago: University of Chicago Press, 1973.

Keck, George, and Sherrill Martin, eds. *Feel the Spirit: Studies in Nineteenth-Century Afro-American Music*. Westport, Conn.: Greenwood Press, 1988.

Kelley, Robin D. G. *Freedom Dreams: The Black Radical Imagination*. Boston: Beacon Press, 2002.

——. *Hammer and Hoe: Alabama Communists during the Great Depression*. Chapel Hill: University of North Carolina Press, 1990.

——. *Race Rebels: Culture, Politics and the Black Working Class*. New York: Free Press, 1994.

——. *Yo' Mama's Dysfunktional: Fighting the Culture Wars in Urban America*. Boston: Beacon Press, 1997.

Kelley, Robin D. G., and Sidney Lemelle. *Imagining Home: Class, Culture and Nationalism in the African Diaspora*. London: Verso Press, 1994.

Kennedy, Louise Venable. *The Negro Peasant Turns Cityward: The Effects of Recent Migrations to Northern Centers*. New York: Columbia University Press, 1930.

Kenney, William Howard. *Chicago Jazz: A Cultural History, 1904–1930*. New York: Oxford University Press, 1993.

Kern, Stephen. *The Culture of Time and Space, 1880–1918*. Cambridge: Harvard University Press, 1983.

Killens, John. *Black Man's Burden*. New York: Trident Press, 1965.

Kimmel, Michael, ed. *Manhood in America: A Cultural History*. New York: Free Press, 1996.

Kinser, Samuel. *Carnival, American Style: Mardi Gras at New Orleans and Mobile*. Chicago: University of Chicago Press, 1990.

Kirby, Jack Temple. *Rural Worlds Lost: The American South, 1920–1960*. Baton Rouge: Louisiana State University Press, 1987.

Kisch, John. *A Separate Cinema: Fifty Years of Black-Cast Posters*. New York: Farrar, Straus and Giroux, 1992.

Kloutman, Phyllis Rauch. *Frame by Frame: A Black Filmography*. Bloomington: Indiana University Press, 1979.

Knupfer, Anne Meis. *Toward a Tender Humanity and a Nobler Womanhood: African American Women's Clubs in Turn-of-the-Century Chicago*. New York: New York University Press, 1996.

Kornweibel, Theodore. *No Crystal Stair: Black Life and the Messenger, 1917–1928*. Westport, Conn.: Greenwood Press, 1975.

——. *"Seeing Red": Federal Campaign against Black Militancy, 1919–1925*. Bloomington: Indiana University Press, 1998.

Kramer, Victor A., and Robert A. Russ. *Harlem Renaissance Re-examined*. Troy, N.Y.: Whitson Publishing, 1997.

Krasner, David. *A Beautiful Pageant: African American Theatre, Drama and Performance in the Harlem Renaissance, 1910–1927*. New York: Palgrave Macmillan, 2002.

———. *Resistance, Parody, and Double Consciousness in African American Theater, 1895–1910*. New York: St. Martin's Press, 1997.

Krehbiel, Henry Edward. *Afro-American Folksong: A Study in Racial and National Music*. 1914. Reprint, New York: Frederick Ungar Publishing, 1962.

Kurtz, Lester P. *Evaluating Chicago Sociology: A Guide to Literature, with an Annotated Bibliography*. Chicago: University of Chicago Press, 1984.

Kusner, David. *A Beautiful Pageant: African American Theatre, Drama, and Performance in the Harlem Renaissance, 1910–1927*. New York: Palgrave-Macmillan, 2002.

Ladd, Tony, and James Mathisen. *Muscular Christianity: Evangelical Protestants and the Development of American Sport*. Grand Rapids, Mich.: Bridgeport Books, 1999.

Lal, Barbara Ballis. *The Romance of Culture in an Urban Civilization: Robert E. Park on Race and Ethnic Relations in Cities*. New York: Routledge, 1990.

Lang, Edith, and George West. *Musical Accompaniment of Moving Pictures: A Practical Manual for Pianists and Organists*. 1920. Reprint, New York: Arno Press, 1970.

Lang, Robert, ed. *The Birth of a Nation*. New Brunswick, N.J.: Rutgers University Press, 1994.

Lange, John Peter. *A Commentary on the Holy Scriptures*. Vol. 6 of *The Old Testament*. New York: Charles Scribner and Sons, 1887.

Larsen, Nella. *Quicksand*. New York: Alfred A. Knopf, 1928.

Lasch-Quinn, Elizabeth. *Black Neighbors: Race and the Limits of the American Settlement House Movement, 1890–1945*. Chapel Hill: University of North Carolina Press, 1993.

Leab, Daniel. *From Sambo to Superspade: The Black Experience in Motion Pictures*. Boston: Houghton Mifflin, 1976.

Lears, T. Jackson. *No Place of Grace: Antimodernism and the Transformation of American Culture, 1890–1920*. New York: Pantheon, 1981.

Lee, Erika. *At America's Gates: Chinese Immigration during the Exclusion Era, 1882–1943*. Chapel Hill: University of North Carolina Press, 2003.

Lemann, Nicholas. *The Promised Land: The Great Black Migration and How It Changed America*. New York: Vintage Books, 1992.

Lemke, Sieglinde. *Primitive Modernism: Black Culture and the Origins of Transatlantic Modernism*. New York: Oxford University Press, 1998.

Lester, Larry, ed. *Black Baseball's National Showcase: The East-West All-Star Game, 1933–1953*. Lincoln: University of Nebraska Press, 2001.

Lester, Larry, Sammy Miller, and Dick Clark. *Black America Series: Black Baseball in Chicago*. Chicago: Arcadia Publishing, 2000.

Levine, Lawrence. *Black Culture and Black Consciousness: Afro-American Folk Thought*. New York: Oxford University Press, 1977.

——. *Highbrow/Lowbrow: The Emergence of Cultural Hierarchy in America*. Cambridge: Harvard University Press, 1988.

——. *The Unpredictable Past: Explorations in American Cultural History*. New York: Oxford University Press, 1993.

Lewis, David J., and Richard Smith. *American Sociology and Pragmatism: Mead, Chicago, Sociology and Symbolic Interactionism*. Chicago: University of Chicago Press, 1980.

Lewis, David Levering. *W. E. B. Du Bois: Biography of a Race, 1868–1919*. New York: Owl Books, 1994.

——. *W. E. B. Du Bois: The Fight for Equality and the American Century, 1919–1963*. New York: Henry Holt and Company, 2000.

——. *When Harlem Was in Vogue*. New York: Oxford University Press, 1981.

Lewis, Earl. *In Their Own Interests: Race, Class and Power in Twentieth-Century Norfolk, Virginia*. Berkeley: University of California Press, 1991.

Lieb, Sandra. *Mother of the Blues: A Study of Ma Rainey*. Amherst: University of Massachusetts Press, 1981.

Lincoln, C. Eric. *The Black Muslims in America*. Trenton, N.J.: Africa World Press, 1961.

Lincoln, C. Eric, and Lawrence H. Mamiya. *The Black Church in the African American Experience*. Durham: Duke University Press, 1990.

Lindberg, Richard. *Chicago by Gaslight: A History of Chicago's Netherworld, 1880–1920*. Chicago: Academy Chicago Publishers, 1996.

Lindner, Rolf. *The Reportage of Urban Culture: Robert Park and the Chicago School*. New York: Cambridge University Press, 1996.

Lipsitz, George. *Class and Culture in Cold War America: A Rainbow at Midnight*. South Hadley, Mass.: J. F. Bergin Publishers, 1982.

Locke, Alain LeRoy. *The Critical Temper of Alain Locke: A Selection of His Essays on Art and Culture*. New York: Garland Publishing, 1983.

——. *The Negro and His Music*. New York: Arno Press, 1936.

——. *The New Negro: Voices of the Harlem Renaissance*. New York: Albert and Charles Boni, 1925.

——. *Race Contacts and Interracial Relations: Lectures on the Theory and Practice of Race*. Washington, D.C.: Howard University Press, 1992.

Lomax, John. *Cowboys Songs and Other Frontier Ballads*. New York: Sturgis and Walton, 1916.

Lomax, Michael. *Black Baseball Entrepreneurs, 1860–1901: Operating by Any Means Necessary*. Syracuse: Syracuse University Press, 2003.

Lott, Eric. *Love and Theft: Blackface Minstrelsy and the American Working Class*. Oxford: Oxford University Press, 1995.

Louis, Joe, with Edna and Art Rust Jr. *Joe Louis: My Life*. New York: Harcourt Brace Jovanovich.

Lowell, John, Jr. *Black Song: The Forge and the Flame*. New York: Macmillan, 1972.

Lubiano, Wahneema, ed. *The House That Race Built: Black Americans, U.S. Terrain*. New York: Pantheon, 1997.

Luker, Ralph. *The Social Gospel in Black and White: American Racial Reform, 1885– 1912*. Chapel Hill: University of North Carolina Press, 1991.

Lutz, Tom. *American Nervousness, 1903: An Anecdotal History*. Ithaca: Cornell University Press, 1991.

MacDonald, J. Fred. *Don't Touch That Dial: Radio Programming in American Life from 1920–1960*. Chicago: Nelson-Hall, 1979.

Macleod, David I. *Building Character in the American Boy: The Boy Scouts, YMCA, and Their Forerunners, 1870–1920*. Madison: University of Wisconsin Press, 1983.

MacRobert, Ian. *The Black Roots of White Racism of Early Pentecostalism in the USA*. New York: St. Martin's Press, 1988.

Madge, John. *The Origins of Scientific Sociology*. Glencoe, Ill.: Free Press, 1962.

Magubane, Bernard. *The Ties That Bind*. Trenton, N.J.: Africa World Press, 1987.

Makdisi, Saree. *Romantic Imperialism: Universal Empire and the Culture of Modernity*. Cambridge: Cambridge University Press, 1998.

Malone, Jaqui. *Steppin' on the Blues: The Visible Rhythms of African American Dance*. Urbana: University of Illinois Press, 1996.

Mangan, J. A., and James Walvin, eds. *Manliness and Morality: Middle-Class Masculinity in Britain and America, 1800–1940*. New York: St. Martin's Press, 1987.

Marable, Manning. *Race, Reform, and Rebellion: The Second Reconstruction in Black America, 1945–1990*. Jackson: University of Mississippi Press, 1991.

Marchand, Roland. *Advertising the American Dream: Making Way for Modernity, 1920–1940*. Berkeley: University of California Press, 1985.

Marks, Carole. *Farewell—We're Good and Gone: The Great Black Migration*. Bloomington: Indiana University Press, 1989.

Marks, Carole, and Diana Edkins, eds. *The Power of Pride: Stylemakers and Rulebreakers of the Harlem Renaissance*. New York: Crown Publishers, 1999.

Marks, Martin Miller. *Music and the Silent Film: Contexts and Case Studies, 1895– 1924*. New York: Oxford University Press, 1997.

Marsh, J. B. I. *The Story of the Jubilee Singers*. London: Hodder and Stoughton, 1877.

Martin, Tony. *Literary Garveyism: Garvey, Black Arts, and the Harlem Renaissance*. Dover: Majority Press, 1983.

——. *Race First: The Ideological and Organizational Struggles of Marcus Garvey and the Universal Negro Improvement Association*. Dover: Majority Press, 1976.

Marwick, Arthur. *Beauty in History: Society, Politics and Personal Appearance, 1500– Present*. London: Thomas and Hudson, 1988.

Mast, Gerald. *A Short History of the Movies*. New York: Macmillan, 1986.

Matthews, Fred. *Quest for an American Sociology: Robert E. Park and the Chicago School*. Montreal: McGill-Queen's University Press, 1977.

Maxwell, William. *New Negro, Old Left: African American Writing and Communism between the Wars*. New York: Columbia University Press, 1999.

May, Lary. *Screening Out the Past: The Birth of Mass Culture and the Motion Picture Industry*. New York: Oxford University Press, 1980.

Mays, Benjamin Elijah, and Joseph William Nicholson. *The Negroes Church*. 1933. Reprint, New York: Arno Press, 1969.

McLoughlin, William. *Revivals, Awakenings and Reform: An Essay on Religion and Social Change in America, 1607–1977*. Chicago: University of Chicago Press, 1978.

McMurray, Linda O. *To Keep the Waters Troubled: The Life of Ida B. Wells*. New York: Oxford University Press, 1998.

Meier, August. *Negro Thought in America, 1880–1915: Racial Ideologies in the Age of Booker T. Washington*. Ann Arbor: University of Michigan Press, 1966.

Mercer, Kobena. *Welcome to the Jungle: New Positions in Black Cultural Studies*. New York: Routledge, 1996.

Meyerowitz, Joanne. *Women Adrift: Independent Wage Earners in Chicago, 1880–1920*. Chicago: University of Chicago Press, 1988.

Mezzrow, Milton "Mezz," and Bernard Wolfe. *Really the Blues*. Garden City, N.Y.: Anchor Books, 1972.

Michaels, Walter Benn. *Our America: Nativism, Modernism and Pluralism*. Durham: Duke University Press, 1955.

Micheaux, Oscar. *The Conquest: The Story of a Negro Pioneer*. Lincoln, Neb.: Woodruff Press, 1913.

———. *The Homesteader*. Sioux City, Iowa: Western Book Supply Company, 1917.

Mignolo, Walter. *The Darker Side of the Renaissance: Literacy, Territoriality, and Colonization*. Ann Arbor: University of Michigan Press, 1995.

Mills, C. Wright. *Power, Politics and People: The Collected Essays*. New York: Ballantine Books, 1963.

Mishkin, Tracy. *The Harlem and Irish Renaissance: Language, Identity, and Representation*. Gainesville: University Press of Florida, 1998.

Mitchell, Reid. *All on Mardi Gras Day: Episodes in the History of New Orleans Carnival*. Cambridge: Harvard University Press, 1995.

Mjagkij, Nina. *Light in the Darkness: African Americans and the YMCA, 1852–1946*. Lexington: University Press of Kentucky, 1994.

Modelski, Tania. *Studies in Entertainment: Critical Approaches to Mass Culture*. Bloomington: Indiana University Press, 1986.

Moore, Robin. *Nationalizing Blackness: Afrocubanismo and Artistic Revolution in Havana, 1920–1940*. Pittsburgh: University of Pittsburgh Press, 1977.

Morris, Calvin S. *Reverdy C. Ransom: Black Advocate of the Social Gospel*. Lanham, Md.: University Press of America, 1990.

Morris, Kenneth. *Improving the Music in the Church*. Chicago: Martin and Morris Music Studio, 1949.

Morrow, Willie. *400 Years without a Comb*. San Diego: Black Publishers, 1973.

Moses, Wilson. *The Golden Age of Black Nationalism, 1850–1925*. Oxford: Cambridge University Press, 1978.

Moss, Alfred. *The American Negro Academy: Voices of the Talented Tenth*. Baton Rouge: Louisiana State University Press, 1981.

Mullen, William. *Popular Fronts: Chicago and African-American Cultural Politics, 1935–1946*. Urbana: University of Illinois Press, 1999.

Mullins, Paul. *Race and Affluence: An Archeology of African America and Consumer Culture*. New York: Kluwer Academic/Plenum Publishers, 1989.

Mumford, Kevin. *Interzones: Black/White Sex Districts in Chicago and New York in the Early Twentieth Century*. New York: Columbia University Press, 1997.

Music of the Sunday School Publishing Board. *Gospel Pearls*. Nashville: Sunday School Publishing Board [of the] National Baptist Convention, USA, 1921.

Naismith, James. *YMCA as Basketball: Its Origins and Developments*. New York: Association Press, 1941. Reprinted as Robert Cheney, ed. *Basketball's Origins: Creative Problem Solving in the Gilded Age*. Cambridge, N.Y.: Bear Publications, 1976.

Negt, Oskar, and Alexander Kluge. *Public Sphere and Experience: Toward an Analysis of the Bourgeois and Proletarian Public Sphere*. Minneapolis: University of Minnesota Press, 1993.

Nesteby, James. *Black Images in American Films, 1896–1954: The Interplay between Civil Rights and Film Culture*. Washington, D.C.: University Press of America, 1978.

Newman, Mark. *Entrepreneurs of Profit and Pride: From Black-Appeal to Radio Soul*. New York: Praeger, 1988.

Nicholls, David. *Conjuring the Folk: Forms of Modernity in African America*. Ann Arbor: University of Michigan Press, 2000.

Nielson, David Gordon. *Black Ethos: Northern Urban Negro Life and Thought, 1890–1930*. Westport, Conn.: Greenwood Press, 1977.

Nielson, Joyce McCarl. *Sex in Society: Perspectives on Stratification*. Belmont, Calif.: Wadsworth, 1978.

Ogren, Kathy J. *The Jazz Revolution: Twenties America and the Meaning of Jazz*. New York: Oxford University Press, 1989.

Oliver, Paul. *Bessie Smith*. London: Cassell Press, 1959.

——. *Songsters and Saints: Vocal Traditions on Race Records*. New York: Cambridge University Press, 1984.

Oriard, Michael. *King Football: Sport and Spectacle in the Golden Age of Radio and Newsreels, Movies and Magazines, the Weekly and the Daily Press*. Chapel Hill: University of North Carolina Press, 2001.

Ortner, Sherry B. *Making Gender: The Politics and Erotics of Gender*. Boston: Beacon Press, 1996.

Ortner, Sherry B., and Harriet Whitehead. *Sexual Meanings: The Cultural Constructions of Gender and Sexuality*. New York: Cambridge University Press, 1981.

Osofsky, Gilbert. *Harlem: The Making of a Ghetto: Negro New York, 1890–1930*. New York: Harper and Row, 1963.

Ostransky, Leroy. *Jazz City: The Impact of Our Cities on the Development of Jazz*. Englewood Cliffs, N.J.: Prentice-Hall, 1978.

Ottley, Roi. *The Lonely Warrior: The Life and Times of Robert Abbott*. Chicago: Henry Regnery, 1955.

Overman, Steven. *The Influence of the Protestant Ethic on Sports and Recreation*. Brookfield: Averbury Press, 1997.

Overton Hygienic Company. *Encyclopedia of Colored People*. N.p., 1922.

Ownby, Ted. *American Dreams in Mississippi: Consumers, Poverty, and Culture, 1830–1998*. Chapel Hill: University of North Carolina Press, 2000.

Painter, Nell Irving. *Exodusters: Black Migration to Kansas after Reconstruction*. New York: Knopf, 1976.

——. *Standing at Armageddon: The United States, 1877–1919*. New York: W. W. Norton, 1987.

Parham, Sarah E. *The Life of Charles F. Parham: Founder of the Apostolic Faith Movement*. Joplin, Mo.: Tri-State Printing Company, 1930.

Paris, Arthur E. *Black Pentecostalism: Southern Religion in an Urban World*. Amherst: University of Massachusetts Press, 1982.

Park, Robert. *Race and Culture*. Glencoe, Ill.: Free Press, 1950.

Park, Robert, and Ernest Burgess. *Introduction to the Science of Sociology*. Chicago: University of Chicago Press, 1921.

Park, Robert, Ernest Burgess, and Roderick McKenzie. *The City: Suggestions for Investigation of Human Behavior in the Urban Environment*. Chicago: University of Chicago Press, 1925.

Parris, Guchard, and Lester Brooks. *Blacks in the City: A History of the National Urban League*. Boston: Little, Brown, 1971.

Patterson, J. O., German R. Ross, and Julia Mason Atkins. *History and Formative Years of the Church of God in Christ with Excerpts from the Life and Works of Its Founder—Bishop C. H. Mason*. Memphis: Church of God in Christ Publishing House, 1969.

Patterson, Lindsay, ed. *Black Films and Filmmakers*. New York: Dodd, Mead, 1975.

Payne, Daniel Alexander. *Recollections of Seventy Years*. New York: Arno Press, 1969.

Peiss, Kathy. *Cheap Amusements: Working Women and Leisure in Turn-of-the-Century New York*. Philadelphia: Temple University Press, 1988.

——. *Hope in a Jar: The Making of America's Beauty Culture*. New York: Henry Holt, 1999.

Pendegrast, Tom. *Creating the Modern Man: American Magazines and Consumer Culture, 1900–1950*. Columbia: University of Missouri Press, 2000.

Penn, Garlan J., and J. W. E. Bowen. *The United Negro: His Problems and his Progress.* 1902. Reprint, New York: Negro Universities Press, 1969.

Penn, Irvine Garland. *The Afro-American Press and Its Editors.* Springfield, Mass.: Wiley, 1891.

Persons, Stowe. *Ethnic Studies at Chicago: 1905–1945.* Urbana: University of Illinois Press, 1987.

Peterson, Robert. *From Cages to Jump Shots: Pro Basketball's Early Years.* New York: Oxford University Press, 1990.

——. *Only the Ball Was White: A History of Legendary Black Ball Players and All-Black Professional Teams.* New York: McGraw-Hill, 1984.

Philpott, Thomas. *The Slum and the Ghetto: Neighborhood Deterioration and Middle Class Reform, 1880–1930.* New York: Oxford University Press, 1978.

Pickens, William. *The New Negro: His Political, Civil, and Mental Status, and Related Essays.* 1916. Reprint, New York: Negro Universities Press, 1969.

Pike, Gustavus. *The Jubilee Singers and Their Campaign for Twenty Thousand Dollars.* London: Hodder and Stoughton, 1873.

Pines, Jim. *Blacks in Films: A Survey of Racial Themes and Images in the American Film.* London: Studio Vista, 1975.

Platt, Anthony. *E. Franklin Frazier Reconsidered.* New Brunswick, N.J.: Rutgers University Press, 1991.

Platt, Harold. *The Electric City: Energy and the Growth of the Chicago Area.* Chicago: University of Chicago Press, 1991.

Pleas, Charles H. *Fifty Years of Achievement from 1906–1956: A Period in History of the Church of God in Christ.* 1956. Reprint, Memphis: Church of God in Christ Publishing House, 1991.

Pollock, J. C. *Moody: A Biographical Portrait of the Pacesetter in Modern Mass Evangelism.* New York: Macmillan, 1963.

Poole, Deborah. *Vision, Race, and Modernity: A Visual Economy of the Andean Image World.* Princeton: Princeton University Press, 1997.

Powell, Richard. *Rhapsodies in Black: Art of the Harlem Renaissance.* Berkeley: University of California Press, 1997.

Puth, Robert C. *Supreme Life: The History of a Negro Life Insurance Company.* New York: Arno Press, 1976.

Putney, Clifford. *Muscular Christianity: Manhood and Sports in Protestant America, 1880–1920.* Cambridge: Harvard University Press, 2003.

Rabateau, Abert J. *Slave Religion: The Invisible Institution in the Antebellum South.* New York: Oxford University Press, 1978.

Rabinowitz, Lauren. *For the Love of Pleasure: Women, Movies and Culture in Turn-of-the-Century Chicago.* New Brunswick, N.J.: Rutgers University Press, 1998.

Radano, Ronald. *Lying Up a Nation: Race and Black Music.* Chicago: University of Chicago Press, 2003.

Radano, Ronald, and Philip V. Bohlman, eds. *Music and the Racial Imagination.* Chicago: University of Chicago Press, 2000.

Rampersand, Arnold. *The Art and Imagination of W. E. B. Du Bois.* Cambridge: Harvard University Press, 1976.

Raushenbush, Winifred. *Robert E. Park: Biography of a Sociologist.* Durham: Duke University Press, 1979.

Reagon, Bernice Johnson. *If You Don't Go, Don't Hinder Me: The African American Sacred Song Tradition.* Lincoln: University of Nebraska Press, 2001.

——, ed. *We'll Understand It Better By and By: Pioneering African-American Gospel Composers.* Washington, D.C.: Smithsonian Institution Press, 1992.

Redkey, Edwin S. *Black Exodus: Black Nationalist and Back to Africa Movements, 1890–1910.* New Haven: Yale University Press, 1969.

Reed, Christopher Robert. *All the World Is Here! The Black Presence at the White City.* Bloomington: Indiana University Press, 2000.

——. *The Chicago NAACP and the Rise of Black Professional Leadership, 1910–1966.* Bloomington: Indiana University Press, 1997.

Reed, Teresa. *The Holy Profane: Religion in Black Popular Music.* Lexington: University Press of Kentucky, 2003.

Reid, Mark. *Redefining Black Film.* Berkeley: University of California Press, 1993.

Reiss, Steven. *City Games: The Evolution of American Urban Society and the Rise of Sports.* Urbana: University of Illinois Press, 1989.

Rich, Doris L. *Queen Bess: Daredevil Aviator.* Washington, D.C.: Smithsonian Institution Press, 1993.

Ricks, George Robinson. *Some Aspects of the Religious Music of the United States Negro: An Ethnomusicological Study with Special Emphasis on the Gospel Tradition.* New York: Arno Press, 1977.

Riis, Thomas Lawrence. *More Than Just Minstrel Shows.* Brooklyn: Institute for Studies of American Music, Brooklyn College of the City University of New York, 1992.

Riley, James A. *The Biographical Encyclopedia of the Negro Baseball Leagues.* New York: Carroll and Graf, 1994.

Robb, Frederick H. H. *The Negro in Chicago: 1779–1927.* Vols. 1–2. Chicago: Washington Intercollegiate Club of Chicago, 1927, 1929.

Roberts, Randy. *Papa Jack: Jack Johnson and the Era of White Hopes.* New York: Free Press, 1983.

Robinson, Cedric. *Black Marxism: The Making of the Black Radical Tradition.* London: Zed Books, 1983.

Robinson, Jantyle Theresa, and Wendy Greenhouse. *The Art of Archibald Motley Jr.* Chicago: Chicago Historical Society, 1991.

Roell, Craig. *The Piano in America, 1890–1940.* Chapel Hill: University of North Carolina Press, 1989.

Rogin, Michael. *Blackface, White Noise: Jewish Immigrants in the Hollywood Melting Pot.* Berkeley: University of California Press, 1996.

———. *Ronald Reagan, the Movie and Other Episodes of Political Demonology.* Berkeley: University of California Press, 1987.

Rogosin, Donn. *Invisible Men: Life in Baseball's Negro Leagues.* New York: Atheneum, 1983.

Rooks, Noliwe. *Hair Raising: Beauty, Culture and African-American Women.* New Brunswick, N.J.: Rutgers University Press, 1996.

———. *Ladies Pages: African American Women's Magazines and the Culture That Made Them.* New Brunswick, N.J.: Rutgers University Press, 2004.

Rose, Tricia. *Black Noise: Rap Music and Black Culture in Contemporary America.* Hanover: Wesleyan University Press, 1994.

Rosen, Ruth. *The Lost Sisterhood: Prostitution in the Progressive Era.* Chicago: University of Chicago Press, 1982.

Rosenberg, Alexander. *Darwinism in Philosophy, Social Science, and Policy.* New York: Cambridge University Press, 2000.

Rosenzweig, Ray. *Eight Hours for What We Will: Workers and Leisure in an Industrial City, 1870–1920.* Cambridge: Cambridge University Press, 1983.

Roses, Lorraine Elena, and Ruth Elizabeth Ran. *Harlem's Glory: Black Women Writing, 1900–1950.* Cambridge: Harvard University Press, 1996.

Ross, Andrew. *No Respect: Intellectuals and Popular Culture.* London: Routledge, 1989.

Ross, Dorothy. *The Origins of American Social Science.* New York: Cambridge University Press, 1991.

Rotundo, E. Anthony. *American Manhood: Transformations of Masculinity from the Revolution to the Modern Era.* New York: Basic Books, 1993.

Rowe, Mike. *Chicago Blues: The City and Its Music.* New York: Da Capo Press, 1981.

———. *Chicago Breakdown.* New York: Da Capo Press, 1975.

Ruck, Rob. *The Tropic of Baseball: Baseball in the Dominican Republic.* 1991. Reprint, Lincoln: University of Nebraska Press, 1999.

Ryan, John. *The Production of Culture in the Music Industry: The ASCAP-BMI Controversy.* Lanham, Md.: University Press of America, 1985.

Rydell, Robert. *All the World's a Fair: Visions of Empire at American International Expositions, 1876–1916.* Chicago: University of Chicago Press, 1984.

Sabneev, Leonid. *Music for the Films: A Handbook for Composers and Conductors.* Translated by S. W. Pring. London: Sir Isaac Pitman and Sons, 1935.

Saffle, Michael. *Perspectives on American Music, 1900–1950.* New York: Garland, 2000.

Sammons, Jeffrey. *Beyond the Ring: The Role of Boxing in American Society.* Urbana: University of Illinois Press, 1990.

Sampson, Henry T. *Blacks in Black and White: A Sourcebook on Black Films.* 2nd ed. Metuchen, N.J.: Scarecrow Press, 1988.

Sandburg, Carl. *The Chicago Race Riots, July 1919.* New York: Harcourt, Brace and Howe, 1919.

Sanders, Cheryl. *Saints in Exile: The Holiness-Pentecostal Movement in the African American Experience.* New York: Oxford University Press, 1996.

Sanjeck, Russell, and David Sanjeck. *American Popular Music Business in the 20th Century*. New York: Oxford University Press, 1991.

Sanky, Ira D. *My Life and the Story of the Gospel Hymns and of Sacred Songs and Solos*. 1907. Reprint, New York: AMS Press, 1974.

Santino, Jack. *Miles of Smiles, Years of Struggle: Stories of the Black Pullman Porters*. Urbana: University of Illinois Press, 1989.

Schatzberg, Rufus, and Robert J. Kelley. *African American Organized Crime: A Social History*. New Brunswick, N.J.: Rutgers University Press, 1996.

Schechter, Patricia. *Ida B. Wells-Barnett and American Reform, 1880–1930*. Chapel Hill: University of North Carolina Press, 2001.

Schiffman, Jack. *Uptown: The Story of Harlem's Apollo Theater*. New York: Cowles Book, 1971.

Schuyler, George. *Black No More: Being an Account of the Strange and Wonderful Workings of Science in the Land of the Free, AD 1933–1940*. College Park, Md.: McGrath Publishing, 1931.

Scott, Daryl Michael. *Contempt and Pity: Social Policy and the Image of the Dominated Black Psyche*. Chapel Hill: University of North Carolina Press, 1997.

Scott, William R. *The Sons of Sheba's Race: African Americans and the Italo-Ethiopian War, 1935–1941*. Bloomington: Indiana University Press, 1993.

Scruggs, Lawson. *Women of Distinction: Remarkable in Works and Invincible in Character*. Raleigh: L. A. Scruggs, 1893.

Seiber, Roy, and Frank Herreman. *Hair in African Art and Culture*. New York: Museum of African Art, 2000.

Shapiro, Herbert. *White Violence and Black Response: From Reconstruction to Montgomery*. Amherst: University of Massachusetts Press, 1988.

Shapiro, Nat, and Nat Hentoff. *Hear Me Talkin' to Ya: The Story of Jazz by the Men Who Made It*. New York: Rinehart, 1955.

Shaw, Stephanie. *What a Woman Ought to Be and Do: Black Professional Women Workers during the Jim Crow Era*. Chicago: University of Chicago Press, 1996.

Shropshire, Kenneth. *In Black and White: Race and Sports in America*. New York: New York University Press, 1996.

Simpson, Anne Key. *Follow Me: The Life and Music of R. Nathaniel Dett*. Metuchen, N.J.: Scarecrow Press, 1993.

———. *Hard Trials: The Life and Music of Harry T. Burleigh*. Metuchen, N.J.: Scarecrow Press, 1990.

Sinclair, Upton. *The Jungle*. New York: Doubleday, Page, 1906.

Singal, Daniel Joseph. *The War Within: From Victorian to Modernist Thought in the South, 1919–1945*. Chapel Hill: University of North Carolina Press, 1982.

Singh, Amritjit, William S. Shiver, and Stanley Brodwin. *The Harlem Renaissance: Revaluations*. New York: Garland, 1989.

Sizer, Sandra. *Gospel Hymns and Social Religion: The Rhetoric of Nineteenth-Century Revivalism*. Philadelphia: Temple University Press, 1978.

Skinner, Elliot. *African Americans and the US Policy toward Africa, 1850–1924*. Washington: Howard University Press, 1992.

Slotkin, Richard. *Gunfighter Nation: The Myth of the Frontier in Twentieth Century America*. New York: Atheneum, 1992.

Small, Albion, and George Vincent. *An Introduction to the Study of Society*. New York: American Books, 1894.

Smith, Charles Hamilton. *The Natural History of the Human Species*. London: Samuel Highly, 1848.

Smith, Dennis. *The Chicago School: A Liberal Critique of Capitalism*. New York: St. Martin's Press, 1988.

Smith, Ruth. *The Life and Works of Thomas Andrew Dorsey: The Celebrated Pianist and Songwriter Poetical and Pictorial*. Chicago: Thomas A. Dorsey, 1935.

Smith, Suzanne. *Dancing in the Streets: Motown and the Cultural Politics of Detroit*. Cambridge: Harvard University Press, 1999.

Smith, Willie "the Lion." *Music on My Mind: Memoirs of an American Pianist*. New York: Da Capo Press, 1974.

Snead, James. *White Screens, Black Images: Hollywood from the Dark Side*. New York: Routledge, 1994.

Snyder, Robert. *The Voice of the City: Vaudeville and Popular Culture in New York*. New York: Oxford University Press, 1989.

Solomon, Mark. *The Cry Was Unity: Communists and African Americans, 1917–1936*. Jackson: University of Mississippi Press, 1998.

Southern, Eileen. *Biographical Dictionary of Afro-American and African Musicians*. Westport, Conn.: Greenwood Press, 1982.

——. *The Music of Black Americans: A History*. New York: W. W. Norton, 1983.

Spear, Allen. *Black Chicago: The Making of a Negro Ghetto, 1890–1920*. Chicago: University of Chicago Press, 1967.

Spencer, Jon Michael. *The New Negroes and Their Music: The Success of the Harlem Renaissance*. Knoxville: University of Tennessee Press, 1997.

Spivey, Donald. *Union and the Black Musician: The Narrative of William Everett Samuels and Chicago Local 208*. Boston: University Press of America, 1984.

Stackhouse, Perry J. *Chicago and the Baptists: A Century of Progress*. Chicago: University of Chicago Press, 1933.

Stansell, Christine. *American Moderns: Bohemian New York and the Creation of a New Century*. New York: Metropolitan Books, 2000.

——. *City of Women: Sex and Class in New York, 1789–1860*. Urbana: University of Illinois Press, 1987.

Starke, Barbara M., ed. *African American Dress and Adornment*. Dubuque, Iowa: Kendall/Hunt, 1990.

Stearns, Marshall. *The Story of Jazz*. New York: Oxford University Press, 1970.

Stecopoulos, Harry, and Michael Uebel, eds. *Race and the Subject of Masculinities*. Durham: Duke University Press, 1997.

Stewart, Jacqueline. *Migrating to the Movies: Cinema and Black Urban Modernity*. Berkeley: University of California Press, 2005.

Stovall, Tyler. *Paris Noir: African Americans in the City of Light*. Boston: Houghton Mifflin, 1996.

Strickland, Arvarh. *History of the Chicago Urban League*. Urbana: University of Illinois Press, 1966.

Stuckey, Sterling. *Slave Culture: Nationalist Theory and the Foundations of Black America*. New York: Oxford University Press, 1987.

Summers, Martin. *Manliness and Its Discontents: The Black Middle Class and the Transformation of Masculinity, 1900–1930*. Chapel Hill: University of North Carolina Press, 2004.

Susman, Warren. *Culture as History: The Transformation of American Society in the Twentieth Century*. New York: Pantheon, 1985.

Synan, Vinson. *The Holiness-Pentecostal Movement in the US*. Grand Rapids, Mich.: William B. Eerdmans, 1971.

Taitt, John. *The Souvenir of Negro Progress: Chicago, 1779–1925*. Chicago: DuSable Association, 1925.

Tate, Claudia. *Psychoanalysis and Black Novels: Desire and the Protocols of Race*. New York: Oxford University Press, 1998.

Taylor, Frank, and Gerald Cook. *Alberta Hunter*. New York: McGraw-Hill, 1987.

Taylor, Frederick Winslow. *The Principles of Scientific Management*. 1912. Reprint, New York: Norton, 1967.

Taylor, Quintard. *In Search of the Racial Frontier: African Americans in the American West, 1528–1990*. New York: W. W. Norton, 1998.

Teele, James E., ed. *E. Franklin Frazier and Black Bourgeoisie*. Columbia: University of Missouri Press, 2002.

Thomas, W. I., and Florian Znaniecki. *The Polish Peasants in Europe and America*. 4 vols. Chicago: University of Chicago Press, 1918–20.

Thompson, E. P. *The Making of the English Working Class*. New York: Vintage Books, 1963.

Thompson, Emily. *The Soundscapes of Modernity: Architectural Acoustics and the Culture of Listening in America, 1900–1933*. Cambridge: MIT Press, 2004.

Thompson, Nathan. *Kings: The True Story of Chicago's Policy Kings and Numbers Racketeers: An Informal History*. Chicago: Bronzeville Press, 2003.

Titon, Jeff Todd. *Early Downhome Blues: A Musical and Cultural Analysis*. Urbana: University of Illinois Press, 1977.

Tobach, Ethel. *The Four Horsemen: Racism, Sexism, Militarism, and Social Darwinism*. New York: Behavioral Publications, 1974.

Toomer, Jean. *Cane*. 1923. Reprint, New York: Harper and Row, 1969.

Trachtenberg, Alan. *The Incorporation of America: Culture and Society in the Gilded Age*. New York: Hill and Wang, 1982.

Travis, Dempsey. *An Autobiography of Black Chicago*. Chicago: Urban Research Institute, 1981.

———. *An Autobiography of Black Jazz*. Chicago: Urban Research Institute, 1983.

Trotter, James M. *Music and Some Highly Musical People*. Boston: Charles T. Dillingham, 1881.

Trotter, Joe William, Jr. *Black Milwaukee: The Making of an Industrial Proletariat, 1915–1945*. Urbana: University of Illinois Press, 1985.

———, ed. *The Great Migration in Historical Perspective: New Dimensions of Race, Class and Gender*. Bloomington: Indiana University Press, 1991.

Tucker, Robert, ed. *The Marx-Engels Reader*. New York: Norton, 1978.

Tuttle, William, Jr. *Race Riot: Chicago in the Red Hot Summer of 1919*. New York: Atheneum, 1970.

Tyler, Bruce Michael. *From Harlem to Hollywood: The Struggle for Racial and Cultural Democracy, 1920–1943*. New York: Garland, 1992.

Vaillant, Derek. *Sounds of Reform: Progressivism and Music in Chicago, 1873–1935*. Chapel Hill: University of North Carolina Press, 2003.

Van Epps-Taylor, Betti Carol. *Oscar Micheaux: Dakota Homesteader, Author, Pioneer Filmmaker: A Biography*. Rapid City, S.D.: Dakota West Books, 1999.

Veblen, Thorsten. *The Theory of the Leisure Class: An Economic Study of Institutions*. New York: Random House, 1961.

Vice Commission of Chicago. *The Social Evil in Chicago*. Chicago: Vice Commission of the City of Chicago, 1911.

Vincent, Ted. *Keep Cool: The Black Activists Who Built the Age of Jazz*. London: Pluto, 1995.

Vincent, Theodore. *Black Power and the Garvey Movement*. Berkeley: Ramparts Press, 1971.

———. *Voices of a Black Nation: Political Journalism in the Harlem Renaissance*. Trenton, N.J.: Africa World Press, 1990.

Wacker, Fred. *Ethnicity, Pluralism, and Race: Race Relations Theory in America before Myrdal*. Westport, Conn.: Greenwood Press, 1983.

Walker, Madam C. J. *The Madam C. J. Walker Beauty Walker Manual: A Thorough Treatise Covering All Branches of Beauty Culture*. Schomburg Center for Research in Black Culture, New York Public Library, Microfilm R-2412 (24).

———. *Textbook of the Madam C. J. Walker Schools of Beauty Culture*. Indianapolis: Walker Manufacturing Company, 1928.

Wall, Cheryl A. *Women of the Harlem Renaissance*. Bloomington: Indiana University Press, 1995.

Wallace, Maurice. *Constructing the Black Masculine: Identity and Ideality in African American Men's Literature and Culture*. Durham: Duke University Press, 2002.

Waller, Gregory A. *Main Street Amusements: Movies and Commercial Entertainment in a Southern City, 1896–1930*. Washington, D.C.: Smithsonian Institution Press, 1995.

Ward, Geoffrey. *Unforgiveable Blackness: The Rise and Fall of Jack Johnson*. New York: Knopf, 2004.

Warren, Joyce W., and Margaret Dickie. *Challenging Boundaries: Gender and Periodization*. Athens: University of Georgia Press, 2000.

Washington, Booker T. *The Negro in Business*. 1906. Reprint, New York: AMS Press, 1971.

———. *Up from Slavery: An Autobiography*. New York: Doubleday, 1902.

Washington, Booker T., N. B. Wood, and Fannie Barrier Williams. *A New Negro for a New Century*. 1901. Reprint, New York: Arno Press, 1969.

Washington, Joseph R., Jr. *Black Sects and Cults*. New York: University Press of America, 1972.

Waters, Enoch P. *American Diary: A Personal History of the Black Press*. Chicago: Path Press, 1987.

Watkins-Owens, Irma. *Blood Relations: Caribbean Immigrants and the Harlem Community, 1900–1930*. Bloomington: Indiana University Press, 1996.

Watson, Steven. *The Harlem Renaissance: Hub of African-American Culture, 1920–1930*. New York: Pantheon Books, 1995.

Webb, Larsen. *The Basketball Man: James Naismith*. Lawrence: University Press of Kansas, 1973.

Weber, Max. *The Protestant Ethic and the Spirit of Capitalism*. New York: Harper Collins, 1930.

Weems, Robert E. *Black Business in the Black Metropolis: The Chicago Metropolitan Assurance Company, 1925–1985*. Bloomington: Indiana University Press, 1996.

Wells-Barnett, Ida B. *Crusade for Justice: The Autobiography of Ida B. Wells*. Edited by Alfreda Duster. Chicago: University of Chicago Press, 1970.

Wendt, Lloyd, and Herman Kogan. *Big Bill of Chicago*. Indianapolis: Bobbs-Merrill, 1953.

Wesley, Charles H. *Negro Labor in the United States, 1850–1925: A Study in American Economic History*. New York: Vanguard Press, 1927.

West, Cornel. *The American Evasion of Philosophy*. Madison: University of Wisconsin Press, 1989.

White, Ronald. *Liberty and Justice for All: Racial Reform and the Social Gospel, 1877–1925*. San Francisco: Harper and Row, 1990.

White, Shane, and Graham White. *Stylin': African American Expressive Culture from Its Beginnings to the Zoot Suit*. Ithaca: Cornell University Press, 1998.

White, Sol. *Sol White's History of Colored Base Ball, with Other Documents on the Early Black Game, 1886–1936*. Compiled and introduced by Jerry Malloy. 1907. Reprint, Lincoln: University of Nebraska Press, 1995.

Whitehead, Charles. *A Man and His Diamonds: A Story of the Great Andrew (Rube) Foster, the Outstanding Team He Owned and Managed, and the Superb League He Founded and Commissioned*. New York: Vintage Press, 1980.

Whitehead, Harriet, and Sherry Ortner, eds. *Sexual Meanings: The Cultural Con-*

structions of Gender and Sexuality. New York: Cambridge University Press, 1981.

Whorton, James. *Crusaders for Fitness: The History of American Health Reformers.* Princeton: Princeton University Press, 1982.

Wiebe, Robert. *The Search for Order, 1877–1920.* New York: Hill and Wang, 1967.

Wiegeman, Robyn. *American Anatomies: Theorizing Race and Gender.* Durham: Duke University Press, 1995.

Wiggins, David, and Patrick Miller, eds. *The Unlevel Playing Field: A Documentary History of the African American Experience in Sport.* Urbana: University of Illinois Press, 2003.

Willett, Julia. *Permanent Waves: The Making of the American Beauty Shop.* New York: New York University Press, 2000.

Williams, Martin. *Griffith, First Artist of the Movies.* New York: Oxford University Press, 1980.

Williams, Vernon J., Jr. *Rethinking Race: Franz Boaz and His Contemporaries.* Lexington: University Press of Kentucky, 1996.

Wilmore, Gayraud. *Black Religion and Black Radicalism: An Interpretation of the Religious History of African Americans.* New York: Doubleday, 1972.

Wils, Sondra Kathryn. *The Messenger Reader: Stories, Poetry, and Essays.* New York: Modern Library, 2000.

Wilson, Elizabeth. *Adorned in Dreams: Fashion and Modernity.* Berkeley: University of California Press, 1985.

Wilson, William H. *The City Beautiful Movement.* Baltimore: Johns Hopkins University Press, 1989.

Wintz, Cary. *Black Culture and the Harlem Renaissance.* Houston: Rice University Press, 1988.

——. *Black Writers Interpret the Harlem Renaissance.* New York: Garland Publishing, 1996.

——. *The Critics and the Harlem Renaissance.* New York: Garland Publishing, 1996.

——. *The Emergence of the Harlem Renaissance.* New York: Garland Publishing, 1996.

——. *The Politics and Aesthetics of "New Negro" Literature.* New York: Garland Publishing, 1996.

——. *Remember the Harlem Renaissance.* New York: Garland Publishing, 1996.

Wolcott, Victoria. *Remaking Respectability: African American Women in Interwar Detroit.* Chapel Hill: University of North Carolina Press, 2001.

Wolters, Raymond. *The New Negro on Campus: Black College Rebellions of the 1920s.* Princeton: Princeton University Press, 1975.

Wood, Junius B. *The Negro in Chicago.* Chicago: Chicago Daily News, 1916.

Woods, E. M. *The Negro in Etiquette.* St. Louis: Buxton and Skinner, 1899.

Woodson, Carter G. *A Century of Negro Migration.* 1916. Reprint, New York: Russell and Russell, 1969.

———. *The Negro in Our History*. Washington, D.C.: Associated Publishers, 1922.

———. *The Negro Professional Man and the Community*. Washington, D.C.: Association for the Study of Negro Life and History, 1934.

Woodson, Carter G., and Lorenzo Green. *The Negro Wage Earner*. 1930. Reprint, New York: Russell and Russell, 1969.

Woodson, Carter G., J. H. Harmon, and Arnett G. Lindsey. *The Negro as Businessman*. College Park, Md.: McGrath, 1921.

Woofter, T. J. *Negro Problems in Cities: A Study Made under the Direction of T. K. Woofter*. 1928. Reprint, New York: Harper and Row, 1969.

Work, John Wesley. *Folk Song of the American Negro*. 1915. Reprint, New York: Negro Universities Press, 1969.

Work, Monroe. *Negro Yearbook and Annual Encyclopedia of the Negro*. Vol. 1. Tuskegee, Ala.: Negro Yearbook Co., 1912.

Wright, Josephine, ed. *New Perspectives on Music: Essays in Honor of Eileen Southern*. Warren, Mich.: Harmonie Park Press, 1992.

Wright, Richard. *Black Boy (American Hunger)*. New York: Harper Perennial Classics, 1998.

———. *Lawd Today!* Boston: Northeastern University Press, 1963.

Wynn, Neil. *The Afro-American and the Second World War*. New York: Holmes and Meier Publishers, 1975.

Yearwood, Gladstone L. *Black Cinema Aesthetics: Issues in Independent Black Filmmaking*. Athens: Ohio University Center for Afro-American Studies, 1982.

———. *Black Film as a Signifying Practice: Cinema, Narration and the African American Aesthetic Tradition*. Trenton, N.J.: Africa World Press, 2000.

Yu, Henry. *Thinking Orientals: Migration, Contact and Exoticism in Modern America*. New York: Oxford University Press, 2001.

Zinn, Howard, Dana Frank, and Robin D. G. Kelley, eds. *Three Strikes: Miners, Musicians, Salesgirls, and the Fighting Spirit of Labor's Last Century*. Boston: Beacon Press, 2000.

Zuck, Barbara A. *A History of Musical Americanism*. Ann Arbor: UMI Research Press, 1980.

ARTICLES

Abrams, Roger. "Phantoms of Romantic Nationalism in Folkloristics." *Journal of American Folklore* (Winter 1993): 3–37.

Adams, John H. "Rough Sketches: A Study of the Features of the New Negro Woman." *Voice of the Negro* 8 (August 1904): 323–27.

Albright, A. "Micheaux, Vaudeville and Black Cast Films." *Black Film Review* 7, no. 4 (1992): 6–9, 36.

Allen, Ernest. "The Cultural Methodology of Harold Cruse." *Journal of Ethic Studies* 5, no. 2 (1977): 26–50.

————. "Identity and Destiny: The Formative Views of the Moorish Science Temple and the Nation of Islam." In *Muslims on the Americanization Path?*, edited by Yvonne Yezbeck Haddad and John Esposito. New York: Oxford University Press, 2000.

————. "When Japan Was 'Champion of the Darker Races': Sakota Takahashi and the Flowering of Black Messianistic Nationalism." *Black Scholar* 24 (1994): 648–718.

Allen, Robert. "Contra the Chaser Theory." *Wide Angle* 3, no. 1 (1979): 4–11.

Altman, Rick. "The Silence of the Silents." *Musical Quarterly* 80 (Winter 1996): 23–46.

Amarillo, Jose. "Mexican American Baseball: Masculinity, Racial Struggle and Labor Politics in Southern California, 1930–1950." In *Sports Matters: Race, Recreation and Culture*, edited by John Bloom and Michael Nevin Willard. New York: New York University Press, 2002.

"Arizona Juanita Dranes." In *Black Women in America: An Historical Encyclopedia*, edited by Darlene Clark Hine. New York: Carlson Publishers, 1990.

Baker, Thomas Nelson. "The Negro Woman." *Alexander's Magazine* 2 (December 15, 1906): 84.

Baldwin, Davarian L. "Black Belts and Ivory Towers: The Place of Race in U.S. Social Thought, 1892–1948." *Critical Sociology* (2004): 397–450.

Barlow, William. "Cashing In: 1900–1939." In *Split Image: African-Americans and the Mass Media*, edited by Janette L. Dates and William Barlow. Washington, D.C.: Howard University Press, 1990.

Barnett, Claude. "The Role of the Press, Radio and Motion Pictures on Negro Morale." *Journal of Negro Education* (Summer 1943).

————. "We Win a Place in Industry." *Opportunity* 7 (March 1929): 82–88.

Bates, Beth Tompkins. "A New Crowd Challenges the Agenda of the Old Guard in the NAACP, 1933–1941." *American Historical Review* 102, no. 2 (April 1997): 340–77.

Bederman, Gail. "Civilization, the Decline of Middle-Class Manliness, and Ida B. Wells Anti-Lynching Campaign, 1892–94." In *Gender and American History since 1890*, edited by Barbara Melosh. New York: Routledge, 1993.

Bell, Bernard. "W. E. B. Du Bois's Struggle to Reconcile Folk and High Art." In *Critical Essays on W. E. B. Du Bois*, edited by William Andrews. Boston: G. K. Hall, 1985.

Bennett, Tony. "A Thousand and One Troubles: Blackpool Pleasure Beach." In *Formations of Pleasure*, edited by Tony Bennett et al. London: Routledge, 1983.

Benyon, Erdmann. "The Voodoo Cult among Negro Migrants in Detroit." *American Journal of Sociology* (July 1934–May 1935): 894–907.

Bernstein, Mathew, and Dana White. " 'Scratching Around' in a 'Fit of Insanity': The Norman Film Manufacturing Company and the Race Film Business in the 1920s." *Griffithiana* 21:62/63 (May 1998): 81–127.

Best, Wallace. "Lucy Madden Smith." In *Women Building Chicago: A Biographical*

Dictionary, edited by Rima Lunin Schultz and Adele Hast. Bloomington: University of Indiana Press, 2001.

———. "Lucy Smith and Pentecostal Worship in Chicago." In *The Religions of the United States in Practice*, edited by Colleen McDannell, 2:11–22. Princeton: Princeton University Press, 2001.

Bobo, Jacqueline. "The Subject Is Money: Reconsidering the Black Film Audience as a Theoretical Paradigm." *Black American Literature Forum* 25, no. 2 (Summer 1991): 421–32.

Bond, George Clement, and John Gibbs. "A Social Portrait of John Gibbs St. Clair Drake: An American Anthropologist." *American Ethnologist* (November 1988).

Bone, Robert. "Richard Wright and the Chicago Renaissance." *Callaloo* 9, no. 3 (1986): 446–68.

Bonner, Marita. "On Being Young—a Woman—and Colored." *Crisis* (December 1925): 63–65.

Boris, Eileen. "Black Women and Paid Labor in the Home: Industrial Homework in Chicago in the 1920s." In *Homework: Historical and Contemporary Perspectives on Paid Labor at Home*, edited by Eileen Boris and Cynthia R. Daniels, 33–52. Chicago: University of Illinois Press, 1989.

Bowser, Pearl. "The Micheaux Legacy." *Black Film Review* 7, no. 4 (1993): 10–14.

———. "Pioneers of Black Documentary Film." In *Struggles for Representation: African American Documentary Film and Video*, edited by Phyllis Klotman, 1–33. Bloomington: Indiana University Press, 1999.

———. "Sexual Imagery and the Black Woman in American Cinema." In *Black Cinema Aesthetics*, edited by Gladstone Yearwood. Athens: Afro-American Studies at Ohio University, 1982.

Bowser, Pearl, and Louise Spence. "Identity and Betrayal: *The Symbol of the Unconquered* and Oscar Micheaux's 'Biographical Legend.'" In *The Birth of Whiteness: Race and the Emergence of U.S. Cinema*, edited by Daniel Bernardi, 57–80. New Brunswick, N.J.: Rutgers University Press, 1996.

———. "Oscar Micheaux's *Body and Soul* and the Burden of Representation." *Cinema Journal* 38, no. 3 (Spring 2000): 3–29.

Boyer, Horace Clarence. "An Analysis of His Contributions: Thomas A. Dorsey, 'Father of Gospel Music.'" *Black World* 23, no. 9 (July 1974): 20–28.

———. "Charles Albert Tindley: Progenitor of Black American Gospel Music." *Black Perspective in Music* 11 (Fall 1983): 103–32.

———. "Contemporary Gospel Music." *Black Perspective in Music* 7 (Spring 1979): 5–58.

———. "Gospel Blues: Origin and History." In *New Perspectives on Music: Essays in Honor of Eileen Southern*, edited by Josephine Wright. Warren, Mich.: Harmonie Park Press, 1992.

———. "'Take My Hand, Precious Lord, Lead Me On.'" In *We'll Understand It Better By and By*, edited by Bernice Johnson Reagon, 141–63. Washington, D.C.: Smithsonian Institution Press, 1992.

Brown, Elsa Barkley. "Negotiating and Transforming the Public Sphere: African American Political Life in the Transition from Slavery to Freedom." *Public Culture* 7, no. 1 (Fall 1994): 107–46.

———. "Womanist Consciousness: Maggie Lena Walker and the Independent Order of St. Luke." *Signs* 14, no. 3 (Spring 1989): 610–33.

Brown, Elsa Barkley, and Greg D. Kimball. "Mapping the Terrain of Black Richmond." *Journal of Urban History* 21 (March 1995): 296–346.

Brown, Jayna. "Pulp Fiction of Oscar Micheaux." *Oscar Micheaux Society Newsletter* (1995): 1–2.

Brownmiller, Susan. "Hair." In *Femininity*, 32–61. New York: Simon and Schuster, 1984.

Bulmer, Martin. "Charles S. Johnson, Robert E. Park and the Research Methods of the Chicago Commission on Race Relations, 1919–1922." *Ethnic and Racial Studies* 4, no. 5 (1981): 289–306.

Bundles, A'Lelia Perry. "Madam C. J. Walker—Cosmetics Tycoon." *Ms. Magazine* (July 1983): 91–93.

Burgos, Adrian. "Playing Ball in a Black and White Field of Dreams: Afro-Caribbean Ballplayers in the Negro Leagues, 1910–1950." *Journal of Negro History* 82, no. 1 (Winter 1997): 67–104.

Burnim, Melonee. "The Black Gospel Music Tradition: A Complex Ideology, Aesthetic and Behavior." In *More Than Dancing: Essays on Afro-American Music and Musicians*, edited by Irene V. Jackson. Westport, Conn.: Greenwood Press, 1985.

———. "Functional Dimensions of Gospel Music Performance." *Western Journal of Black Studies* 12, no. 2 (1988): 112–21.

Burroughs, Nannie H. "Not Color but Character." *Voice of the Negro* 1 (July 1904): 277–79.

Calt, Stephen. "The Anatomy of a 'Race' Label—Part I." *78 Quarterly* 1 (1988): 9–23.

———. "The Anatomy of a 'Race' Label—Part II." *78 Quarterly* 1 (1989): 11–30.

———. "Paramount, Part 2: The Mayo Williams Era." *78 Quarterly* 1 (1989): 11–30.

Canty, Inez. "Jesse Binga." *Crisis* 34 (December 1927).

Caponi-Tabery, Gena. "Jump for Joy: Jump Blues, Dance, and Basketball in 1930s African America." In *Sports Matters: Race, Recreation and Culture*, edited by John Bloom and Michael Nevin Willard. New York: New York University Press, 2002.

Captain, Gwendolyn. "Enter Ladies and Gentleman of Color: Gender, Sport, and the Ideal of African American Manhood and Womanhood during the Late Nineteenth and Twentieth Centuries." *Journal of Sports History* 18, no. 1 (Spring 1991): 81–102.

Carbine, Mary. "'The Finest outside the Loop': Motion Picture Exhibition in Chicago's Black Metropolis, 1905–128." *Camera Obscura* 23 (1990): 9–41.

Carby, Hazel. "'It Jus' Be's Dat Way Sometime': The Sexual Politics of Women's Blues." *Radical America* 20, no. 4 (June–July 1986): 9–24.

——. "Policing the Black Woman's Body in an Urban Context." *Critical Inquiry* 18 (Summer 1992): 738–55.

Clark-Lewis, Elizabeth. " 'This Work Had an End': African-American Domestic Workers in Washington, D.C., 1910–1940." In *"To Toil the Lifelong Day": America's Women at Work, 1780–1980*, edited by Carol Groneman and Mary Beth Norton, 196–213. Ithaca: Cornell University Press, 1987.

Coben, Stanley. "The Assault on Victorianism in the Twentieth Century." *American Quarterly* 27 (November 1975): 604–28.

Cohen, Lizabeth. "Encountering Mass Culture at the Grassroots: The Experience of Chicago Workers in the 1920s." *American Quarterly* 41, no. 1 (March 1989): 6–33.

Contee, Clarence. "Du Bois, the NAACP, and the Pan-African Congress of 1919." *Journal of Negro History* 57 (January 1972): 13–28.

Conyers, John. "Carter Goodwin Woodson's Biographical Sketch." In *Carter G. Woodson*, edited by James Conyers. New York: Garland, 2000.

Costonie, Toni. "Memories of an Early Salon." *Shoptalk* (Spring 1984).

Cox, Oliver Cromwell. "Race, and Caste: A Distinction." *American Journal of Sociology* 50, no. 5 (1945): 360–68.

——. "The Racial Theories of Robert E. Park and Ruth Benedict." *Journal of Negro Education* 13, no. 4 (Spring 1944): 452–63.

Cripps, Thomas. "The Birth of a Race Company: An Early Stride toward a Black Cinema." *Journal of Negro History* 59, no. 1 (January 1974): 28–37.

——. "The Making of *The Birth of a Race*: The Emerging Politics of Identity in Silent Movies." In *The Birth of Whiteness: Race and the Emergence of U.S. Cinema*, edited by Daniel Bernardi, 38–55. New Brunswick, N.J.: Rutgers University Press, 1996.

——. "Paul Robeson and Black Identity in the Movies." *Massachusetts Review* 11 (Summer 1970).

——. " 'Race Movies' as Voices of the Black Bourgeoisie: The Scar of Shame." In *American History / American Film: Interpreting the Hollywood Image*, edited by John E. O'Connor and Martin A. Jackson. New York: Ungar, 1987.

——. "The Reaction of the Negro to the Motion Picture *Birth of a Nation*." *Historian* 25 (May 1963): 344–62.

Cruz, Jon. "Testimonies and Artifacts: Elite Appropriations of African American Music in the Nineteenth Century." In *Viewing, Reading, Listening: Audiences and Cultural Reception*, edited by Jon Cruz and Justin Lewis. San Francisco: Westview Press, 1994.

Dalfume, Richard. " 'The Forgotten Years' of the Negro Revolution." *Journal of American History* 55 (June 1968): 90–106.

Daniel, Vattel. "Ritual and Stratification in Chicago Negro Churches." *American Sociological Review* 7 (June 1942): 352–61.

DeCaro, F. A., and Tom Ireland. "Every Man a King: Worldview, Social Tension and Carnival in New Orleans." *International Folklore Review* 6 (1988): 58–65.

Diawara, Manthia. "Black Spectatorship: Problems of Identification and Resistance." In *Black American Cinema*, edited by Manthia Diawara, 211–20. New York: Routledge, 1993.

Dorsey, Thomas A. "From Bawdy Songs to Hymns." *Guideposts* (December 1950): 8. Scrapbook clippings from vertical files of the Schomburg Collection.

———. "Gospel Music." In *Reflections on Afro-American Music*, edited by Dominique-Rene de Lerma. Kent, Ohio: Kent State University Press, 1973.

———. "Ministry of the Music in the Church." In *Improving the Music in the Church*, edited by Kenneth Morris. Chicago: Martin and Morris Music Studio, 1949.

Drake, St. Clair. "Churches and Voluntary Associations in the Chicago Negro Community." Works Projects Administration, 1940, Vivian G. Harsh Research Collection of Afro-American History and Literature, Carter G. Woodson Regional Library, Chicago Public Library.

Du Bois, W. E. B. "The African Roots of War." *Atlantic Monthly* 115 (May 1915): 707–14.

———. "Let Us Reason Together." *Crisis* 18 (September 1919): 231.

———. "The Problem of Amusement." *Southern Workman* 26 (September 1897). Reprinted in *W. E. B. Du Bois on Sociology and the Black Community*, edited by Dan Green and Edwin Driver. Chicago: University of Chicago Press, 1978.

———. "The Religion of the American Negro." 1900. Reprinted in *W. E. B. Du Bois on Sociology and the Black Community*, edited by Dan Green and Edwin Driver. Chicago: University of Chicago Press, 1978.

———. "Returning Soldiers." *Crisis* 18 (May 1919): 13.

Duckett, Alfred. "On His 75th Anniversary: An Interview with Thomas A. Dorsey." *Black World* 23 (July 1974): 4–19.

Dvořák, Antonín. "Music in America." *Harper's New Monthly Magazine* 90 (February 1895).

Early, Gerald. "The Black Intellectual and the Sport of Prizefighting." In *The Culture of Bruising: Essays on Prizefighting, Literature and Modern American Culture*. Hopewell, N.J.: Ecco Press, 1994.

Egonu, Iheanachor. "Les Continents and the Francophone Pan-Negro Movement." *Phylon* 42 (September 1981): 245–54.

Elder, Arlene. "Oscar Micheaux: The Melting Pot on the Plains." *Old Northwest: A Journal of Regional Life and Letters* 2, no. 3 (September 1976): 299–307.

Eliot, T. S. "The Waste Land." In the *Complete Poems and Plays, 1909–1950*. New York: Harcourt and Brace, 1962.

Epstein Barbara. "Family, Sexual Morality and Popular Movements in Turn-of-the-Century America." In *Powers of Desire: The Politics of Sexuality*, edited by Ann Snitow, Christine Stansell, and Sharon Thompson. New York: Monthly Review Press, 1983.

Evans, Linda. "Claude A. Barnett and the Associated Negro Press." *Chicago History: The Magazine of the Chicago Historical Society* 12, no. 1 (Spring 1983).

Evans, William L. "The Negro in Chicago Industries." *Opportunity* 1, no. 2 (February 1923): 15–17.

Fidler, R. L. "Historical Review of the Pentecostal Outpouring in Los Angeles at the Azusa Street Mission in 1906." *International Outlook* (Jan.–March 1963).

Filene, Benjamin. " 'Our Singing Country': John and Alan Lomax, Leadbelly, and the Construction of an American Past." *American Quarterly* 43 (1991).

Fisher, Miles Mark. "Organized Religion and the Cults." *Crisis* 44 (January 1937): 8–10, 29, 30.

Fisher, S. Mattie. "Olivet as a Christian Center." *Missions* 10, no. 3 (March 1919): 199–202.

Fishkin, Shelley Fischer. "The Borderlands of Culture: Writing by W. E. B. Du Bois, James Agee, Tillie Olsen, and Gloria Anzaldua." In *Literary Journalism in the Twentieth Century*, edited by Norman Sims. New York: Oxford University Press, 1993.

Flug, Michael. "Marjorie Stewart Joyner." In *Notable Black American Women, Book II*, edited by Jesse Carney Smith, 336–70. Detroit: Gale Research, 1996.

Fontenot, Chester, Jr. "Oscar Micheaux, Black Novelist and Filmmaker." In *Vision and Refuge: Essays on the Literature of the Great Plains*, edited by Virginia Faulkner. Lincoln: University of Nebraska Press, 1982.

Foster, Andrew. "How to Pitch." In Sol White, *Sol White's Official Baseball Guide*, in *Sol White's History of Colored Base Ball, with Other Documents on the Early Black Game, 1886–1936*, compiled and introduced by Jerry Malloy. 1907. Reprint, Lincoln: University of Nebraska Press, 1995.

Foucault, Michel. "Of Other Spaces." *Diacritics* 16, no. 1 (Spring 1986): 22–27.

Frazier, E. Franklin. "La Bourgeoisie Noire." In *Anthology of American Negro Literature*, edited by V. F. Calverton. New York: Modern Library, 1929.

———. "Chicago: A Cross Section of Negro Life." *Opportunity* 7, no. 3 (March 1929): 70–73.

———. "Durham: Capital of the Black Middle Class." In *The New Negro: Voices of the Harlem Renaissance*, edited by Alain Locke. New York: Albert and Charles Boni, 1925.

Gaines, Jane. "*The Birth of a Nation* and *Within Our Gates*: Two Tales of the American South." In *Dixie Debates: Perspectives on Southern Culture*, edited by Richard King, Richard Taylor, and Helen Taylor. New York: New York University Press, 1996.

———. "Fire and Desire: Race, Melodrama and Oscar Micheaux." In *Black American Cinema*, edited by Manthia Diawara. New York: Routledge, 1993.

Garon, Paul. "Blues and the Church: Revolt and Resignation." *Living Blues: A Journal of the Black American Blues Tradition* 1 (Spring 1970): 18–23.

Gates, Henry Louis. "The Trope of a New Negro and the Reconstruction of the Image of the Black." *Representations* 24 (Fall 1988): 129–55.

Gatewood, Willard B. "Booker T. Washington and the Ulrich Affair." *Journal of Negro History* (January 1970): 29–44.

Gehr, Richard. "One-Man Show." *American Film* 16, no. 5 (May 1991): 34–40.

Gems, Gerald. "Blocked Shot: The Development of Basketball in the African American Community of Chicago." *Journal of Sports History* (Summer 1995): 135–48.

George, Louis. "Beauty Culture and Colored People." *Messenger* 2 (July 1918): 18.

Gibson-Hudson, Gloria. "The Norman Film Manufacturing Company." *Black Film Review* 7, no. 4 (1992): 16–20.

Gilmore, Al-Tony. "Jack Johnson and White Women: The National Impact." *Journal of Negro History* 58 (January 1973): 18–38.

Goddard, Terell. "The Black Social Gospel in Chicago, 1896–1906: The Ministries of Reverdy C. Ransom and Richard R. Wright Jr." *Journal of Negro History* 84 (Summer 1999): 22–46.

Gomery, Douglas. "Movie Audiences, Urban Geography and the History of American Film." *Velvet Light Trap* 19 (1982): 23–29.

———. "Movie Theaters for Black Americans." In *Shared Pleasures: A History of Movie Presentation in the United States*. Madison: University of Wisconsin Press, 1992.

Granger, Lester. "The National Negro Congress—An Interpretation." *Opportunity* 14 (May 1936).

Green, Adam. "The Rising Ride of Youth: Chicago's Wonder Books and the 'New' Black Middle Class." In *The Middling Sorts: Explorations in the History of the American Middle Class*, edited by Burton Beldstein and Robert Johnson, 239–55. New York: New York University Press, 2001.

Green, J. Ronald. "The Micheaux Style." *Black Film Review* 7, no. 4 (1993): 32–34.

———. "Micheaux vs. Griffith." *Griffithiana* 60/61 (1997): 32–49.

———. " 'Twoness' in the Style of Oscar Micheaux." In *Black American Cinema*, edited by Manthia Diawara. New York: Routledge, 1993.

Griffiths, Alison, and James Latham. "Film and Ethnic Identity in Harlem, 1896–1915." In *American Movie Audiences: From the Turn of the Century to the Early Sound Era*, edited by Melvyn Stokes and Richard Maltby. London: BFI, 1999.

Gunning, Tom. "The Cinema of Attraction[s]." *Wide Angle* 8, nos. 3–4 (1986): 63–70.

Hall, Stuart. "Notes on Deconstructing the 'Popular.' " In *People's History and Socialist Theory*, edited by Raphael Samuel, 227–49. London: Routledge, 1981.

Haller, Mark A. "Policy Gambling, Entertainment, and the Emergence of Black Politics: Chicago from 1900 to 1940." *Journal of Social History* 24, no. 4 (Summer 1991): 719–40.

Hamm, Charles. "Dvořák in America: Nationalism, Racism, and National Race." In *Putting Popular Music in Its Place*. New York: Cambridge University Press, 1995.

Hanchard, Michael. "Afro-Modernity: Temporality, Politics, and the African Diaspora." *Public Culture* 11, no. 1 (1999): 245–68.

Hannah, Clayton. "Dr. Thomas A. Dorsey, Patriot of Gospel Music in the 20th Century." *Gospel World* (July–Aug. 1980): 27.

Hansen, Chadwick. "Social Influences on Jazz Style: Chicago, 1920–1930." *American Quarterly* 12, no. 4 (1960): 493–507.

Haraway, Donna. "Teddy Bear Patriarchy: Taxidermy in the Garden of Eden, New York City, 1908–1936." *Social Text* (Winter 1984–85): 20–64.

Harris, David. "The Mass Media: Politics and Popularity." In *From Class Struggle to the Politics of Pleasure: The Effects of Gramscianism on Cultural Studies*. New York: Routledge, 1992.

Harris, Neil. "Great American Fairs and American Cities: The Role of Chicago's Columbian Exposition." In *Culture Excursions: Marketing Appetites and Cultural Tastes in Modern America*. Chicago: University of Chicago Press, 1990.

Harrison, Max. "Boogie-Woogie." In *Jazz: New Perspectives on the History of Jazz by Twelve of the World's Foremost Jazz Critics and Scholars*, edited by Nat Hentoff and Albert McCarthy. New York: Rineheart, 1959.

Hartt, Rollin Lynde. "The New Negro, When He's Hit, He Hits Back!" *Independent* 15 (January 1921): 59–60, 76.

Havig, Alan. "The Commercial Amusement Audience in Early 20th Century American Cities." *Journal of American Culture* (Spring 1982): 1–19.

Hennessey, Thomas J. "The Black Chicago Establishment, 1919–1930." *Journal of Jazz Studies* 2 (December 1974): 15–45.

Herbert, Janis. "Oscar Micheaux: A Black Pioneer." *South Dakota Review* (Spring 1973): 62–69.

Higginbotham, Evelyn Brooks. "Rethinking Vernacular Culture: Black Religion and Race Records in the 1920s and 1930s." In *The House That Race Built: Black Americans, U.S. Terrain*, edited by Wahneema Lubiano. New York: Pantheon, 1997.

Hine, Darlene Clark. "Black Migration to the Urban Midwest: The Gender Dimension, 1915–1945." In *The Great Migration in Historical Perspective: New Dimensions of Race, Class and Gender*, edited by Joe William Trotter Jr., 127–46. Bloomington: Indiana University Press, 1991.

Hoberman, J. "Bad Movies." *Film Comment* 16, no. 4 (July–Aug. 1980): 7–12.

Holloman, Laynard. "On the Supremacy of the Negro Athlete in White Athletic Competition." *Psychoanalytic Review* (April 1943): 162.

hooks, bell. "Micheaux: Celebrating Blackness." *Black American Literature Forum* 25, no. 2 (Summer 1991): 315–60.

———. "Reconstructing Black Masculinity." In *Black Looks: Race and Representation*. Boston: South End Press, 1992.

Howe, Daniel Walker. "American Victorianism as a Culture." *American Quarterly* 27 (November 1975): 507–32.

Hughes, C. Alvin. "The Negro Sanhedrin Movement." *Journal of Negro History* 69 (Winter 1984): 1–13.

Hughes, Langston. "The Negro Artist and the Racial Mountain." *Nation* 122 (June 23, 1926): 692–94.

——. "The Negro Speaks of Rivers." *Crisis* (June 1921): 71.

Humphrey, Mark. "Holy Blues: The Gospel Tradition." In *Nothing but the Blues: The Music and Musicians*, edited by Lawrence Cohn. New York: Abbeville Press, 1993.

Hurd, Michael, and Stan C. Spence. "Halftime: The Band Be Kickin'!" In *Black College Football, 1892–1992: One Hundred Years of History, Education, and Pride*, edited by Michael Hurd. Virginia Beach: Donning, 1993.

Hurston, Zora Neale. "Concert." In *Folklore, Memoirs, and Other Writings*. Edited by Cheryl Wall. New York: Library of America, 1995.

Jafa, Arthur. "The Notion of Treatment: Black Aesthetic and Film." In *Oscar Micheaux and His Circle: African-American Filmmaking and Race Cinema of the Silent Era*, edited by Pearl Bowser, Jane Gaines, and Charles Musser, 12–15. Bloomington: Indiana University Press, 2001.

Johnson, Charles. "Editorial." *Opportunity* (March 1929): 69.

——. "How Much of the Migration Was a Flight from Persecution?" *Opportunity* 1, no. 9 (September 1923): 273–75.

——. "These 'Colored' United States, VIII—Illinois: Mecca of the Migrant Mob." *Messenger* (December 1923).

Kelley, Robin D. G. "Notes on Deconstructing the Folk." *American Historical Review* 97, no. 5 (December 1992): 1400–8.

——. "The Riddle of the Zoot: Malcolm Little and Black Cultural Politics during World War II." In *Malcolm X: In Our Own Image*, edited by Joe Wood. New York: St. Martin's Press, 1992.

——. "Without a Song: New York Musicians Strike Out against Technology." In *Three Strikes: Miners, Musicians, Salesgirls, and the Fighting Spirit of Labor's Last Century*, edited by Howard Zinn, Dana Frank, and Robin D. G. Kelley. Boston: Beacon Press, 2000.

Kellogg, Peter J. "Civil Rights Consciousness in the 1940s." *Historian* 42 (November 1979): 18–41.

Kimmel, Michael. "Men's Responses to Feminism at the Turn of the Century." *Gender and Society* 1, no. 3 (September 1987): 261–83.

Klarlund, Susan. "The Origins of Racism: The Critical Theory of Oliver C. Cox." *Mid-American Review of Sociology* 18, nos. 1–2 (1994).

Kolodin, Irving. "The Dance Band Business: A Study in Black and White." *Harpers Magazine* (June 1941): 72–82.

Korstad, Robert, and Nelson Lichtenstein. "Opportunities Found and Lost: Labor, Radicals, and the Early Civil Rights Movement." *Journal of American History* 75 (December 1988): 786–811.

Kreiling, Albert. "The Commercialization of the Black Press and the Rise of Race News in Chicago." In *Ruthless Criticism: New Perspectives in U.S. Communication History*, edited by William Solomon and Robert McChesney, 176–203. Minneapolis: University of Minnesota Press, 1993.

———. "The Rise of the Black Press in Chicago." *Journalism History* 4, no. 4 (Winter 1977–78): 132–36, 156.

Lanier-Seward, Adrienne. "A Film Portrait of Black Ritual Expression: The Blood of Jesus." In *Expressively Black: The Cultural Basis of Ethnic Identity*, edited by Geneva Gay and Willie L. Baber. New York: Praeger, 1987.

Latham, Charles, Jr. "Madam C. J. Walker and Company." *Traces of Indiana and Midwestern History* 1, no. 3 (Summer 1989): 29–40.

Lax, John. "Chicago's Black Jazz Musicians in the '20s." *Journal of Jazz Studies* 1, no. 2 (1974): 107–27.

Lears, T. Jackson. "The Concept of Cultural Hegemony: Problems and Possibilities." *American Historical Review* 90 (June 1985): 567–93.

Lenin, V. I. "Of Capitalism and Agriculture." In *Collected Works*. 45 vols. Edited by George Hanna. Translated by Yuri Sdobnikov. Moscow: Progress, 1960–70.

LeRoy, Greg. "The Founding Heart of A. Philip Randolph's Union: Milton P. Webster and Chicago's Pullman Porters Organize, 1925–1937." *Labor's Heritage* 3, no. 3 (July 1991): 22–43.

Levine, Lawrence. "The Concept of the New Negro and the Realities of Black Culture." In *The Unpredictable Past: Explorations in American Cultural History*. New York: Oxford University Press, 1993.

Levine, Lawrence, Robin D. G. Kelley, Natalie Zemon Davis, and T. Jackson Lears. "AHR Forum." *American Historical Review* 97 (December 1992): 1369–426.

Lewis, Earl. "To Turn as on a Pivot: Writing African Americans into a History of Overlapping Diasporas." *American Historical Review* 100 (June 1995): 765–87.

Light, Ivan. "Immigrant and Ethnic Enterprise in North America." *Ethnic and Racial Studies* 7 (April 1984): 195–216.

———. "Numbers Gambling among Blacks: A Financial Institution." *American Sociological Review* 42 (December 1977): 892–904.

Lipsitz, George. "Mardi Gras Indians: Carnival and Counter-Narrative in New Orleans." In *Time Passages: Collective Memory and American Popular Culture*, edited by George Lipsitz. Minneapolis: University of Minnesota Press, 1990.

Locke, Alain. "Our Little Renaissance." In *Ebony and Topaz: A Collectanea*, edited by Charles S. Johnson. New York: Opportunity, National Urban League, 1927.

Lomax, John. "'Sinful Songs' of the Southern Negro." *Musical Quarterly* 20 (April 1934): 177–87.

Lomax, Michael. "Black Entrepreneurship in the National Pastime: The Rise of Semiprofessional Baseball in Black Chicago, 1890–1915." *Journal of Sports History* 25, no. 1 (Spring 1998): 43–64.

Lombardo, Robert. "The Black Mafia: African-American Organized Crime in Chicago, 1890–1960." *Crime, Law, and Social Change* 38 (2002): 33–65.

Lott, Eric. "Double V, Double-Time: Bebop's Politics of Style." *Callaloo* 11, no. 3 (1988): 597–605.

Massa, Ann. "Black Women in the 'White City.'" *Journal of American Studies* (December 1974): 319–37.

Maultsby, Portia K. "The Role of Scholars in Creating Space and Validity for Ongoing Changes in Black American Culture." In *Black American Culture and Scholarship: Contemporary Issues*, edited by Bernice Johnson Reagon. Washington, D.C.: Smithsonian Institution Press, 1985.

Maxwell, William J. "The Proletarian as New Negro: Mike Gold's Harlem Renaissance." In *Radical Revisions: Rereading 1930s Culture*, edited by Bill Mullen and Sherry Linkon. Urbana: University of Illinois Press, 1996.

May, Lary. "Apocalyptic Cinema: D. W. Griffith and the Aesthetics of Reform." In *Screening Out the Past: The Birth of Mass Culture and the Motion Picture Industry*. New York: Oxford University Press, 1980.

McCarthy, Kathleen D. "Nickel Vice and Virtue: Movie Censorship in Chicago, 1907–1915." *Journal of Popular Film* 5 (1976): 37–55.

McKay, Claude. "If We Must Die." *Liberator* 2 (July 1919): 21.

McKinley, John. "Anthony Overton: A Man Who Planned for Success." *Reflexus* 1 (April 1925).

Meier, August. "Negro Class Structure and Ideology in the Age of Booker T. Washington." *Phylon* 23 (Fall 1963): 258–66.

Mercer, Kobena. "Black Hair/Style Politics." *New Formations* 3 (Winter 1987): 33–54.

Mercer, Kobena, and Issace Julien. "Race, Sexual Politics and Black Masculinity: A Dossier." In *Male Order: Unwrapping Masculinity*, edited by Rowena Chapman and Jonathan Rutherford. London: Lawrence and Wishart, 1988.

Merritt, Russell. "Nickelodeon Theaters, 1905–1914: Building an Audience for the Movies." In *The American Film Industry*, edited by Tino Balio, 59–79. Madison: University of Wisconsin Press, 1976.

Metheny, Eleanor. "Some Differences in Bodily Proportions between American Negro and White Male College Students as Related to Athletic Performance." *Research Quarterly* 10 (December 1939): 41–53.

Mignolo, Walter. "The Darker Side of the Renaissance: Colonization and the Discontinuity of the Classical Tradition." *Renaissance Quarterly* 45, no. 4 (Winter 1992): 808–28.

Miller, Patrick. "The Anatomy of Scientific Racism: Racialist Responses to Black Athletic Achievement." *Journal of Sports History* 25, no. 1 (Spring 1998): 119–51.

———. "To 'Bring the Race along Rapidly': Sport, Student Culture, and Educational Mission at Historically Black Colleges during the Interwar Years." *History of Education Quarterly* 35 (Summer 1995): 111–34.

Miller, Zane. "Pluralism, Chicago Style: Louis Wirth, The Ghetto, The City and 'Integration.'" *Journal of Urban History* (May 1992): 251–80.

Mitchell, Elmer. "Racial Traits in Athletics." *American Physical Education Review* (March 1922): 93–95; (April 1922): 151–52; (May 1922).

Mjagkij, Nina. "True Manhood: The YMCA and Racial Advancement, 1890–1930." In *Men and Women Adrift: The YMCA and the YWCA in the City*, edited by Nina Mjagkij and Margaret Spratt, 138–59. New York: New York University Press, 1997.

Mongold, Jeanne Conway. "Annie Minerva Turnbo Malone." In *Notable American Women: The Modern Period*, edited by Barbara Sicherman and Carol Hurd Green. Cambridge: Harvard University Press, 1980.

Mooney, Amy. "Representing Race: Disjunctures in the Work of Archibald Motley Jr." *Museum Studies: The Art Institute's Journal* 24, no. 2 (1999): 163–79.

Moore, Fred. "How to Keep Women at Home." *Colored American Magazine* (January 1908): 7–8.

Moses, Wilson J. "Domestic Feminism, Conservatism, Sex Roles and Black Women's Clubs, 1863–1896." *Journal of Social and Behavioral Sciences* (Fall 1978): 166–77.

———. "The Lost World of the Negro, 1895–1919: Black Literary and Intellectual Life before the 'Renaissance.' " *Black American Literature Forum* 21 (Spring–Summer 1987): 61–64.

Musser, Charles. "Nickels Count: The Rise of Storefront Theaters." In *The Emergence of Cinema: The American Screen to 1907*. New York: Scribner, 1990.

Muwakkil, Salim. "Art vs. Ideology: The Debate over Positive Images." *Black Film Review* 2 (Summer 1986): 26–27.

Nance, Susan. "Mystery of the Moorish Science Temple: Southern Blacks and American Alternative Spirituality in 1920s Chicago." *Religion and American Culture* 12, no. 2 (Summer 2002): 123–66.

———. "Respectability and Representation: The Moorish Science Temple, Morocco, and Black Public Culture in 1920s Chicago." *American Quarterly* 54, no. 4 (December 2002): 623–59.

Neal, Larry. "Uncle Rufus Raps on the Squared Circle." *Partisan Review* (1972).

"Negro Class Structure and Ideology in the Age of Booker T. Washington." *Phylon* 23 (Fall 1963): 268–66.

Ninkovich, Frank. "Theodore Roosevelt: Civilization as Ideology." *Diplomatic History* 10 (Summer 1986): 21–45.

Ohmann, Richard. "Where Did Mass Culture Come From? The Case of Magazines." *Berkshire Review* (1981): 85–101.

O'Neal, Jim, and Amy O'Neal. "Living Blues Interview: Georgia Tom Dorsey." *Living Blues: A Journal of the Black American Blues Tradition* 20 (March–April 1975): 17–34.

"Our Far Flung Challenge." *Crusader* 1 (September 1919): 8.

Owen, Chandler. "The Cabaret—A Useful Social Institution." *Messenger* 4 (August 1922): 461.

Patterson, Tiffany Ruby, and Robin D. G. Kelley. "Unfinished Migrations: Reflections on the African Diaspora and the Making of the Modern World." Special issue, *African Studies Review* 43 (April 2000): 11–45.

Perkins, Linda. "Impact of the Cult of True Womanhood on the Education of Black Women." *Journal of Social Issues* 39, no. 3 (September 1983): 17–28.

Peterson, Bernard. "A Filmography of Oscar Micheaux: America's Legendary Black Filmmaker." In *Celluloid Power: Social Film Criticism from "The Birth of a Nation" to "Judgment at Nuremberg,"* edited by David Platt, 113–41. Metuchen, N.J.: Scarecrow Press, 1992.

——. "The Films of Oscar Micheaux: America's First Fabulous Black Filmmaker." *Crisis* 86, no. 4 (1979): 136–41.

Powell, Richard J. "Sartor Africanus." In *Dandies: Fashion and Finesse in Art and Culture*, edited by Susan Fillin-Yeh. New York: New York University Press, 2001.

Powers, Thomas. "The Page Fence Giants Play Ball." *Chronicle: The Quarterly Magazine of the Historical Society of Michigan* (Spring 1983).

Radano, Ronald. "Denoting Difference: The Writing of the Slave Spirituals." *Critical Inquiry* 22, no. 3 (Spring 1996): 506–44.

——. "Hot Fantasies: American Modernism and the Idea of Black Rhythm." In *Music and the Racial Imagination*, edited by Ronald Radano and Phillip V. Bohlman. Chicago: University of Chicago Press, 2001.

——. "Soul Texts and the Blackness of Folk." *Modernism/Modernity* 2, no. 1 (January 1995): 71–95.

Randolph, A. Philip, and Chandler Owen. "The Cause of and Remedy for Race Riots." *Messenger* 2 (September 1919): 14–21.

Rathbun, F. G. "The Negro Music of the South." *Southern Workman* 22 (1893).

Regester, Charlene. "Black Films, White Censors: Oscar Micheaux Confronts Censorship in New York, Virginia and Chicago." In *Movie Censorship and American Culture*, edited by Francis Couvares. Washington, D.C.: Smithsonian Institution Press, 1996.

——. "Oscar Micheaux on the Cutting Edge: Films Rejected by the New York State Motion Picture Commission." *Studies in Popular Culture* 17, no. 2 (1995).

——. "Oscar Micheaux's *Body and Soul*: A Film of Conflicting Themes." In *In Touch with the Spirit: Black Religious and Musical Expression in American Cinema*, edited by Phyllis Klotman and Gloria Gibson-Hudson, 59–71. Bloomington: Indiana University Press, Black Film Archive, 1994.

——. "Oscar Micheaux's Multifaceted Portrayals of the African American Male: The Good, the Bad, and the Ugly." *Studies in Popular Culture* 17, no. 2 (April 1995): 17–27.

——. "Oscar Micheaux the Entrepreneur: Financing *The House behind the Cedars*." *Journal of Film and Video* 49, nos. 1–2 (Spring/Summer 1997): 17–27.

Rochberg-Halton, Eugene. "Life, Literature and Sociology in Turn-of-the-Century Chicago." In *Consuming Visions*, edited by Simon Bronner. New York: Norton, 1989.

Roosevelt, Theodore. "The Strenuous Life." 1901. Reprinted in *The Strenuous Life: Essays and Addresses*. St. Clair Shores, Mich.: Scholarly Press, 1970.

Rose, Tricia. "Black Texts/Black Contexts." In *Black Popular Culture*, edited by Gina Dent. Seattle: Bay Press, 1992.

Rusch, Bob. "Georgia Tom Dorsey Interview." *Cadence: The American Review of Jazz and Blues* 4 (November 1978).

Rushing, Andrea Benton. "Hair-Raising." *Feminist Studies* 14, no. 2 (Summer 1988): 325–35.

Ryan, Mary P. "Gender and Public Access: Women's Politics in 19th Century America in Craig Calhoun." In *Habermas and the Public Sphere*, edited by Craig Calhoun. Cambridge: MIT Press, 1992.

Sammons, Jeffrey. " 'Race' and Sport: A Critical, Historical Examination." *Journal of Sports History* 21, no. 3 (Fall 1994).

Samuelson, Time. "From Ragtime to Real Estate: Joe Jordan's Career as a Chicago Real Estate Developer." *Rag-Time Ephemeralist* 3 (2001): 201–9.

Sayre, Helen B. "Making Over Poor Workers." *Opportunity* 1, no. 2 (February 1923): 17–18.

Schmidt, Francis, and Harold Fitzgerald. "The New Open Game." *Saturday Evening Post* 5 (October 1935).

Scott, Emmett J. "Leisure Time and the Colored Citizen." *Playground* 18 (January 1925): 593–96.

———, ed. "Letters of Negro Migrants of 1916–1918." *Journal of Negro History* 4 (July 1919): 290–340.

———, ed. "More Letters of Negro Migrants of 1916–1918." *Journal of Negro History* 4 (Oct. 1919): 412–75.

Scott, Julius. "Black Nationalism and the Italo-Ethiopian Conflict, 1934–1936." *Journal of Negro History* 63, no. 2 (1978): 118–34.

Shaw, Malcolm. "Arizona Dranes and Okeh." *Storyville* 27 (February 1970).

Simmons, Christina. "African Americans and Sexual Victorianism in the Social Hygiene Movement." *Journal of the History of Sexuality* 4, no. 1 (1993): 51–75.

Singh, Nikhil Pal. "Culture/Wars: Recoding Empire in an Age of Democracy." *American Quarterly* (September 1998): 471–522.

Sitkoff, Harvard. "Racial Militancy and Interracial Violence in the Second World War." *Journal of American History* 58 (December 1971): 661–81.

Smith, Thomas. "Outside the Pale: The Exclusion of Blacks from the National Football League, 1934–1946." *Journal of Sports History* 15, no. 1 (Winter 1988): 255–81.

Smith-Rosenberg, Carroll, and Charles Rosenberg. "The Female Animal: Medical and Biological Views of Women and Their Role in Nineteenth Century America." In *From Fair Sex to Feminism: Sport and Socialization of Women in Post-Industrial Eras*, edited by J. A. Mangan and Robert J. Park. London: Frank Cass, 1987.

Snead, James. "Images of Blacks in Black Independent Cinema." In *Blackframes: Critical Perspectives on Black Independent Cinema*, edited by Mbye Cham and Claire Andrade-Watkins. Cambridge: MIT Press, 1988.

Stanfield, John H. "The 'Negro Problem' within and beyond the Institutional Nexus of Pre–World War I Sociology." *Phylon* (1982): 187–201.

Stepan, Nancy L., and Sander Gilman. "Appropriating the Idioms of Science: The Rejection of Scientific Racism." In *The Bonds of Race: Perspectives on Hegemony and Resistance*, edited by Dominick LaCapra. Ithica: Cornell University Press, 1999.

Streible, Dan. "The Harlem Theatre: Black Film Exhibition in Austin, Texas: 1920–1973." In *Black American Cinema*, edited by Manthia Diawara, 221–36. New York: Routledge, 1993.

———. "Race and the Reception of Jack Johnson Fight Films." In *The Birth of Whiteness: Race and the Emergence of U.S. Cinema*, edited by Daniel Bernardi, 170–200. New Brunswick, N.J.: Rutgers University Press, 1996.

Strickland, Arvarh. "The Superfluous Negro." *New Republic* 7 (June 24, 1916): 187–88.

Swanson, Richard. "The Acceptance and Influence of Play in American Protestantism." *Quest*, monograph 11 (December 1968).

Taylor, Clyde. "The Re-birth of the Aesthetic in Cinema." In *The Birth of Whiteness: Race and the Emergence of U.S. Cinema*, edited by Daniel Bernardi, 15–37. New Brunswick, N.J.: Rutgers University Press, 1996.

Taylor, Graham. "Public Recreations Facilities: Recreation Developments in Chicago Parks." *Annals of the American Academy of Political and Social Science* 35 (March 1910).

Taylor, Paul C. "Malcolm's Conk and Danto's Colors; or Four Logical Positions Concerning Race, Beauty and Aesthetics." In *Beauty Matters*, edited by Peg Zeglin Brand. Bloomington: Indiana University Press, 2000.

Taylor, Ula. "From White Kitchens to White Factories: The Impact of World War I on African-American Working Women in Chicago." *Ufahamu: Journal of the African Activist Association* (1985).

Thomas, W. I. "The Psychology of Race Prejudice." *American Journal of Sociology* 9 (1904): 593–611.

———. "Race Psychology: Standpoint and Questionnaire with Particular Reference to the Immigrant and the Negro." *American Journal of Sociology* 17 (July 1912): 725–75.

Thompson, E. P. "Time, Work-Discipline and Industrial Capitalism." *Past and Present* 38 (December 1967): 56–97.

Tillman, Katherine. "Paying Professions for Colored Girls." *Voice of the Negro* (January–February 1907): 54–55.

Vaillant, Derek. "Sounds of Whiteness: Local Radio, Racial Formation, and Public Culture in Chicago, 1921–1935." *American Quarterly* 54 (March 2002): 25–66.

Vincent, Ted. "The Community That Gave Jazz to Chicago." *Black Music Research Journal* 12 (1992): 43–55.

Wacker, Fred. "An American Dilemma: The Racial Theories of Robert E. Park and Gunnar Myrdal." *Phylon* 37, no. 2 (Summer 1976): 117–25.

Waller, Greg. "Another Audience: Black Moviegoing, 1907–1916." *Cinema Journal* 31, no. 2 (Winter 1992): 3–25.

Webster, Milton P. "Organized Labor among Negroes in Chicago." In *The Negro in Chicago: 1779–1927*, vols. 1–2, edited by Frederick H. H. Robb. Chicago: Washington Intercollegiate Club, 1929.

Weinrott, Lester. "Chicago Radio: The Glory Days." *Chicago History* 3 (Spring–Summer 1974): 14–22.

Wells, Ida B., and Frederick Douglass. *The Reason Why the Colored American Is Not in the World's Columbian Exposition*. In *Selected Works of Ida B. Wells-Barnett*, edited by Trudier Harris. New York: Oxford University Press, 1991.

White, Walter. "Chicago and Its Eight Reasons." *Crisis* 18, no. 6 (October 1919): 294–97.

Wiggins, David K. " 'Great Speed but Little Stamina': The Historical Debate over Black Athletic Superiority." *Journal of Sports History* 16 (Summer 1989): 158–85.

Wiggins, William. "Jack Johnson as Bad Nigger: The Folklore of His Life." *Black Scholar* (January 1971): 43–44.

Williams, Brett. "The South in the City." *Journal of Popular Culture* 16 (1982): 30–41.

Williams, Christopher. "Forms and Ideologies." In *Realism and the Cinema: A Reader*. London: Routledge, 1980.

Williams, Fannie Barrier. "The Club Movement among Colored Women in America." In *A New Negro for a New Century*, edited by Booker T. Washington, N. B. Wood, Fannie Barrier Williams, 396–97. Chicago: American Publishing House, 1900.

———. "The Colored Girl." *Voice of the Negro* 2 (June 1905): 400–403.

———. "Social Bonds in the 'Black Belt' of Chicago." *Charities* 15 (October 1905–March 1906): 40–44.

———. "The Woman's Part in a Man's Business." *Voice of the Negro* 1 (June 1904): 543–47.

Williams, Vernon J., Jr. "Franz Boaz's Paradox and the African American Intelligentsia." In *African Americans and Jews in the Twentieth Century: Studies in Convergence and Conflict*, edited by V. P. Franklin, Nancy L. Grant, Harold M. Kletnik, and Genna Rae McNeil. Columbia: University of Missouri Press, 1998.

Williams-Jones, Pearl. "Afro-American Gospel Music: A Crystallization of the Black Aesthetic." *Ethnomusicology* 19 (September 1975): 374–85.

Willis, Susan. "I Shop Therefore I Am: Is There a Place for Afro-American Culture in Commodity Culture?" In *Changing Our Own Words: Essays on Criticism, Theory and Writing by Black Women*, edited by Cheryl Wall. New Brunswick, N.J.: Rutgers University Press, 1989.

Wittner, Lawrence. "The National Negro Congress: A Reassessment." *American Quarterly* 22, no. 4 (Winter 1970): 883–901.

Wolcott, Victoria. "The Culture of the Informal Economy: Numbers in Inter-war Black Detroit." *Radical History Review* 69 (Fall 1997): 46–75.

———. "Mediums, Messages, and Lucky Numbers: African-American Spiritualists and Numbers Runners in Inter-war Detroit." In *Geography of Identity*, edited by Patricia Yeager, 273–306. Ann Arbor: University of Michigan Press, 1996.

Woodson, Carter G. "Fifty Years of Negro Citizenship as Qualified by the United States Supreme Court." *Journal of Negro History* 6, no. 1 (January 1921): 1–53.

———. "The Insurance Business among Negroes." *Journal of Negro History* 14, no. 2 (April 1929): 202–26.

Work, John W. "Changing Patterns in Negro Folk Songs." *Journal of American Folklore* 62 (1949): 281–90.

———. "Negro Folk Song." *Opportunity* (October 1923). Reprinted in *The Opportunity Reader: Stories, Poetry, and Essays from the Urban League's Opportunity Magazine*, edited by Sondra Kathryn Wilson, 336–42. New York: Modern Library, 1999.

Ziemer, Linda. "Chicago's Negro Leagues." *Chicago History* 23, no. 3 (Winter 1994): 36–51.

PAPERS, THESES, AND DISSERTATIONS

Attwood, J. H. "The Attitude of Negro Ministers of the Major Denominations in Chicago toward the Fact of Division between Negro and White Churches." Ph.D. diss., University of Chicago, 1930.

Beekman, Scott Michael. "This Judas Iscariot: Cyril Briggs and the African Blood Brotherhood's Relationship with Marcus Garvey and the Universal Negro Improvement Association, 1918–1922." Ph.D. diss., Ohio State University, 1998.

Best, Wallace. "Passionately Human, No Less Divine: Racial Ideology and Religious Culture in the Black Churches of Chicago, 1916–1963." Ph.D. diss., Northwestern University, 2000.

Blair, Cynthia. "Vicious Commerce: African American Women's Sex Work and the Transformation of Urban Space in Chicago, 1850–1915." Ph.D. diss., Harvard University, 1999.

Boyer, Horace Clarence. "The Gospel Song: A Historical and Analytical Survey." Ph.D. diss., University of Rochester, Eastman School of Music, 1964.

Brooks, Dwight. "Consumer Markets and Consumer Magazines: Black America and the Culture of Consumption, 1920–1960." Ph.D. diss., University of Iowa, 1991.

Bryant, Leo M. "Negro Insurance Companies in Chicago." M.A. thesis, University of Chicago, 1934.

Buchanan, Singer Alfred. "A Study of the Attitudes of the Writers of the Negro Press toward the Depiction of the Negro in Plays and Films, 1930–1965." Ph.D. diss., University of Michigan, 1968.

Burnim, Mellonee. "The Black Gospel Music Tradition: A Symbol of Ethnicity." Ph.D. diss., Indiana University, 1980.

Caldwell, Lewis A. H. "The Policy Game in Chicago." M.A. thesis, Northwestern University, 1940.

Carlson, Gustav G. "Number Gambling: A Study of a Culture Complex." Ph.D. diss., University of Michigan, 1940.

Cox, Oliver Cromwell. "The Origins of Direct-Action Protest among Negroes [in Chicago], 1932–1933." Unpublished ms., 1963. Microfiche copy at Kent State University Libraries.

Daniel, Vattel. "Ritual in Chicago's South Side Churches for Negroes." Ph.D. diss., University of Chicago, 1940.

Dargan, William Thomas. "Congregational Gospel Songs in a Black Holiness Church: A Musical and Textual Analysis." Ph.D. diss., Wesleyan University, 1982.

Davis, Ralph Nelson. "The Negro Newspaper in Chicago." M.A. thesis, University of Chicago, 1939.

de Quattro, Leah. "Popular Music as a Site of Agency, Labor and Discourse: Black Cultural Production in Liverpool." B.A. thesis, Boston College, 2003.

Edmerson, Estelle. "A Descriptive Study of the American Negro in U.S. Professional Radio, 1922–1955." M.A. thesis, University of California, Los Angeles, 1954.

Fisher, Miles Mark. "History of Olivet Baptist Church of Chicago." M.A. thesis, University of Chicago, 1922.

Foreman, Ronal Cilfford. "Jazz and Race Records, 1920–32: Their Origins and Their Significance for the Record Industry and Society." Ph.D. diss., University of Illinois, 1968.

Graham, Sandra J. "The Fisk Jubilee Singers and the Concert Spirituals." Ph.D. diss., New York University, 2001.

Green, Adam. "Selling the Race: Cultural Production and Notions of Community in Black Chicago, 1940–1955." Ph.D. diss., Yale University, 1998.

Harris, Michael Wesley. "The Advent of Gospel Blues in Black Old-Line Churches in Chicago, 1932–33: As Seen through the Life and Mind of Thomas Dorsey." Ph.D. diss., Harvard University, 1982.

Heap, Chad. " 'Slumming': Sexuality, Race, and Urban Commercial Leisure, 1900–1940." Ph.D. diss., University of Chicago, 2000.

Hunter, Herbert. "The Life and Work of Oliver C. Cox." Ph.D. diss., Boston University, 1981.

Hunter, Jerome. " 'Don't Buy from Where You Can't Work': Black Urban Boycott Movements during the Depression, 1929–1941." Ph.D. diss., University of Michigan, 1977.

Hunter, Tera. "Household Workers in the Making: Afro-American Women in Atlanta and the New South, 1861 to 1920." Ph.D. diss., Yale University, 1990.

Jackson, Irene V. "Afro-American Gospel Music and Its Social Setting with Special Attention to Roberta Martin." Ph.D. diss., Wesleyan University, 1974.

Jackson, Jerma. "Testifying at the Cross: Thomas Dorsey, Sister Rosetta Tharpe and the Politics of African-American Sacred and Secular Music." Ph.D. diss., Rutgers University, 1995.

Kailil, Timothy. "The Role of the Great Migration of African-Americans to Chicago in the Development of Traditional Black Gospel Piano of Thomas Dorsey." Ph.D. diss., Kent State University, 1993.

Kincheloe, Samuel C. "The Prophet." Ph.D. diss., University of Chicago, 1929.

Kreiling, Albert. "The Making of Racial Identities in the Black Press: A Cultural Analysis of Race Journalism in Chicago, 1878–1929." Ph.D. diss., University of Illinois, 1973.

Lerner, Daniel. "Visions of a Sporting City: 'Shadowball' and Black Chicago, 1887–1952." Ph.D. diss., Michigan State University, 2002.

Lewis, Hylan. "Social Differentiation in the Negro Community." M.A. thesis, University of Chicago, 1936.

Lindstrom, Julie Ann. " 'Getting a Hold Deeper in the Life of the City': Chicago Nickelodeons, 1905–1914." Ph.D. diss., Northwestern University, 1998.

Logsdon, Joseph. "Reverend A. J. Carey and the Negro in Chicago Politics." M.A. thesis, University of Chicago, 1961.

Lomax, Michael. "Black Baseball, Black Community, Black Entrepreneurs: The History of the Negro National and Eastern Colored Leagues, 1880–1930." Ph.D. diss., Ohio State University, 1996.

Lovett, Leonard. "Black Holiness-Pentecostalism: Implications for Ethics and Social Transformation." Ph.D. diss., Emory University, 1978.

Luckett, Moya T. "Cities and Spectators: A Historical Analysis of Film Audiences in Chicago, 1910–1915." Ph.D. diss., University of Wisconsin, 1995.

Makalani, Minkah. "For the Liberation of Black People Everywhere: The African Blood Brotherhood, Black Radicalism, and Pan-African Liberation in the New Negro Movement." Ph.D. diss., University of Illinois, 2004.

Nelson, Douglas J. "For Such a Time as This: The Story of Bishop William J. Seymour and the Azusa Street Revival, a Search for Pentecostal/Charismatic Roots." Ph.D. diss., University of Birmingham, England, 1981.

Nimmons, Julius F. "Social Reform and Moral Uplift in the Black Community: Social Settlements, Temperance and Social Purity." Ph.D. diss., Howard University, 1991.

Pascoe, William Wesley. "Seasons in the Sun: The Negro Baseball Leagues." Ph.D. master's thesis, Department of History, University of Western Ontario, 1994.

Reed, Christopher R. "A Study of Black Politics and Protest in Depression-Era Chicago, 1930–1939." Ph.D. diss., Kent State University, 1982.

Robinson, Gwendolyn. "Race, Class and Gender: A Transcultural, Theoretical, and Sociohistorical Analysis of Cosmetic Institutions and Practice to 1920." Ph.D. diss., University of Illinois-Chicago, 1984.

Shopshire, James Maynard. "A Socio-historical Characterization of the Black Pentecostal Movement in America." Ph.D. diss., Northwestern University, 1975.

Smith, Hubert W. "Three Negro Preachers in Chicago: A Study in Religious Leadership." M.A. thesis, University of Chicago, 1935.

Sotiropoulos, Karen. "Staging Race: Black Cultural Politics before the Harlem Renaissance, 1893–1915." Ph.D. diss., Graduate Center of City University of New York, 2000.

Spaulding, Norman. "History of Black Oriented Radio in Chicago, 1929–1963." Ph.D. diss., University of Illinois, 1981.

Stewart, Jacqueline. "Migrating to the Movies: The Emergence of Black Urban Film Culture, 1893–1920." Ph.D. diss., University of Chicago, 2000.

Strong, Samuel. "Social Types in the Negro Community of Chicago: An Example of the Social Type Method." Ph.D. diss., University of Chicago, 1940.

Sutherland, Robert Lee. "An Analysis of Negro Churches in Chicago." Ph.D. diss., University of Chicago, 1930.

Taylor, Theman. "Cyril Briggs and the African Blood Brotherhood: Effects of Communism on Black Nationalism, 1919–1935." Ph.D. diss., University of California, Santa Barbara, 1981.

Thorson, Theodore Winton. "A History of Music Publishing in Chicago, 1850–1960." Ph.D. diss., Northwestern University. 1961.

Tinney, James S. "A Theoretical and Historical Comparison of Black Political and Religious Movements." Ph.D. diss., Howard University, 1978.

Wells, Patricia. "Historical Overview of the Establishment of the Church of God in Christ." Ph.D. diss., International Seminary, 1989.

Wolcott, Victoria. "Remaking Respectability: African American Women and the Politics of Identity in Interwar Detroit." Ph.D. diss., University of Michigan, 1995.

Work, Monroe. "Negro Real Estate Holders." M.A. thesis, University of Chicago, 1903.

FILMS

Birth of a Nation. Dir. D. W. Griffith. 1915.

Birthright. Dir. Oscar Micheaux. 1924.

Body and Soul. Dir. Oscar Micheaux. 1924.

The Girl from Chicago. Dir. Oscar Micheaux. 1933.

The Homesteader. Dir. Oscar Micheaux. 1919.

The Phantom of Kenwood. Dir. Oscar Micheaux. 1933.

Symbol of the Unconquered. Dir. Oscar Micheaux. 1920.

Underworld. Dir. Oscar Micheaux. 1936.

Veiled Aristocrats. Dir. Oscar Micheaux. 1932.

Within Our Gates. Dir. Oscar Micheaux. 1920.

VIDEO RECORDINGS

Bowser, Pearl, and Pamela Thomas. *Midnight Ramble: Oscar Micheaux and the Story of Race Movies.* Alexandria, Va.: Northern Light Productions, 1994.

King, George. *Goin' to Chicago.* San Francisco: California Newsreel, 1994.

Moving North to Chicago. Princeton, N.J.: Films for the Humanities and Sciences, 1991.

Nelson, Stanley. *The Black Press: Soldiers without Swords*. San Francisco: Half Nelson Recordings, 1998.

——. *Two Dollars and a Dream*. New York: Filmmakers Library, 1987.

Nueremburg, George T. *Say Amen Somebody*. Carmel, Calif.: Pacific Arts Video Records, 1993.

That's Black Entertainment. Huntsville, Tex.: Skyline Entertainment. Distributed by Video Communications, Inc., 1989.

Too Close to Heaven: The History of Gospel Music. 3 vols. Rutgers, N.J.: Films for the Humanities and Sciences, 1996.

AUDIO RECORDINGS

Arizona Dranes, 1926–1928. Herwin Records, 210.

Deep River: The Songs and Spirituals of Harry Burleigh. Northeastern Classical Arts, 1995.

Dorsey, Thomas Andrew. *Professional Thomas Andrew Dorsey, The Maestro Sings: A Music and Photo History*. Sound of Gospel Records, 1980.

Johnson, Robert. "Sweet Home Chicago." Recording of first of five sessions, November 23, 1936, San Antonio, Texas. On *The Complete Recordings*, CBS 467246 2.

Preachin' the Gospel: Holy Blues. Columbia Records, Roots n' Blues Series, CK46779, 1991.

Smith, Bessie. "Soft Pedal Blues." *Bessie Smith: The Complete Recordings*. Columbia #14075-D, 1925.

Tharpe, Sister Rosetta. *Sincerely Sister Rosetta Tharpe: Sacred and Secular Gospel-Blues-Jazz*. Rosetta Records, Women's Heritage Series, RR 1317, 1988.

Tom, Georgia. *Complete Recorded Works in Chronological Order*. Vol. 2. RST Records, BCCD-6022, 1922.

Wade in the Water. Tape 17. Washington, D.C.: National Public Radio, 1994.

Index

Abbott, Robert, 42, 49, 77, 112, 145, 212; popularizing of term "race" by, 14, 15; as cultural critic, 29, 37; in Micheaux film, 153. See also *Chicago Defender*

Absorption/distraction, 103, 104, 106

Adams, Minnie, 101, 105, 108

Advertisements: beauty, 54–56, 68–70, 75; by Kashmir, 81–84; theater, 100, 103, 105–6; movie, 131, 137–38, 145–48; film industry, 133; amusement, 210, 228

African American migrants: as consumers, 5–7, 38–39; old settler resistance to, 9, 97; Chicago as destination for, 14; attempts at disciplining behavior of, 31–32, 34, 37, 106–7, 159–60, 163; employment opportunities for, 39–41, 62, 165; influence on black film culture, 94; leisure activities paralleling experience of, 104; white anxieties concerning, 122–23; and rise of black gospel music, 163–70; religious practices of, 166–67, 183

African Americans: assertion of right to public space by, 2–4, 95–96, 225; turn to mass marketplace by, 8–9; internationalism of, 10–12, 83, 115–16; and primitivism, 12, 157, 160–61, 173–74; discrimination against, 23, 25, 95–97, 99, 209–10; racial "temperament" of, 27, 35; as amusement participants, 39, 44–45, 51, 92, 95, 104–8, 140, 165, 212, 225–26

African American soldiers, 96; returning from World War I, 11; in beauty advertisement, 83; on film, 102, 118, 126, 134–35, 145

African American women: employment opportunities for, 29, 40–41, 55, 62–64, 165; and respectability, 31–32, 56–64; as Walker agents, 73–75, 77; as objects of race pride, 81–83, 116; and sexuality, 107; as evangelists, 166, 168–69. *See also* Black beauty culture

Ali, Noble Drew, 41

All Nations Pentecostal Church, 166, 168, 188. *See also* Smith, Elder Lucy

All Negro Hour (radio show), 43, 48

Apex Club, 50

Appomattox Club, 36, 202

Armstrong, Lillian Hardin "Lil'", 44, 48

Armstrong, Louis, 48, 138, 206

Association for the Study of Negro Life and History (ASNLH), 35

As the World Rolls On (film), 136

Barnett, Claude, 36, 66, 67, 81, 83, 147. *See also* Kashmir Chemical Company

Baseball, 39, 227; and policy, 49, 217; on

CPSIA information can be obtained
at www.ICGtesting.com
Printed in the USA
LVHW052041180123
737396LV00003B/196

9 780807 857991